# MAKING TROUBLE

# MAKING TROUBLE

essays

on gay

history,

politics,

and the

university

●

john d'emilio

●

routledge

new york & london

Published in 1992 by

Routledge
An imprint of Routledge, Chapman and Hall, Inc.
29 West 35 Street
New York, NY 10001

Published in Great Britain by

Routledge
11 New Fetter Lane
London EC4P 4EE

Interior Design by Karen Sullivan

Printed in the United States of America

**Library of Congress Cataloging in Publication Data**

D'Emillo, John, 1948–
    Making trouble : essays on gay history, politics, and the
university / John D'Emillo.
        p.   cm.
    Includes bibliographical references.
    ISBN 0-415-90509-5     ISBN 0-415-90510-9 (pbk.)
    1. Gay liberation movement—United States—History.
2. Homosexuality and education—United States. 3. Homosexuality—
United States.   I. Title.
HQ76.8.U5D447   1992
305.9'0664—dc20                                        92-10049
                                                          CIP


**British Library cataloguing in publication data also available.**

*In memory of*
*Ken Dawson*
*(1946–1992)*

# CONTENTS

CONTENTS

CONTENTS

# ACKNOWLEDGMENTS

---

Writing the acknowledgments for a book is the pleasurable last task that finishes the project. In this case, however, I wonder: how, in a volume whose contents were written over a period of almost twenty years, do I include all those who influenced me and my work? Rather than risk exclusion through forgetfulness, I will limit my expressions of gratitude to those whose help was critical in putting this collection together.

The University of North Carolina at Greensboro granted me a year's research leave from teaching, during which I conceived this volume and saw it through to completion. The Center for Advanced Study in the Behavioral Sciences in Stanford, California, kindly invited me to be a Fellow during the academic year 1990–91 (funding for my fellowship was provided by the National Endowment for the Humanities, Grant #RA-20037-88, and the Andrew W. Mellon Foundation). The Center is unmatched in the environment it offers for intellectual work; my being there for a year made every task associated with this project a pleasure. The staff of the Center were consistently helpful in all matters large and small. I particularly want to thank Kathleen Much for her skill as an editor, and Lynn Gale for making my entrance into the computer age so painless. I also benefitted from my participation in the Center's seminar "States, Culture, and Social Movements."

Members of the seminar read a draft of the essay "After Stonewall," and their comments helped me to revise it. I am especially grateful to Jacquelyn Hall and Gaea Leinhardt, each of whom went beyond the call of collegiality in reading and dissecting some of my work.

The proximity of the Center to San Francisco allowed me to join for a year in the life of one of the most vibrant gay and lesbian communities that has ever existed. What that meant specifically is that I was able to participate in a yearlong reading group with three other gay and lesbian scholars—Allan Bérubé, Estelle Freedman, and Nancy Stoller. Our animated discussions of our own work and that of others, as well as the way our talk bounced naturally from professional to personal to political concerns, reminded me of why I do the work that you see here and why it is important. Their comments on some of the essays written expressly for this volume improved the final product.

From the beginning I have seen my writing as embedded in a movement for social change. I continue to gain strength from the many women and men who are activists in the lesbian and gay movement in the United States. In the last few years, my comrades in activism have been the board of directors and staff of the National Gay and Lesbian Task Force. Our time together is sometimes stormy, as one would expect of an organization committed to making a difference, and always rewarding and inspirational.

There are three special debts of gratitude. Thanks are due to the other members of the Four Tops group; they know who they are. Peter Skutches read through the entire manuscript and provided astute suggestions about the structure and organization of this volume. About Jim Oleson, with whom I have cast my lot for the last eleven years, I can never say enough. Even during the many months of separation that my fellowship entailed, he continued to be the ballast that keeps me steady.

Finally, the dedication is an expression of my affection and respect for Ken Dawson. One of the 150,000 casualties of the AIDS epidemic in this country, he died while this book was in press. Each death from AIDS is intolerable, and his especially so. His reach was wide, and his vision larger than most. For many, Ken was the motor that propelled us forward and kept us on track. Over the last few years, he was my closest buddy in thinking about issues of justice and social change, and I miss him.

# BY WAY
# OF INTRODUCTION

## NOTES FROM ONE GAY LIFE

---

Each fall, for several years running, my elementary school teachers assigned as a writing exercise the essay "What I Want to Be When I Grow Up." The year I became an altar boy and was admitted to the mysteries of the sacristy, I wrote of my desire to be a priest and serve God. Another time I picked accounting, because my dad had told me that's the profession he would have entered if he had gone to college. In the sixth grade, fascinated by a story I had read about a rural Missouri family, I declared my intention of becoming a farmer—an odd choice for a city boy who had never seen a live chicken, cow, or hog, and for whom vegetables were something purchased at Safeway. Needless to say, I never wrote an essay about being a gay historian, gay activist, or gay writer.

I

Before I could be any of those things I had to become gay. This was not a simple assignment. Growing up in the Bronx in the 1950s, in an ethnic working-class neighborhood and in a world that was intensely Catholic, I had nothing to point me in that direction. Sure, I engaged in various kinds of sex play with my friends from St. Raymond's School, but I did that with girls and boys both. Sex made a formal appearance only as a prohibition—as something that priests and nuns and lay teachers would occasionally warn us against. Otherwise, it was something that young ones discovered together, apart from the world of adults, without quite knowing what we were exploring.

I don't know what my life would have been like if I had followed my friends to a neighborhood high school in the Bronx. But I didn't. In the eighth grade I took the competitive exam for admission to Regis, a Jesuit-run boys' high school in Manhattan. The school's endowment allowed everyone to attend on full scholarship and, among Catholics in the New York area, admission carried great prestige. Regis promised upward mobility for a small number of working-class Catholic kids. Everyone who graduated went to college, and the school proudly counted the number of scholarships that its students won each year. My mother had been grooming me for that exam almost from the moment I learned to read; the day I received my acceptance letter was one of great joy for my family.

It was only seven miles by subway from the Bronx to the Upper East Side of Manhattan where Regis was located, but in many ways the distance was as wide as that from Earth to Mars. The school cultivated among us a sense of elitism: it was a privilege to go to Regis, we were special and different, and we would go far. Because students converged on the school from a radius of thirty miles, we depended on each other. Between travel and classes and extracurricular activities, many of us spent twelve hours a day away from home; this was sometimes true of our weekends as well. Add three hours each night for homework, and you can see that Regis was an all-consuming experience.

Nothing about this Jesuit environment intentionally pointed me toward a gay world. But intellectual sophistication was highly prized, and this meant that as teenagers, I and my friends read novels by James Baldwin and J. D. Salinger and Mary McCarthy. In the pages of *Another Country* and *The Group,* gay characters made an appearance. Tragedy and alienation engulfed them, and I absorbed those lessons, but at least now there was something to which I could attach my own sexual feelings. We also made forays into midtown Manhattan where we saw European art films and Broadway plays. The latter were clean as a whistle, but on the streets outside I saw my first homosexuals (which is the word I would have used then)—"three young men, thin as toothpicks, with long teased hair, mascara, rouge, and powder on their faces, their fingers fluttering in front of them," as I describe them in the essay in this volume about Women Against Pornography (see chapter 16). As with so many of my other early instances of "discovery," I wonder now just how I *knew* they and I had something in common. No one had ever spoken to me about drag queens, or effeminacy, or homosexuality, or the connections among them. Yet I knew. And I was as fascinated as I was repelled by the knowledge.

It wasn't the world of literature and the arts, to which Regis introduced me, that launched my gay life, however. Rather, it was the daily commute on the New York City subway. Before Stonewall and gay liberation, and maybe even now, the subways were a place where men's eyes locked, where the back of a hand brushed against a thigh, and where the legs of strangers sitting next to one another pressed together for a second too long when the train lurched to a stop. Again, I wonder how I knew. I, and so many of the gay men I met in the succeeding years, would wax lyrical about our sixth gay sense, about the sharply honed ability we all possessed to recognize "members of the tribe." Now I think that's all hogwash. It ignores the hundreds of legs that didn't press back and eyes that didn't return the gaze.

In any case, I discovered sex—in the subways, in deserted lots, and alongside highways in the Bronx. In Grand Central Terminal and Times Square and Bryant Park. In movie theaters in Manhattan. And always without names being exchanged. The sex was fast, explosive, and terrifying. To every encounter I brought the fear of being found out and, because I had read *Advise and Consent,* the fear of being blackmailed. Little matter that these men, in having sex with a minor, had far more to lose than I did.

It was not an edifying way for an adolescent to experience his sexual awakening. The encounters themselves ranged from gentle and generous to brutishly exploitative. But worse was the fact that I had no sense of an alternative. Desire drove me forward and I headed toward the only marked point on the map.

I was also tortured by guilt. From the age of fifteen I don't think an hour passed without my sexual sins intruding into my consciousness. I was thoroughly Catholic. In high school I went to Mass three times a week, prayed every day, and participated in spiritual retreats. I went to confession as often as I could—I *had* to, or else face the anxiety provoked by images of hell. In the days between sin and absolution, I worried that I might fall in front of an onrushing train, be struck by a cab in Manhattan, or die in my sleep.

And yet through all of this I had fun. High school was a golden time. I had friends to die for. Regis stretched me intellectually every day. I traveled around the country to speech and debate tournaments, and carried home trophies almost every weekend. I honed oratorial skills that I now use to delight gay audiences when I speak about our history, and learned the rigors of logical reasoning that today help me to construct plausible and compelling historical arguments.

For all the guilt it induced, my Catholicism was almost a source of strength. I may have trembled before God the Father, but I loved Jesus and Mary and knew that they loved me too. I was entranced by the courage and compassion displayed by my favorite saints. The passion for justice that animates my activism, my writing, and my teaching came from the Church. The belief that every human life is precious and worthy of respect, and that I always need to strive to do what is right, remains with me. The individuals whom I most respected—the priests and seminarians who taught me in school—seemed to embody the best of the human spirit. I wanted to be just like them.

Religious fervor and my admiration for these men provoked my first coming out beyond the curtains of the confessional. Each October, the seniors at Regis traveled to a seminary in upstate New York for a three-day spiritual retreat. I had, over the previous few years, intermittently considered entering the priesthood. Now, the bucolic setting, the mandated silence, the prayers, sermons, and devotional exercises—all these combined to elicit spiritual longings for a life of religious commitment. But what to do about my homosexual urges?

The retreat master, Father Burns, was a kindly white-haired Irish priest who exuded grandfatherly understanding. A night of intense prayer convinced me to approach him about my "vocation," the name we used for a calling to the priesthood, *and* about my trepidations. It was not an easy moment. I explained my situation, as euphemistically as I could, yet also with more honesty than I had imagined possible. He gently questioned me about a number of things, and finally asked:

"Do you like children?"

"Yes, Father, I do. Very much."

"Well then, son, you couldn't possibly be a homosexual. A homosexual would hate children. He would find them repulsive because they were the issue of the sacred love of a man for a woman."

I wanted release from my adolescent sexual drives desperately enough that I welcomed his message. He encouraged me in my vocation and advised me to talk openly with Father McGuire, the guidance counselor at school, who would walk me through the steps necessary to enter the Jesuit Order after graduation. Over the next months I had frequent sessions with Father McGuire, about spiritual matters and about sex. I prayed, I exercised restraint, I reported my triumphs over temptation—and I made sure that I went to a confessor other than Father McGuire whenever my best intentions failed me.

At one point, I was sent to a priest/psychiatrist in Brooklyn. He conducted a day's worth of interviews and psychological tests to determine whether I was "really" a homosexual. I remember his administrating the Rorschach test. To my horror, inkblot after inkblot seemed to contain a penis, of various sizes and in various states of tumescence. I knew I couldn't acknowledge this, so I improvised:

one was the Empire State Building, another a rocket being launched from Cape Canaveral, a third resembled the shape of the Florida peninsula. During a lunch-hour break, I wandered around downtown Brooklyn and eventually found myself sitting on the promenade in Brooklyn Heights with a glorious view of lower Manhattan. Suddenly I realized that the same men were passing back and forth in front of me. I had stumbled upon a gay cruising area. I fled back to the office.

As it turned out, I was accepted into the Jesuits. My homosexuality, everyone seemed to agree, was not deeply rooted. With prayer and self-discipline, it would fade. (I still wonder how to interpret this outcome: As a comment on the ineptitude of psychiatry? On the effectiveness of my deceit? On the church's desperation for priests?) But I couldn't go through with it. I took my Catholicism seriously enough—that is, I accepted the Church on its own terms—so that, while I was willing to dissemble with a priest, I wasn't foolish enough to try to trick God, or myself. The decision came with some regrets. My closest friends were all entering the seminary; the Jesuits promised the kind of commitment and challenge that I was reaching for, as well as the safety of a community that would be there not only for the rest of my life but for all eternity. I explained to Father McGuire that I didn't feel confident enough of my vocation. I had yet to be fully tested, I said. I needed to find out whether I had the spiritual strength to resist the enticements of a secular life and to avoid the temptations that the real world would throw in my path. If, after four years at Columbia, I still felt the calling, I would take it up again.

In retrospect I see the decision to go to Columbia as a choice shaped by the unfolding of my gay desires. It was not quite the norm in the mid-1960s for the smartest Catholic boys to attend elite secular colleges; only three years earlier did Regis begin sending the transcripts of its seniors to non-Catholic schools. Had I gone to Fordham, I would have lived at home with too many constraints on my behavior. Georgetown offered distance, but in a Catholic environment and away from the few corners of gay geography I had discovered. Columbia provided the best of all possible worlds. I'd be living on campus, but close enough to my family to pop home for dinner. I'd have freedom of movement and could explore the city, including those "near occasions of sin," as the Catholic prayer for contrition phrased it, that I was pledging to avoid.

2

My undergraduate years were, at the time and in memory, the most confusing and disorienting of my life. Some of that confusion can be explained as the pain attached to coming out in a pre-Stonewall world; part of it was attributable to the campus turmoil of those years and the Damoclean threat of the draft. But much of it, and certainly far more than I could articulate at the time, came from the unfamiliar cultural and class milieu into which I was thrown. At age eighteen, I still had experienced only a small layer of the social pyramid. My classmates at St. Raymond's, with wrinkled and stained white shirts, were "lower class"; a friend whose father was a high school teacher qualified as "well-to-do." Like many kids who came of age in the ethnic tangle of New York City, I believed the world was made up of Catholics and Jews—except for one Lutheran family who lived next door to my grandparents. In my education, the Reformation had not been a blow for human freedom. Until college, I managed not to recognize that Protestants not only were the majority in the United States, but that they also owned much of the country.

At Columbia they were unavoidable. They were visible as preppies, wearing clothes I couldn't afford and owning a wardrobe that could fill my room at home. They exuded ease and confidence. They traveled on vacations and went out on both weekend nights. Their monthly allowances from home were larger than my wages from the two jobs I worked to meet the cost of an Ivy League education. Except for those monthly checks, they seemed unburdened by family relationships. They also seemed unencumbered by religion. I resented them without knowing why.

I also had other more pressing worries staring me in the face. If I wanted to pit myself against the temptations of a secular world, Columbia was the place to be. The first book I was assigned to read, for an orientation-week discussion group led by a Protestant campus minister who told us that God was dead, was Norman O. Brown's *Life Against Death:* it left me speechless. My dorm floor turned out to be "drug central" for the campus; I was so naive that it was spring semester before I learned that the cloud of smoke in the corridor didn't come from pipe tobacco. My peers talked openly about the girls they were having sex with (I may have been engaging in sex with men, but I knew it was wrong *and* I didn't talk about it). All in all, it was a stressful, agonizing year.

But it was Columbia's famed Western Civilization course that did me in. I find it ironic that conservative critics of present-day curriculum reform defend Western Civ in the name of transmitting our cultural traditions. In my case, it performed an act of demolition. I came into the class steeped in the values and historical teleology of Catholicism; by the end, I was on the road to agnosticism. The readings from the ancient world were fine. The Jesuits had taught me Latin and Greek, and Plato's sensibility seemed Catholic in everything but name. Medieval philosophy was old hat. When we read Augustine, I patiently explained to the class the difference between predestination and foreknowledge. The next week, Aquinas's

proofs of God's existence comforted me immensely. But the Enlightenment proceeded to shake my intellectual foundations. After David Hume disproved the
existence of God, and after I failed in a paper to disprove his proofs, I became one
more lost Catholic soul. I retained for a while longer a vague allegiance to the idea
of God, and the life of Jesus continued to carry resonance for me, but the Church,
its rituals, and its theology I discarded. The process was emotionally tumultuous,
yet also surprisingly brief. Once done, I never reconsidered.

It is easier for me to sort through issues of causation when I write about history
than when I examine my own life. Did I let go of the Church so quickly because
of the power of my late-adolescent sexual desires? Certainly many gay men
and lesbians have pursued homosexual experience while retaining their Catholic
identities. Some have been tortured by guilt because of it; others have creatively
reinterpreted Catholicism to suit their lives. What I can say for sure is that leaving
the Church forced me to devise my own ethics. It also lightened considerably the
load of guilt that I carried into my sexual explorations and consequently made it
a good deal easier to go in search of a more substantial gay life.

And search I did. One Friday evening, while waiting in line with friends outside
an East Side movie theater, I noticed a surprising number of men, to my eyes gay,
walking up and down along Third Avenue: it soon became my first street cruising
area. I discovered that the crowd of opera lovers who spent Saturday night and
Sunday morning at the Met waiting for standing-room tickets was heavily laced
with homosexuals. I developed a passion for opera and, for a year or two, became
something of a regular there; the lobby of the Met was the closest thing to a
community center that I found until gay liberation. A man I met there took me
under his wing and introduced me to my first gay bars—Julius, on West 10th
Street, and another place in the Village. I didn't like them much and so didn't go
back, but they were a revelation to me. I stumbled upon the places on campus
where gay men did their cruising—the coffee house in the basement of my dorm,
and the upper floors of Butler Library.

Virtually all of the visual images of gay experience that I can conjure up from
those days are shaded in darkness. On one level the explanation is simple. It *was*
often dark when I did my cruising. I spent more nighttime hours looking for . . .
sex? . . . love? . . . closeness? . . . comfort? . . . someone with whom I could talk
without censorship? . . . than I care to remember. And more often than not
returned with none of the above. But something other than the hour accounts for
the dimmed prospect of those times. I said that detaching from the Church had
lifted a good deal of the burden of guilt, and that is true. But the fear stayed. Every
moment spent in quest of a homosexual connection remained encased in a mind-
numbing terror—of discovery, and of the calamities that would ensue if I were

discovered. The terror simultaneously dulled and sharpened my senses. To move ahead, I had to blot out as much feeling as I could and, as a result, often saw myself as blanketed by a dense, impenetrable fog. At the same time, whenever I cruised or was in a public space with another gay man, I was acutely, sharply, conscious of *everything* that was happening around me, and absolutely attuned to the finest nuances of behavior. I *had* to be: What if a family member or friend or acquaintance should happen upon me? What if a cop was somewhere nearby? What if the man I was cruising was a homicidal maniac? You might think this a melodramatic extravagance, but to an eighteen-year-old bookish kid from a good Italian family in the Bronx, those fears were all too real.

Although I recall terror as defining the emotional tone of that period, my most vivid particular memories are those of the men who, whether by chance or intention, opened a window of hope for me. There was José, an extraordinarily handsome Cuban man whom I met in Butler Library. He took me to his efficiency apartment in a nearby brownstone and, as we stripped naked, I noticed the gold crucifix around his neck. The juxtaposition of sacred symbol and profane act shocked me. Desperately confused and in a voice that spoke worlds of pain, I asked him how he could do that. His puzzlement forced me to explain: "How can you wear a crucifix when we're about to do something like this? Jesus died for us. How can you mock him like that?" His reply was simple: "But Jesus loves me, too," was all he said. I remember Sal, an Italian man about twice my age who had recently returned to school and was bursting with enthusiasm about everything he was reading. We talked intensely about literature and philosophy. Our falling into bed seemed just another form of passion into which we easily and naturally slipped.

Most of all, I remember Luis, another Cuban emigré and also Catholic, who saw straight through to the heart of my interior struggle and found a way to help. Getting up from bed, after we'd had sex and had talked for a time, he went to his bookshelf and reached for a well-thumbed copy of Oscar Wilde's *De Profundis,* which he gave to me. Later, alone in my room, I read it through in a single sitting, absorbing the story of Wilde's relationship with Alfred Douglas and the circumstances by which it had landed him in prison. I don't know what Wilde's intentions were, what narrative strategy he had in mind as he composed the essay in jail. But the lofty eloquence of his prose, the way he interpreted the character of Jesus as he discoursed on love, and, most of all, his peroration—"whatever is realized is right"—allowed me to turn a corner. I think it fair to say that it saved my life.

Reading Wilde must have primed me for love because that summer, between my freshman and sophomore years, I fell in love with a man for the first time.

Ron was a twenty-nine-year-old travel agent, a WASP from the Midwest with four years of naval service behind him and a perfect—to my eyes—swimmer's body. I met him one evening as I was exiting the subway at Lexington and 51st Street. When I saw him turn around to look at me, I promptly got another token and followed him into the train. It was a mad infatuation, based on nothing more than my own need to have an object for my affections and to have my desires purified by cloaking them in the mantle of love.

The relationship, such as it was, introduced me to another slice of the gay world. Ron moved in a circle of what I now would call "piss-elegant queens." Preoccupied with status, they had pretensions to culture and sophistication. Ron sang in the choir of St. Bartholomew's Episcopal Church on Park Avenue. Our dates often consisted of a Sunday brunch with his friends at the Cattleman (where we got plastered on all the champagne we could drink), followed by a late afternoon concert at church. He took me to cocktail parties and to candlelit dinners cooked by friends. I learned to drink as much as they did. I scraped together the money to buy at least a few items of the sort of clothes Ron wore. I worked to improve my Bronx-bred table manners. But we were badly mismatched. He didn't quite know what to do with this kid who'd latched on to him and, eventually, my infatuation faded.

Still, the experience with Ron did leave me hungering for a relationship. In the spring of 1968, while many Columbia students were preparing to make history by occupying university buildings and calling a campuswide strike, I was engaging in a courtship with a graduate student. To Billy I attached for the first time the word "lover," which is how partners were well-nigh universally described then. The relationship developed gradually (at least by gay time) over a period of many weeks, and lasted almost until I graduated two years later.

Billy had been gay in New York for almost ten years before our meeting. He lived in the Village, in a spanking-new white highrise on the corner of West 10th Street and Greenwich. He introduced me to a Village gay life whose contours were much broader and whose density was much thicker than anything I'd yet encountered. On a typical evening or weekend-afternoon date in the spring, we might get a cup of coffee and buttered roll from Tor's, a gay coffeeshop on the corner, and sit on a parked car on Greenwich Avenue or a stoop on Christopher Street, watching gay men cruise by. I was astounded by the numbers. Though lots of men would make the circuit several times in a night, there were always new faces. The scene also had something of a small-town quality to it: Billy was friend or acquaintance to quite a few of the men, and they would stop to chat, share gossip, and catch up on events in their lives. Many of them were former tricks and that, too, was new to me—that a sexual encounter might slide in time into friendship. My experience had been so wrapped up in guilt and fear that it never occurred to me that bonds such as these might form. Billy took me to gay bars and restaurants; he showed me the trucks along the river's edge as well as other Village cruising areas. Slowly I was incorporated into his gay life. For the first time, something akin to ordinary, everyday good spirits was grafted to my homosexuality.

The relationships with Ron and then with Billy also provoked a series of coming-out experiences. Previously, I had come out to some priests at Regis. During my first year at Columbia, when life seemed especially intolerable, I wrote alcohol-induced letters to my friends in the seminary confessing my anguish. But now I had good news to tell, and at times it seemed irrepressible. I don't want to give a false impression: I didn't exactly bounce into the dorm rooms of my friends and joyously proclaim, "I'm a homosexual." I approached each one somberly, and let him know I had something serious I needed to talk about. But once it was clear that my friends weren't going to recoil in horror—and none of them did—then my need to talk broke through all restraints and I probably did babble away. One of them, Jack Collins, with whom I had also gone through high school, came out to me as well. Twenty-odd years later, as the chair of the first gay and lesbian studies department in the United States, Jack would invite me to address its inaugural conference; the speech I gave is included in the second section of this volume (see chapter 10).

These breaks with discretion also meant that by and by, I began to meet other gay students in the dorms. Gradually I became part of a small circle of undergraduates, all of whom were trying to fashion a gay life. A couple of them, Gerry and Rob, already possessed the quick wit and skills in verbal dueling that many gay men cultivated. This meant, in part, that they were always dropping clues about their sexuality for other dorm residents to pick up. I was more reticent, but my approving laughter and the time we spent together meant that I was acquiring a semipublic "identity by association."

I have a tendency to draw overly broad conclusions from what social scientists would call an "inadequate data base." Nonetheless, I am struck now by what my own experiences suggests of a rift opening, in the years just before Stonewall, between two generations of gay men. When I contrast our behavior in the dorm, or my acts of self-revelation to friends, with the way both Ron and Billy, each ten years older than I, managed their sexual identity, the differences are stark. Each of them maintained a sharp divide between their gay worlds and all other relationships; they had told no heterosexuals that they were gay. For instance, soon after Billy and I met, we discovered that we were booked on the same Columbia charter flight to Europe that summer. He was planning to travel with two straight friends, a married couple named Hillary and Larry. By the time we left, I had been absorbed into his itinerary, and the four of us spent much of the summer together. Never a word was spoken about my and Billy's relationship, though it must have seemed odd for this nineteen-year-old to be attached to their party. It was often tense and awkward, but it apparently never occurred to Billy that these two *close* friends should be privy to his secret.

I don't know what made me and my dorm buddies do it differently. I certainly wasn't about to divulge my homosexuality to the world, but I was determined to stretch the boundaries of discretion, if only because it felt emotionally untenable to do otherwise: I'd have gone crazy if I'd held it all in. The simplest—and, probably, most profound—way to explain it is through reference to "the times." By 1967 and 1968, the sense of breaking through barriers permeated college life. Some of that came from political struggle around race, and the war, and student power. Some of it was cultural, a cluster of values expressed through music, drugs, styles of dress and hair, *and* sexuality. There was an openness, a climate of tolerance, and an acceptance of things new and different that made it safe to speak my secret and made my friends authentically curious to hear about my world rather than be repelled by it. I suspect that, in dorm rooms and other settings across the country, many young men and women were engaged in similar acts of personal disclosure. Stonewall would soon make this a collective endeavor and transform the meaning of what we were doing. For the moment, I and others were on the cusp of something new, straining toward a world that was waiting to be born.

The times were shaping me in other ways, too. Columbia between 1966 and 1970 was awash with the antiwar and racial politics sweeping over the nation's campuses. Though much of my extracurricular energy focused on crafting a gay life, I was also caught in the political turmoil. In the essay "Not a Simple Matter," I describe myself as "a bit player—maybe only an extra," in the cast of thousands that the antiwar movement was mobilizing. Even that much was a miracle, considering my upbringing. All the adults in my family were conservative Cold Warriors; they'd voted for Goldwater in 1964. In high school speech tournaments, I declaimed about the strategic hamlet program and the hope it offered for victory in Vietnam.

Columbia exposed me to a side of the story absent from the pages of *U.S. News and World Report*. During orientation week, besides learning that God was dead, I listened as Jim Shenton delivered to the freshman class an antiwar address that packed more wallop than almost any speech I've ever heard. Shenton was a radical history professor. Later, in graduate school, I studied with him and often turned to him for mentoring; he enthusiastically encouraged my pursuit of gay history. That night, in an oration that seemed to pour from his lips spontaneously, but which must have been meticulously prepared, he set up a dramatic confrontation between policymakers justifying war in phrases rife with national chauvinism, and an elected official whose opposition was framed in the loftiest American ideals. He named no names until the very end, when he socked us with his punch line: the dissenter was Abraham Lincoln speaking against war with Mexico. It was my first acquaintance with the power of history to reshape contemporary opinion.

Just as it didn't take long to pry me loose from the Church, it didn't require much effort to let go of my family's politics. By the end of my freshman year I was marching against the war. SDS was too intimidating and alien for me to feel at home there; I couldn't follow much of their political rhetoric, and they were very, very angry. Instead, I gravitated toward radical pacifist circles. I participated in ecumenical services against the war, and fasts in front of the White House. I was trained as a draft counselor to help young men avoid military service, and I took part in guerrilla activities against New York City's draft boards. I developed a healthy skepticism toward "the system" and its leaders—toward university presidents whose untruths were exposed when radical students rifled through the files in their offices, and toward a corporate press whose journalism mangled the events I was witnessing.

Through all of this there was my personal struggle with the draft. Today, in my undergraduate course on the 1960s, I can manage to explain to my students the labyrinthine workings of the Selective Service System. It is more difficult to communicate the emotional stress experienced by the male undergraduates of a generation ago who were subject to its whims. For me, the closest analogue— hardly illuminating for my students in Greensboro—is the experience of being gay in pre-Stonewall times: never far from my conscious thoughts, ever poised to provoke anxiety, erupting unpredictably like pimples on the face of a helpless teenager, which is exactly what many of us were.

I knew I could get out by declaring my homosexuality, but to me that seemed the path of moral cowardice. Instead, I decided fairly early on to seek conscientious objector status. But my parents were the rub. Draft boards were not exactly rushing to give CO classifications to young men. They had to be incontrovertibly persuaded of one's sincerity and convictions. Without support from my parents, my effort would be pointless. The first time I raised the issue, they both became outraged. Over the next two years, we engaged in emotionally lacerating arguments that, twenty-five years later, it still hurts to recall. (I am *sure,* now, that some of my very unpacifistic vehemence came from the rupture that my unacknowledged gayness was provoking in our relationship.) At the eleventh hour, they yielded. Reluctantly my mom wrote a letter in which she recalled how I never played with the toy gun-and-holster set I'd received one Christmas; my dad movingly told of his own conflicts, unknown to me, over military service during World War II.

In the end, the agony proved moot. Nixon instituted a lottery system and I drew a lucky number. Then, called for my draft physical, I unexpectedly flunked it because of the lingering effects of a childhood accident. When I telephoned home from Fort Hamilton, my God-and-country mother broke into sobs; she hadn't wanted her son sacrificed after all.

Perhaps in calmer times the transition from college into the "real world" of adult responsibilities might have been easier. But those weren't placid times. For months I had been having a recurrent nightmare. A huge brick wall loomed in front of me. I knew that I had to make it to the other side. I would try to run to one end or the other, but the wall kept lengthening, always stretching out several yards ahead of me. I would try to climb over it, scratching my way up its surface, but falling before my hands could grasp the top. The future was on the other side, but I could never see what it looked like.

The previous fall, as I had been struggling with my draft board, I had also applied to graduate schools and was accepted into Johns Hopkins, my school of choice. The first year of the program, to begin that summer, would have taken me to Italy. For months I'd been assuming that, instead, I would have to spend two years as a conscientious objector doing alternative service work somewhere in the United States. Now, having flunked my physical, I was free to do whatever I wanted. But I couldn't. Those last months before graduation, I was tense as a coiled wire. There were the dealings with the draft. I was breaking up with Billy. The Cambodia invasion, and the killings at Kent State and Jackson State, provoked the largest wave yet of student protest. The days and nights were filled with guerrilla action in the street. In the pressure-cooker atmosphere of Morningside Heights, it felt as if the world were braced to explode. I remember coming home one day after demonstrations in front of the induction center on Whitehall Street in Lower Manhattan. One of my roommates, Judy, was home. Sitting on the edge of her bed, we tried to make sense of the events around us until finally, giving up, we just held each other and cried. The world seemed too chaotic and I was too distraught to embark on anything like a straight-line path toward maturity. I turned down my graduate school admissions. I started checking the job ads in the *Village Voice,* found one for a library position in Brooklyn, was hired, and agreed to start at a $100 a week a few days after graduation.

That's the official story. It's the one I told my friends and my parents, and the one I told myself. But there was a gay subtext to those months of decision making, one that I barely admitted to myself, let alone to anyone else. Each bit of information I'd acquired about gay life in New York, each bar and cruising area, each gay friend I'd made, and each friend I'd told—each was like a buoy, something to grab hold of to stay afloat. The prospect of swimming to another shore—in this case, Italy—

was too risky. I think I sensed that the type of student who would be in a program studying international affairs would be "straighter" than my radical Columbia friends. A new country, a new culture, a new language, and no gay markers. I wouldn't survive.

As it turned out, my job perfectly suited me. After weeks of accumulating hints, my boss and I each scoped out that the other was gay, and that made everything easier. Joe also had leftish leanings and had added periodicals like *Radical America, Socialist Revolution, Ramparts,* and *New Left Review* to the library's holdings. Until then, my "radicalism" had been of the heart rather than the head: the war provoked revulsion in me, the men responsible for it were monsters, and there was something wrong with a system that could allow it to happen. Now I had time for reading of my choosing, and some of the most thoughtful left-wing writing was passing across my desk. I devoured it. Following up the footnotes, I encountered the work of William Appleman Williams and other New Left historians. Though I had studied European history in college, I hadn't read a book on U.S. history since high school. Now I was hooked. I recalled Shenton's antiwar address and remember thinking, "this stuff could change the world." I reapplied to graduate school, this time only to Columbia so that I wouldn't have to leave New York, and the next fall I was back on Morningside Heights.

The other great benefit of the job was Tomás. I encountered him one morning on a subway platform, as I waited for the train to take me to work. He was stunningly attractive and for several days I remained obsessed with his image. The next week, when I saw him again standing at the same place, I approached and invited him to dinner. Thereafter, we spent every night together for four years. Toward the end of our first summer of coupledom, I began moving my few possessions—clothes, books, records—into his apartment. Being with him was so natural that I didn't ask, and we didn't discuss or negotiate it. Our living together seemed preordained.

It requires a stretch of imagination to recall now how saturated with love I was that summer, and for most of the succeeding four years. It is much easier to identify how Tomás reshaped my relationship to my gayness. Despite the breaks with discretion that I'd made, I still separated the world into those who knew and those who didn't. Now, with my life entwined in his, I no longer knew how to conceal who I was. Since promiscuous self-revelation seemed equally impossible, I simply jettisoned those friendships in which I felt I didn't dare speak the truth, as I describe in the essay "Graduation Day" (see chapter 12). Once done, this task of letting go left my life thoroughly gay.

At the time, I don't think I experienced these various ruptures as a great loss. The connection with Tomás was so intense that it compensated for a lot. Tomás's world was rich and engaging. Today I travel in circles where "diversity" is a primary value; much conscious thought goes into the "struggle" to create multicultural environments at work and in movement organizations. Twenty years ago, Tomás's life embodied that ideal, and he didn't seem to expend much effort to make it happen. His network of friends and acquaintances, which was very large, ranged across race and ethnicity, education and occupation, and age. He was also out to his family. Though he didn't see his parents often, as the eldest in a large Puerto Rican family he retained the love and respect of his siblings, and we saw them and his nieces and nephews a lot. The ties to his family were also just one aspect of something larger: heterosexuals were likewise incorporated into this variegated social milieu. Tomás, in other words, was fully out of the closet before gay liberation had touched him.

This different kind of gay world that I was entering also seemed to be in transition. How do I know that, you might ask, since I was entering it for the first time? Because Tomás was the pacesetter in his circle, and I watched as others followed his lead. When I met him, his hair was combed out into a huge Afro; over the next couple of years, his male friends grew their hair too. He was the first man I'd ever seen who wore an earring; before long, other ears got pierced. Tomás, whose education had stopped with a vocational-track diploma from a New York high school, had managed to land a white-collar job with an airline. The work was secure, it paid decently, and it allowed him to travel a lot. Not long before I met him, he had given that up, gone to work for NYU to qualify for tuition credit, and was preparing to start school full-time, which meant taking on student loans and living on a lot less money than he'd grown accustomed to. Soon, others in his group "dropped out" to one extent or another, making do with fewer of the creature comforts of American consumerism in exchange for the promise of more personal freedom.

All of this was happening in New York in 1970 and 1971, after Stonewall, when gay liberation was there for the taking. But it wasn't the movement that was provoking change in Tomás and those around him. When I met him, in June of 1970, I'd heard that a march to commemorate the first anniversary of Stonewall was planned for later in the month. I raised with Tomás and some of his friends the possibility of going. But the idea of "fags marching," which is how one of them framed it, sent them into stitches, and I beat a hasty retreat. Rather, their lives were in motion from the impact of the counterculture which, by the early 1970s, was bursting free of its roots among middle-class white youth and sweeping over the population. As taken up by Tomás and others, it was denuded of any explicitly political content, but the effects were nonetheless profound. Individuals were trying to redirect their lives beyond the grooves into which they had slipped, or been channelled. Allegiance to these antimaterialistic and personally expressive values constituted an exciting bond, a commonality that, at least for a time, was flattening other social differences, particularly those of race and class, but also of sexual identity.

Two other features of this social world deserve mention, though I find myself hesitating to introduce these topics in the "just say no" climate of today. One was drug use. Hallucinogenics such as LSD and mescaline were integral to the innovations people were making in their lives. Under the influence of LSD, the densest material objects seemed quite literally to dissolve. Out of the rubble piles one might reconstruct reality. "Trips" were often planned carefully to achieve maximum effect, to allow for the exploration of psychic frontiers. Marijuana was consumed more casually and more frequently: it calmed one so thoroughly that the prospect of living without a career, with less money, and with fewer lifetime goals seemed palatable.

The other feature was sexual experimentation. Through my own work and that of others in recovering the social history of gay life, I know now what should have been obvious—that we were not the first gay men to have group sex or be nonmonogamous. However, that history was hidden then, and the larger social practice of relegating sex to a private sphere made us unaware of what might have come before us. Even in our own lives, some of us in the past had been "unfaithful" to lovers, or experienced group sex in places like the baths or the trucks or city parks at night. But now there was an *intentionality* to our pursuit; it was driven by an evolving, self-consciously created belief system evocative of the counterculture.

I vividly recall listening with Tomás to a Jefferson Airplane song, "Triad," about the struggle to open a relationship, whose refrain was "why can't we be three?" We grappled with the question and its implications. Weren't we committed to eliminating acquisitiveness and possessiveness in our lives? Wasn't a lover a "possession"? If love was good, why restrict it to only one? Why couldn't we be three . . . or four . . . or more? The logic seemed irrefutable.

And so we tried. We had sex with other men, and told one another about it. We introduced our other partners to each another. We tried to bring them into the more intense everyday relationship that we shared. We had group sex. Sometimes we embarked on these adventures enthusiastically. At other times we approached them more gingerly, when feelings of jealousy or insecurity stormed into our lives. At still other times we pulled back altogether, when it seemed too much to handle. Since we lived in a collective household after our first year together, our roommates' partners were drawn into this ever-expanding network of tricks, former tricks, affairs, ex-lovers, friends, and acquaintances. We created a densely packed gay life.

With gay liberation spreading through New York's gay worlds, it was inevitable that, at some point, one of the men who passed through our door would bring the movement with him. I don't quite remember how Bert Hansen entered our lives, but he proved to be the perfect emissary. Just a handful of years older than I, he taught history at Fordham's experimental college and lived a few blocks north of us, on the edge of Harlem, in a group household as complicated as ours. One day, after we'd known each other a few months, he told me about an informal meeting to discuss the topic of gays in academic life and invited me to come. My life would never be the same again.

3

Because most of the essays in the second section of this collection touch in one way or another on the story of the Gay Academic Union, it would be repetitive for me to tell it here. "The Universities and the Gay Experience" (see chapter 6) recounts the events of GAU's first several months without the distortion of two decades of reinterpretation; other essays at least begin to suggest its significance in launching gay scholarship and the move toward gay studies. Here I want to mention a couple of other issues, one general and the other personal to me.

I learned through my work with GAU (and have had the lesson confirmed in every other gay group I have been a part of) that gay organizations are extraordinarily complex, intricate, and bewildering creatures regardless of what their stated purpose may be. Two of GAU's goals, for instance, were to oppose discrimination against gay people in academia, and to foster scholarship and the teaching of gay studies. Admittedly, these are not easy goals to achieve, as the passage of time has revealed. They are, however, fairly straightforward and relatively simple to define, and ought to have pointed us in a clear direction.

But gay and lesbian organizations are never simply about their mission statements. Because everyone who participates is at some stage of coming into their sexuality and coming out about their identity, we approach the organizational environment with a host of other agendas that often remain unarticulated. Old memories of ridicule and rejection, the desire for love, sex, and intimacy, the search for home and family, the struggle to fashion an identity free of the corrosive assumptions of a homophobic culture—all these converge at the meeting site. We carry into the movement as well the accumulated grievances of our other social identities. We bring a worldview, a set of assumptions about society and social change that we graft to the goals of the organization or to the discussion at hand.

No wonder the atmosphere is often thick with emotion. The greatest surprise of all is that, despite this, we have managed to accomplish as much as we have.

Because GAU coalesced in the early years of gay liberation, many of us were new to the movement, new to its stance of gay pride, and new to the daunting imperative to come out. This made our gatherings all the more intense, our expectations all the greater. Meetings, whether of a conference planning committee or of a consciousness-raising group (of which there were many) were sometimes exhilarating, sometimes explosive, and often cathartic. We were engaged in acts of creation. Far more seemed to ride on our words and actions than whether the universities abolished discrimination. If in the eyes of any member the organization took a wrong turn, our identity, our home, our life seemed at stake.

If these observations seem abstract or overly intellectualized, let me illustrate what I mean with an example. In the early GAU, one of the recurring topics of debate (a very mild word to describe these discussions) was bisexuality. I no longer remember who said what or where I stood on the issue. But I can't forget the atmosphere—emotions boiling over, veins on necks standing out as individuals strained to be heard above the din, my own fear that my new gay home was about to crumble for reasons that I could not comprehend. It was as if the room were suddenly crowded by a trainload of former lovers who had betrayed each of us by crossing back to "the other side." Who could theorize rationally about human sexuality under these circumstances?

As for me, that first meeting, which marked my entry into the movement, was—and remains—the most significant event in my life. While the years since then have certainly not moved forward in anything like a straight line, I am nonetheless most impressed by the continuities of the last twenty years. The world of the movement is not the same as gay life. It is bound together not only by a shared oppression, but by a shared commitment to do something about it, by an indignation at injustice, and by a profound discontent with things as they are. From my entry into the GAU I can trace the beginnings of friendships that continue today. My life radiates outward from those relationships (and the many that have since been added) and from the enterprise that binds us together.

In practical terms, this meant that my gayness, my activism, and my inchoate professional life became all of a piece. I had entered a graduate program in U.S. history, as had other students of that era, at a moment when many of the mass movements of the 1960s were dissolving. I, and others, had some cloudy notion that the writing and teaching of history could become a site for social change. A generation of New Left scholars was reshaping our understanding of the nation's past. The new social history was restoring a voice to the dispossessed and making history something other than an account of elite white men's lives.

When it was time to embark on my dissertation, I picked a gay topic, an almost unheard-of decision in 1974. From my vantage point today, the choice appears so inevitable that it seems hardly worth a comment. But it wasn't so then. I obsessed over it. The worries weren't about the implications for my career to which, quite honestly, I rarely gave a thought. Rather, to write gay history made it well-nigh impossible not to be out of the closet. It was a step that, if I took it, promised to force a whole series of future coming-out encounters—to my professors, to my parents, to anyone who asked the common question "and what do you do?" This was certainly the right course of action in the eyes of movement ideologues, but they wouldn't be there at the dinner table with my mom and dad. In the end, I took the plunge, preferring the stress of disclosure to the complications of a bifurcated life. Once made, the decision wedded me more closely to the fate of the movement. And, my choice to discover and write about the history of pre-Stonewall activism reflected my own absorption in issues of activism and social change. (That absorption also took its toll on my relationship with Tomás. Already suffering lacerations from our experiments with a new sexual ethic, it collapsed under the tension of my immersion in a movement world and his disdain for it. The personal and the political did not always mix well.)

Some of the essays in this volume—"The Supreme Court and the Sodomy Statutes," "Making and Unmaking Minorities," and "After Stonewall" (see chapters 14, 13, and 20, respectively)—express a concern, or comment upon, the evolution of gay male activism in the 1970s from a radical liberation perspective to a reformist gay rights politics. GAU became just one of the many sites where these tensions were played out. One form this took was conflict over the relationship between feminism and the gay movement. Each resolution of the issue in favor of acknowledging the intertwined nature of sexism and homophobia was eviscerated by the next infusion of men into the organization who hadn't been through consciousness-raising on gender oppression. Toward the end of 1975, most of the women in GAU simply walked out, tired of having to cover the same ground again and again. Another battle line formed between men whose radical identification led us to see gay liberation as one piece of a larger project of social change and men who sought to detach gay issues from all other concerns. When GAU's conference planners, keenly interested in Sergeant Leonard Matlovich and his challenge to the military's exclusion policy, invited him to address our 1975 annual conference, it provoked a major debate over the purpose and direction of the organization. Most of the radical men chose to leave. For those of us who had come of age in the antiwar movement, it seemed a betrayal to honor someone who had proclaimed, "I love the military."

Looking back on that experience, I see this withdrawal as one example of an all-too-frequent pattern: radicals abandoning organizations whose limited goals or reform-oriented politics seem too narrow for our social vision. Since we provided much of the energy and much of the drive in GAU—and in other groups as well— our leaving only furthered the conditions we bemoaned. After our departure, the organization became even less dynamic and less effectual. These reflections come long after the fact, however; they are shaped, in part, by observing the different and more productive choices that many gay and lesbian radical activists—renamed "progressives" in the 1980s—have made in more recent years. In 1975, we preferred to wear the mantle of political purity, and hence departed.

That same fall I was invited by Jonathan Katz to join a number of other GAU expatriates in a gay men's study group, convened to explore the utility of Marxist theory for understanding gay oppression. We met weekly for a period of almost two years and slogged our way through a number of classic texts: *The Communist Manifesto, Origins of the Family, Eighteenth Brumaire, The German Ideology, What Is To Be Done?,* and volume one of *Capital.* Needless to say, we did not find a well-articulated sexual politics. But I came away from those readings and discussions with tools for intellectual analysis that still inform the gay history I write.

For years I had been reading works of history produced by radical scholars. Almost uniformly, their conclusions were more persuasive than those elaborated by liberal or conservative historians. But the means by which they built their arguments out of the mass of historical evidence always eluded me. In my seminar papers, I could not reproduce their logical power. To my eyes, my efforts seemed weakly imitative.

A few months into the study group there came a flash of intellectual recognition (I *know* how Catholic this sounds, like Paul's conversion on the road to Damascus). Reading *The German Ideology,* I understood that Marxism was less about the particular conclusions one drew—any one of which could be endlessly debated— and more about a method of analysis that was both dialectical and materialist. Because this was the 1970s rather than the 1930s, and because I was being influenced by the New Left rather than the Stalinist Old Left, it was possible for me to absorb a Marxist method that left ample room for issues of culture and consciousness, matters of great significance in the construction of a gay historical literature.

Our study group did more than read. Naming ourselves the Gay Socialist Action Project, we sought opportunities to keep the militant spirit of radical gay liberation alive. We helped organize noisy demonstrations outside the Democratic Convention which met in New York City that summer. We put together a gay contingent for the counter-Bicentennial march held in Philadelphia. Our most emotionally gratifying action came when we pulled off a perfectly executed disruption—a "zap" in the parlance of the times—of a panel on male homosexuality held at the New York Academy of Medicine and containing a collection of the most retrograde homophobic psychoanalysts. We were in touch with other collectives of gay male radicals in Los Angeles, San Francisco, Toronto, Chicago, and elsewhere.

All of these activities included Tony, my roommate at the time. I had first met him when the GAU was forming. A community organizer who had worked in East Harlem for most of the 1960s, Tony had separated from his wife and the children they had raised, and, like many other men who had contained their homosexuality in the pre-Stonewall era, was coming out. He had lived with me and Tomás for a few months before moving to Berlin and now, three years later, was returning to New York. For seven years after that we shared not only a home but also intellectual interests, a political worldview, and the excitement of being gay in New York during the years when the gay male subculture was being re-created in its post-Stonewall and pre-AIDS form. Tony had a lifetime dedication to social justice issues. He worked tirelessly to assure high-quality day care for the children of working-class families and thrived on embarrassing the city's rigid social service bureaucracy. From Tony I learned a good deal about organizing and strategizing change and, less tangibly, about making a commitment to continuing the work of social change even when circumstances seem unfavorable. At financially strapped times in my life as a volunteer activist/graduate student, he kept me afloat by hiring me to work in the child advocacy agency he headed.

Tony was also partner in the creation of our weekly open house for gay men. I described this informal institution in the essay "Saturday Night" (see chapter 15). From 1976 until the mid-1980s we opened our apartment to our gay friends, and their friends, made endless amounts of spaghetti and chili and beef stew, and socialized, talked politics, planned actions, and just had a good time. Our place became a watering hole for gay activists from around the country, particularly for those of a leftish persuasion who were passing through New York. When we moved into a larger apartment and were joined by another GAU buddy, David Roggensack, the numbers grew to fill the extra space. In an odd way, these weekly occasions evoked for me the gatherings of my extended family at my grandmother's house every Sunday, throughout my childhood and adolescence. Rain or shine, Grandma would be there and so would the rest of us. Now we were making a gay extended family for ourselves. With our closest friends we cooked Thanksgiving feasts and shared other holiday gatherings.

Tony and I initiated our open house to resolve the "Saturday Night Fever" dilemma: how to make sure we had plans and had fun on Saturday night. In many ways it was a self-conscious alternative to the increasingly expensive commercial-ized leisure that the city offered. But, as I suggested in the essay I wrote at the time, our lives flowed in and out of movement settings, self-created social environments like our open house, and the public gay subculture that flowered in the 1970s. Social, sexual, and political worlds overlapped. Tonight's trick might metamorphose into tomorrow's friend or movement co-conspirator; a movement acquaintance might reappear among the tangle of male bodies in the steam room of the St. Mark's baths.

To Tony I owe one other debt of gratitude. Through him I met Dorothy Stoneman, as dynamic and inspiring a social change advocate as anyone I know. Dorothy, too, had been a community organizer in Harlem and East Harlem during the 1960s, focusing on issues of education and community control of schools. Like other radicals from the sixties, she was searching for ways to extract lessons from those years and fashion them into a dynamic new strategy. When I met her late in 1975, she was—with great chutzpah—preparing to launch a new political party. The movements of the 1960s, she reasoned, had settled for a strategy of protest and backed away from the issue of power. Dorothy was convinced that there was a reservoir of experience and passion still afloat in those post-Watergate times. In fresh, visionary language, completely devoid of stale left-wing rhetoric, she dared to sketch a fifty-year plan for transforming America.

It was impossible not to be attracted by Dorothy's magnetic energy. Much of what she said corresponded to my own values and beliefs. I was also looking for a setting for my activism in which my gayness would be integrated into a larger whole. I proved to be one of her most enthusiastic recruits. For the next four years, we talked almost daily, saw each other several times a week, and participated in the creation and execution of a host of community organizing projects— expanding access to day care for low-income families; developing neighborhood improvement projects conceived by and employing jobless teenagers of color; mobilizing against violence against women; creating community-based theaters— that were to be the foundation upon which a political party would be built.

Dorothy also believed that many of the best-intentioned efforts at making change collapsed under the accumulated emotional stress and material pressures that activists lived with. We needed, she argued, a tool for personal growth that would sustain our moral and political commitments. Dorothy introduced into all our work the practice of Reevaluation Counseling. RC or, as it is commonly called, co-counseling, was just then spreading across the country, along with many other human potential philosophies. But unlike most of the other methods afloat in the 1970s, which appealed to middle-class self-absorption, RC grounded its approach in a liberation perspective. It saw the limitations people experienced in their lives—whether they be depression, powerlessness, low self-esteem, or discourage- ment—as results of the endless onslaught of oppression. Many things drew me to its practice: RC proposed that ordinary folks could be easily trained to give one another effective help; its low cost made access to it democratic; its view of human nature was optimistic; its faith in the ability of people to make change was boundless. I was also attracted to it by the effects I observed. As I and the other activists I was working with began to have regular co-counseling sessions, I watched us resolve conflicts that had seemed intractable, take on challenges that had once seemed daunting, and dream bolder dreams. I was hooked and, in a short time, co-counseling became thoroughly integrated into my life.

Dorothy became mentor to me. From her I learned what seem, in retrospect, to be simple, basic skills, but ones which have proved enormously valuable: how to plan an agenda for a meeting; present proposals that can be debated and revised, rather than permit unstructured chaos to prevail; create structures that allow everyone's thinking to be heard; craft a consensus out of a score of ornery, independent minds. Though as a group we never figured out how to build a political party, we all became more effective and committed activists, with a legacy of successful local community endeavors.

**4**

These activities held a good deal more appeal and drama for me than did the plodding work of dissertation research. My allegiance to the academic world was, at best, tenuous; only the conviction that the movement would be strengthened by the retrieval of its hidden early history kept me at it. I was also frankly discouraged by what seemed the insurmountable obstacle of finding sources to construct anything like a coherent narrative. I'd spent a year reading through every issue of *Mattachine Review, The Ladder, One Magazine,* and *Vector,* the main publications of the pre-Stonewall movement. The work was more frustrating than illuminating. Many articles were unsigned or only initialled; many other writers used pseud-onyms. How was I to find people to interview, or to locate the records of organizations that no longer existed and whose papers had never been collected?

Jonathan Katz was, by this time, most of the way through the work of writing his ground-breaking book, *Gay American History.* He had collected some oral histories to include in it; one of them was with Harry Hay. Jonathan told me what seemed then to be an unbelievable story of Hay, a Communist, founding the gay movement with a group of other leftists. Jonathan also had names and phone numbers of several pre-Stonewall activists from California. With those in hand, I set out for a research trip to the West Coast.

The months of work in California shaped the contours for what became *Sexual*

*Politics, Sexual Communities,* my book on the movement before Stonewall. Until then, I had assumed that I would be writing a work of contemporary history: a few chapters on what happened before gay liberation, and half or more of the book describing the birth and growth of a radical gay and lesbian politics. Now I was learning that the pre-Stonewall story was rich and engrossing enough to be a study in itself. I conducted about three dozen interviews, some lasting as long as fourteen hours and stretching over several sessions. Almost every person I talked with pointed me toward several more, and each subject gave a fascinating account of activism in less hospitable times. Since some of them, like Jim Kepner and Dorr Legg, had saved virtually every piece of paper that passed through their hands in the 1950s and 1960s, they were also providing the manuscript collections that would allow me to match memory against the documentary record.

Though everything I was finding was new and riveting, the story of the early Mattachine Society, which I later wrote up for *Body Politic* and which appears in this collection as "Dreams Deferred" (see chapter 2), captured my heart and my political soul. I'd heard bits of it from Jonathan, and interviews with Kepner and Legg provided me with more details, but a visit of several days with Harry Hay at his home in New Mexico unfolded a tale of Communist gay organizers working in secret during the McCarthy era. Harry is a wonderful storyteller and the yarn he recounted was certainly one that I wanted to believe. But I was troubled by the relative scarcity of documents from those earliest years of activism. How much of what I was hearing was wishful thinking—his *and* mine—and how much deserved to be called "history"? The issue troubled me for weeks until, one day in San Francisco, I was sitting in the garage of Don Lucas, a Mattachine activist, poring through boxes of records that he had saved. One of them contained documents from the early Mattachine—enough of them so that I could begin the laborious task of testing the recollections of my informants against the paper trail that, miraculously, had survived.

The trip to California was significant in another, more enduring way. It was an important time in my relationship with Estelle, who had become my closest friend and intellectual collaborator. I planned my research trip to coincide with Estelle's move to the West Coast for a teaching job; we drove cross-country together. Her being in California was like having a bit of the security of home while I was doing research, and we could talk through much of the material I was uncovering while it was fresh and new in my mind. For her, my presence nearby was an important support as she set up a life away from her friends and family in the East.

I had met Estelle soon after I entered the graduate program at Columbia, where she was already a student. Since we never had any classes together and since she moved out of the city after my first year in school, our paths crossed only occasionally—on campus, and at extracurricular work sessions to put out the graduate student newsletter. We became friends only gradually, over a period of three years. Perhaps because I knew she was a feminist and was studying women's history, I told Estelle—while she waited for a bus on Amsterdam Avenue—about my work with the GAU even before I had decided to write my dissertation on a gay topic. Later, after she had come out to me, she would tell me about riding away as I stood there, and pondering why I had chosen *her* for this information.

Our points of commonality were many: we had each spent our undergraduate years on Morningside Heights during the era of student protests; we were each preparing to pioneer in new fields of historical study; we had each been affected to one degree or another by countercultural values; we were each grappling in our lives with the critiques of gender and sexuality that feminists in the early 1970s were propounding. Our friendship seemed like a continuing conversation, punctuated by the interruptions that geographic distance dictated, about the possibilities for remaking intimate relationships. Many of the issues of sexual freedom that Tomás and I had wrestled with—about open relationships, about balancing commitments, about dealing with jealousy and possessiveness, about where sexual pleasure ought to fit in a life—were grist for our mill. But with a twist. Now I was in dialogue with a woman, and Estelle approached those issues from a different point on the spectrum.

The growing closeness between us was making our relationship the place where I absorbed the meaning of feminism as something more than a politics of formal gender equality. Adding sex to our friendship, as we first did during the summer after I had broken up with Tomás, raised the emotional stakes for me considerably. In a sense, it transformed the relationship into a site where the most personal issues of gender and sexual politics were played out. We were hardly unique in this since feminism was percolating through the intimate lives of many women and men in the 1970s. But we were also embarking on this erotic journey as a gay man and a lesbian. I suspect there were others doing the same thing, but we sure didn't know of any.

What that meant is that we entered a new closet just as we were each exiting another. I was enmeshed in a gay male milieu that placed homosexual expression at the heart of who we were. The lesbian community was defining its identity— and its politics—in gender separatist terms. For both groups bisexuality, as I had been told in the GAU, was a "copout." There seemed to be little space for a relationship such as ours. All around us, gay men and lesbians were engaged in spirited collective discussions about life, love, and sex. We, meanwhile, had to puzzle through questions of our own, without the benefit of a shared discourse: how would each of us negotiate this relationship in our respective worlds? What did our sexual connection mean for my gay identity, or for Estelle's lesbian identity? Should the time come that one or both of us entered a longterm, same-sex partnership, how would we have to adjust our sexual relationship? How would these future lovers feel about our commitment to one another?

Many gay men and heterosexual women have commented on how gay men are unlike other men: more sensitive and expressive, less sexist, not quite as caught in all the trappings of male conditioning. No doubt this is true for some of us in some aspects of our lives. But we are also male as well as gay, and in one crucial area we are often more male than thou. In our sexuality, ironically the place that stigmatizes us as different, many of us come closest to embodying the male stereotype. We can be quite cavalier and careless about sex, relentless in our pursuit of it, treating it as a thing to get rather than a bond to be shared. No questions asked, no tears shed, each responsible only to himself.

This male approach to sex clashed with Estelle's feminism in a number of ways. For instance, in the brave new world of sexual freedom that gay men were trying to create, disease was common. Responsible behavior meant getting tested for syphilis and gonorrhea every three months, taking tetracycline as prescribed, and telling our partners—when we knew who they were—to get tested. At the same time, feminists were critiquing a health system in which women's bodies were an afterthought, and a sexual revolution that made women pay the price of male freedom. Needless to say, Estelle was not interested in sharing the results of my bathhouse philandering. The issue was not one of sexual exclusivity versus promiscuity, but rather of responsibility and the deeply gendered way in which we understood its meaning.

With Estelle I also experienced not only my first sexual relationship with a woman, but my first one to grow out of an already-established intimacy. In my gay experience, sexual attraction had always preceded a relationship. If the erotic energy was strong enough, or if we discovered other areas of affinity, maybe then a bond would grow. By contrast, sex was now serving as an extension of our caring, another layer of intimacy resting on several more. This imparted a richness to our time together that was missing from much of my gay erotic life.

Over time this provoked in me questions about what I was doing. I don't want to give the wrong impression: by most standards, my life during those years would not have been considered chaste. But a space had opened between the norms of the public gay male subculture and, if not my behavior, at least my own inner musings about sex, love, and intimacy.

As Estelle and I evolved a commitment to one another that we each considered permanent, one outcome was that I made repeated trips to San Francisco in order to nurture and sustain our connection. San Francisco in the mid-to-late 1970s was home to the grandest gay experiment of them all. The community was larger and more visible, its political influence greater, and its institutions more extensive than in any other city. I remember one visit early in 1978 when, in just two weeks, I went to more gay theater, films, and readings than in a year in New York. As I wrote about these in my journal, I drew an analogy with the importance of Harlem in the 1920s for the African–American experience. American blacks coming together in such great numbers in an urban setting produced a vibrant culture and politics, even in the midst of oppression. So, too, in San Francisco, something of historic significance was happening.

I returned to San Francisco for a stay of several months in the spring of 1979. By that time, my articles on the radical origins of the Mattachine Society had appeared in the *Body Politic* and given me, in certain small activist circles, minor celebrity status. Katz's *Gay American History* had been out for more than two years, and was spurring an interest in community-based historical research. Estelle told me about a collection of people with whom she was meeting to discuss gay and lesbian history. All of them—Allan Bérubé, Amber Hollibaugh, Jeff Escoffier, Gayle Rubin, Eric Garber—have gone on to produce important work and have helped to shape the debates about sexual politics that occurred in the 1980s.

Those months changed profoundly the social context in which I pursued gay history. It was now becoming a collaborative, collective enterprise to which more of us were deeply committed—to the work and to each other. With Allan, especially, I established an intimate connection. Our lives overlapped in a number of ways. Close in age, we both came from ethnic working-class families, had experienced the campus turmoil of the 1960s and, influenced both by our family backgrounds and the counterculture, had mastered the art of living on very little money. Allan guided me on long walks in which we explored the nooks and crannies of San Francisco, all the while engaging in animated, nonstop conversations about gay history and politics. I remember well his excitement—and mine—when a precious cache of letters written by gay soldiers during World War II fell into his possession. It launched him on a ten-year project that at last has found expression in his book, *Coming Out Under Fire.*

My time in San Francisco coincided with critical events in the political life of the city. I arrived in the midst of the trial of former city supervisor Dan White, who had assassinated Harvey Milk, the city's first openly gay supervisor, and George Moscone, the mayor. When the jury handed down the lightest possible sentence, it triggered a riot. The crowd that formed spontaneously in the Castro and marched to City Hall exhibited more raw rage than anything I'd encountered in the 1960s. Speaker after speaker tried to calm the crowd with words about "gay love," and were booed. In my memory only one, Amber, spoke to the anger that was waiting to erupt. She validated the emotions that were churning in all of us; we were right to feel incensed at this miscarriage of justice. It was my first experience of Amber's uncanny ability to read an audience, to think on her feet, and to crystallize the political sentiment of a crowd. I was staying at the time on Castro Street with Cleve Jones, who had been an aide to Harvey Milk. Later that night, after the riot at City Hall, we watched from his building as the police ran wild. We pulled one gay man, bleeding from a mauling by the police, into his apartment. All in all, it was a sobering—and exhilarating—night.

What I witnessed that night, and over the succeeding days, allowed me to read my historical research in a new light. I saw how dependent the movement was on the subculture; in reality, the subculture, or community, was the sea in which activists swam. Much of the crowd that gathered in front of City Hall had poured out of the bars when they heard about the jury's verdict. Many of them were the much-maligned "clones" whom many activists criticized—those allegedly apolitical gay men with short-cropped hair and mustaches, wearing the uniform of flannel shirt, Levis, and bomber jacket, and having Nautilus-perfect bodies. In the collective experience of the bars and larger subculture, political consciousness clearly germinated, ready to flower under certain conditions.

In my research I had noted how the movement before Stonewall seemed to develop further in San Francisco than in any other city—an interesting fact for which I had only the tautological explanation that San Francisco was the gay capital of the United States. Now, with my interest piqued by contemporary events, I began to search more deeply. Clues whose meaning had eluded me became significant. I uncovered an interlocking set of events and circumstances—the Beat presence in San Francisco and its gay subtext, patterns of state harassment, and gay-related scandals involving police corruption—that provoked activism within the pre-Stonewall bar world. Out of this I was able to fashion a story of San Francisco's gay social and political history, appearing in this volume as "Gay Politics, Gay Community" (see chapter 4).

The city that year was also the setting for the creation of a vibrant community-based history project. During the months when the San Francisco Lesbian and Gay History Project was taking shape, we saw instance after instance of the role history could play in building a community and shaping contemporary political understandings. Allan Berube gave the first presentation of his slide show about women who had passed as men in early San Francisco, *Lesbian Masquerade,* before a packed audience at the Women's Building. It was a grand celebration, and immediately netted the history project new recruits to our collective cultural enterprise. Later that summer, Amber, Jeff Escoffier, and I participated in a panel discussion of history and politics called "Spontaneous Combustion." A couple of hundred lesbians and gay men listened to us describe the evolution since the 1950s of bar life, police harassment, and political activism in San Francisco. It put the White Night riots in a larger framework, making the police violence on Castro Street seem less like an aberration and more like an expression of a long historical pattern.

One other feature of those months stands out in my mind: they were the first time in years that I participated in activity involving lesbians and gay men together. The gay world in which I came of age in the 1960s and early 1970s, though it crossed ethnic, racial, and class lines, was rigidly segregated by sex. Although GAU made efforts at creating a gender-mixed organization, it ultimately failed. Thereafter, my ties with lesbians were restricted to Estelle, and a very small number of acquaintances. Now, in the history project, men and women were working together, and learning from one another. Perhaps it was because history, at least one step removed from contemporary passions, was neutral ground on which to meet. More important, I think, was the fact that the political climate in San Francisco was changing in those years. The work in 1978 against the Briggs Initiative (a ballot measure that would have removed from the public schools open gays and lesbians as well as anyone who "advocated" the naturalness of homosexuality) had pulled lesbians and gay men into a common political struggle that deepened after the trauma of the assassination and the trial.

I returned to New York not only with new friends and new insights but also with a much stronger commitment to history. The number of us who were doing it was growing, and the bonds between us were strong. Many of us saw ourselves as "cultural worker[s] in a liberation movement," as I later wrote in "Not a Simple Matter" (see chapter 8). We formed a tight little community, scattered across the country.

By the early 1980s there were also small indicators of change in the academic world. An organization like GAU had ceased to be the main site in which gay and lesbian academics organized. Instead, women and men in a variety of fields were forming caucuses in their professional associations, such as the Modern Language Association, the American Historical Association, the American Psychological Association, and others. Scholars were presenting their research on lesbian and gay topics at the annual conferences in their disciplines. A few university presses and trade publishers were beginning to solicit manuscripts.

These gains also came with perils. Would even a modicum of acceptance tear the guts out of our work? If the reference point for those of us with at least a foot in the academic world became our professional colleagues or our tenure commit- tees, would we have to tame the passion that the movement fanned in us? These were very real issues for me. My world was based in the movement, not in the academy, even though I maintained my registration at Columbia year after year after year.

Though I continued to work on my history of the pre-Stonewall movement and was publishing pieces in various movement publications, I never seemed to be able to complete my book. Etched sharply in my mind is a November afternoon in 1980, at the apartment of my co-counseling partner in Brooklyn. In the midst of a session in which I was complaining about how stuck I felt, I realized that, once again, fear was shaping my choices. To finish my dissertation would put me face-to-face with several issues I preferred to avoid: would anyone hire me as an openly gay historian? Could I deal with piles of rejection letters? Did I want the stress of coming out, year after year, to new cohorts of students? Could I combine a professional career with an activist's commitment to radical social change? Was I prepared to leave the security of my New York gay world? I determined to bite the bullet. Over the next year I finished and revised the manuscript, got a book contract, and began applying for teaching positions, wondering whether I would succeed and knowing that success would mean big changes in my life.

In the past, I had had opportunities to leave New York but always pulled back, unwilling to risk losing the only shreds of gay life that I knew. Now I was part of a world grown visible, and I had ties to many parts of the country. My life in New York, though rich and satisfying, also had its difficulties. One involved the mundane matter of money. Neither gay history nor gay activism were paying propositions (though that would change by the mid-1980s as the movement began to generate full-time organizing jobs). In the early 1970s, with a rent-controlled apartment, it was still possible for me to live on less than three hundred dollars a month and, quasi-hippie that I then was, I perfected the skills of making do with very little. By the early 1980s, I was in my mid-thirties, the cost of living had skyrocketed, and even I was beginning to experience consumer deprivation: all of my possessions other than books could fit in a mid-sized station wagon.

There were other things. The gay movement in New York was at a low ebb, not yet transfigured by the demands of the AIDS epidemic. AIDS itself, however, was making its menacing presence felt. For my last eighteen months in the city, it was impossible to be with other gay men and not have the conversation focus on AIDS. There was no helpful information, no knowledge of what we could do to protect ourselves, no way of finding out—other than by becoming deadly ill—whether we were infected and what that meant. I and many of my friends were emotionally frazzled, obsessed by any new speck that appeared on our bodies. Even a little geographic distance from one of the epicenters of the epidemic seemed attractive. Finally, it was during this time that I entered—with more care and thoughtfulness than had often been the case—into an intimate relationship. Jim and I had been together for over two years when I got the job offer from the University of North Carolina at Greensboro. He said that he would relocate with me, and so we moved.

My stay in Greensboro has continued now for eight years. I am absorbed in it enough that I lack the distance to see it critically; there is also a rhythm and regularity to teaching that makes these years seem all of a piece. Certainly the move meant dramatic change. Outside of the Triangle area (Durham, Chapel Hill, and Raleigh), North Carolina in 1983 did not call itself home to much of a gay and lesbian movement or community. My experience of gay life in Greensboro has been that it is an interesting hybrid of pre- and post-Stonewall consciousness, institutions, and practice. Though activism has now spread to other parts of the state, especially since the 1987 March on Washington, gays and lesbians are not yet a visible, easily identifiable part of Greensboro's everyday affairs. Overall, the social climate remains less than welcoming. For instance, virtually every time I have appeared as a gay activist on local television or in the newspaper, I have received telephone death threats.

After so many years of immersion in New York's gay world, it has been interesting to move almost to the other extreme. In Greensboro, being an activist and contributing to a process of social change have come to have different meanings for me. I am often the only openly gay man that many of the people around me have ever met. In my classes, students encounter the social history of gay men and lesbians as a natural part of the nation's experience. They also come face-to-face with *me*. Over the years, I have developed a reputation as a good teacher. Depending on which course they take from me, they (affectionately, I think) spread the word either about the professor of sex or the wild radical. Whatever the case, they and others who get to know me at least come to learn that gays are not monsters. In 1991 it exasperates me that, as a society, we are still at that stage, yet I know that it is a first, necessary step on a longer journey.

I also continue to be part of a much broader collective effort at change, whether in the academy or in the nation at large. Overall, the lesbian and gay movement, and the subset of it which is creating a vibrant body of knowledge about our experience, has grown enormously in the last several years. The final essay in this collection, "After Stonewall" (see chapter 20), tries to account for this, and many of the essays in the section on the university describe some of the recent moves in the area of gay studies. In the last three years, the National Gay and Lesbian Task Force has been the setting for expressing my most overtly activist energies. Working closely with these smart, dynamic, committed men and women reminds me not only that much work remains to be done, but also that the changes which, together, we have all wrought in the last generation have already exceeded anything I might have imagined when I was first coming out in the mid-1960s.

The essays that follow display the range of concerns and topics that my writing has reflected. The first section, on history, begins with "Capitalism and Gay Identity" (see chapter 1), a broad interpretive framework for understanding modern gay history. The next three essays touch on particular aspects of the post–World War II history of the United States: the radical origins of the gay movement in the Cold War era; the persecutions and witch-hunts of the McCarthy years; and the evolution of the San Francisco community from the 1940s through the 1970s (see chapters 2–4). All of these were written in the late 1970s and early 1980s, and are products of my research on the pre-Stonewall homophile movement. The last piece in the section, recently done, surveys the historical literature of the 1970s and 1980s on male homosexuality, and attempts to assess where we are and what we know.

Part Two focuses on the university as a setting for some of our lives, our work, and our political energies. Except for "The Universities and the Gay Experience," written in 1974 and recounting the early history of the Gay Academic Union (see chapter 6), all of the articles are of relatively recent vintage. This reflects not only the contours of my own life, in which the academic world did not begin to figure prominently until the mid-1980s, but also the timing of progress in lesbian and gay studies. More is happening now than ten years ago, and the pace of change seems to be accelerating. The essays address a number of different concerns: a campus agenda for activism, the development of gay studies, issues of strategy for institutionalizing our work, and my own reflections on the state of things within the world of historians.

The final section contains pieces written over a fifteen-year period about various issues, events, and experiences in the life of the movement. The first, "Making and Unmaking Minorities" (see chapter 13), was an effort to relate the findings of some gay and lesbian historians to larger issues of strategy that the movement confronts. Those in the middle deal with topics such as the Supreme Court, pornography, the Names Project Quilt, and the perils of an emotion-driven politics (see chapters 14, 16–18). The final essay, "After Stonewall" (see chapter 20), is my first attempt to apply my gaze as a historian to the movement of the last two decades. Unlike the other writing in the collection, it is very much a work-in-progress and seems a fitting place to close the book.

PART ONE

# REWRITING HISTORY

# I

# CAPITALISM AND
# GAY IDENTITY

——————

*This essay is a revised version of a talk I gave before several gay audiences during 1979 and 1980. I was searching for a large historical framework in which to set the history of the pre-Stonewall movement. Why, I wanted to know, did a movement begin only in 1950, when many of the elements of gay and lesbian oppression stretched much farther back in time? Michel Foucault in* The History of Sexuality *and Jeffrey Weeks in* Coming Out *had each argued that "the homosexual" was a creation of the nineteenth century, but without convincingly specifying why or how this came to be. I wanted to be able to ground social construction theory, which posited that gay identity was historically specific rather than universal, in concrete social processes. Using Marxist analyses of capitalism, I argued that two aspects of capitalism—wage labor and commodity production—created the social conditions that made possible the emergence of a distinctive gay and lesbian identity. I was not trying to claim that capitalism* causes *homosexuality nor that it* determines *the form that homosexual desire takes.*

*The essay had political motivation as well. Early gay liberationists had argued that sexuality was malleable and fluid ("polymorphously perverse") and that homosexuality and heterosexuality were both oppressive social categories designed to contain the erotic potential of human beings. By the late 1970s this belief was fading. In its place, gay activists laid claim to the concept of "sexual orientation," a fixed condition established early in life, if not at birth. This perspective was immediately useful in a political environment that sought "rights" for "minorities," but it also fudged some troubling issues, which the conclusion to this essay addresses.*

Reprinted with permission from *Powers of Desire: The Politics of Sexuality,* eds. Ann Snitow, Christine Stansell, and Sharon Thompson (New York: Monthly Review Press, 1983), 100–113.

For gay men and lesbians, the 1970s were years of significant achievement. Gay liberation and women's liberation changed the sexual landscape of the nation. Hundreds of thousands of gay women and men came out and openly affirmed same-sex eroticism. We won repeal of sodomy laws in half the states, a partial lifting of the exclusion of lesbians and gay men from federal employment, civil rights protection in a few dozen cities, the inclusion of gay rights in the platform of the Democratic Party, and the elimination of homosexuality from the psychiatric profession's list of mental illnesses. The gay male subculture expanded and became increasingly visible in large cities, and lesbian feminists pioneered in building alternative institutions and an alternative culture that attempted to embody a liberating vision of the future.

In the 1980s, however, with the resurgence of an active right wing, gay men and lesbians face the future warily. Our victories appear tenuous and fragile; the relative freedom of the past few years seems too recent to be permanent. In some parts of the lesbian and gay male community, a feeling of doom is growing: analogies with McCarthy's America, when "sexual perverts" were a special target of the right, and with Nazi Germany, where gays were shipped to concentration camps, surface with increasing frequency. Everywhere there is a sense that new strategies are in order if we want to preserve our gains and move ahead.

I believe that a new, more accurate theory of gay history must be part of this political enterprise. When the gay liberation movement began at the end of the 1960s, gay men and lesbians had no history that we could use to fashion our goals and strategy. In the ensuing years, in building a movement without a knowledge of our history, we instead invented a mythology. This mythical history drew on personal experience, which we read backward in time. For instance, most lesbians and gay men in the 1960s first discovered their homosexual desires in isolation, unaware of others, and without resources for naming and understanding what they felt. From this experience, we constructed a myth of silence, invisibility, and isolation as the essential characteristics of gay life in the past as well as the present. Moreover, because we faced so many oppressive laws, public policies, and cultural beliefs, we projected this into an image of the abysmal past: until gay liberation, lesbians and gay men were always the victims of systematic, undifferentiated, terrible oppression.

These myths have limited our political perspective. They have contributed, for instance, to an overreliance on a strategy of coming out—if every gay man and lesbian in America came out, gay oppression would end—and have allowed us to ignore the institutionalized ways in which homophobia and heterosexism are reproduced. They have encouraged, at times, an incapacitating despair, especially

4

at moments like the present: how can we unravel a gay oppression so pervasive and unchanging?

There is another historical myth that enjoys nearly universal acceptance in the gay movement, the myth of the "eternal homosexual." The argument runs something like this: Gay men and lesbians always were and always will be. We are everywhere; not just now, but throughout history, in all societies and all periods. This myth served a positive political function in the first years of gay liberation. In the early 1970s, when we battled an ideology that either denied our existence or defined us as psychopathic individuals or freaks of nature, it was empowering to assert that "we are everywhere." But in recent years it has confined us as surely as the most homophobic medical theories, and locked our movement in place.

Here I wish to challenge this myth. I want to argue that gay men and lesbians have not always existed. Instead, they are a product of history, and have come into existence in a specific historical era. Their emergence is associated with the relations of capitalism; it has been the historical development of capitalism—more specifically, its free-labor system—that has allowed large numbers of men and women in the late twentieth century to call themselves gay, to see themselves as part of a community of similar men and women, and to organize politically on the basis of that identity.[1] Finally, I want to suggest some political lessons we can draw from this view of history.

What, then, are the relationships between the free-labor system of capitalism and homosexuality? First, let me review some features of capitalism. Under capitalism workers are "free" laborers in two ways. We have the freedom to look for a job. We own our ability to work and have the freedom to sell our labor power for wages to anyone willing to buy it. We are also freed from the ownership of anything except our labor power. Most of us do not own the land or the tools that produce what we need, but rather have to work for a living in order to survive. So, if we are free to sell our labor power in the positive sense, we are also freed, in the negative sense, from any other alternative. This dialectic—the constant interplay between exploitation and some measure of autonomy—informs all of the history of those who have lived under capitalism.

As capital—money used to make more money—expands so does this system of free labor. Capital expands in several ways. Usually it expands in the same place, transforming small firms into larger ones, but it also expands by taking over new areas of production: the weaving of cloth, for instance, or the baking of bread. Finally, capital expands geographically. In the United States, capitalism initially took root in the Northeast, at a time when slavery was the dominant system in the South and when noncapitalist Native American societies occupied the western half of the continent. During the nineteenth century, capital spread from the Atlantic to the Pacific, and in the twentieth, U.S. capital has penetrated almost every part of the world.

The expansion of capital and the spread of wage labor have affected a profound transformation in the structure and functions of the nuclear family, the ideology of family life, and the meaning of heterosexual relations. It is these changes in the family that are most directly linked to the appearance of a collective gay life.

The white colonists in seventeenth-century New England established villages structured around a household economy, composed of family units that were basically self-sufficient, independent, and patriarchal. Men, women, and children farmed land owned by the male head of the household. Although there was a division of labor between men and women, the family was truly an interdependent unit of production: the survival of each member depended on the cooperation of all. The home was a workplace where women processed raw farm products into food for daily consumption, where they made clothing, soap, and candles, and where husbands, wives, and children worked together to produce the goods they consumed.

By the nineteenth century, this system of household production was in decline. In the Northeast, as merchant capitalists invested the money accumulated through trade in the production of goods, wage labor became more common. Men and women were drawn out of the largely self-sufficient household economy of the colonial era into a capitalist system of free labor. For women in the nineteenth century, working for wages rarely lasted beyond marriage; for men, it became a permanent condition.

The family was thus no longer an independent unit of production. But although no longer independent, the family was still interdependent. Because capitalism had not expanded very far, because it had not yet taken over—or socialized—the production of consumer goods, women still performed necessary productive labor in the home. Many families no longer produced grain, but wives still baked into bread the flour they bought with their husbands' wages; or, when they purchased yarn or cloth, they still made clothing for their families. By the mid-nineteenth century, capitalism had destroyed the economic self-sufficiency of many families, but not the mutual dependence of the members.

This transition away from the household family-based economy to a fully developed capitalist free-labor economy occurred very slowly, over almost two centuries. As late as 1920, fifty percent of the U.S. population lived in communities of fewer than 2,500 people. The vast majority of blacks in the early twentieth century lived outside the free-labor economy, in a system of sharecropping and tenancy that rested on the family. Not only did independent farming as a way of life still exist for millions of Americans, but even in towns and small cities women continued to grow and process food, make clothing, and engage in other kinds of domestic production.

But for those people who felt the brunt of these changes, the family took on new significance as an affective unit, an institution that provided not goods but emotional satisfaction and happiness. By the 1920s among the white middle class, the ideology surrounding the family described it as the means through which men and women formed satisfying, mutually enhancing relationships and created an environment that nurtured children. The family became the setting for a "personal life," sharply distinguished and disconnected from the public world of work and production.[2]

The meaning of heterosexual relations also changed. In colonial New England the birth rate averaged over seven children per woman of childbearing age. Men and women needed the labor of children. Producing offspring was as necessary for survival as producing grain. Sex was harnessed to procreation. The Puritans did not celebrate heterosexuality but rather marriage; they condemned all sexual expression outside the marriage bond and did not differentiate sharply between sodomy and heterosexual fornication.

By the 1970s, however, the birth rate had dropped to under two. With the exception of the post–World War II baby boom, the decline has been continuous for two centuries, paralleling the spread of capitalist relations of production. It occurred even when access to contraceptive devices and abortion was systematically curtailed. The decline has included every segment of the population—urban and rural families, blacks and whites, ethnics and WASPs, the middle class and the working class.

As wage labor spread and production became socialized, then, it became possible to release sexuality from the "imperative" to procreate. Ideologically, heterosexual expression came to be a means of establishing intimacy, promoting happiness, and experiencing pleasure. In divesting the household of its economic independence and fostering the separation of sexuality from procreation, capitalism has created conditions that allow some men and women to organize a personal life around their erotic/emotional attraction to their own sex. It has made possible the formation of urban communities of lesbians and gay men and, more recently, of a politics based on sexual identity.

Evidence from colonial New England court records and church sermons indicates that male and female homosexual behavior existed in the seventeenth century. Homosexual behavior, however, is different from homosexual identity. There was, quite simply, no "social space" in the colonial system of production that allowed

**7**

men and women to be gay. Survival was structured around participation in a nuclear family. There were certain homosexual acts—sodomy among men, "lewd-ness" among women—in which individuals engaged, but family was so pervasive that colonial society lacked even the category of homosexual or lesbian to describe a person. It is quite possible that some men and women experienced a stronger attraction to their own sex than to the opposite sex—in fact, some colonial court cases refer to men who persisted in their "unnatural" attractions—but one could not fashion out of that preference a way of life. Colonial Massachusetts even had laws prohibiting unmarried adults from living outside family units.[3]

By the second half of the nineteenth century, this situation was noticeably changing as the capitalist system of free labor took hold. Only when individuals began to make their living through wage labor, instead of as parts of an interdepen-dent family unit, was it possible for homosexual desire to coalesce into a personal identity—an identity based on the ability to remain outside the heterosexual family and to construct a personal life based on attraction to one's own sex. By the end of the century, a class of men and women existed who recognized their erotic interest in their own sex, saw it as a trait that set them apart from the majority, and sought others like themselves. These early gay lives came from a wide social spectrum: civil servants and business executives, department store clerks and college professors, factory operatives, ministers, lawyers, cooks, domestics, hoboes, and the idle rich; men and women, black and white, immigrant and native-born.

In this period, gay men and lesbians began to invent ways of meeting each other and sustaining a group life. Already, in the early twentieth century, large cities contained male homosexual bars. Gay men stalked out cruising areas, such as Riverside Drive in New York City and Lafayette Park in Washington. In St. Louis and the nation's capital, annual drag balls brought together large numbers of black gay men. Public bathhouses and YMCAs became gathering spots for male homosexuals. Lesbians formed literary societies and private social clubs. Some working-class women "passed" as men to obtain better-paying jobs and lived with other women—forming lesbian couples who appeared to the world as husband and wife. Among the faculties of women's colleges, in the settlement houses, and in the professional associations and clubs that women formed, one could find lifelong intimate relationships supported by a web of lesbian friends. By the 1920s and 1930s, large cities such as New York and Chicago contained lesbian bars. These patterns of living could evolve because capitalism allowed individuals to survive beyond the confines of the family.[4]

Simultaneously, ideological definitions of homosexual behavior changed. Doc-tors developed theories about homosexuality, describing it as a condition, some-thing that was inherent in a person, a part of his or her "nature." These theories did not represent scientific breakthroughs, elucidations of previously undiscovered areas of knowledge; rather, they were an ideological response to a new way of organizing one's personal life. The popularization of the medical model, in turn, affected the consciousness of the women and men who experienced homosexual desire, so that they came to define themselves through their erotic life.[5]

These new forms of gay identity and patterns of group life also reflected the differentiation of people according to gender, race, and class that is so pervasive in capitalist societies. Among whites, for instance, gay men have traditionally been more visible than lesbians. This partly stems from the division between the public male sphere and the private female sphere. Streets, parks, and bars, especially at night, were "male space." Yet the greater visibility of white men also reflected their larger numbers. The Kinsey studies of the 1940s and 1950s found significantly more men than women with predominantly homosexual histories, a situation caused, I would argue, by the fact that capitalism had drawn far more men than women into the labor force, and at higher wages. Men could more easily construct a personal life independent of attachments to the opposite sex, whereas women were more likely to remain economically dependent on men. Kinsey also found a strong positive correlation between years of schooling and lesbian activity. College-educated white women, far more able than their working-class sisters to support themselves, could survive more easily without intimate relationships with men.[6]

Among working-class immigrants in the early twentieth century, closely knit kin networks and an ethic of family solidarity placed constraints on individual autonomy that made gayness a difficult option to pursue. In contrast, for reasons not altogether clear, urban black communities appeared relatively tolerant of homosexuality. The popularity in the 1920s and 1930s of songs with lesbian and gay male themes—"B. D. Woman," "Prove It on Me," "Sissy Man," "Fairey Blues"—suggests an openness about homosexual expression at odds with the mores of whites. Among men in the rural West in the 1940s, Kinsey found extensive incidence of homosexual behavior, but, in contrast with the men in large cities, little consciousness of gay identity. Thus even as capitalism exerted a homogenizing influence by gradually transforming more individuals into wage laborers and separating them from traditional communities, different groups of people were affected in different ways.[7]

The decisions of particular men and women to act on their erotic/emotional preference for the same sex, along with the new consciousness that this preference made them different, led to the formation of an urban subculture of gay men and lesbians. Yet at least through the 1930s this subculture remained rudimentary, unstable, and difficult to find. How, then, did the complex, well-developed gay community emerge that existed by the time the gay liberation movement exploded?

The answer is to be found in the dislocations of World War II, a time when the cumulative changes of several decades coalesced into a qualitatively new shape.

The war severely disrupted traditional patterns of gender relations and sexuality, and temporarily created a new erotic situation conducive to homosexual expression. It plucked millions of young men and women, whose sexual identities were just forming, out of their homes, out of towns and small cities, out of the heterosexual environment of the family, and dropped them into sex-segregated situations—as GIS, as WACS and WAVES, in same-sex rooming houses for women workers who relocated to seek employment. The war freed millions of men and women from the settings where heterosexuality was normally imposed. For men and women already gay, it provided an opportunity to meet people like themselves. Others could become gay because of the temporary freedom to explore sexuality that the war provided.[8]

The gay men and women of the 1940s were pioneers. Their decisions to act on their desires formed the underpinnings of an urban subculture of gay men and lesbians. Throughout the 1950s and 1960s the gay subculture grew and stabilized, so that people coming out then could more easily find other gay women and men than in the past. Newspapers and magazines published articles describing gay male life. Literally hundreds of novels with lesbian themes were published.[9] Psychoanalysts complained about the new ease with which their gay male patients found sexual partners. And the gay subculture was not to be found just in the largest cities. Lesbian and gay male bars existed in places like Worcester, Massachusetts, and Buffalo, New York; in Columbia, South Carolina, and Des Moines, Iowa. Gay life in the 1950s and 1960s became a nationwide phenomenon. By the time of the Stonewall Riot in New York City in 1969—the event that ignited the gay liberation movement—our situation was hardly one of silence, invisibility, and isolation. A massive, grass-roots liberation movement could form almost overnight precisely because communities of lesbians and gay men existed.

Although gay community was a precondition for a mass movement, the oppression of lesbians and gay men was the force that propelled the movement into existence. As the subculture expanded and grew more visible in the post–World War II era, oppression by the state intensified, becoming more systematic and inclusive. The Right scapegoated "sexual perverts" during the McCarthy era. Eisenhower imposed a total ban on the employment of gay women and men by the federal government and government contractors. Purges of lesbians and homosexuals from the military rose sharply. The FBI instituted widespread surveillance of gay meeting places and of lesbian and gay organizations, such as the Daughters of Bilitis and the Mattachine Society. The Post Office placed tracers on the correspondence of gay men and passed evidence of homosexual activity on to employers. Urban vice squads invaded private homes, made sweeps of lesbian and gay male bars, entrapped gay men in public places, and fomented local witch-hunts. The danger involved in being gay rose even as the possibilities of being gay were enhanced. Gay liberation was a response to this contradiction.

Although lesbians and gay men won significant victories in the 1970s and opened up some safe social space in which to exist, we can hardly claim to have dealt a fatal blow to heterosexism and homophobia. One could even argue that the enforcement of gay oppression has merely changed locales, shifting somewhat from the state to the arena of extralegal violence in the form of increasingly open physical attacks on lesbians and gay men. And, as our movements have grown, they have generated a backlash that threatens to wipe out our gains. Significantly, this New Right opposition has taken shape as a "pro-family" movement. How is it that capitalism, whose structure made possible the emergence of a gay identity and the creation of urban gay communities, appears unable to accept gay men and lesbians in its midst? Why do heterosexism and homophobia appear so resistant to assault?

The answers, I think, can be found in the contradictory relationship of capitalism to the family. On the one hand, as I argued earlier, capitalism has gradually undermined the material basis of the nuclear family by taking away the economic functions that cemented the ties between family members. As more adults have been drawn into the free-labor system, and as capital has expanded its sphere until it produces as commodities most goods and services we need for our survival, the forces that propelled men and women into families and kept them there have weakened. On the other hand, the ideology of capitalist society has enshrined the family as the source of love, affection, and emotional security, the place where our need for stable, intimate human relationships is satisfied.

This elevation of the nuclear family to preeminence in the sphere of personal life is not accidental. Every society needs structures for reproduction and childrear-ing, but the possibilities are not limited to the nuclear family. Yet the privatized family fits well with capitalist relations of production. Capitalism has socialized production while maintaining that the products of socialized labor belong to the owners of private property. In many ways, childrearing has also been progressively socialized over the last two centuries, with schools, the media, peer groups, and employers taking over functions that once belonged to parents. Nevertheless, capitalist society maintains that reproduction and childrearing are private tasks, that children "belong" to parents, who exercise the rights of ownership. Ideologically, capitalism drives people into heterosexual families: each generation comes of age having internalized a heterosexist model of intimacy and personal relationships.

Materially, capitalism weakens the bonds that once kept families together so that their members experience a growing instability in the place they have come to expect happiness and emotional security. Thus, while capitalism has knocked the material foundation away from family life, lesbians, gay men, and heterosexual feminists have become the scapegoats for the social instability of the system.

This analysis, if persuasive, has implications for us today. It can affect our perception of our identity, our formulation of political goals, and our decisions about strategy.

I have argued that lesbian and gay identity and communities are historically created, the result of a process of capitalist development that has spanned many generations. A corollary of this argument is that we are not a fixed social minority composed for all time of a certain percentage of the population. There are more of us than one hundred years ago, more of us than forty years ago. And there may very well be more gay men and lesbians in the future. Claims made by gays and nongays that sexual orientation is fixed at an early age, that large numbers of visible gay men and lesbians in society, the media, and the schools will have no influence on the sexual identities of the young, are wrong. Capitalism has created the material conditions for homosexual desire to express itself as a central component of some individuals' lives; now, our political movements are changing consciousness, creating the ideological conditions that make it easier for people to make that choice.

To be sure, this argument confirms the worst fears and most rabid rhetoric of our political opponents. But our response must be to challenge the underlying belief that homosexual relations are bad, a poor second choice. We must not slip into the opportunistic defense that society need not worry about tolerating us, since only homosexuals become homosexuals. At best, a minority group analysis and a civil rights strategy pertain to those of us who already are gay. It leaves today's youth—tomorrow's lesbians and gay men—to internalize heterosexist models that it can take a lifetime to expunge.

I have also argued that capitalism has led to the separation of sexuality from procreation. Human sexual desire need no longer be harnessed to reproductive imperatives, to procreation; its expression has increasingly entered the realm of choice. Lesbians and homosexuals most clearly embody the potential of this spirit, since our gay relationships stand entirely outside a procreative framework. The acceptance of our erotic choices ultimately depends on the degree to which society is willing to affirm sexual expression as a form of play, positive and life-enhancing. Our movement may have begun as the struggle of a "minority," but what we should now be trying to "liberate" is an aspect of the personal lives of all people— sexual expression.[10]

Finally, I have suggested that the relationship between capitalism and the family is fundamentally contradictory. On the one hand, capitalism continually weakens the material foundation of family life, making it possible for individuals to live outside the family, and for a lesbian and gay male identity to develop. On the other, it needs to push men and women into families, at least long enough to reproduce the next generation of workers. The elevation of the family to ideological preeminence guarantees that a capitalist society will reproduce not just children, but heterosexism and homophobia. In the most profound sense, capitalism is the problem.[11]

How do we avoid remaining the scapegoats, the political victims of the social instability that capitalism generates? How can we take this contradictory relationship and use it to move toward liberation?

Gay men and lesbians exist on social terrain beyond the boundaries of the heterosexual nuclear family. Our communities have formed in that social space. Our survival and liberation depend on our ability to defend and expand that terrain, not just for ourselves but for everyone. That means, in part, support for issues that broaden the opportunities for living outside traditional heterosexual family units: issues like the availability of abortion and the ratification of the Equal Rights Amendment, affirmative action for people of color and for women, publicly funded daycare and other essential social services, decent welfare payments, full employment, the rights of young people—in other words, programs and issues that provide a material basis for personal autonomy.

The rights of young people are especially critical. The acceptance of children as dependents, as belonging to parents, is so deeply ingrained that we can scarcely imagine what it would mean to treat them as autonomous human beings, particularly in the realm of sexual expression and choice. Yet until that happens, gay liberation will remain out of our reach.

But personal autonomy is only half the story. The instability of families and the sense of impermanence and insecurity that people are now experiencing in their personal relationships are real social problems that need to be addressed. We need political solutions for these difficulties of personal life. These solutions should not come in the form of a radical version of the pro-family position, of some left-wing proposals to strengthen the family. Socialists do not generally respond to the exploitation and economic inequality of industrial capitalism by calling for a return to the family farm and handicraft production. We recognize that the vastly increased productivity that capitalism has made possible by socializing production is one of its progressive features. Similarly, we should not be trying to turn back the clock to some mythic age of the happy family.

We do need, however, structures and programs that will help to dissolve the

13

boundaries that isolate the family, particularly those that privatize childrearing. We need community- or worker-controlled day care, housing where privacy and community coexist, neighborhood institutions—from medical clinics to performance centers—that enlarge the social unit where each of us has a secure place. As we create structures beyond the nuclear family that provide a sense of belonging, the family will wane in significance. Less and less will it seem to make or break our emotional security.

In this respect gay men and lesbians are well situated to play a special role. Already excluded from families as most of us are, we have had to create, for our survival, networks of support that do not depend on the bonds of blood or the license of the state, but that are freely chosen and nurtured. The building of an "affectional community" must be as much a part of our political movement as are campaigns for civil rights. In this way we may prefigure the shape of personal relationships in a society grounded in equality and justice rather than exploitation and oppression, a society where autonomy and security do not preclude each other but coexist.

## NOTES

1. I do not mean to suggest that no one has ever proposed that gay identity is a product of historical change. See, for instance, Mary McIntosh, "The Homosexual Role," *Social Problems* 16 (1968): 182–92; Jeffrey Weeks, *Coming Out: Homosexual Politics in Britain* (New York: Quartet Books, 1977). It is also implied in Michel Foucault, *The History of Sexuality, vol. 1: An Introduction,* trans. Robert Hurley (New York: Pantheon, 1978). However, this does represent a minority viewpoint and the works cited above have not specified how it is that capitalism as a system of production has allowed for the emergence of a gay male and lesbian identity. As an example of the "eternal homosexual" thesis, see John Boswell, *Christianity, Social Tolerance, and Homosexuality* (Chicago: University of Chicago Press, 1980), where "gay people" remains an unchanged social category through fifteen centuries of Mediterranean and Western Europe history.

2. See Eli Zaretsky, *Capitalism, the Family, and Personal Life* (New York: Harper & Row, 1976); and Paula Fass, *The Damned and the Beautiful: American Youth in the 1920s* (New York: Oxford University Press, 1977).

3. Robert F. Oaks, " 'Things Fearful to Name': Sodomy and Buggery in Seventeenth-Century New England," *Journal of Social History* 12 (1978): 268–81; J. R. Roberts, "The Case of Sarah Norman and Mary Hammond," *Sinister Wisdom* 24 (1980): 57–

62; and Jonathan Katz, *Gay American History* (New York: Crowell, 1976), 16–24, 568–71.

4. For the period from 1870 to 1940 see the documents in Katz, *Gay American History,* and idem *Gay/Lesbian Almanac* (New York: Crowell, 1983). Other sources include Allan Bérubé, "Lesbians and Gay Men in Early San Francisco: Notes Toward a Social History of Lesbians and Gay Men in America," unpublished paper, 1979; Vern Bullough and Bonnie Bullough, "Lesbianism in the 1920s and 1930s: A Newfound Study," *Signs* 2 (Summer 1977): 895–904.

5. On the medical model see Weeks, *Coming Out,* 23–32. The impact of the medical model on the consciousness of men and women can be seen in Louis Hyde, ed., *Rat and the Devil: The Journal Letters of F. O. Matthiessen and Russell Cheney* (Hamden, Conn.: Archon, 1978), 47, and in the story of Lucille Hart in Katz, *Gay American History,* 258–79. Radclyffe Hall's classic novel about lesbianism, *The Well of Loneliness,* published in 1928, was perhaps one of the most important vehicles for the popularization of the medical model.

6. See Alfred Kinsey et al., *Sexual Behavior in the Human Male* (Philadelphia: W. B. Saunders, 1948) and *Sexual Behavior in the Human Female* (Philadelphia: W. B. Saunders, 1953).

7. On black music, see "AC/DC Blues: Gay Jazz Reissues," Stash Records, ST-106 (1977) and Chris Albertson, *Bessie* (New York: Stein and Day, 1974); on the persistence of kin networks in white ethnic communities see Judith Smith, "Our Own Kind: Family and Community Networks in Providence," in *A Heritage of Her Own,* eds. Nancy F. Cott and Elizabeth H. Pleck (New York: Simon & Schuster, 1979), 393–411; on differences between rural and urban male homoeroticism see Kinsey et al., *Sexual Behavior in the Human Male,* 455–57, 630–31.

8. The argument and the information in this and the following paragraphs come from my book *Sexual Politics, Sexual Communities: The Making of a Homosexual Minority in the United States, 1940–1970* (Chicago: University of Chicago Press, 1983). I have also developed it with reference to San Francisco in "Gay Politics, Gay Community: San Francisco's Experience," *Socialist Review* 55 (January–February 1981): 77–104.

9. On lesbian novels see the *Ladder,* March 1958, 18; February 1960, 14–15; April 1961, 12–13; February 1962, 6–11; January 1963, 6–13; February 1964, 12–19; February 1965, 19–23; March 1966, 22–26; and April 1967, 8–13. The *Ladder* was the magazine published by the Daughters of Bilitis.

10. This especially needs to be emphasized today. The 1980 annual conference of the National Organization for Women, for instance, passed a lesbian rights resolution that defined the issue as one of "discrimination based on affectional/sexual preference/ orientation," and explicitly disassociated the issue from other questions of sexuality such as pornography, sadomasochism, public sex, and pederasty.

11. I do not mean to suggest that homophobia is "caused" by capitalism, or is to be found only in capitalist societies. Severe sanctions against homoeroticism can be found in European feudal society and in contemporary socialist countries. But my focus in this essay has been the emergence of a gay identity under capitalism, and the mechanisms specific to capitalism that made this possible and that reproduce homophobia as well.

# 2

# DREAMS DEFERRED

## THE BIRTH AND BETRAYAL
## OF AMERICA'S FIRST
## GAY LIBERATION MOVEMENT

––––––––––––––

*"Dreams Deferred" was the first piece of gay historical writing that I published. I chose to send it to the* Body Politic, *a radical gay liberation monthly based in Toronto, because I respected the members of the collective and because they had already published historical work, such as Jim Steakley's study of the early German gay movement.*

*I doubt that any research and writing gave me as much satisfaction as the work that resulted in this three-part series of articles. The pleasure came, in large part, from the surprise of discovery and the knowledge that readers would be surprised as well. That something so unlikely—gay male Communists being the founders of the gay movement in the United States—could actually be true pleased me no end. The discrediting epithet of "commie-pinko-fag" had to be revisited: not only were there some, but the whole gay movement was in their debt.*

*The editors of* the Body Politic *wanted a dramatic story and I wrote it to highlight the drama that was inherent in the events. The conclusion suggests some of the ways that this bit of gay history held personal significance for me.*

Reprinted from the Body Politic, *November 1978, December–January 1978–79, and February 1979.*

On a Saturday afternoon early in November 1950, five men met at the home of Henry Hay in the Silver Lake district of Los Angeles, California. They were discussing for the first time a proposal Hay had written which had as its focus "the heroic objective of liberating one of our largest minorities and guaranteeing them self-respecting citizenship." After several hours of animated discussion and exhilarating conversation, the others left Hay with the promise to meet again in a few days. All of them were pledged to secrecy.

The need for secrecy flowed from two very different sources. All of the men were homosexuals, and they were discussing the liberation of the gay minority in the United States. In mid-twentieth-century America, homosexuals were well advised to keep their sexual preferences secret. Discovery virtually guaranteed that a man or woman would be ostracized by family and friends, denied most means of earning a decent living, and consigned to a marginal existence.

But the five men who met that November afternoon had another, just as pressing, reason for exercising caution. Two of them were members of the Communist Party; a third had been an active party member in the Midwest after World War II; and the other two might well have been described as fellow travelers. It was difficult enough to be gay in postwar America; to be a communist or communist sympathizer compounded the danger.

Despite the odds against it, however, a homosexual emancipation movement did take root in the America of the 1950s. Several months after their first meeting, the five leftist homosexuals founded the Mattachine Society. The name "Mattachine" was chosen after Hay told the others of the mysterious wandering figures by that name who, during the Middle Ages, performed at festivals wearing masks, and whom Hay suspected might have been homosexuals.

The founding of the Mattachine Society in Los Angeles in 1951 marked the radical beginning of a continuous history of gay political organization in the United States. How was it that a movement to liberate the gay minority had its start in an era of intense repression, in a decade best remembered for its stultifying conformity? How did it happen that the founders of the movement were men whose political beliefs and affiliations placed them far from the mainstream of American politics? How did their Marxist worldview influence the form and direction of the early Mattachine Society? How were the Society's radical beginnings to be betrayed by later events? And why is it that the early history of the Mattachine is barely known?

I

Henry Hay was the man most responsible for the founding of the Mattachine Society. Born of American parents in England in 1912, he spent his early childhood in Chile, where his father was a mining engineer for Anaconda Copper. The family returned to the United States in 1917, and Hay spent the rest of his childhood and adolescence in southern California. After graduating from Los Angeles High School in 1929, he entered Stanford University in the fall of 1930. At Stanford, Hay developed an interest in drama and returned to Los Angeles without completing his studies in order to pursue an acting career. In the depression-ridden years of the early 1930s, Hay found it difficult to secure steady work as an actor, and when a friend asked him to join a group of agitprop (agitation/propaganda) players, he accepted the invitation.

Hay's participation in the agitprop company awakened in him a political consciousness. The street performances at the sites of strikes and other demonstrations were "dangerous stuff," he said. "The Red Squad was always busting things up." He remembered the players narrowly escaping arrest on several occasions. Soon after joining the agitprop company, Hay was taken to a Communist Party study group by some of his actor friends. Though he understood little of the theory being discussed, he admired the seriousness of the party members whom he met and enjoyed the theater which he discovered the party was sponsoring. Early in 1934, Hay joined the Communist Party.

Hay might well have been one of the many party recruits who joined hastily and as quickly fell away were it not for his experiences during the summer of 1934. A strike by West Coast longshoremen in May had escalated in San Francisco into a stoppage of all maritime workers, and the Communist Party sent Hay and many other Los Angeles members to aid in the strike effort. Early in July, violence erupted as employers tried to open the port with scab labor. When the governor called out the national guard, labor leaders appealed for a general strike. In the heady days which ensued, Hay's commitment to the party was born.

"The strike was just something tremendous!" Hay remembers with excitement. "That did it! It was pure emotion, a gut thing. You couldn't have been a part of that and not have your life completely changed."

For the next fifteen years, Hay's life revolved around the Communist Party. Initially assigned to the artists' and writers' branch of the party, he continued to do agitprop theater as well as to participate in many of the party's mass organizations. Active in the Los Angeles chapter of People's Songs Inc (PSI), a leftist organization of songwriters and musicians, Hay represented PSI at the People's Educational Center, a worker education project whose directors ranged from American Federation of Labor (AFL) representatives to Communist Party members. Early in 1948, Hay began teaching a class at the Center on the history of popular music.

Hay's commitment to the party also profoundly affected the shape of his personal life. When he joined in 1934, Hay was an active homosexual. Becoming aware of his sexual attraction to men during his adolescence, he had gradually discovered the male homosexual subculture in Los Angeles and San Francisco and slowly begun the process of accepting his sexuality. Joining the party led Hay to question his choice. The Communists shared the society's general condemnation of "sexual deviance" and, in the total world of the party, Hay found it difficult to incorporate his sexual identity. Deciding to suppress his homosexuality, Hay in 1938 married a party member with whom he had worked closely for a long time. "I determined that I would simply close a book and never look back. For fourteen years I lived in an exile world," he reminisced. Unable, however, to make a complete break with his homosexual inclinations, Hay occasionally had sexual encounters with men. But he deliberately isolated himself from gay social circles and ostensibly conformed to society's—and the party's—sexual mores.

An unexpected occurrence during the summer of 1948 upset this precarious equilibrium. The Communist Party was concentrating much of its effort that summer on Henry Wallace's presidential bid—a third-party effort organized by some liberal Democrats and leftists who opposed the Cold War policies of the Truman administration. Hay was working on the campaign while continuing to do research for his history of music class at the People's Educational Center.

Early in August, Hay attended a party where he was expecting to meet another musicologist. When he arrived he found, to his surprise, that all of the guests were gay. Hay began talking about the Wallace campaign, and before long he and several others were jokingly spinning out the design of an organization to mobilize gay men behind Wallace's Progressive Party. Calling it "Bachelors for Wallace," they imagined the group gathering support among male homosexuals in return for a sexual privacy plank in the Wallace platform.

Although Bachelors for Wallace never moved beyond the stage of idle talk, this chance discussion set in motion in Hay a reevaluation of his personal life. He now began to perceive that homosexuality might contain the potential for political organizing and, in the months that followed, he mulled over the idea of a gay organization. Hay began to realize that "somehow or another, my life as a heterosexual, a pseudo-heterosexual, was coming to an end. Suddenly I was forced to admit that the relentless difference between me and the world of my choice had grown imperceptibly into an unscalable barrier."

But the imminent break with his past had its exhilarating side, too. Hay saw that he would be bringing "to my own people magnificent experience and training in organization and in struggle which I had learned on the other side." He would be using the organizing skills he had acquired in the Communist Party to launch a homosexual emancipation movement.

For the next two years Hay cautiously pursued his still hazily defined scheme for homosexual organization. Hesitating to plunge into the endeavor carelessly, he sounded out the opinions of his professional acquaintances—doctors, lawyers, ministers, educators—about the "plight" of homosexuals. Some of them expressed the conviction that society's treatment of homosexuals was regrettable, but when Hay pushed the subject further by suggesting that something ought to be done, their responses were surprisingly similar: should homosexuals organize for social justice, then they would consider lending their support. To Hay it was becoming clear that a campaign for the rights of homosexuals would have to be initiated by homosexuals themselves.

Sometime during the spring of 1950, Hay elicited his first signs of interest when he spoke to Bob Hull and Chuck Rowland about his idea. Hull was a student in Hay's music class; Rowland was Hull's roommate and closest friend. The three men met one evening at a concert and Hay, who suspected that the pair were gay, decided to broach the subject of a homosexual rights organization. As it turned out, the three men had more in common than their homosexuality, since Rowland and Hull had also been members of the Communist Party.

Rowland was born and raised in a small town in South Dakota. He too grew up feeling isolated by homosexual urges which he could discuss with no one. Going away to college at the University of Minnesota in Minneapolis provided the opportunity for him to come out, to meet other men like himself, and begin the process of self-acceptance. But Minneapolis and the university there in the 1930s also provided fertile soil for the growth of political activism. Rowland found himself participating in the campus disturbances of those years, including demonstrations in support of the Loyalists in the Spanish Civil War and against compulsory military training for students.

Hull attended the university in the same years as Rowland, although the two men did not know each other as students. Hull had a graduate degree in chemistry, but had passed by a career in science in favor of pursuing his interest in music. When he met Rowland in 1940, he was just beginning to break into Twin Cities music circles as a pianist. The two men became lovers and, when that relationship ended, moved easily into a close friendship that would last for twenty years.

Rowland served in the army during World War II, and toward the end of the war, while still in the service, he became a charter member of the American Veterans Committee (AVC). The AVC tended to attract New Deal liberals and progressives who were determined, as Rowland described it, "to build a world in our own idealistic image." The organization was especially active in campaigning for adequate housing, the retention of postwar price controls, and in opposing racial discrimination. After his discharge, Rowland became a field representative for the AVC in the Midwest and helped organize chapters in cities throughout the region.

Despite his ability as both organizer and administrator, Rowland did not remain with the American Veterans Committee for long. The anti-Communism of the postwar years reached that organization early, and from the national headquarters in New York City came cries of communist infiltration. When the AVC leadership began screening members signed up by the midwestern office, Rowland was at first "incredulous, and then mad," after which he himself moved to the left. His own queries established the fact that there were indeed Communists among AVC organizers, but in his opinion they invariably turned out to be the most dedicated workers and soundest strategists.

Rowland decided to join the party (recruiting his friend, Hull, in the process) and, when he was finally forced out of the veterans' organization for his politics, he returned to Minneapolis to work as executive secretary of the branch office of American Youth for Democracy (AYD), a Communist-dominated organization. Late in 1948 Rowland migrated to Los Angeles, at the same time abandoning his active involvement in the party. Hull followed Rowland to Los Angeles toward the end of 1948. Maintaining his party affiliation, he joined one of its cultural units and participated in the activities of the People's Educational Center, where Hay was teaching.

Hull and Rowland were both excited by Hay's suggestions for a homosexual organization and a few more conversations about it ensued. Their informal discussions ended, however, as abruptly as they had begun. After the conclusion of Hay's music class, the men lost contact with one another and Hay was once again left alone with his plan.

The disappearance of Rowland and Hull, in fact, was due to more than the conclusion of Hay's class, although Hay did not know it at the time. According to Rowland, he, Hull, and another Communist Party member left the country in the late spring of 1950 and "departed for Mexico, where we had decided to spend the rest of our lives." In describing their motives, Rowland said, "That was not just a wild, romantic spree; we were fleeing the witch-hunts along with thousands of other Americans from all parts of the country. On several occasions since then I've met previously unknown people who spoke of that crazy summer of 1950 when everyone became a refugee in Mexico."

Although Rowland most likely exaggerated the numbers, the incident points to the depth of the fear and panic felt by many Communists and their sympathizers at the height of the postwar anti-communist hysteria. By the end of the summer, however, Rowland and Hull had returned to Los Angeles, chastened after several aimless months in Mexico, having decided that their flight was "ridiculous."

Early in July 1950, Hay met Rudi Gernreich at a rehearsal of the Lester Horton Dance Theatre. A costume designer and dancer with Horton's company, Gernreich had fled with his mother from Austria in 1938 to escape the Nazis' genocidal persecution of Jews. Settling in Los Angeles, he joined Lester Horton's dance group in 1942. He found the company an intensely political milieu, as Horton's dance pieces frequently had social injustice as their theme, and troupe members who did not share these concerns quickly left. At the time of his initial meeting with Hay, Gernreich was performing in *The Park,* a dramatization of police brutality toward Mexican–American youths, and *Brown County,* a story of a fugitive slave.

Hay spoke to Gernreich about his idea for a political organization to defend the rights of homosexuals. When he expressed interest, Hay resolved to commit his scheme to paper and wrote a lengthy prospectus of the proposed organization. Upon reading it a few days later, Gernreich enthusiastically committed himself to the venture. After almost two years of cautious effort Hay at last had found his first recruit.

Eager to begin, Hay and Gernreich faced the difficult problem of how to attract others to what was potentially a dangerous undertaking. In an attempt to locate homosexual leftists, they took copies of "America's Peace Poll," an anti–Korean War petition being circulated by the Communist Party, to the gay male beaches in Los Angeles and Santa Monica. During the next two months, the two men collected the signatures of several hundred homosexuals opposed to the war. But when they used the opportunity also to talk about the government investigations of homosexuals in federal employment and to suggest that something ought to be done, Hay and Gernreich encountered a terrified silence: no one was willing to risk exposure of his sexual identity by joining a homosexual rights organization.

Hull, meanwhile, had enrolled in another of Hay's music classes and Hay, who had been somewhat puzzled by the sudden termination of their earlier discussions, decided to show Hull the prospectus he had written in July. Hull and Rowland passed it on to another gay friend, Dale Jennings, a writer active in campaigns to defend the civil rights of Japanese–Americans. Hull arranged a meeting for them with Hay, and on a Saturday afternoon in November 1950, the five men—Hay, Gernreich, Hull, Rowland, and Jennings—gathered at Hay's home to discuss the formation of a homosexual rights organization.

Frequent meetings over the next several months led to the formation of the Mattachine Society. As the first organization in what would become a nationwide movement, the early Mattachine Society had several features that reflected the leftist orientation of its founders and that would distinguish it from most of its successor organizations: it had a secret, cell-like, and hierarchical structure; it developed an analysis of homosexuals as an oppressed cultural minority; and, as a corollary of that analysis, the Mattachine Society pursued a strategy for social change that rested on mass action by homosexuals.

The founders' perception of a need for secrecy grew out of the specific political climate in which they lived. By 1950 American Communists and their sympathizers were an embattled, increasingly isolated political minority, subject to severe repression. In the five years since World War II, the popular front of the 1930s, in which Communists, New Deal liberals, and other radicals frequently worked together, had fragmented. The Truman administration's hard-line foreign policy toward the Soviet Union had spawned a rabid anti-Communist crusade in the United States. Although its most extreme expression was found among right-wing Republicans and conservative Democrats, liberals also actively promoted domestic anti-Communism.

In 1947 Truman established a loyalty program for federal employees and the Justice Department issued a lengthy list of allegedly subversive organizations. A number of Congress of Industrial Organizations (CIO) unions were purging Communists from positions of leadership while the national CIO had taken the step of expelling entire unions and certain statewide affiliates. Some liberal Democrats had formed the Americans for Democratic Action to distinguish themselves from those who were "soft on communism."

In 1949, Communist Party leaders were indicted under the Smith Act for supposedly conspiring to overthrow the government by violent means, and the following year, in September 1950, Congress passed a tough new Internal Security Act requiring party members and front organizations to register with the Justice Department and providing for the internment of Communists during periods of national emergency. With the Korean War raging in Asia, the threat of internment loomed large. Following the lead of the federal government, many states enacted laws aimed at suppressing the Communist Party.

To the founders of the Mattachine Society, the attacks on radicals were not an abstraction: Rowland had experienced the effects of anti-Communism in his work with the American Veterans Committee; Jennings's involvement with Japanese–Americans in California made him appreciate the threat of internment; Gernreich had fled his native country to escape a fascist regime bent on exterminating not only an entire people but leftists as well.

Above all, Hay was acutely conscious of the growing climate of repression. With much of his party work centered around cultural activities, he was aware of the targeting of leftists in Hollywood by the House Un-American Activities Committee (HUAC). California, moreover, had its own anti-communist investigating committee whose head, Jack Tenney, came from Los Angeles, and which held highly publicized hearings throughout the postwar years. The two organizations in which Hay was most active, People's Songs and the People's Educational Center, had already come under official scrutiny.

Hay and the others also felt themselves under attack as homosexuals. By 1950 the anti-Communist crusade included "moral perverts" among its targets. In February 1950, Under Secretary of State John Peurifoy testified before a Senate committee that the State Department had uncovered homosexuals among its employees. Over the next several months the Senate pursued this revelation and ultimately issued a report that recommended the dismissal of homosexuals as security risks from government and defense-related employment. One result of the investigation was that the number of homosexuals dismissed from government service increased sharply. Figures in the Senate report indicate that dismissals increased tenfold in 1950 over the preceding three years.

The prospectus that Hay had written in July 1950 for a homosexual rights organization, and which served as the starting point for the founders' early discussions, revolved around his awareness of government repression. Taking off from the Communist Party's thinking of the time, which saw the country moving rapidly toward fascism, Hay gave its analysis quite a different twist by placing the plight of the homosexual at the center of contemporary American politics. After drawing an analogy to Nazi rule in Germany, where homosexuals were "ruthlessly exterminated," he went on to warn against an "encroaching American fascism" which "seeks to bend unorganized and unpopular minorities into isolated fragments." The full significance, he wrote, "of government indictments against Androgynous Civil Servants lies in the legal establishment of a type of GUILT BY ASSOCIATION" which the accused cannot disprove. If the government succeeds in isolating and attacking the homosexual minority, it will have a weapon, Hay argued, which "can be employed as a threat against any and every man and woman in our country to insure thought control and political regimentation." While this danger made it imperative for homosexuals to organize, it also pointed to a need for caution. Hay's prospectus suggested that membership be by careful recommendation only, that all members be sworn to protective secrecy, and that they remain anonymous to the community at large and to each other.

The structure that the five men ultimately devised for the Mattachine Society reflected their own intense fear of repression as well as their recognition of the need to provide security for their homosexual constituents. As its model it drew heavily upon the experience of Hay—and to some extent of Rowland and Hull— in the Communist Party, where secrecy, hierarchical structures and centralized leadership predominated.

They created a pyramid of five "orders" of membership, with increasing levels of responsibility as one ascended the structure and with each order having one or two representatives from higher orders of the organization. As the membership of the Mattachine Society grew, the orders were expected to subdivide into separate cells so that each layer of the pyramid could expand horizontally. With the number of cells increasing, members of the same order but in different cells would be largely unknown to one another. Organizational coherence would come primarily through the representatives of the higher order. A single fifth order consisting of the founders would provide the Mattachine Society with a centralized leadership whose policies flowed downward through the lower orders. Initially, the founders acted as both fifth and first order; the intermediate orders were to be filled gradually as they recruited new members into the organization.

Recruitment into the Mattachine came through a series of semipublic discussion groups whose focus was some aspect of homosexuality. Run by the first order (which were also called "guilds"), they were open to anyone who cared to attend, and members of the guilds, as well as participants in the discussion groups, were encouraged to invite their gay friends and acquaintances. Attending a discussion group, however, did not make one a member of the Mattachine Society. In fact, the concern over secrecy was such that the first-order members who led the groups did it unobtrusively so that the discussions appeared informal and spontaneous. After someone attended regularly for some time, contributed significantly to the content of the discussion, and showed an ability to lead groups skillfully, a member would, in confidence, inform that individual about the Mattachine Society and invite him or her to join a first-order guild and become a member of the organization.

The founders also brought to their planning meetings a concern for ideology that grew out of their leftist politics. Although Communist ideology in the mid-twentieth century largely ignored questions of human sexuality, and certainly did not describe the persecution of homosexuals as something to be fought, the worldview of its adherents rested on an analysis of society that saw injustice as rooted in the social structure. Exploitation and oppression came not from simple prejudice or misinformation, but from deeply embedded structural relationships.

Hay himself was well-read in Marxist literature, and the other four, according to Rowland, had at least "some coloration of Marxism" in their thinking. This led them to reject a narrowly pragmatic approach to the problems of the homosexual, one that focused only on a set of reform goals, and instead pushed them to seek a theoretical explanation of the sources of the homosexual's inferior status. The concern with theory as a guide to action—a standard feature of Marxist thought—set them apart from the leaders of the movement who emerged later in the 1950s and who had no contact either with the Communist Part or with Marxism. These later spokespersons tended to reiterate a single theme: they had neither an analysis of the sources of the oppression of gay women and men, nor any sense of strategy. They expected to change society's treatment of lesbians and homosexuals simply by plugging away at prejudice.

The founders' lack of an already developed analysis of the oppression of homosexuals forced them to generate one by scrutinizing the main source of information available to them—their own lives. Throughout the winter of 1951 the five men met frequently to share their personal histories. They exchanged stories of coming out, of discovering cruising places and bars, of the years of loneliness. Trying to make some collective sense out of their individual experiences, they posed such questions as: How did one become a homosexual? Were homosexuals sick as the medical profession claimed? Was it possible to overcome the isolation and invisibility of the gay population and organize homosexuals? Were homosexuals, perhaps, a minority group, or merely a conglomeration of individuals sharing nothing but a sexual orientation?

Out of these discussions an analysis gradually emerged of the sources of the oppression of homosexuals. Pointing to the heterosexual nuclear family as the "established vehicle for the outlet of social impulses," the founders of the Mattachine Society argued that it constituted a "socially predetermined pattern" for human relationships. Raised in families as virtually all Americans were, men and women unquestioningly accepted as "natural," a system of social roles "which equates male, masculine, man only with husband and Father and which equates female, feminine, woman only with wife and Mother."

Homosexuals "did not fit the patterns of heterosexual love, marriage and children upon which the dominant culture rests." Excluded from the basic use of society, the family, they found themselves "an enclave within society . . . an undesirable and despicable group worthy only of ridicule and rebuke." With no socially approved models for their lifestyle, homosexuals "mechanically superimposed the heterosexual ethic on their own situation in empty imitation of dominant patterns." The result was a daily existence predicated upon "self-deceit, hypocrisy, and charlatanism and a sense of value distorted, inadequate, and undesirable."

Victimized by a "language and culture that does not admit the existence of the Homosexual Minority," and that viewed their sexual behavior as an individual aberration or personal moral failing, homosexuals remained largely unaware that their efforts to adjust to society constituted "a culture in itself" and that they were in fact "a social minority imprisoned within a dominant culture."

Their definition of homosexuals as a minority group suggested to the founders an initial course of action. Committed to a Marxist worldview that saw progressive social change occurring through the mobilization of masses of people with common interests, they were at first stymied by traditional thinking about homosexuality:

27

if "sexual deviance" was merely a personal problem, on what basis did one organize a mass movement of homosexuals? But if the ideology itself was a primary agent of oppression, then the first task of a homosexual emancipation movement was to challenge the internalization of that ideology by homosexuals, to develop among the gay population a consciousness of itself as an oppressed minority. Out of that consciousness homosexuals could then evolve a "highly ethical homosexual culture and lead well-adjusted, wholesome, and socially productive lives." And, from the cohesiveness that such a process would stimulate, the founders expected to forge, in time, a unified movement of homosexuals ready to fight against their oppression.

The semipublic discussion to which the founders were inviting their friends and acquaintances eventually led to the addition of James Gruber and Konrad Stevens to the group of five. Gruber was a student at Occidental College in Los Angeles; Stevens, his lover, was a photographer. Appearing at one of the gatherings during the winter of 1951, they exhibited an interest and enthusiasm lacking in other participants. Rowland approached them after the gathering, told them about the effort to form a homosexual rights organization, and invited them to the next closed meeting. Gruber and Stevens, now intrigued, accepted the offer.

Both men retained vivid recollections of their first meeting with the others. Unlike the original five, they had never been involved in political causes, and certainly had not had contact with Communists. Stevens remembered that there was "definitely a political atmosphere" to the discussion. Gruber was, in his own words, "terrified by it all." There was a lot of Communist jargon being used, he recalled, and in the McCarthy era even a familiarity with such terms made one suspect. "What am I getting into?" he wondered. But he was also attracted by the sense of justice in what was being said, and by the end of the evening the two men were firmly committed to the as-yet-unformed organization.

With the involvement of Gruber and Stevens, the Mattachine Society finally took shape. Their presence forced others to abandon the jargon of the left and to frame their ideas in language accessible to non-Marxists. In April 1951, they wrote a succinct, one-page document that set out clearly the goals of the organization and incorporated some of their thinking about homosexuals as a minority. During the spring they formally agreed on the secret structure of five orders of membership and made a renewed effort to revive the discussion group that they were still running. After the first feeble attempts of the winter and spring, the groups suddenly started to catch on and proliferate as summer approached.

A questionnaire that the fifth-order members compiled during the spring facilitated the discussion groups. The document, several pages long, covered a wide range of subjects. Few of the participants in the Mattachine had ever been systematically asked questions about their sexual and social lives before, and the questionnaire fueled endless discussions. Group members shared with each other the pain of discovering their sexual identities as well as the strengths which survival in a hostile society had produced. Together they imagined how life might be different, how a gay subculture might emerge that provided emotional support and sustenance, and how homosexuals might act to change social attitudes.

Although similar in some ways to the consciousness-raising groups popularized by the women's and gay liberation movements of the late 1960s and early 1970s, the Mattachine discussion groups existed in a far different social and political climate. In the early 1950s there were no mass protest movements to support an individual's challenge to the status quo. Nor was there a much-publicized counterculture to legitimize alternative lifestyles. Instead, an atmosphere of insecurity and vulnerability infected the entire gay subculture. Rumors of bar raids, mass arrests, and the loss of government jobs were endemic, and individuals who ventured to a Mattachine group brought these fears with them. Konrad Stevens recalled that most of the initial participants were "petrified at the government getting a list of names and fully expected that the cops would come barging in and arrest everybody." Many of those who attended the meetings used pseudonyms at first.

Despite these fears, the discussion groups thrived. Time itself, the ongoing, biweekly meetings at which there were no raids, alleviated the fear of exposure. Friendships formed among those who attended regularly, and the groups took on the character of intimate gatherings rather than political meetings. But mostly, the discussion groups were successful in drawing fearful gays into an organizational network because they offered a clear alternative to the traditional patterns of the gay subculture.

The impact of these gatherings upon the individuals was startling. Geraldine Jackson, who became an active first-order guild member, recalled how "people were able to bloom and be themselves. It was something we didn't know before. At last there was the opportunity to say what you wanted to say and feel accepted."

"All of us had known a whole lifetime of not talking, of repression," said James Gruber. "Just the freedom to open up, that's what it was all about. We had found a sense of belonging, of camaraderie, of openness in an atmosphere of tension and distrust. A family feeling came out of it, a nonsexual emphasis. It was a brand new idea. Just that is what kept the organization going."

The founders, however, expected the discussions to be more than an evening's haven from a hostile society. They intended them to be forums in which members of the gay minority developed a consciousness of their social oppression and a cohesiveness among themselves that would make political action possible. Hay described the discussion groups as the setting in which "to fashion a homosexual

29

ethic whereby homosexuals can begin to conceive, comprehend, form themselves into a minority in fact."

By the early autumn of 1951 the seven fifth-order members, no longer able to handle the multiplying discussion groups, began to establish first-order guilds. They carefully selected from the groups individuals whom they invited to become guild members. Wishing to imbue them with a sense a special purpose, the fifth order devised what one member described as "almost a religious ceremony" to initiate members. Standing in a circle and holding hands in a candlelit room, new and old members pledged themselves to the work ahead: "Our interlocking, sustaining and protecting hands guarantee a reborn social force of immense and simple purpose. We are resolved that our people shall find equality of security and production in tomorrow's world. We are sworn that no boy or girl, approaching the maelstrom of deviation, need make that crossing alone, afraid and in the dark ever again. In these moments we dedicate ourselves once again to each other in the immense significance of such allegiance, with dignity and respect, proud and free."

For women and men who remembered well the loneliness and fear of their own coming out, the power of these sentiments inspired an intense loyalty. "You felt like you had a mission in the world," Geraldine Jackson recalled. "You felt that you were doing something terribly worthwhile for our people." "No one felt that our rituals were empty, frivolous or lugubrious," echoed Chuck Rowland, "and I think the reason is that they were not any of those things. They solemnized a dedication, a devotion, and a promise."

With the discussion groups and guilds functioning smoothly, the fifth order turned its attention to the large, uncharted area of political action. Their first public action was a modest, undramatic one. Brutal incidents of police harassment of the Chicano community in Los Angeles had received considerable attention in the press, and mounting pressure for an official investigation of police practices had finally succeeded in forcing the city government to hold public hearings. The founders of the Mattachine Society attended the hearings and spoke in favor of disciplinary action against offending policemen. The rationale for their participation was their conviction that all socially oppressed minorities had something in common.

A few weeks later the issue of police abuses arose again, but this time it struck close to home. Late in February 1952, one of the Mattachine's founders, Dale Jennings, became a victim of police entrapment. Arrested by a plainclothes officer who accosted him in a Los Angeles park, Jennings was charged with lewd and dissolute behavior. He had little inkling that the arrest would precipitate a plunge into public action and mark a watershed in the history of the early Mattachine Society.

## 2

"Then there was the badge and the policeman was snapping the handcuffs on me with the remark, 'Maybe you'll talk better with my partner outside.' "

"I was forced to sit in the rear of a car on a dark street for almost an hour while three officers questioned me," Jennings later was to write. "It was a peculiarly effective type of grilling. They laughed a lot among themselves. Then, in a sudden silence, one would ask, 'How long have you been this way?' I refused to answer. I was scared stiff. Then more laughter and shop talk and another sudden question. At last the driver started the car up. Having expected the usual beating before, now I was positive it was coming—out in the country somewhere. They drove over a mile past the suburb of Lincoln Heights, then slowly doubled back. During this time they repeatedly made jokes about police brutality, and each of the three instructed me to plead guilty and everything would be all right. The first officer had approached me at five to nine in the park, I was booked at eleven-thirty and not allowed to send out a message until three in the morning."

Finally released on bail, Jennings called his Mattachine Society associates, who hastily scheduled an emergency meeting. They listened carefully as Jennings, tense and still shaken by the experience, described what had happened. But while he bemoaned his inevitable conviction as a felon, the others responded differently. Harry Hay, his eyes lighting up, argued forcefully that Jennings's arrest was the chance they had been waiting for. After much debate they decided to fight the charges and use the arrest to expose police entrapment practices against homosexuals. It would be the first major plunge into public action for the fledgling organization.

Through Hay's Communist Party contacts, the fifth order hired George Shibley, a radical lawyer from Long Beach who had a reputation, Hay recalled, as a "good fighting attorney." An Armenian by birth, Shibley had achieved local notoriety during World War II as the defense attorney for a group of Mexican–American youths who were arrested on trumped-up murder charges. Although Shibley knew little about gay life, he agreed to take the case.

In many long conferences the fifth-order members educated him about the problems experienced by homosexuals and together they decided on the strategy to pursue. Jennings would admit in court that he was a homosexual, but plead not guilty to the charges of lewd and dissolute behavior. It was a courageous—and dangerous—stand to take, since popular prejudice equated homosexuality with lewdness and immorality. To admit one's homosexuality in court risked almost certain conviction on the charges. But the Mattachine founders had resolved to challenge the practices that victimized the gay minority.

Wishing to build a large public campaign in support of Jennings, the fifth order decided to mobilize the discussion groups around the issue and, throughout the spring of 1952, the upcoming trial became the prime topic at the groups. To the dismay of the guild members who were leading the discussions, participants were at first reluctant to rally around the case. Many of them simply assumed that if Jennings were arrested, he must have been guilty. As Jennings wryly commented later, "Innocent people don't get into such a situation. Nice people just don't get arrested!"

The Mattachine leadership, however, took the position that innocence or guilt was irrelevant to the question of support. The law itself was unjust, they argued, and needed to be questioned, and the abusive police practices toward homosexuals must be stopped. They argued persuasively. In time, the entire Mattachine Society mobilized itself in support of Jennings.

Still hesitant about exposing the Mattachine Society to public view, the fifth order adopted a standard Communist Party organizing tactic and created an ad hoc committee, the Citizens Committee to Outlaw Entrapment, to publicize the case. Its task was not an easy one. Despite press releases and letters to radio and television stations and to newspapers, a complete news blackout prevailed, the first of many that the gay movement would confront in the coming decades.

With no prospects of media coverage, the Citizens Committee decided to use the informal communications network of the gay male subculture to make the upcoming trial known. The leadership wrote several flyers about the case and circulated them throughout Los Angeles.

Mattachine's membership distributed the leaflets, probably the first ones in the country's history to raise the homosexual issue, in areas frequented by homosexuals. They handed them out at gay beaches in Santa Monica and at bars in Los Angeles. They deposited them in restrooms known to be cruised by gay men. And they plastered them on park benches and at bus stops in homosexual areas of the city. They also arranged meetings with gay shop owners in West Hollywood, talked to them about the issue, and elicited their cooperation in informing their homosexual patrons about the case. Hay humorously recalled that the Mattachine even had a couple of supermarket clerks in the Hollywood area who surreptitiously dropped flyers into the packages of their gay customers!

The literature of the Citizens Committee argued its case in forthright, compelling terms. All of the committee's flyers, though prominently featuring the specifically homosexual aspect of the case, emphasized the threat which entrapment of homosexuals posed for all citizens. One piece of literature declared that it was "not only idle, but dangerous, for the community at large to placidly assume that illegal police techniques as practiced against the Homosexual Minority are special and confined." On the contrary, the techniques of "blackmail, intimidations, shakedown, entrapment, search and seizure without warrant, incarceration without charge currently employed against homosexuals can be wielded against the entire community."

Jennings deserved support, the committee reasoned, because "the issue is civil rights. The issue is the restoration of basic citizenship guarantees, rights and privileges equally for everybody. Deny the homosexual basic protections as a citizen, and you'll have set up the very machinery which will deny yourselves these rights. The moment you establish second class citizenship categories, you too are headed for that class. We're all in the same boat!"

Their arguments struck a responsive chord. The Citizens Committee was soon receiving a flood of mail with financial contributions to defray legal fees and requests for information about what else could be done.

When the trial began on June 23, 1952, Jennings admitted under Shibley's questioning that he was a homosexual, while denying that he was guilty of the charges against him. At the close of the proceedings, Shibley delivered a speech to the jurors which Hay characterized as "a militant exposition of what it is like to be a homosexual in today's sociopolitical climate." After thirty-six hours of deliberation, the jury reported that it was hopelessly deadlocked, with one member holding fast to a verdict of guilty. The rest voted straight acquittal. The judge ordered a retrial, but a few days later the district attorney's office decided to drop all charges against Jennings. Given the prevalent attitudes toward "sexual deviance," the Citizens Committee was justified in calling the outcome "a GREAT VICTORY for the homosexual minority."

Jennings's trial marked a watershed in the history of the early Mattachine Society. Chuck Rowland recalled that after the Jennings victory, "Mattachine really took off. From the months when we had nothing, we moved into a broad sunlit upland filled with whole legions of eager gays. Mattachine was suddenly in. No combination of people in our limited leadership could handle them."

Word of the Mattachine spread like wildfire. Discussion groups that had fifteen or twenty members were deluged by as many newcomers. Groups subdivided, only to repeat the process a few weeks later as the number of participants continued to multiply. The network of discussion groups soon had spread throughout Southern California. By the beginning of 1953, they extended along the coast from the beach communities north of Santa Monica south to San Diego, and inland to San Bernardino. New guilds were formed to handle the proliferating discussion groups, and the structure of the Mattachine expanded to include second-order units. In May 1953, the fifth order estimated that over 2,000 people were participating in the Society's activities.

The Mattachine Society also grew beyond its Southern California place of origin. In February 1953, a young man named Gerry Brissette who worked as a lab technician at the University of California at Berkeley wrote a letter of inquiry to the Mattachine Society. Describing himself as a pacifist who was active in the Fellowship of Reconciliation, he spoke of his "dream of freedom" for homosexuals. "I am with you all the way," his letter concluded. At the invitation of Rowland, Brissette came to Los Angeles in March to meet with the fifth-order members. He returned to Berkeley eager to start the Mattachine Society there. Before long, discussion groups had spread from Berkeley to Oakland and to San Francisco, with sixty or more persons coming to meetings. As Brissette wrote to Rowland, gays continued to "flock to us in hordes, hungry, anxious, eager to do something, say something, get started."

With the growth in membership came the expansion of activities. Well-established discussion groups began assuming new functions. One group, composed mostly of faculty members at UCLA, embarked upon a program of reading in the natural and social sciences in an attempt to make sense of then current theories about homosexuality. Another began surveying literature with homosexual characters and themes. Others compiled clipping files on contemporary sexual mores, and most of them gathered written statements from participants who had suffered abusive police behavior, with the goal of assembling massive documentation of illegal and discriminatory police practices.

The most significant development, however, was the decision in October 1952 by a few members of one discussion group to launch publication of a homosexual magazine. In the midst of one person's telling of his unfortunate experiences at the hands of the police, someone declared, "There ought to be some way of letting more people know these things." When another participant suggested that homosexuals needed their own magazine, several members volunteered to remain behind to explore the idea further. More talks were scheduled.

Several years later, an issue of the magazine described the process of birth during these meetings: "What would be its name? This was a tedious, wearying hassle, over endless cups of coffee. The 'dignified and ambiguous' school argued against the 'let's-be-frank' group." Guy Rousseau, a young black member of the discussion group, finally came up with a quote from Thomas Carlyle which provided both name and masthead slogan: "A mystic bond of brotherhood makes all men one." More decisions followed. *ONE* magazine would be issued monthly. It would not be mimeographed. It would be printed and have the best format that could be managed. There would be essays, scientific articles, original fiction, poetry, and reprints from classics. In short, concluded the later account, "it was to be neither a tract nor a pamphlet, but a real magazine." Three months later in January 1953, the first issue of *ONE,* featuring a simple grey cover with purple lettering, was ready for distribution.

The publication of *ONE* constituted a major step forward for the young movement. The Jennings cast vividly demonstrated that homosexuals could not depend on the press or other media to publicize their grievances. The gay women and men who established *ONE* intended it as a forum where the gay minority could present its views to the public and to other homosexuals and lesbians. Although *ONE* was formally independent of the Mattachine Society , most of the editorial board were members of the organization and Dale Jennings served as the magazine's first editor. Early issues of *ONE* prominently featured articles about the Mattachine Society, and the network of discussion groups provided the editors with a large pool of subscribers and potential customers. Within a few months, *ONE*'s sales had surpassed 2,000 copies per month, with a readership substantially larger than that. The magazine was also circulating, as the letters to the editor revealed, among gays throughout the country.

The experience of the Citizens Committee to Outlaw Entrapment emphasized, for the leaders, the need to have a mechanism apart from the secret structure of the organization to mediate between the anonymous membership and the larger society. Shortly after the Jennings case ended, the fifth order decided to incorporate in California as a not-for-profit educational organization called the Mattachine Foundation. They saw the Foundation as a means of advancing their work in several ways: it would allay the fears and questions of the many newcomers about who was sponsoring the discussion groups and other activities; it would offer an acceptable front for reaching out to the society, especially to professionals and public officials; and it could become the vehicle for conducting research into homosexuality and for using the results as part of the campaign for the rights of the gay minority.

Rowland wrote a concise, four-page pamphlet introducing the foundation. Using the findings of the Kinsey study of male sexual behavior to emphasize the scope of the problem, the pamphlet declared that 150,000 male homosexuals resided in the Los Angeles area alone. "Homosexuals are not," it emphasized, "insane, stupid, willfully perverted, unnatural, or socially incompetent. They are neither uncommon nor queer. BUT HOMOSEXUALS AS SUCH HAVE ONLY LIMITED SOCIAL AND LEGAL RIGHTS—in fact, our whole society is organized to keep them completely oppressed." The pamphlet announced the formation of the Mattachine Foundation by a "group of Los Angeles citizens" to conduct research, promote education, and encourage understanding of an important social phenomenon.

"The Mattachine Foundation," Rowland concluded, "looks toward the time the homosexual minority will live a well-oriented, socially productive life, with pride and without fear, will develop its own standards of ethics and conventions suitable to its needs and in conformity with the best interests of society, and will make a huge, recognized addition to the productiveness and social consciousness of our City, our State and our Country."

The fifth order had modest success in obtaining professional backing for the foundation. Through members James Gruber and Konrad Stevens, they arranged a meeting with the writer Christopher Isherwood and with a research psychologist from UCLA, Dr. Evelyn Hooker. Both professed support for what the Mattachine leaders were attempting, although they declined to join the board of directors. Isherwood, according to Stevens, bowed out on the grounds that he was not a "joiner," but he did contribute money to the foundation and informed others of its existence. Hooker, who was just beginning her studies of male homosexuality, felt that membership would compromise her research in the eyes of her colleagues. She did keep in close touch with her Mattachine friends, however, and in 1953, Mattachine provided her with a large pool of gay men for her study of the male homosexual personality. Other efforts secured the involvement of a clergyman, Wallace de Ortega Maxey, pastor of the First Universalist Church in Los Angeles, which supported a variety of political causes, and a physician from San Bernardino, Richard Gwartney.

Increasingly confident of the course they were taking, Mattachine's leaders decided to use the cover of the foundation to raise the homosexual issue in local elections. To candidates for the Los Angeles Board of Education they sent a letter which charged the public school system with "a high percentage of responsibility for the social tragedy" of the homosexual minority and asked candidates for their position on "nonpartisan" counseling on homosexuality in the high schools. In another letter to aspirants for mayor, city council and board of supervisors, they outlined the "growing body of evidence" indicating that the Los Angeles police were engaging in "explicitly unlawful" practices against homosexuals and polled candidates on their attitudes toward a range of law enforcement techniques. Although few candidates responded to the questionnaire, the Mattachine's founders considered it an important step to take.

As fifth-order members, foundation directors, participants in the first- and second-order units, and leaders of discussion groups, the founders saw their lives almost consumed by these activities. In two and one-half years, the tiny group of leftist homosexuals had built a thriving, rapidly expanding organization. Konrad Stevens recalled that, for a time after the Jennings trial, "We were meeting very often. We just lived Mattachine. We didn't do anything else. We never went anywhere just for pleasure. When we went, it was organizing." From being "pioneers in a hostile society," Rowland wrote to Hay, the leadership could claim that they had "set a movement in motion."

But the spectacular growth of the Mattachine Society also created other problems for the leaders that demanded solution. Rapid expansion strained the organization's structure and weakened the cohesion which the fifth order valued so highly. As the discussion groups proliferated, the need for leadership forced the guilds to loosen the procedures for initiation into membership.

The original emphasis on a "consensus of principle," on agreement that homosexuals were indeed an oppressed minority who needed to engage in collective political action, gave way before the simple requirement of having enough guild members to lead each of the discussion groups. Men and women who had only recently attended their first discussion meetings found themselves invited to join the guilds and to assume responsibility in an organization whose structure, purpose, and leadership remained enshrouded in mystery.

Under these circumstances the secret, cell-like structure of the Mattachine Society hampered the organization. Instead of seeing it as a mechanism to protect them from exposure, newer members feared it as a device to manipulate them. Within the guilds, dissension surfaced with an alarming frequency; pressure mounted to reorganize the Mattachine Society in an open, democratic form.

### 3

The question of reorganization provoked the first serious split among the members of the fifth order. Their carefully nurtured unanimity collapsed as they debated the merits of restructuring. A special weekend conference held in February 1953 to work out a solution fell apart in acrimony. Tensions were so high that some members were barely speaking to one another.

Rowland, Hull, Stevens, and Martin Block—the one newcomer admitted to the fifth order since the founding of the Mattachine—argued strongly for an aboveground membership organization. In a letter to Hay, Rowland reminded him that secrecy had never been an end in itself, but rather a tactical response to the fear of joining a gay organization. Now, he said, the Mattachine's efforts had created "a qualitatively new situation in which even our Junior Chamber of Commerce Laguna Group (the exact type of group the secrecy of the Society was designed to protect)," favored openness. Much had changed since their first meeting in 1950, he went on, and "a radical approach" was required.

"Three years ago," Rowland wrote, "we were pioneers in a hostile society, and we had to take elaborate precautions to insure our safety and that of others. Today we have such diverse elements as Gwartney, Don Frey, Tommy, the swishy Long Beach crowd, and you. Our pioneering has created a whole new situation and it is in this situation that we must all act and act intelligently or we will lose our leadership, all our aims, and our purposes." Rowland told Hay that he would introduce at the next meeting of the fifth order a motion to call a convention and propose a constitution for a newly structured Mattachine Society. "Whether you like it or not," he concluded, "the subject of discussion for today is reorganization."

Hay adamantly disagreed and instead argued that opening up the Society would weaken it irreparably. Hay's position grew out of the distrust he felt toward many of the newcomers. Their attraction to the Mattachine, he believed, came from a narrow concern for their own security. The successful defense of Dale Jennings made them see the organization merely as a means of protection in case they personally ran afoul of the law. But they had little if any sense of solidarity with other oppressed gays and no allegiance, Hay felt, to the long-term goal of building a powerful, militant mass movement for homosexual rights.

In response to Rowland's letter, Hay reminded him that from the start the basic objective of the Mattachine Society had been the "integration of our minority as a group." The malcontents who were pressuring for an open organization, he said, "don't give a shit about the homosexual minority and want assimilation (passing, by Christ!) made respectable." To Rowland's claim that reorganization was a radical solution Hay countered: "No, Chuck! this move isn't radical, it's betrayal. You can't build a democratic society on a bunch of diversified individualists going nowhere."

Before the fifth order could resolve its differences, a red-baiting newspaper column on the Mattachine Foundation gave the debate a sudden urgency. Los Angeles journalist Paul Coates had received a copy of the Mattachine Foundation's letter and questionnaire to local candidates. "This is an election year," wrote Paul V. Coates in his *Los Angeles Mirror* column early in 1953. "Anything can happen. And yesterday, something did. The already harassed and weary candidates for office were whacked with a broadside from a strange new pressure group. An organization that claims to represent the homosexual voters of Los Angeles is vigorously shopping for campaign promises. Questionnaires have been sent to all candidates by the Mattachine Foundation, Inc., a group which pointedly hints . . . potential support of 150,000 to 200,000 homosexuals in this area. . . . But it's an odd thing. I checked the State Division of Corporations and the County Clerk's offices. There is no record of a Mattachine Corporation.

"If I belonged to that club, I'd worry.

"I learned that the articles of incorporation were drawn up by an attorney named Fred M. Snider, who was an unfriendly witness at the Un-American Activities hearings. Snider is the legal advisor for Mattachine, Inc. Homosexuals have been found to be bad security risks in our State Department. They're a scorned part of the community. It's not inconceivable that they might band together for their own protection. Eventually they might swing tremendous power.

"A well-trained subversive could move in and forge that power into a dangerous political weapon.

"To damn this organization before its aim and directions are more clearly established would be vicious and irresponsible. Maybe the people who founded it are sincere. It will be interesting to see."

It is important to remember the context in which the Coates column appeared. Senator Joseph McCarthy, who had become chairman of the Government Operations Committee and its permanent subcommittee on investigations in January 1953, was at the height of his influence. In February, he began his investigation into alleged Communist influence in the State Department, its overseas information program, and the Voice of America, an investigation which received widespread publicity. The House Un-American Activities Committee, moreover, which had conducted numerous inquiries into Communist influence in Hollywood over the preceding six years, was in Los Angeles in March and April 1953 and held public hearings on the operations of the Communist Party in Los Angeles.

The Coates column hit the Mattachine Society where it was most vulnerable and its charges provoked a swift, vocal reaction throughout the organization. One Los Angeles discussion group, having set aside its scheduled topic, appealed to the foundation's directors to "make themselves known" and bring an end to "subterfuge." A recalcitrant Laguna group called for "a loyalty oath as a condition of membership" in the Mattachine, and backed its demands with a refusal to contribute funds to the foundation.

Marilyn Rieger, a guild member from Los Angeles, wrote a forceful letter to the foundation in which she reported that "many members of the meetings feel that Mr. Coates asked legitimate questions and that explanations are definitely in order." To continue working for a cause, Rieger said, she needed "complete faith in the people who set forth the policies, principles, aims and purposes." Should the directors fail to respond, she announced her intention of writing to Sacramento and to the state bar association in order to pursue the disturbing revelations in the Coates article.

With pressures upon them escalating rapidly, the fifth order acted decisively. Burying whatever doubts remained about restructuring, it called a "democratic convention" of all members of the Mattachine Society. The "deliberately complicated" secret structure "has served its function well," the invitation declared, and "the time is ripe for a democratic organization to move forward into greater spheres." The fifth order proposed that the convention be held on April 11 and 12, 1953, at the Reverend Maxey's Universalist Church in Los Angeles, draw up a constitution, adopt bylaws, and elect officers for an open membership organization.

Despite the assured tone of the invitation, the fifth order approached the event apprehensively. As Rowland wrote to Gerry Brissette, the Mattachine's leader in Northern California, "there has been a very considerable, delayed reaction to the Coates article," and he and the other fifth order members were reluctant to predict the final outcome. Although flexible on matters of structure, the fifth order had resolved to hold firm in two areas: the new Society must pledge itself to "the necessity of concerted action and of its members accepting a consciousness of their existence" as a minority; and it must resist the hue and cry for a declaration of anti-Communism. In forceful terms, Rowland informed Brissette that, "come hell or high water, we will oppose all ideas of a non-communist statement by any group using the name Mattachine. We, as individuals, will have nothing to do with any group which has a loyalty oath as a condition of membership. Our position is that a fight against the House Un-American Activities Committee is our fight, in our interests. I am convinced that this is the correct course of action, and I believe that we who are doing organizational work must take a very strong stand on this issue from the first." Although he offered the opinion that "the Mattachine movement will live and grow," Rowland also revealed his personal fear that there "may be a split at the convention" over the Communist issue.

Little did Rowland know that the convention would set in motion drastic changes that would transform the Mattachine Society from a radical, visionary gay organization into a conservative, closeted, and self-effacing one.

4

A charged and emotional atmosphere permeated the opening of the April constitutional convention. The delegates, numbering over one hundred women and men, were well aware of the historic importance of the event. To the best of their knowledge, they were attending the first public gathering of homosexuals and lesbians in the United States. It was a gathering faced with an immensely significant task—to create an open membership organization pledged to achieve equality for gay men and women.

But an undercurrent of tension also ran through the hall. Besides the reasonable fear at daring to meet publicly, there was also the unease of knowing that the convention had been scheduled hastily in response to a crisis. Many of the participants waited nervously for their first view of the mysterious fifth-order members who had founded the Mattachine Society.

Chuck Rowland began the session with a rousing keynote speech that argued for a recognition of homosexuals as an oppressed cultural minority. "We must disenthrall ourselves of the idea," he said, "that we differ only in our sexual directions and that all we want or need in life is to be free to seek the expression of our sexual desires as we see fit." "The heterosexual mores of the dominant culture have excluded us," he continued, and "as a result of this exclusion, we have developed differently than have other cultural groups." Homosexuals faced the challenge of developing "a new pride—a pride in belonging, a pride in participating in the cultural growth and social achievements of the homosexual minority." Once this challenge was accepted, Rowland declared, "the prospect is not at all bleak, for with this pride will come a new confidence that we can make our own, significant cultural contribution to the world in the interests of humanity."

With scarcely a pause, Harry Hay followed with a spirited defense of Mattachine attorney Fred Snider's refusal to testify before the House Un-American Activities Committee. He reminded the audience that witnesses could invoke Fifth Amendment privileges regarding self-incrimination only if they refused to answer all questions. Had Snider responded to questions about his own political beliefs and affiliations, he would also have had to divulge information about individuals and organizations with which he was associated, including the Mattachine Society and its members.

"How would you feel," Hay asked, "about placing your trust in a lawyer who had spilled his guts concerning himself, his friends and his clients?" Hay emphasized that everyone in the hall had compelling reasons to worry about their names being divulged to government investigators: gay women and men had been judged "basic security risks and therefore unemployable by the Government," and in fact were being purged from federal jobs. Clearly, he argued, it was in their interest to defend the Fifth Amendment rights of everyone regardless of political belief.

Provocative as the speeches were, little overt conflict erupted in response to them. The fifth order effectively circumvented open dissent by dividing the participants into small working groups to draft a constitution and bylaws. The plan produced nothing but chaos, however, since few committees completed their work and those that did found their various proposals lacking in consistency. At the final session, the delegates voted to elect a committee to fashion the partial drafts into a coherent document and to present the results at a second convention scheduled for late May.

The first convention's outcome produced a mixed reaction from the Mattachine's leadership. Perhaps because the fifth order had approached the event with such apprehension, it mistakenly interpreted the relative calm of the proceedings as a victory. Chuck Rowland optimistically wrote Gerry Brissette, Mattachine's leader in Northern California, that the opposition had been effectively isolated. Though he expected "some rumbles from them at the next session," Rowland confidently predicted that they would not succeed.

Brissette, however, held a less sanguine view. He had noticed with alarm the quiet maneuvering of "a real evil minority at the Convention." The opposition had hopes, he wrote, "of winning our whole delegation over to their side and even proposed delights of the bed to win us over." Brissette warned that, "smarting under their rejection, they might return even better organized," and he implored Rowland to "come to the next session well prepared" to counter them.

Brissette's assessment proved accurate. The deceptive calm of the April meeting masked a significant development. The convention had brought together the separate orders and allowed dissatisfied members scattered among several guilds to meet for the first time. At the convention, and in the intervening weeks before the May session, the opposition to the Mattachine leadership began to coalesce.

Kenneth Burns, a Los Angeles guild member, emerged as the de facto leader of the conservative minority. Burns presided over a guild whose members, according to one of them, were "politically conservative and closety" and which had reacted vehemently to the Paul Coates column. They had been as upset, one member recalled, by the Mattachine's questionnaire to local political candidates as they had been by the innuendos of Communist subversion, and felt that any direct political action was likely to destroy the organization. Nor did they look with favor on Rowland and Hay's opening speeches which "shocked, angered, and infuriated" them. Burns, who was a safety engineer for the Carnation Company, looked the part of a "Brooks Brothers executive type." He was young and sexually attractive, with a soft-spoken manner that commanded attention. Burns had an ability, one participant recalled, "to get people to quiet down and let their emotions cool." His adeptness with the labyrinthine rules of parliamentary procedure quickly distinguished him from the mass of delegates, who selected Burns to chair the interim committee charged with drafting a constitution.

Burns was joined on the committee by Marilyn Rieger, another guild member from Los Angeles. Unlike Burns, whose guild was virtually unanimous in its opposition to the fifth order's control, Rieger found herself isolated. Although she had mobilized her discussion group to challenge the Mattachine leadership, her guild was led by Martin Block, a member of the fifth order who retained the allegiance of the rest of the guild. At the convention, Rieger and Burns quickly made contact and together quietly canvassed other delegates to garner their support.

They found a receptive listener in Hal Call, a San Francisco delegate. Call had a degree in journalism from the University of Missouri and had worked for a number of midwestern newspapers. Arrested in Chicago in 1952 on a homosexual morals charge, Call was subjected to what he described as "the completely and utterly corrupt" workings of the Chicago police and judicial system where male homosexuals were "fair game for every cop who wanted to make his arrest record better." As a result of his arrest he lost his job and migrated to San Francisco, where he joined the first Mattachine discussion group in the city.

Gruff and aggressive in manner, the outspoken Call came to the convention already suspicious of the fifth order. The keynote speeches did nothing to allay his fears, and the whispered rumors emanating from Burns's guild that Rowland was a Communist youth organizer aroused Call's ire. After meeting Burns and Rieger, he returned to San Francisco bent on purging the Mattachine of its allegedly subversive elements.

It was the May convention which witnessed the first concerted challenge to the fifth order. The opposition had come prepared to do battle with the founders for control of the Mattachine Society. They intended, according to Call, to "read out of the roll-call most of the founding members."

The opposition staked out its position early when Rieger delivered an extended critique of the minority group concept. "We know we are the same," she began, "no different than anyone else. Our only difference is an unimportant one to the heterosexual society, unless we make it important." Rieger argued that the emphasis on a homosexual culture would only accentuate the hostility of society, and she pleaded with the delegates to reject it. Equality for gay women and men would come, she said, "by declaring ourselves by integrating not as homosexuals but as people, as men and women whose homosexuality is irrelevant to our ideals, our principles, our hopes and aspirations." Only then, she concluded, will we "rid the world of its misconceptions of homosexuality and homosexuals."

Rieger's argument had obvious flaws. To claim that homosexuality was an unimportant difference—in the face of laws, government policy, religious beliefs, medical opinion, and popular prejudice that said otherwise—clearly missed the mark. Whatever persuasiveness her position carried came not from its logic or its grounding in fact, but from its emotional appeal. Gay men and women in mid-twentieth-century America lived with an ever-present awareness of their "difference," of being set apart from society. When Rieger said to the audience that "we are first and foremost people," she tapped a deeply felt need on the part of many delegates to have their humanity affirmed.

Although the gay minority thesis more accurately described the situation of lesbians and homosexuals, the emphasis which its proponents placed on being different aroused the antagonism of individuals who yearned for nothing more than simple acceptance of who they were. It mattered little that advocates of a minority group analysis saw their position as tactical, as a means for homosexual men and women eventually to achieve equality. For the present it raised the specter of a more pronounced separation from an already hostile culture.

The opposition's issue-oriented debate was merely a prelude, however, to an unrestrained red-baiting. The San Francisco delegation in particular, led by Hal Call and a newly recruited friend of his, David Finn, attacked the fifth order for their political affiliations. Playing upon the anti-communist fears of the early 1950s, Call introduced a motion approved by the entire San Francisco membership that "a very strong statement concerning our stand on subversive elements" be inserted into the new constitution. "We are already being attacked as Communistic," he reminded his audience, and the proposed article "guarantees us that we will not be infiltrated by Communists." Should anyone make such charges again, he argued, "we can insist that it be printed and our stand would then be clear."

Not restricting himself to parliamentary maneuvering, Call used every available opportunity to abuse Chuck Rowland, whom he especially disliked. Finn, too, joined the fray with a blanket accusation of Communist Party membership against the Mattachine Foundation directors. Though their attacks antagonized more delegates than they persuaded, they added an element of personal bitterness and factionalism that soured the proceedings.

After the first day's sessions, the fifth-order members met to assess the situation and to plan a response. Vehement as the opposition was, the leadership had nonetheless emerged victorious on every vote. The convention had defeated Call's motion for an anti-Communist declaration and approved a preamble to the organization's constitution that affirmed the need for a homosexual minority to develop "a highly ethical homosexual culture." Yet their victory was a hollow one. The founders had every reason to believe that the red-baiting would continue and they recognized its capacity to destroy the still-fragile movement.

"We were aware," James Gruber recalled, "that Communism had become a burning issue. We all felt, especially Harry, that the organization and its growth was more important than any of the founding fathers. The Mattachine had grown beyond our control and it had reached the point where we had to turn it over to other people. There was no guarantee that they would continue with what the organization started, but we couldn't help it."

The next afternoon, Rowland addressed the convention. The Mattachine Foundation's directors had decided to dissolve, he informed them, and to allow the new organization to retain the name. The fifth-order members, moreover, did not wish to seek office in the restructured Mattachine Society. Rowland's announcement received a wide round of applause.

The rest was anticlimactic. The convention abandoned the secret structure of orders and guilds and approved a simple membership organization, with a Coordinating Council elected by the membership and a series of organization-wide committees focused on particular areas of work—legal, legislative, publications, public relations, and research. Semiautonomous regional branches of the Mattachine Society, called "Area Councils," would elect their own officers and be represented on the Coordinating Council. The unit for membership participation was the task-oriented chapter, similar in focus to the committees but working on a local level. Among the officers elected by delegates were the leaders of the opposition—Ken Burns, Marilyn Rieger, and David Finn.

## 5

The May convention initiated changes in the Mattachine Society reaching far beyond the simple transfer of leadership from one group to another. Over the next several months the new officers firmly imprinted their mark on the organization. Methodically erasing every trace of the founders' influence, they charted a direction that was distinctively their own. Cautious, fearful, and conservative, they brought the Mattachine Society almost to the point of collapse.

Despite their claim that the Mattachine Society was "non-political," that it espoused "no isms," Burns, Rieger, Call, and the reset of the newly elected leadership proceeded from a set of interlocking, mutually reinforcing assumptions that gave their actions coherence and that formed as definite a worldview as that held by Hay and the other leftist founders. Decisively rejecting the notion of a homosexual minority, they took the contrary view that "the sex variant is no different from anyone else except in the object of his sexual expression." Where Hay had attributed the oppression of homosexuals to structural causes—to their exclusion from the heterosexual nuclear family—the Mattachine leadership believed that "discrimination, derision, prejudice, and the denial of civil rights" arose instead from "false ideas about the variant."

In claiming as they did that the pervasive sanctions against homosexuality resulted from misinformation and a lack of objective scientific fact, Burns and the others were led to conclude that the Mattachine's "greatest and most meaningful contribution" to the liberation of homosexuals "will consist of aiding established and recognized scientists, clinics, research organizations and institutions by furnishing material for their work in studying sex variation problems."

The reliance on professionals as the agents of social change pushed them to abandon collective, militant action by homosexuals themselves. Terrified of provoking a hate-inspired campaign against gays, they shifted responsibility for mounting political action away from the Mattachine Society and instead placed it upon the individual. Their desire for social acceptance made them hostile to the idea of a homosexual culture and to the effort to fashion an "ethic" for gay life. Instead, the leadership urged homosexuals to adjust to a "pattern of behavior that is acceptable to society in general and compatible with the recognized institutions of home, church, and state."

In sum, accommodation replaced militancy, collective effort gave way to individual action, the affirmation of one's own integrity yielded to the wisdom of experts. Under its new officers, the Mattachine Society pursued respectability and abandoned the quest for self-respect.

The impact of the new leadership's perspectives hit the discussion groups first. Conceived by Hay as a place in which to forge homosexuals into a cohesive, self-respecting, and self-conscious minority, they no longer had an integral place in the Mattachine Society, and the overwhelming majority of the one hundred or so groups withered and died. The reason was more than structural. Under Burns, the discussion groups became a "means of therapy" for homosexuals so that they could learn to lead "well-adjusted" lives. By reinforcing rather than contradicting the ideology of sickness and moral turpitude, the discussion groups ceased to inspire and hold on to their participants. The San Diego group, for example, collapsed within weeks after the May convention. In the Los Angeles area, the far-flung network of discussion groups shriveled into a mere handful.

A few of the discussion groups with some of the early Mattachine Society's most active members reconstituted themselves as task-oriented chapters. Rowland and Stevens, for instance, remained active in a Los Angeles chapter that voted to take on entrapment cases. Under their leadership the group agreed to search out cases "of significance to the whole minority, and to fight the charges aggressively." But Burns and the Coordinating Council vetoed the chapter's decision.

The Mattachine Society's new attorney, David Ravin, advised the leadership that "the very existence of a Legal Chapter, if publicized to society at large, would intimidate and anger heterosexual society. It would be detrimental to the

Mattachine Society to let the public know of the existence and activities of the Legal Chapter; and it would probably bring more pressure on the Society if the heterosexual felt that the homosexual, whom he hates, was trying the change the laws to suit himself."

Burns accepted Ravin's estimation and argued that the Mattachine Society had to "consider what the outside society feels toward us at this time." Afraid to challenge the law and its enforcement, the Coordinating Council cautioned the membership to be "realistic" and to recognize that the organization was "not yet strong enough to embark upon an aggressive program." Instead, it offered to refer entrapment victims to sympathetic and reputable lawyers.

Fear also inhibited them from seeking penal code reform. Despite the fact that the Mattachine Convention had authorized the creation of a legislative committee to pursue sodomy law repeal, the leadership sidestepped the issue. David Finn, the chairman of the committee, along with Call, a committee member, effectively forestalled action. In August 1953 they published a pamphlet outlining the organization's policies that declared: "Any organized pressure on lawmakers by members of the Mattachine Society as a group would only serve to prejudice the position of the Society. It would provide an abundant source of hysterical propaganda with which to foment an ignorant, fear-inspired anti-homosexual campaign." Instead, they proposed for the Mattachine a policy of "merely acquainting itself" with legislation. Insensitive to the real risks which individual action without organizational support entailed for homosexuals, they informed members that the "burden of activity must rest upon the individual."

The full-scale retreat from independent action stemmed, in part, from the acceptance by the leadership of society's evaluation of themselves. "We didn't have much confidence at that time," Burns later acknowledged. "We felt we had to work through people who could better present what homosexuality was all about—better than ourselves. We made a definite decision that by working through research projects and people in education and religion that we would get acceptance." And, as Call conceded, "we felt we had to work through professionals to give ourselves credibility. To be just an organization of upstart gays we would have been shattered and ridiculed and put down."

This eagerness, as Call put it, "to ride on the shirttails of a psychiatrist, a psychologist, a clergyman, a lawyer" reinforced the conservative, self-deprecating spirit of the leadership. Alfred Kinsey, for instance, with whom the society was in contact, advised the Mattachine's officers to avoid the "special pleas for a minority group" and to restrict themselves to aiding "qualified research experts." Evelyn Hooker, too, cautioned that reference to homosexuals as a minority was "a misnomer," and dismissed the question of gay identity and consciousness since "only the mode of sexual behavior would differentiate and distinguish a homosexual." Burns used such counsel to underline the judiciousness of his conservative leadership. "Responsible persons in public life tell us," he wrote, that if the Mattachine society does not "grow up with good manners and an attitude of responsibility, we can only expect to fail."

As a connecting thread through each of these separate decisions ran a vehement anti-Communism. The new leadership of the Mattachine Society had originally coalesced around their shared fear of "subversive" influences, a concern that continued to bind them together and to motivate their actions. Despite the firm control that they had over the organization, Burns, Call, Rieger and others remained preoccupied with demonstrating the Mattachine's loyalty and projecting an image of unalloyed Americanism.

Just two weeks after the May 1953 convention, Finn wrote to Burns that the FBI contacted him in San Francisco. Finn reportedly gave the government investigators copies of the Mattachine constitution and detailed the efforts of himself and others to purge the Society of any Communist elements. Though Burns later announced that the organization had "expressed itself satisfactorily to the FBI," an inordinate amount of the Coordinating Council's attention continued to revolve around the Communist issue rather than around building a homosexual rights organization. Stemming as much from their fear of exposure as from a genuine anti-Communism, their hysteria boomeranged and heightened the membership's concern for its own safety. In ordering local chapter leaders to tell their members not to speak to investigators, the officers awakened worries that might otherwise have lain dormant. Worse, it led them to take arbitrary actions that made a mockery of the democratic procedures which supposedly justified their concerns.

Despite the clearly expressed rejection by the membership at the May convention of any declaration of anti-Communism, the Mattachine leadership unilaterally published such statements. Both the Los Angeles and San Francisco Area Councils released pamphlets under the Society's name which announced that the Society was "unalterably opposed to Communists and Communist activity." Determined to give substance to their words, the pamphlets made further statements which, in the effort to prove the Mattachine's anti-Communism, tied its hands as a homosexual rights organization. "Homosexuals," the Los Angeles group wrote, "are not seeking to overthrow or destroy any of society's existing institutions, laws or mores, but to be assimilated as constructive, valuable, and responsible citizens." The implications of the position were devastating. How were homosexuals to be assimilated as valuable citizens when the institutions, laws, and mores of society precluded that possibility?

The leadership's action did not pass without criticism. James Kepner, a Los

Angeles member who had joined Burns's guild just before the April convention, wrote an angry letter to the Los Angeles officers with the full support of his chapter. Kepner had briefly been a Communist Party member after World War II until his expulsion for homosexuality. Though he retained neither affection nor loyalty toward the Communist Party, he found the pamphlets in question "degrading." They constituted "the same sort of limitation of thought and action which already plagues us as homosexuals, and additionally would constitute a cheap genuflection toward our most rabid enemies. For McCarthy and his ilk, who hate Communists and homosexuals so equally they can't tell them apart, it would be worse than useless for us to deny being one while admitting being the other." Kepner failed to get the offending pamphlets withdrawn, but his letter did serve to hint at the invisible and somewhat pathetic motivation for the anti-Communist hysteria—the unarticulated belief that, by affirming their loyalty, homosexuals could mitigate the hatred and persecution which the crusade against internal subversion had intensified.

The conflict between the remnants of the old Mattachine and the emerging direction of the new leadership peaked in November 1953 at an organization-wide convention. Burns and the other officers came prepared to jettison whatever survived of the founders' influence and to complete the transition begun in the spring. The balance of power in the organization had now shifted. When Burns spoke, he did so as head of the Mattachine Society.

The leadership successfully disposed of what was left of the founders' perspective. Still chafing over the preamble, adopted in May, which committed the Society to developing "a highly ethical homosexual culture," Burns urged the convention to eliminate "that very peculiar language which the influence of the old leadership at the last convention forced upon us." In its place he offered, and the membership accepted, a statement which not only dropped the reference to a homosexual culture, but also avoided any mention of homosexuals! Burns also proposed, again successfully, a resolution declaring that "the basic limitations of an organization such as the Mattachine Society are of a nature which would preclude its effectually pursuing any direct, aggressive action." Instead, the organization accepted as policy that it would "limit its activities to contacting, enlisting and working with and through established persons, institutions, and organizations which command the highest possible public respect and influence."

Though the changes proposed by Burns were accepted, the debate surrounding them provoked an uproar. When Rowland attempted to speak against revising the preamble, Dave Finn, who was acting as parliamentarian and who was perhaps the most vituperative of the red-baiting leadership, ruled him out of order. Finn then erupted angrily that he would turn over to the FBI the names of everyone in attendance if the convention failed to reject the "communistic" principles imposed by the old leadership. His announcement created havoc. Kepner recalled jumping to his feet and demanding that Finn be thrown out. Many others were outraged that anyone would dare violate the almost sacred guarantee of anonymity. Burns deftly called for a recess and, after tempers had time to cool, sidestepped the issue which Finn's threat raised by simply attributing the outburst to the emotional heat engendered by the debate.

Finn's behavior, however, did upset the scenario planned by Burns and some of the other officers. They had prepared a number of resolutions to deal with the question of "subversive" elements within the Mattachine Society. One simply declared that "this society unconditionally subscribes to the American creed." Another, a loyalty oath, required each member to sign a statement that "I believe it is my duty to my country to love it; to support its constitution; to obey its laws; to respect its flag; and to defend it against all enemies." A third resolution mandated the creation of a "Committee for Investigating Communist Infiltration" with the power to summon any member before it and to suspend anyone who failed to answer "satisfactorily" questions concerning Communist Party membership. It remains unclear whether the majority of the delegates opposed the resolutions out of conviction, or out of anger at the attempt at intimidation or, perhaps, because Finn's threat put into bold relief the menace of such rabid sentiments. But they did defeat all of the resolutions aimed at extirpating "subversive" influences.

The convention, however, closed a chapter in the history of the Mattachine Society. Despite the rejection of loyalty oaths and other paraphernalia of the McCarthy era, the membership had decisively abandoned the radical, militant impulse which had characterized the first years of the organization.

The context in which they did so—amid red-baiting attacks on the integrity of some of the members—cost them dearly. Since the early summer, the organization's work had been "immeasurably hampered," as Burns himself admitted, by a series of resignations coming from officers and members who shared the politics and the vision of the founders. "Too many committees," the chairman of the Los Angeles Area Council, John Loy, glumly reported in 1953, are "at present trying to function with a minimum of personnel." In September, Gerry Brissette and almost all of the East Bay membership in Northern California left the organization, distressed by the widening gulf between, as he put it "those of us who had more of a movement idea and the group who wanted to be respectable."

The November convention accelerated the process. Kepner recalled that for many in attendance, the bitter fighting was "a devastating experience. Probably a majority of those who attended the Convention never came back." Konrad Stevens, who finally left the organization after the convention, described his reasons: "It was dull and wasting time. The fighting, the beginnings, the revolution was over. I felt we were dragging our feet. Everything was so watered down that nothing courageous would ever be done. They wanted to do nice things to make society accept them."

Others agreed. Ben Tabor, an officer in Southern California, submitted his resignation to Burns shortly after the convention. There were, he wrote, "two premises which comprise the essence of our organization. We are predominantly an organization of homosexuals and we are interested primarily in demanding our civil rights. But from where I sit, it looks like the Coordinating Council is devoting all its time to denying both of these premises."

Ironically, the convention's outcome also failed to satisfy many of the Mattachine's most conservative members. After the defeat of the loyalty oath, Guy Van Alstyne, who headed the Mattachine's research committee and had been responsible for its developing contacts with professionals, announced his resignation. "It can be regarded as the sheerest madness," he said, "for me to act officially in a movement which seeks to encourage respect for those who have been linked with subversion." To John Loy, the rejection of the resolutions signaled that the membership had "no sense of responsibility," and he too resigned. Marilyn Rieger, one of the leaders of the opposition in the spring, relinquished her position on the Coordinating Council a few days later, merely citing "personal reasons."

Over the next year and a half, the Mattachine Society continued to decline in size. At its first annual convention in May 1954, only forty-two members were in attendance. Burns attempted to put a happy face on the situation by telling his audience that "what the Society requires of members is quality—not quantity," but it was hard to mask the startling change from a year earlier when the organization had been expanding rapidly and thriving. The turnout for the annual meeting the following year was even smaller.

In its pursuit of a respectable image for itself and for the homosexual, the Mattachine offered little to attract its gay constituency. In place of consciousness-raising, challenges to police practices, political action, and efforts to achieve penal code reform, the organization sponsored activities—blood drives, the collection of clothes, books, and magazines for hospitals, and the like—to demonstrate that homosexuals were solid citizens. The leadership expended its energy denouncing indecent public behavior and dissociating itself from those who contributed to the "delinquency" of minors. The Society witnessed the sorry spectacle of members investigating and exposing each other's private lives under the guise of preserving the Mattachine's good reputation, as if any homosexual in the 1950s had a reputation to protect.

The Mattachine Society had opted for a strategy of interminable waiting for public enlightenment. It was an approach that depended upon members of the very professions that had helped create and maintain destructive attitudes toward homosexuals. It urged homosexuals themselves not to work to change the community mores that restrict their lives, but instead to adapt to them. How one could do this, and still remain a homosexual, the new leadership never answered.

The outcome of the Mattachine Society's internal struggle was almost inevitable and cannot be understood in isolation from larger currents in postwar American society and politics. By 1953, the Cold War anti-Communist crusade had succeeded in driving leftists from hard-won positions of influence in the labor movement, in blacklisting them from the motion picture industry, silencing them in the schools, and crippling most of the organizations in which Communists played an important role. As a result, not only had Communists become an insignificant force in the United States, but for a time the country as a whole appeared to have reached a consensus which left little room for militant movements for social change. Under these conditions, one could hardly expect that a small band of leftists would retain leadership in a movement that by its nature was offensive to most Americans of whatever political persuasion.

The predictability of the outcome, however, should not obscure its disastrous impact upon the Mattachine Society and upon the movement which the Mattachine initiated. In abandoning the perspectives of Hay, Rowland, and the other founders, the organization's new leadership discarded several elements that would prove crucial for a successful gay movement: the recognition that the oppression of homosexuals had structural roots that ran deeper than simple prejudice; the bold rejection of the complex of theories and attitudes that labeled homosexual behavior as sin, sickness, or crime; the espousal of a self-affirming pride in one's gay identity; the determined assertion that gay life could be ethical and dignified and that a gay culture had something of value to contribute to the society as a whole; and the conviction that only mass collective action by homosexuals themselves could initiate significant changes in the status of the gay population.

By contrast, the conservative, essentially accommodationist course pursued by Burns, Call, and the other successors to the founders left the Mattachine without a dynamic strategy for achieving its goal of equality for gays, and with little appeal among its natural constituency.

6

Certain question remain: Why do most gay people of the 1970s, including gay liberationists, remain so ignorant of an important piece of our history? What happened in the intervening years between 1953 and Stonewall? Did the movement continue to pursue the lifeless, stagnant course set for it by Burns, Call, and others like them? What about the personal histories of the founders, the seven men who provided the energy, insight, and inspiration that sustained the early Mattachine Society?

Our ignorance of the radical roots of the early gay movement in the United States is a compelling example of our oppression. The failure of those efforts meant, in effect, that twenty years later the system of gay oppression survived intact. The silence and invisibility which, until recently, surrounded our lives, extended to our history, including its most precious parts—the organized attempts not only to survive but to fight back and to use our gayness, as Chuck Rowland once said, "in the interests of humanity."

But it is also important for us to realize that the history of the early Mattachine Society has remained hidden not solely because of external forces. The individuals who took hold of the Mattachine in 1953 systematically buried every trace of its left-wing origins. Accounts of the early history that were printed in the *Mattachine Review* and passed on to newer members later in the 1950s told merely of a semisecret organization that had grown so rapidly that it outlived its initial structure. The changes of 1953 are painted as the triumph of the democratic strivings of the membership and as a sign of the maturing of the movement.

One cannot help but draw an analogy with the American labor movement of the 1930s, whose enormous achievements owed much to the commitment, daring, and sustained efforts of thousands of Communist Party members. Not only were they, too, ruthlessly purged during the Cold War era, but their contributions have also been ignored and denied. As gays, we have shared a fate with others whose radical history of struggle, organization, and visionary outlook lay buried for years under the homogenized "consensus" history written by academics and journalists in the 1950s and 1960s.

The intervening years of the homophile movement, as the gay activists of the 1950s and 1960s called it, were not so bleak as the outcome of the Mattachine's internal fighting might suggest. Change, growth, and development did take place. In 1955 the Daughters of Bilitis (DOB) was founded in San Francisco, adding a distinctive, autonomous lesbian voice to the movement. In 1958 *ONE* magazine, which retained some of the militancy of the early Mattachine Society, had its right to publish affirmed by the U.S. Supreme Court. The Mattachine and DOB grew beyond their California origins and set up chapters in several American cities.

During the 1960s, East Coast activists Franklin Kameny and Barbara Gittings took positions far in advance of their time. Both had not only the self-confidence to denounce the proclamations of the medical establishment as charlatanism and quackery, but also the determination to tackle the discriminatory policies of the federal bureaucracy, and the courage to demonstrate in public for gay rights. In San Francisco the Society for Individual Rights (SIR), founded in 1964, became a mass organization with more than 1,000 members. By the time of Stonewall, nearly fifty American gay organizations existed, in every part of the country except the South.

The movement had adopted the slogan "Gay is good"; the *Advocate* (far different from what it has become) had started publishing in Los Angeles and was relentlessly exposing the everyday oppression of gay men; *The Ladder,* the monthly magazine of the Daughters of Bilitis, had moved decisively in the direction of feminism; Troy Perry had founded what would become in the 1970s the biggest gay organization in the United States, the Metropolitan Community Church.

The Stonewall Riot did not create a gay liberation movement out of nothing; the seeds had already started to sprout by the time the police raided the Christopher Street bar. Stonewall was the catalyst that allowed gay women and men to appropriate to themselves the example, insight, and inspiration of the radical movements of the 1960s—black power, the new left, the counterculture and, above all, feminism—and take a huge leap forward toward liberation.

Though the movement as a whole continued to grow during the 1950s and 1960s, for many of the leaders of the early Mattachine it all but ended with the events of 1953. According to James Gruber, the impact was that of a "personal calamity." Some of them—Gruber, Stevens, Hull and Gernreich—dropped out of the movement altogether, disillusioned by the experience. Bob Hull later committed suicide. For a time, Dale Jennings and Chuck Rowland transferred their energy to *ONE* magazine. But Jennings, who had risked much for a cause that had now repudiated him, grew increasingly bitter, withdrew into private life, and disavowed the movement. Rowland, impatient with the task of publishing a monthly magazine, attempted to organize homosexuals once again, this time by starting a "gay church," only to be subjected to ridicule by many of his friends. When his effort collapsed, he sank into alcoholism for many years before successfully rehabilitating himself and resuming a long-interrupted teaching career.

Harry Hay, too, was profoundly affected by the turn of events. In the autumn of 1951, when it appeared that the Mattachine Society would become an all-consuming effort, he had gone to his wife, Anita, and to his party superiors to tell them of his work. The relevation led to the breakup of a thirteen-year marriage and to the severance of his Communist Party ties. Deprived of what had been the main props of his life, Hay had plunged into his new commitment, fully expecting that it would become the focus of his life. With that also taken from him, the once energetic, enthusiastic Hay suffered a paralyzing nervous breakdown and came close to committing suicide.

In the pre-Stonewall era, Hay never again engaged in sustained organizational work in the gay movement, but the liberation of homosexuals remained his overriding concern. During the 1950s and 1960s he surfaced from time to time, pleased at the opportunity "to begin rocking the boat toward Christopher Street by scandalously declaring, at decorously-conducted Homophile conferences, that Gays were different from everybody else except in bed." To a movement that remained reformist, he tried to communicate a radical sense of gay identity, of how the "gay window" on the world held something of enormous significance for humanity as a whole.

With the birth of radical gay liberation in the last decade, Hay feels that his own work has been vindicated and that the message of the early Mattachine Society has been reborn. He warns, however, of the danger of the gay movement's losing its most revolutionary visions in the quest for what he calls "the chimera of Gay civil rights." "I would like to feel," he says, "that Gay Lib isn't dead, that it's only derailed since it allowed itself to become a Thunder-Mug planted to geraniums in the middle-class parlors of Gay Democratic Clubs. It's time for the Gay Visionaries and Poets and Dreamers to create a new chemistry, to fan up a new incandescence, to lift the veil on a new dream."

Hay himself has become something of a folk hero to a younger generation of gay male radicals. An interview in Jonathan Katz's *Gay American History,* an appearance in the film *Word Is Out,* and a stream of visiting activists from around the country are slowly giving Hay the recognition he deserves.

When I began my research three years ago into the early history of the gay movement, I had little idea of what I would uncover. I also had little idea of what "gay history" could mean to me personally, a gay socialist of the 1970s.

These explorations into our past have been an intensely emotional journey. Of Hay, whom I visited for several days at his home in rural New Mexico, and of Rowland, with whom I have had an extensive correspondence, I could say that I fell in love, though that phrase barely touches the depth and variety of feeling that I have for them. I was three years old when they wrote the Mattachine initiation ceremony: "No boy or girl, approaching the maelstrom of deviation, need make that crossing alone, afraid, and in the dark ever again." They were talking about me.

We have a special need for history. Raised as we were in heterosexual families, we grew up and discovered our gayness deprived of gay ancestors, without a sense of our roots. We need to create and carry with us a living awareness of gay generations, to incorporate in our consciousness not only the organized struggle of our predecessors, but the everyday struggle to survive that our ancestors engaged in. We need to affirm and appreciate our past, not in some abstract way, but as it is embodied in living human beings.

Just as a knowledge of our history can strengthen us today, the way we carry on that tradition validates those who came before us. Maybe Chuck Rowland, in a letter he wrote to me during my research, should have the final word:

"You say, John, that you are grateful and filled with love for me. You won't feel the need to apologize for these feelings when I say: What the hell, man, you're my son, blood of my blood, flesh of my flesh, in a deeper, truer sense than any literal blood or flesh could possibly be! You represent our future and our fulfillment. You are the greatest and finest progeny we could ever have aspired to conceive when we met in our little, fear-struck rooms filled with brave words and great dreams back in the 1950s."

# 3

# THE HOMOSEXUAL MENACE

## THE POLITICS OF SEXUALITY IN COLD WAR AMERICA

────────────

*The persecutions of gay men and lesbians during the McCarthy era are the essential political context for understanding the work of Harry Hay and his colleagues, described in the previous essay, in launching a gay freedom struggle in the United States. The 1950s were a grim period for gay men and lesbians. Neither before nor since has oppression against us been so intensely concentrated. "The Homosexual Menace" traces the history of that era.*

*I also intended that this exploration of a particular moment of gay history would begin to suggest the importance of including the study of homosexuality into the larger work of interpreting the history of the United States. Knowledge of this episode, I am convinced, can give us a more nuanced and accurate perception of Cold War America. Sexuality, gender, and the family are not separate, isolated subjects, but integral to understanding the whole of a society's history.*

Reprinted with permission from *Passion and Power: Sexuality in History*, eds. Kathy Peiss and Christina Simmons (Philadelphia: Temple University Press, 1989), 226–240.

Over the last two decades, new social historians, feminist historians, and historical demographers together have shifted the focus of the discipline away from its traditional concern with politics, war, and diplomacy toward an examination of what might broadly be called the private realm. Gradually, this reorientation has expanded to include the sexual. Community studies, the reconstruction of family life, examination of marriage patterns and fertility rates, the investigation of the domestic sphere in which many women moved, the exploration of popular culture, and other topics often intersect at the point of sexuality. Historians have pursued these connections and are now directing more attention than ever before to the study of erotic life.

Meanwhile, events since the 1960s have alerted us to the importance of sexuality as an area of political contention. Eroticism in contemporary America is clearly more than a private matter. During the 1970s both women's liberation and gay liberation became major social forces in part by their assertion that the personal is political. They succeeded in mobilizing millions of women and men around sexual concerns. In local, state, and national politics, issues of abortion and reproductive rights, rape, sexual harassment, and homosexuality stimulated intense debate, and in many cases substantive changes in policy and public attitudes took place. By the late 1970s, moreover, the victories of the feminist and gay movements had provoked a backlash. A well-organized, well-financed movement, often referred to as the New Right and strongly grounded in Christian fundamentalism, attempted to erase the changes of the previous few years. With sexual issues as its motivating force, the New Right provided much of the energy behind Ronald Reagan's successful campaign for the presidency. During the 1980s sexuality moved even closer to center stage in American politics, as the issues of abortion, gay rights, pornography, and, most recently, AIDS, have polarized Americans.

The contemporary scene certainly suggests that it is worth investigating the intersection of sexuality and politics in the American past—how sexuality has worked its way into politics and, conversely, how politics has impinged upon sexual expression. In this essay I would like to turn attention to the 1950s, the decade when Cold War tensions were at their height, and explore a moment when the American political system seized upon one particular aspect of sexual life. Throughout these years the state mobilized considerable resources against homo-sexuals and lesbians. The image of the homosexual as a menace to society sharpened in the 1950s and the sanctions faced by gay men and women intensified. In the first part of the essay I will examine the anti-homosexual campaigns of the Cold War era and then move on to suggest what lay behind them.

I

Homosexuality made its unexpected debut as an issue of Cold War domestic politics in February 1950. During hearings before the Senate Appropriations Committee, Under Secretary of State John Peurifoy mentioned that most of the ninety-one employees who had been dismissed for reasons of "moral turpitude" were homosexuals.[1] The revelation could hardly have come at a less fortunate time for the Truman administration or for gay Americans. The previous few months had witnessed a series of events that encouraged the exploitation of fears about national security—the Communist victory in China, the detonation of an atom bomb by the Soviet Union, the conviction of Alger Hiss on charges of perjury, and the trial in New York of Judith Coplon for espionage. A few days before Peurifoy testified, Senator Joseph McCarthy had delivered his famous Wheeling, West Virginia, speech in which he claimed that the State Department was riddled with Communists. Eager to discredit President Truman and the Democrats, Republicans saw in Peurifoy's remarks another opportunity to cast doubt upon the administration's competence to safeguard the nation's security.[2]

In the succeeding months the danger posed by "sexual perverts" became a staple of partisan rhetoric. Several Republican senators charged that homosexuals had infiltrated the executive branch of the government and that the Truman administration had failed to take corrective action. Governor Thomas Dewey of New York, the Republican presidential candidate in 1948, accused Truman of condoning the presence of sex offenders on the federal payroll. When the officer in charge of the District of Columbia vice squad testified at a Congressional hearing that thousands of "sexual deviates" worked for the government, pressure for an investigation built. Finally, in June 1950 the Senate authorized a formal inquiry into the employment of "homosexuals and other moral perverts" in government.[3]

The report that the Senate released in December 1950 painted a threatening picture of homosexual civil servants. Significantly, the senators never questioned the assumption that government employment of gay men and women was undesirable; instead, they treated it as a self-evident problem. The investigating committee offered two closely connected arguments to buttress its conclusion that homosexuals should be excluded from government service. The first pertained to the "character" of the homosexual who allegedly lacked "emotional stability" and whose "moral fiber" had been weakened by sexual indulgence. Homosexuality took on the form of a contagious disease that threatened the health of anyone who came near it. Even one "sex pervert in a Government agency," the committee warned,

> tends to have a corrosive influence upon his fellow employees. These perverts will frequently attempt to entice normal individuals to engage in perverted practices. This is particularly true in the case of young and impressionable people who might come under the influence of a pervert. . . . One homosexual can pollute a Government office.

The second rationale for exclusion concerned the danger of blackmail. "The social stigma attached to sex perversion is so great," the committee noted, that blackmailers made "a regular practice of preying upon the homosexual." Already morally enfeebled by sexual indulgence, homosexuals would succumb to the blandishments of the spy and betray their country rather than risk the exposure of their sexual identity. The only evidence the committee provided to support its contention was the case of an Austrian intelligence officer early in the twentieth century.[4]

The homosexual menace remained a theme of American political culture throughout the McCarthy era. In committee hearings legislators persistently interrogated federal officials about the employment of "sex perverts." Right-wing organizations combined charges of Communist infiltration with accusations about sex offenders on the government payroll.[5] Lee Mortimer, a columnist for the Hearst-owned *New York Daily Mirror*, published a series of sensationalistic "Confidential" books that capitalized on the homosexual issue. Lesbians, according to Mortimer, formed cells in schools and colleges that preyed upon the innocent. They infiltrated the armed services, where they seduced, and sometimes "raped," their peers. Mortimer warned that "10,000 faggots" had escaped detection and that the government remained "honeycombed in high places with people you wouldn't let in your garbage wagons." The pens of right-wing ideologues transformed homosexuality into an epidemic infecting the nation, actively spread by Communists to sap the strength of the next generation.[6]

The Senate report, as well as the rhetoric and articles on homosexuality, served as prelude to the imposition of heavier penalties against gay men and women. During the 1950s the web of oppression tightened around homosexuals and lesbians. An executive order barred them from all federal jobs, and dismissals from government service rose sharply. The military intensified its purges of gay men and lesbians. The Post Office tampered with their mail, the FBI initiated widespread surveillance of homosexual meeting places and activities, and urban police forces stepped up their harassment.

Dismissals from civilian posts in the federal government increased as soon as the sexual pervert issue arose. From 1947 through March 1950, they had averaged only five per month, but in the next six months the figure increased twelvefold. Within weeks after Eisenhower's inauguration, the Republican president issued an executive order that made homosexuality sufficient and necessary grounds for disbarment from federal employment. In addition, all applicants for government jobs faced security investigations, and the number of homosexuals and lesbians who never made it past the screening process far exceeded those whose employment was terminated. States and municipalities, meanwhile, followed the lead of the federal government in demanding moral probity from their personnel. The states also enforced rigorous standards in the licensing of many professions. Corporations under government contract applied to their workers the security provisions of the Eisenhower administration. The Coast Guard enforced a similar system of regulations for merchant sailors, longshore workers, and other maritime laborers. One study in the mid-1950s estimated that over 12,600,000 workers—more than twenty percent of the labor force—faced loyalty-security investigations.[7]

The military, too, intensified its search for homosexuals and lesbians in its ranks. During the late 1940s discharges for homosexuality averaged slightly over 1,000 per year. But in the atmosphere of heightened concern for national security that the Cold War provoked, even the military worked overtime to purge homosexuals. Separations averaged 2,000 per year in the early 1950s and rose to over 3,000 by the beginning of the next decade. Exploiting the sense of terror and helplessness that an investigation provoked, military authorities often trampled upon the rights of gay and nongay personnel alike.[8] Late in 1950, for example, the military began a "housecleaning" of lesbians at its bases in the South. As one corporal under investigation reported:

> Eleven girls were called in and questioned as to their alleged homosexuality . . . The girls being sick of the worry and strain of being under suspicion and being promised by a very likable chap Capt. Dickey of the OSI (Office of Special Investigation) that they would receive General Discharges if they confessed, all proceeded to do so and after confessing were informed that it wasn't enough to incriminate only themselves—they must write down also someone else with whom they had homosexual relations—this done they waited and at the end of January they were all out with Undesirables.

Altogether, at least three dozen women received separations at Lackland, Kessler, and Wright-Patterson Air Force Bases. The cost in human suffering hidden behind these numbers, and the thousands of other discharged women and men, defies calculation. Two of the women caught in the investigation mentioned earlier committed suicide; the others carried a burden that one study called "a life stigma."[9]

Since most homosexuals and lesbians could mask their identity, the presumption that they imperiled national security led the government to adopt extraordinary measures to break their cover. In 1950 the FBI, responsible for supplying the Civil Service Commission with information on government employees and applicants, established liaisons with police departments throughout the country. Not content merely to screen particular individuals, it adopted a preventive strategy that justified widespread surveillance. Cooperative vice squad officers supplied the bureau with records of morals arrests, regardless of the disposition of a case. Regional FBI offices clipped press articles about the gay subculture, gathered data on gay bars, compiled lists of other places frequented by homosexuals, and infiltrated gay rights organizations such as the Mattachine Society and the Daughters of Bilitis. Agents sometimes exhibited considerable zeal in using the information they collected.[10] In an affidavit submitted to the American Civil Liberties Union, one former employee of the federal government described how the FBI hounded him for over a decade after he left his civil service job. Agents informed his employers and coworkers about the man's sexual identity, and he experienced merciless ridicule at work. When an arm injury left him disabled, he was denied vocational retraining by the state of Illinois because of his homosexuality. As late as the early 1960s, FBI agents visited him at home in an effort to extract the names of homosexual acquaintances.[11]

The Post Office, too, participated in extralegal harassment. Using obscenity statutes as a rationale, the department established a watch on the recipients of physique magazines and other gay male erotica. Postal inspectors joined pen pal clubs that were often used by male homosexuals as a way of meeting one another, began writing to men they believed might be gay, and if their suspicions proved correct, placed tracers on the victim's mail to locate other homosexuals. A professor in Maryland and an employee of the department of highways in Pennsylvania lost their jobs after the Post Office revealed to their employers that the men received mail implicating them in homosexual activity.[12]

The highly publicized labeling of lesbians and homosexuals as moral perverts and national security risks, and the antigay policy of the federal government, gave local police forces across the country free rein in harassing them. Throughout the 1950s lesbians and gay men suffered from unpredictable, brutal crackdowns. Women generally encountered the police in and around lesbian bars while men also faced arrest in public cruising areas, but even the homes of gay men and women lacked immunity from vice squads. Newspaper headlines would strike fear into the heart of the gay population by announcing that the police were combing the city for nests of deviates. Editors often printed names, addresses, and places of employment of men and women arrested in bar raids.[13] Arrests were substantial in many cities. In the District of Columbia they topped 1,000 per year during the early 1950s; in Philadelphia misdemeanor charges against lesbians and homosexuals averaged one hundred per month. Arrests fluctuated enormously as unexpected sweeps of gay bars could lead to scores of victims in a single night. New York, New Orleans, Dallas, San Francisco, and Baltimore were among the cities that witnessed sudden upsurges in police action against homosexuals and lesbians in the 1950s. A survey of male homosexuals conducted by the Institute for Sex Research revealed how far police action extended into the gay world: twenty percent of the respondents had encountered trouble with law enforcement officers.[14]

In some localities the concern about homosexuality became an obsession. In Boise, Idaho, the arrest of three men in November 1955 on charges of sexual activity with teenagers precipitated a fifteen-month investigation into the city's male homosexual subculture. A curfew was imposed on Boise's youth, and the city brought in an outside investigator with experience in ferreting out homosexuals. Over 150 news stories appeared in the local press, and newspapers in neighboring states gave prominent coverage to the witch-hunt. Gay men fled Boise by the score as the police called in 1,400 residents for questioning and pressured homosexuals into naming friends.[15]

The issue of homosexuality also surfaced repeatedly in Florida throughout the 1950s and early 1960s. In Miami in 1954, the murder of two homosexuals by "queerbashers" who had picked up their victims in a gay bar led the mayor to reverse a long-standing policy of closing his eyes to the existence of the establishments. In a strange twist, the individuals most in need of protection became the targets of the police, who made sweeps of the bars and beefed up their patrols of local parks and beaches. The Miami City Council passed a law mandating special attendants in movie theaters to protect youth and another that prohibited establishments selling liquor from employing or serving homosexuals. In testimony before a Senate committee investigating juvenile delinquency, the mayor of Miami called for an amendment to the so-called white slavery act so that homosexuals could be prosecuted under it. A special file containing the names of those arrested on homosexual-related charges was circulated to police departments throughout southern Florida.[16] In 1958 concern spread to the state legislature as a special committee spearheaded a sensationalistic investigation in Gainesville. The committee collected several thousand pages of testimony, grilled hundreds of witnesses, and exhibited few compunctions about releasing information based on hearsay and unsubstantiated accusations. Sixteen staff and faculty members of the University of Florida eventually lost their positions on charges of homosexuality; significantly, all of them had been active in the civil rights movement in Florida.[17]

2

Although the preoccupation with "sexual perversion" appears, in retrospect, bizarre and irrational, the incorporation of gay women and men into the demonology of the McCarthy era required little effort. According to right-wing ideologues, leftist teachers poisoned the minds of their students; lesbians and homosexuals corrupted the bodies of the young. Since Communists bore no identifying physical characteristics, they were able to infiltrate the government and commit treason against their country. Bereft of integrity, they exhibited loyalty only to an alien ideology that inspired fanatical passion. Homosexuals, too, could escape detection and thus insinuate themselves into every branch of the government. The slaves of their sexual passions, they would stop at nothing to gratify their desires until the satisfaction of animal needs finally destroyed their moral sense. Communists taught their children to betray their parents; "mannish" women mocked the ideals of marriage and motherhood. Lacking toughness, the effete men of the eastern establishment lost China and Eastern Europe to the enemy, while weak-willed, pleasure-obsessed homosexuals—"half-men"—feminized everything they touched and sapped the masculine vigor that had tamed a continent. The congruence between the stereotypes of Communists and homosexuals made the scapegoating of gay men and women a simple matter.

Still, the special targeting of homosexuals and lesbians during the Cold War marked a significant departure from the past. Although it grew out of a centuries-long cultural tradition that was clearly hostile to homoerotic activities, there was no model for it in America's history. In 1920, for instance, the Senate investigated "immoral conditions" of a homosexual nature at the naval training station in Newport, Rhode Island. In important ways the political context resembled that of the McCarthy era—a world war had recently ended, a major Communist revolution had taken place, the nation was in the midst of a red scare, and Republicans were trying to discredit a Democratic administration. Yet, although the Senate report expressed intense loathing for homosexuals, it reserved its strongest condemnation for the methods used to entrap them and made no effort to arouse an anti-homosexual campaign.[18]

The need to explain the scapegoating of gay men and lesbians becomes even more apparent when one recalls that the initial attacks grew out of the belief that the vulnerability of homosexuals to blackmail made them likely candidates for treason. The threat to security informed the Senate investigation into their employment by the government, pushed the government to exclude them from its service, and rationalized the widespread surveillance by the FBI. Yet at no time during this period did the government present evidence to sustain its contention about blackmail. How then does one explain the massive mobilization of resources at every level of government to unmask the homosexual menace? Why did the 1950s witness so great an intensification of the penalties directed at lesbians and gay men? The answer, I think, may be found by looking at the changes in sexual expression, gender roles, and family stability that occurred in the previous two decades.

Taken together, the Great Depression and World War II seriously disrupted family life, traditional gender arrangements, and patterns of sexual behavior. The prolonged economic dislocations of the 1930s led to a significant drop in both marriage and birth rates. The inability of young adults to find stable employment and achieve financial independence from parents forced a postponement of marriage. The discrimination that married women in particular faced in the labor market encouraged young single women to remain unwed. Although birth rates had been declining steadily for over a century, the depression years witnessed an acceleration of this trend. Extreme economic hardship may have drawn some families together, but it also certainly meant that many young women and men never realized their expectation of a family of their own.[19]

Wartime brought the return of prosperity and full employment and, for a short time in the early 1940s, a rush toward marriage and childbearing. But far more significant were the disruptions caused by war. Families endured prolonged separations, divorce and desertion occurred more frequently, and the trend toward sexual permissiveness accelerated. Juvenile delinquency emerged as a perplexing social problem, and the rate of premarital pregnancy and illegitimacy rose. Women, especially those who were married and had children, entered the workforce in unprecedented numbers. They not only took the low-paying jobs traditionally available to them, but also filled positions that were normally occupied by men and that promised them financial security. At the same time the widespread use of psychiatrists by the government during the war enormously increased the prestige and influence of the profession. The emphasis of mental health professionals on family dynamics as a source of individual maladjustment focused concern on the instability of family life.[20]

World War II also marked a critical turning point in the social expression of homosexuality. It created a substantially new "erotic situation" that led to a sudden coalescence of an urban gay subculture in the 1940s. The war plucked millions of young men and women, whose sexual identities were just forming, out of their homes, out of towns and small cities, and away from the heterosexual environment of the family, and dropped them into essentially sex-segregated situations—as GIs, as WACs and WAVEs, in same-sex roominghouses for women workers who had relocated to find employment. Wartime society freed millions of the young from the settings where heterosexuality was normally encouraged. For men and women who were already gay, the war provided the opportunity to meet persons like themselves, while others were able to act on erotic desires they might otherwise have denied. World War II was something of a nationwide "coming out" experience for homosexuals and lesbians.[21]

The evidence to support this contention is accumulating as the exploration of the social history of the gay subculture progresses. Lisa Ben, for instance, came out during the war. Leaving the small California farming community where she was born and raised, she came to Los Angeles to find work and lived in a women's boardinghouse. There, she met for the first time lesbians who took her to gay bars and introduced her to other gay women. Donald Vining, a young man with lots of homosexual desire but few gay experiences, moved to New York during the war and worked at a large YMCA. His diary reveals numerous erotic adventures with soldiers, sailors, marines, and civilians who were also away from home. Even oppression could have positive side effects. When Pat Bond, a lesbian from Davenport, Iowa, was caught up in a purge of lesbians from the WACs in the Pacific, she did not return to Iowa. She stayed in San Francisco and became part of a community of lesbians.[22]

These changes added up to more than the sum of the individual biographies. Lesbians and gay men in association with one another created institutions to bolster their identity. Places as diverse as San Jose, Denver, Kansas City, Buffalo, and Worcester, Massachusetts, had their first gay bars in the 1940s. The immediate postwar period also witnessed a minor efflorescence of gay male and lesbian literature. The social expression of homosexual behavior took on a substantially new form during these years as a stable urban gay subculture appeared in many American cities.[23]

Finally, the publication in 1948 of the Kinsey study of male sexual behavior put in bold relief concerns about American sexual morality. The release of the huge scientific tome was the publishing event of the year. The book remained high on the best-seller list for several months, sold a quarter of a million copies, and received widespread attention in the press, popular magazines, and specialized journals. Most men, the study found, were sexually active by age fifteen. Premarital and extramarital sex was typical rather than exceptional, and virtually all men had violated the law at least once in pursuit of an orgasm. Worst of all, perhaps, were Kinsey's conclusions about the incidence of homosexuality. Over a third of his sample had had at least one adult homosexual experience, homoerotic activity predominated for at least a three-year period in one of eight cases, and four percent of American men were exclusively homosexual. The sexual portrait of the American male that the Kinsey study sketched could only have horrified moral conservatives.[24]

The disruptions created by depression and war, as well as the evolution of a stable gay subculture, did not occur in isolation. From the 1920s to the 1950s, the place of sexuality in American life was also changing in profound ways. Influenced by the spread of Freudianism, marital advice literature highlighted the importance of erotic pleasure in achieving a successful marriage. Youth were enjoying greater autonomy in sexual matters. A school-based peer culture, the availability of the automobile, and innovations in mass culture allowed them to date and go steady without the chaperonage of adults. The success of the birth control movement in making contraceptives more widely available helped sustain the shift to a sexuality that was nonprocreative and, increasingly, nonmarital. And, after World War II, the spread of pornography beyond its traditional place in a marginal, illicit underground accentuated the flux in sexual values.[25]

### 3

Government policymakers and business leaders approached the end of World War II with two overriding and interlocking concerns. With memories of the Great Depression still vivid, they set their minds on achieving a stable international order and a prosperous domestic economy. Postwar conditions, however, did not augur well for either goal. The Soviet Union retained hegemony in Eastern Europe, civil wars raged in China and Greece, the economy of Western Europe was in ruins, and Communists were making a serious bid for power in Italy and France. At home, the first year of peace brought a wave of strikes in basic industries, and labor militancy threatened to escalate. Inflation immediately after the war was followed later in the decade by recession.

The policies that political leaders pursued in the international arena helped to condition their response to domestic instability. The rhetoric about Communist aggression abroad inevitably fed concerns about subversion at home and justified extraordinary measures. As American Communists were pushed beyond the pale of political legitimacy, the fragile popular front of the 1930s in which New Deal liberals, progressives, and Communists worked together collapsed. The attorney general's list of subversive organizations destroyed the effectiveness of many reform efforts, and labor militancy declined as Communists were expelled from positions of union leadership. The House Un-American Activities Committee's highly publi-cized hearings inhibited the expression of dissent in the field of education and in cultural activity. The political spectrum both shifted to the right and narrowed considerably in the postwar years.[26]

Accompanying these efforts were a series of initiatives that one can reasonably describe as a politics of personal life tailored to restore a different form of domestic tranquility. Some of these measures were decidedly benevolent. A generous GI Bill of Rights and federal home mortgages, for instance, subsidized millions of young men so that they could more easily and quickly assume the role of husband and father. Other measures fell on the side of coercion, psychological or otherwise. Even before the war ended, women faced a barrage of propaganda informing them that their jobs really belonged to men and extolling the virtues of marriage and childrearing. In the media, pictures of sparkling, well-equipped kitchens occupied by young mothers with babies dangling from their arms replaced images of women in hardhats surrounded by heavy machinery. Popular psychology books and women's magazines equated femininity with marriage and motherhood. Where these methods failed, employers could simply fire women, since female workers lacked the support of either organized labor or federal antidiscrimination statutes. From 1944 to 1946 the number of women workers fell by four million.[27]

Most extreme, however, were those currents that induced fear and promised punishment. For example, an extensive popular literature in the late 1940s described the grave threat that a surge in sex crimes posed to the women and children of America. Just as hidden enemies imperiled the security of the nation, dangerous criminals lurking in the shadows menaced the postwar family. J. Edgar Hoover himself sounded the alarm, and a dozen states convened special commissions to find ways of containing the sexual psychopath. Eventually, more than half the states passed sexual psychopath laws. Those enacted at the height of the Cold War tended to wreak havoc on constitutional rights.[28]

When placed in this context, the Cold War era's preoccupation with the homosexual menace appears less like a bizarre, irrational expression of McCarthyism and emerges, instead, as an integral component of postwar American society and politics. The anti-homosexual campaigns of the 1950s represented but one front in a widespread effort to reconstruct patterns of sexuality and gender relations shaken by depression and war. The targeting of homosexuals and lesbians itself testified to the depth of the changes that had occurred in the 1940s since, without the growth of a gay subculture, it is difficult to imagine the homosexual issue carrying much weight. The labeling of sexual deviants helped to define the norm for men and women. It raised the costs of remaining outside the traditional family even as other, nonpunitive approaches encouraged a resurgence of traditional male and female roles. There was a congruence between anti-Communism in the sphere of politics and social concern over homosexuality. The attempt to suppress sexual deviance paralleled and reinforced the efforts to quash political dissent.

Finally, one should note the unintended consequence of the McCarthy era campaigns. In marshaling the resources of the state and the media against the more extensive gay subcultures of midcentury, political and moral conservatives unwittingly helped weld that subculture together. The penalties directed at gay men and lesbians grew so intense that they fostered a collective consciousness of oppression. Thus, in the 1950s a gay emancipation movement first took shape, spreading slowly until the political radicalism of the 1960s infiltrated the gay world. By the end of the 1960s, a resurgent feminism and a militant gay liberation movement would usher in a new era of sexual politics, assaulting the policies and practices of Cold War America.

**NOTES**

1. *New York Times*, 1 March 1950, 1. A more detailed discussion of these events may be found in John D'Emilio, *Sexual Politics, Sexual Communities: The Making of a Homosexual Minority in the United States, 1940–1970* (Chicago: University of Chicago Press, 1983), ch. 3.

2. See Athan Theoharis, *Seeds of Repression: Harry S. Truman and the Origins of McCarthyism* (Chicago: Quadrangle Books, 1971); Alan Harper, *The Politics of Loyalty: The White House and the Communist Issue, 1946–52* (Westport, Conn.: Greenwood Publishing, 1969); Robert Griffith and Athan Theoharis, eds., *The Specter: Original Essays on the Cold War and the Origins of McCarthyism* (New York: Franklin Watts, 1974); Allen Weinstein, *Perjury: The Hiss-Chambers Case* (New York: Knopf, 1978); and David M. Oshinsky, *A Conspiracy So Immense: The World of Joe McCarthy* (New York: Free Press, 1983).

3. For discussions of the "sexual pervert" issue see *New York Times*, 9 March 1950, 1; 15 March 1950, 1; 19 April 1950, 25; 25 April 1950, 5; 26 April 1950, 3; 5 May 1950, 15; 20 May 1950, 8; 15 June 1950, 6. See also the series of articles by Max Lerner in the *New York Post*, 10–23 July 1950.

4. U.S. Senate, 81st Cong., 2nd Sess., Committee on Expenditures in Executive Departments, *Employment of Homosexuals and Other Sex Perverts in Government* (Washington, D.C.: 1950). The quotations may be found on pages 3–5.

5. *New York Times*, 28 March 1951, 2; 26 June 1953, 4; 13 April 1953, 20; *Senator McCarthy's Methods*, a pamphlet published by the Committee for McCarthyism of the Constitutional Educational League, New York City, 1954, copy in Herbert Lehman papers, Columbia University.

6. Lee Mortimer, *Washington Confidential Today* (New York: 1952; Paperback Library ed., 1962), 110–19; Jack Lait and Lee Mortimer, *U.S.A. Confidential* (New York: Crown Publishers, 1952), 43–45.

7. *Employment of Homosexuals*, 7–9, 12–13; Executive Order 10450, reprinted in the *Bulletin of the Atomic Scientists* (April 1955): 156–58; *New York Times*, 4 January 1955,

15; Eleanor Bontecou, *The Federal Loyalty-Security Program* (Ithaca, N.Y.: Cornell University Press, 1953), 272–99, 323–35; Ralph S. Brown, Jr., *Loyalty and Security: Employment Tests in the United States* (New Haven: Yale University Press, 1958), 256–60; Karl M. Bowman and Bernice Engle, "A Psychiatric Evaluation of the Laws of Homosexuality," *Temple Law Quarterly Review* 29 (1956): 299–300. The twenty percent figure comes from Ralph S. Brown, Jr., "Loyalty-Security Measures and Employment Opportunities," *Bulletin of the Atomic Scientists* (April 1955): 113–17.

8.  *Employment of Homosexuals*, 8; Colin Williams and Martin Weinberg, *Homosexuals and the Military: A Study of Less Than Honorable Discharge* (New York: Harper & Row, 1971), 31–36, 45–47, 53; Clifford A. Dougherty and Norman B. Lynch, "The Administrative Discharge: Military Justice?" *George Washington Law Review* 33 (1964): 498–528; Jerome A. Susskind, "Military Administrative Discharge Boards: The Right to Confrontation and Cross-Examination," *Michigan State Bar Journal* 46 (1965): 25–32.

9.  Barbara J. Scammell to ACLU, 15 February 1951, and June Fusca to ACLU, 16 March and 23 April 1951, all in General Correspondence, Vol. 16, 1951, ACLU papers, Princeton University. The phrase "life stigma" comes from Williams and Weinberg, *Homosexuals and the Military*, 36. See also Allen Bérubé and John D'Emilio, "The Military and Lesbians during the McCarthy Years," *Signs* 9 (1984): 759–75.

10. See J. Edgar Hoover, "Role of the FBI in the Federal Employee Security Program," *Northwestern University Law Review* 49 (1954): 333–47. The information on the FBI surveillance program comes from several hundred pages of documents obtained from the FBI under the Freedom of Information Act, File Classification Nos. 94-843, 94-1001, 94-283, 100-37394, and 100-45888.

11. B. D. H., "Personal and Confidential History," in General Correspondence, Vol. 43, 1964, ACLU papers.

12. The postal surveillance did not come to light until the mid-1960s. See Alan Reitman to Affiliates, Memo, 1 September 1965; Ernest Mazey to Reitman, 10 September 1965; and Spencer Coxe to Reitman, 5 August 1965, all in General Correspondence, Vol. 1, 1965, ACLU papers. See also *New Republic*, 21 August 1965, 6–7; *Newsweek*, 13 June 1966, 24.

13. With the exception of the Boise scandal, discussed below, local police activities against gay men and women did not receive coverage beyond the pages of local papers. It is, accordingly, a laborious process to uncover incidents of harassment. The most accessible sources are the publications of gay organizations which, beginning in the mid-1950s, covered police practices extensively. *ONE* magazine is by far the best source, with news items from around the country, but the *Ladder* and the *Mattachine Review* are also valuable sources. James Kepner, who wrote articles on police practices for *ONE*, has saved the clippings from local newspapers that readers sent to him. The clippings may be found in the National Gay Archives in Los Angeles.

14. On the District of Columbia see *Employment of Homosexuals*, 15–19; *Kelly v. US.*, 194 F.2d 150 (D.C. Circuit, 1952); 90 A.2d 233 (D.C. Munic. Ct. App., 1952); *McDermott*

v. *US.*, 98 A .2d 287 (D.C. Munic. Ct. App., 1953). On Philadelphia, see Council on Religion and the Homosexual, *The Challenge and Progress of Homosexual Law Reform* (San Francisco: 1968), 18. On New York, see *ONE* (November 1953): 19, and Lee Mortimer's columns in the *Daily Mirror*, 12 August 1959, 3 November 1959, and 26 January 1960. On New Orleans, see Elly Bulkin, "An Old Dyke's Tale: An Interview with Doris Lunden," *Conditions: Six* (1980): 18. On San Francisco, see the *Ladder* (November 1956): 5. On Baltimore, see *ONE* (April 1955): 14, and (December 1955): 10, and *Baltimore Evening Sun*, 3 and 5 October 1955, clippings in National Gay Archives. On other cities, see *ONE* (November 1955): 8; (November 1958): 17; (December 1958): 15; and (June 1959): 13. For the ISR survey, see John H. Gagnon and William Simon, *Sexual Conduct* (Chicago: Aldine, 1973), 138–39.

15.   On Boise, see *Time*, 12 December 1955, 12; John Gerassi, *The Boys of Boise* (New York: Macmillan, 1966), 109–19; *Washington Mattachine Newsletter* (January 1957) 1–3.

16.   On Miami, see "Miami Junks the Constitution," *ONE* (January 1954): 16–21, and "Miami Hurricane," *ONE* (November 1954): 4–8; John Orr to Herbert Levy, 13 September 1954, in General Correspondence, Vol. 19, 1954, ACLU papers. See also the extensive collections of clippings from the *Miami Herald* and the *Miami Daily News*, August and September 1954, National Gay Archives.

17.   Weekly Bulletin 2015, 26 October 1958; Stuart Simon to Charlie Johns, 5 February 1959; clippings; and other material on the Johns Committee in General Correspondence, Vol. 55, 1959, ACLU papers. For the final report of the investigation, which continued for several years, see *Homosexuality and Citizenship in Florida: A Report of the Florida Legislative Investigating Commiteee* (Tallahassee: 1964).

18.   U.S. Senate, 67th Cong., 1st Sess., Committee on Naval Affairs, *Alleged Immoral Conditions at Newport (R.I.) Naval Training Station* (Washington, D.C.: 1921).

19.   For demographic information on the 1930s, see Conrad and Irene Taeuber, *The Changing Population of the United States* (New York: J. Wiley, 1958), and Joseph Spengler, *Facing Zero Population Growth* (Durham, N.C.: Duke University Press, 1978). On the economic status of women, see William Chafe, *The American Woman* (New York: Oxford University Press, 1972), 58–65, 81–88, 107–11.

20.   On domestic society during the war years, see Richard Polenberg, *War and Society* (Philadelphia: Lippincott, 1972); Francis Merrill, *Social Problems on the Home Front* (New York: Harper, 1948); Ruth Milkman, "Women's Work and the Economic Crisis: Some Lessons from the Great Depression," in *A Heritage of Her Own*, eds. Nancy F. Cott and Elizabeth H. Pleck (New York: Simon & Schuster, 1979); William Chafe, *The American Woman*, chs. 6–8; Geoffrey Perrett, *Days of Sadness, Years of Triumph* (New York: Coward, McCann & Geoghegan, 1973); Roy Hoopes, *Americans Remember the Home Front* (New York: Hawthorn Books, 1977); and Richard R. Lingeman, *Don't You Know There's a War On?* (New York: Putnam, 1970). On psychiatry, see Rebecca

Schwartz Greene, "The Role of the Psychiatrist in World War II" (Ph.D. dissertation, Columbia University, 1977), and William C. Menninger, *Psychiatry in a Troubled World* (New York: Macmillan, 1948).

21. On the impact of World War II on homosexual expression, see Allan Bérubé, *Coming Out Under Fire* (New York: Free Press, 1990). The description of wartime and military life as a new "erotic situation" comes from Williams and Weinberg, *Homosexuals and the Military*, 57.

22. Leland Moss, "An Interview with Lisa Ben," *Gaysweek*, 23 January 1978, 14–16, and Lisa Ben, interview with the author, 9 January 1977, Los Angeles; Donald Vining, *A Gay Diary, 1933–1946* (New York: Pepys Press, 1979); Pat Bond, in Nancy and Casey Adair, *Word Is Out: Stories of Some of Our Lives* (San Francisco: New Glide Publications, 1978), 55–65.

23. On the spread of gay bars, see Gene Tod, "Gay Scene in Kansas City," *Phoenix* (Newsletter of the Phoenix Society of Kansas City) (August 1966): 5–6; Karla Jay and Allen Young, eds., *Lavender Culture* (New York: Jove/HBJ Publications 1979), 146–54. On literature, see Roger Austen, *Playing the Game: The Homosexual Novel in America* (Indianapolis: Bobbs-Merrill, 1977), 93–142, and Jeannette Foster, *Sex Variant Women in Literature*, 2nd ed. (Baltimore: Diana Press, 1975), 324–41.

24. Alfred Kinsey et al., *Sexual Behavior in the Human Male* (Philadelphia: W. B. Saunders, 1948), 301, 392, 499, 585, 610–66. For discussions of Kinsey and his work, see Wardell Pomeroy, *Dr. Kinsey and the Institute for Sex Research* (New York: Harper & Row, 1972); Paul Robinson, *The Modernization of Sex* (New York: Harper & Row, 1976), 42–119; and Regina Markell Morantz, "The Scientist as Sex Crusader: Alfred C. Kinsey and American Culture," *American Quarterly* 29 (1977): 563–89. For the opinion of one moral conservative, see Henry P. Van Dusen, "The Moratorium on Moral Revulsion," *Christianity and Crisis*, 21 June 1948, 81.

25. See John D'Emilio and Estelle Freedman, *Intimate Matters: A History of Sexuality in America* (New York: Harper & Row, 1988), chs. 11 and 12.

26. On anti-Communist measures and the isolation of the Communist Party in the postwar period, see David Caute, *The Great Fear: The Anti-Communist Purge under Truman and Eisenhower* (New York: Simon & Schuster, 1978); Griffith and Theoharis, eds., *The Specter*; Norman Markowitz, *The Rise and Fall of the People's Century* (New York: Free Press, 1973); Lawrence S. Wittner, *Cold War America* (New York: Praeger, 1974); and Joseph Starobin, *American Communism in Crisis, 1943–1957* (Cambridge: Harvard University Press, 1972).

27. On women's and men's roles in the postwar decade, see Mary P. Ryan, *Womanhood in America* (New York: New Viewpoints, 1975), 298–303, 316–20, 335–38; Chafe, *The American Woman*, 174–95; Sara Evans, *Personal Politics* (New York: Knopf, 1979), 3–14; Betty Friedan, *The Feminine Mystique* (New York: Norton, 1963); Peter Filene, *Him/Her/Self* (New York: Harcourt Brace Jovanovich, 1975), 169–202; Joe L. Dubbert,

*A Man's Place: Masculinity in Transition* (Englewood Cliffs, N.J.: Prentice-Hall, 1979), 230–55.

28.   See Estelle B. Freedman, "Uncontrolled Desires: The Response to the Sexual Psychopath, 1920–1960," *Journal of American History* 74 (June 1987): 83–106. For a sampling of the popular literature, see J. Edgar Hoover, "How Safe is Your Daughter," *American Magazine* (July 1947): 32–33; "Biggest Taboo: Crimes Committed by Sexually Maladjusted," *Collier's*, 15 February 1947, 24; "What Can We Do About Sex Crimes?," *Saturday Evening Post*, 11 December 1948, 30–31; "Terror in the Cities," *Collier's*, 11 November 1949, 13–15; and "Murder as a Sex Practice," *American Mercury* (February 1948): 144–50. Among the state commission reports are Commission to Study Sex Offenses, *The Sex Offender and the Criminal Law: Report to the Governor and the General Assembly of Virginia* (Richmond: 1951); Interim Commission of the State of New Hampshire to Study the Cause and Prevention of Serious Sex Crimes, *Report* (Concord: 1949); Joint State Government Commission of Pennsylvania, *Sex Offenders: A Report to the General Assembly* (Harrisburg: 1951); and Michigan Governor's Study Commission on the Deviated Criminal Sex Offender, *Report* (Lansing: 1950). For critiques of the laws, see Edwin H. Sutherland, "The Sexual Psychopath Laws," *Journal of Criminal Law and Criminology* 40 (1950); 543–54; Bowman and Engle, "A Psychiatric Evaluation"; Bowman and Engle, "Sexual Psychopath Laws," in *Sexual Behavior and the Law*, ed. Ralph Slovenko (Springfield, Ill.: Thomas, 1965); Alan Swanson, "Sexual Psychopath Statutes: Summary and Analysis," *Journal of Criminal Law, Criminology and Police Science* 51 (1960): 215–35.

# 4

# GAY POLITICS,
# GAY COMMUNITY

## SAN FRANCISCO'S EXPERIENCE

---

*This article practically wrote itself. Witnessing the "White Night Riots" and the political ferment in San Francisco in the spring and summer of 1979 dramatized the value of knowing a community's history. I supplemented the research that I had done on San Francisco in the 1950s and 1960s with work on the 1970s to trace the evolution of the city's gay and lesbian movement as well as the connections between political activism and the community's growth. It was through these events that I came to see clearly the utter dependence of activists on a well-developed set of community institutions, particularly the bars, in order to be able to mobilize in self-defense.*

*"Gay power" has grown in San Francisco in the years since 1980, and the community needs someone who will trace in far greater detail than I have done its history in the twentieth century.* Reprinted with permission from *Socialist Review* 55 (January–February 1981): 77–104.

For gay men and for lesbians, San Francisco has become akin to what Rome is for Catholics: a lot of us live there and many more make the pilgrimage. The gay male subculture in San Francisco is more visible and more complex than in any other city. Mainstream media from CBS to *Playboy* find it newsworthy enough to explore, expose, and vilify. Though most of the publicity has focused on the gay male presence, lesbians in the Bay Area also sustain more institutions than their sisters elsewhere. San Francisco is one of the very few cities where lesbians are residentially concentrated enough to be visible. For gay men and for lesbians, San Francisco is a special place.

The gay community in San Francisco and its politics have been a long time in the making. Surveying its history can tell us much not just about one city, but about the emergence of sexual minorities generally, about shifting forms of oppression and changing political strategies.

## THE HISTORICAL BACKGROUND

The distinction between behavior and identity is critical to an understanding of contemporary gay male and lesbian life. Jeffrey Weeks described it well in *Coming Out: Homosexual Politics in Britain.* "Homosexuality has existed throughout history," he wrote. "But what have varied enormously are the ways in which various societies have regarded homosexuality, the meanings they have attached to it, and how those who were engaged in homosexual activity viewed themselves. . . . As a starting point we have to distinguish between homosexual behaviour, which is universal, and a homosexual identity, which is historically specific—and a comparatively recent phenomenon."

In colonial America, in the family-centered household economy of the North, heterosexual relations and individual survival meshed, as production was based on the cooperative labor of husband, wife, and their children. Where forced labor predominated, white indentured servants and black slaves were deprived of the most basic control of their own bodies. In either setting, the presence of lesbians and gay men is literally inconceivable. Though evidence of homosexual activity in the colonial era survives (mainly through the court records that detailed its punishment), nothing indicates that men or women could make their erotic/ emotional attraction for the same sex into a personal identity. The prevailing ideology reflected the facts of social existence. Homosexual behavior was labeled a sin and a crime, a discrete act for which the perpetrator received punishment, in this world and the next. In preindustrial America, heterosexuality remained undefined because it was truly the only way of life.

The decisive shift in the nineteenth century to industrial capitalism provided the conditions for a homosexual and lesbian identity to emerge. As a free-labor system, capitalism pulled men and women out of the home and into the market- place. Throughout the nineteenth and twentieth centuries, capital expanded its sway over more aspects of material life and began producing as commodities goods that were once made in the home. Free labor and the expansion of commodity production created the context in which an autonomous personal life could develop. Affection, personal relationships, and sexuality increasingly entered the realm of "choice," seemingly independent and disconnected from how one organized the production of goods necessary for survival. Under these conditions, men and women could fashion an identity and a way of life out of their sexual and emotional attraction to members of the same sex. As industrial capitalism extended its hegemony, the potential for homosexual desire to coalesce into an identity grew. Not only had it become possible to be a lesbian or a homosexual: as time passed, more and more men and women could embody that potential.

Beginning in the last third of the nineteenth century, evidence points to the appearance of gay men and women. Meeting places, rudimentary institutions, and friendship networks dotted the urban landscape. The medical profession "discovered" the homosexual, a new, exotic human type. The lead taken by the medical profession in reconceptualizing homosexuality as a condition that inheres in a person, rather than as a criminal, sinful act, was less a sign of scientific progress than an ideological response to a changing social reality: some women and men were structuring their lives in a new way. During the first half of the twentieth century, the institutions and networks that constituted the subculture of gay men and lesbians slowly grew, stabilized, and differentiated themselves. This process occurred in an oppressive context. Those who engaged in homosexual activity were severely punished if they were caught; the culture devalued homosexual expression in any form; and lesbians and gay men were denied information about the lives of their own kind and about their sexuality.

Capitalist society differentiates and discriminates according to gender, class, and race. The evolution of gay life reflects those processes. For instance, in building upon its patriarchal origins, capitalism drew more men than women out of the home and into the paid labor force, and at higher wages. The potential for men to live outside the heterosexual family unit has been, consequently, proportionately greater, and the difference is reflected in the contrasting incidence rates for homosexuality among men and women in the Kinsey studies. Also, given that the public space of cities is male space, it is not surprising that gay male life has been significantly more public than lesbian life.

## POSTWAR SAN FRANCISCO

The slow, gradual evolution of a gay identity and of urban gay subcultures was immeasurably hastened by World War II. The social disruption of the war years allowed the almost imperceptible changes of several generations to coalesce into a qualitatively new shape. World War II was something of a nationwide coming-out experience. It properly marks the beginning of the nation's, and San Francisco's, modern gay history.

The war uprooted tens of millions of American men and women, plucking them from families, small towns, and the ethnic neighborhoods of large cities and depositing them in a variety of sex-segregated, non-familial environments. Most obvious among these were the armed services, but the home front also departed from the heterosexual norm of peacetime society with millions of women entering the labor force, often working and lodging in all-female space. Young men and women who, in normal times, might have moved directly from their parents' home into one with their spouse, experienced years of living away from kin, and away from the intimate company of the opposite sex. For a generation of Americans, World War II created a setting in which to experience same-sex love, affection, and sexuality, and to discover and participate in the group life of gay men and women. For some it simply confirmed a way of living and loving they had already chosen. For others, it gave meaning to little-understood desires, introduced them to men and women with similar feelings, and thus allowed them to "come out." For still others, the sexual underside of the war years provided them with experiences they otherwise would not have had and that they left behind when the war ended.

If the war years allowed large numbers of lesbians and gay men to discover their sexuality and each other, repression in the postwar decade heightened consciousness of belonging to a group. One component of Cold War politics was the drive to reconstruct traditional gender roles and patterns of sexual behavior. Women experienced intense pressure to leave the labor force and return home to the role of wife and mother. Homosexuals and lesbians found themselves under virulent attack: purges from the armed forces; Congressional investigation into government employment of "perverts"; disbarment from federal jobs; widespread FBI surveillance; state sexual psychopath laws; stepped-up harassment from urban police forces; and the inflammatory headlines of the metropolitan press warning residents of the danger of sex "deviates" in their midst. The tightening web of oppression in McCarthy's America helped to create the minority it was meant to isolate.

The war and its aftermath also decisively shaped the gay history of San Francisco, initiating a process that has made the city a unique place for lesbians and gay men. As a major port of departure and return for servicemen and women destined for the Pacific theater (and, later, for the postwar occupation of Japan and the fighting in Korea), and as an important center of war industry, the Bay Area's charm and physical beauty were exposed to large numbers of young, mobile Americans. Many stayed after demobilization; others later returned. Between 1940 and 1950 the population of San Francisco, which had declined during the 1930s, grew by over 125,000.

The growth included a disproportionate number of lesbians and gay men, many of whom had reasons for settling in San Francisco specific to their sexual identities. The sporadic, unpredictable purges from the armed forces in the Pacific had the effect of depositing lesbians and homosexuals, sometimes hundreds at a time, in San Francisco with dishonorable discharges. Unable or unwilling to return home in disgrace to family and friends, they stayed to carve out a new gay life. California, moreover, was the one state whose courts upheld the right of homosexuals to congregate in bars and other public establishments. Though the police found ways around the decision and continued to harass gay bars, the ruling gave to bars in San Francisco a tiny measure of security lacking elsewhere. By the late 1950s about thirty gay male and lesbian bars existed in the city, perhaps more than in New York. Such small advantages were significant, and over the years the individual decisions to settle in San Francisco created a qualitative difference in the shape of gay life. Census statistics hint at the degree to which San Francisco, even before the 1970s, was attracting a gay populace. From 1950 to 1960 the number of single-person households doubled and accounted for 38 per cent of the city's residence units.

Under the combined impact of the war, the publication in 1948 of the Kinsey study of male sexual behavior, the persecutions of the McCarthy era, and the wide currency that a growing civil rights movement was giving to the concept of minority group status, some gay men and lesbians took the first steps toward building a political movement of their own. In 1950, a small group of male homosexuals who were members of the Communist Party or fellow travelers formed the Mattachine Society in Los Angeles. Initially a secret underground organization, it developed a radical analysis of homosexuals as an oppressed cultural minority and sought to build a mass, militant movement of homosexuals working for their own emancipation. Though the founders were eventually purged and the philosophy and goals of the group transformed, the Mattachine did, at least, survive. In 1953 a branch was formed in San Francisco. Three years later, the organization's national office moved there and its monthly magazine, *Mattachine Review*, was published out of San Francisco. In 1955 several lesbians founded the Daughters of Bilitis, a lesbian political group, in San Francisco. DOB also published a monthly magazine, *The Ladder*, and tried, with limited success, to set up chapters in other cities.

Throughout the 1950s, the "homophile" movement remained small and fragile. The combined membership of DOB and Mattachine in San Francisco probably never exceeded two hundred (yet no other American city reached even that number during the decade). Hostile as the social climate of the 1950s was to a gay movement, and notwithstanding the personal courage that involvement in a lesbian or gay male organization required, the feeble size of the movement stemmed in no small part from the political choices made by homophile leaders. Mattachine and DOB reflected the accommodationist, conformist spirit of the Eisenhower era. They assiduously cultivated an image of middle-class respectability and denied that they were organizations of homosexuals, instead claiming that they were concerned with the problem of the "variant." They expected social change to come through the good offices of professionals—doctors, lawyers, ministers, and psychologists. They saw their task primarily as one of educating the professionals who influenced public opinion and only secondarily as one of organizing lesbians and gay men. In defining prejudice and misinformation as the problem, both DOB and Mattachine often found themselves blaming the victim. DOB regularly counseled lesbians to grow their hair long and wear dresses, and Mattachine firmly dissociated itself from the stereotypical promiscuous sexuality of male homosexuals, in one instance even applauding the local police for rounding up gay men who frequented the restroom of a railroad terminal. Neither organization had kind words for the milieu of the gay bars, though they would have done well to consider why the bars were packed while their membership rolls remained tiny.

Despite these limitations, one cannot dismiss the work of DOB and Mattachine in making San Francisco what it is today. More copies of *The Ladder* and *Mattachine Review* were distributed in San Francisco than elsewhere. The city had more women and men doing gay "political" work than any other. They made contact with a significant number of professionals, and initiated a dialogue that was a crucial step in changing antigay attitudes. As the national headquarters of both organizations, San Francisco attracted gay men and lesbians.

Though a militant, grass-roots nationwide liberation movement of lesbians and gay men did not emerge until the end of the 1960s, San Francisco alone witnessed the beginnings of militancy and a mass politics several years earlier (at least among gay men). San Francisco was the first city to see the barrier between the "movement" and the gay subculture break down. The impetus for this pre-Stonewall wave of gay politics did not come from leadership exerted by already-existing homophile organizations. Instead, it emerged out of the subculture of bars, and resulted from a set of circumstances unique to San Francisco: the "Beat" scene in North Beach; two well-publicized, politically embarrassing homosexual-related scandals; and a three-year-old, intensive police crackdown against homosexuals.

San Francisco in the 1940s and 1950s was the setting for an underground literary movement of poets and writers who saw themselves as cultural dissenters from the dominant ethos of Cold War America, trying to express through verse their opposition to the bland conformity and consumerism of the postwar era. By the mid-1950s, the bohemian literary scene in North Beach began attracting Beat writers like Allen Ginsberg. Word of what was happening spread and the San Francisco poets slowly reached a wider audience.

After 1957, however, what had begun as a small, underground literary movement was suddenly transmuted by the media into a nationwide generational rebellion against everything that America held sacred. The summer witnessed the trial of Lawrence Ferlinghetti, the owner of City Lights bookstore, on charges of selling obscene literature, Ginsberg's *Howl*. Simultaneously, Jack Kerouac's *On the Road* was published. Over the next two years the media turned a spotlight on the Beat rebellion and on North Beach, the setting of the most visible, concentrated Beat subculture. Whatever the Beats were really about soon was overshadowed by the sensationalistic portrayal of them in the press and in magazines. As writers and as a social movement, they received almost universal condemnation. *Look* accused the Beats of turning "the average America's value scale . . . inside out." The local press descended on North Beach, with the *Examiner* and the *Chronicle* running lurid series that exposed the boozing, drug-crazed, orgiastic, and sexually perverse daily life of San Francisco's Beatniks. In a way that tended to become self-fulfilling, North Beach was labeled the "international headquarters" of the Beat generation.

The visibility of the Beat subculture in North Beach had a major impact upon gay consciousness in San Francisco. Despite the hostile intent behind the media's portrayal of the Beat scene as rife with "sexual perversion," the characterization had important elements of truth. Many of the central figures of the literary renaissance in San Francisco were gay men—Robert Duncan, Jack Spicer, Robin Blaser, and, of course, Ginsberg—and through their work they carved out a male homosexual cultural space. Ginsberg's *Howl*, which became a local best-seller after the obscenity trial, openly acknowledged homosexuality. In describing gay male sexuality as joyous, delightful, and even holy, Ginsberg did in fact turn American values "inside out." The geography of the two subcultures, moreover, overlapped considerably, with the Beats centered in North Beach, and many of the city's gay male and lesbian bars stretching from North Beach over to the Tenderloin and to the Polk Street area.

Most important, to the extent that there was a coherent philosophy behind the Beat protest, it resonated with the experience of gays in the 1950s. The Beats were rebelling against the "straight" ethos of Cold War society—career, home and family, suburban bliss—an ethos that excluded lesbians and gay men. They gloried in their "deviant" lifestyles. When Paul Goodman, whose *Growing Up Absurd* was one of the few serious critical treatments of the Beats, described the "structural characteristics" of Beat society, he could just as easily have been referring to gay and lesbian life: outcastness; facing prejudice; protective exclusiveness; in-group loyalty; fear of the cops; exotic, or at least not-standard-American, art and folkways. The Beats provided a different lens through which homosexuals and lesbians could view their lives—as a form of protest against a stultifying lifestyle and set of values.

While the Beats exerted their subtle influence upon the self-image of San Francisco's gay population, two homosexual-related scandals rocked the city. In the midst of the 1959 mayoral campaign, one of the candidates, Russell Wolden, accused incumbent mayor George Christopher and his chief of police Thomas Cahill of allowing San Francisco to become "the national headquarters of the organized homosexuals in the United States." Wolden's charges, based on the fact that Mattachine and DOB were located in San Francisco, made front-page headlines for several days. Political figures and the local press vigorously denied the charges, but the affair made the entire city aware of the homophile organizations in its midst.

The following spring, the city was treated to another extensive discussion of the gay presence in San Francisco when a "gayola" scandal hit the police department. Several gay bar owners, fed up with making monthly payoffs to the police, reported to the district attorney a long history of extortion. One detective and a state liquor department investigator were caught with marked money and pleaded guilty. Several other indicted members of the SFPD opted for a jury trial that dragged on throughout the summer. All of them were, naturally, acquitted, but the scandal seriously embarrassed the police department and the Christopher administration.

Taken together, the Beat phenomenon and the homosexual scandals were giving San Francisco an unwelcome reputation as the home for the nation's "deviates" and "rebels." By 1959, the police had increased their patrols in North Beach and were systematically harassing Beat gathering places and individuals. The following year, immediately after the conclusion of the gayola trials, the police, with the support and encouragement of the mayor, shifted their attention to the city's gay population and began an extended, brutal crackdown against almost every public manifestation of homosexuality. Felony convictions of gay men, which stood at zero in the first half of 1960, rose to twenty-nine in the next six months and jumped to seventy-six in the first six months of 1961. Misdemeanor charges against gay women and men stemming from sweeps of the bars ran at an estimated forty to sixty per week during 1961. In August 1961 the police conducted the biggest gay bar raid in the city's history, arresting eighty-nine men and fourteen women at the Tay-Bush Inn. By October the state alcoholic beverage control department had revoked the licenses of twelve of the city's thirty gay bars and had initiated proceedings against another fifteen. Every one of the bars that testified against the police department during the gayola inquiry was shut down. The police, backed by the city's press, intensified surveillance of gay male cruising areas such as Buena Vista Park and Union Square. Vice squad officers raided theaters showing male homosexual porn films and confiscated thousands of volumes of gay male and lesbian pulp fiction.

Police harassment of gay bars was not new. In the 1950s, it was endemic to the gay male and lesbian subculture of American cities. What was novel about the San Francisco police crackdown was the social context in which it took place. The scandals of 1959 and 1960 led to an unprecedented degree of public discussion of homosexuality. As one veteran local reporter put it, "San Francisco parents were uncomfortably alone among the fathers and mothers of America in having to field such questions from 11 and 12 year olds as 'Daddy, what is a homosexual?' " Just as important, the stepped-up harassment followed upon the growing awareness of the Beat rebellion and its subtle impact on gay consciousness in San Francisco. Thus, the conditions were present to encourage a political response to the antigay campaign.

The response did not come from the existing homophile organizations. Both DOB and Mattachine were too enmeshed in the accommodationist politics of the 1950s and too caught in the quest for respectability to spark a resistance to attacks on aspects of gay life that both organizations deplored as unseemly. Instead, the first wave of rebellion emerged directly out of the bar subculture and out of the one bar, the Black Cat, where gay men, bohemian nonconformity, and police harassment most clearly converged.

Located on Montgomery Street a few blocks from the center of North Beach, the Black Cat had a long history as a bohemian meeting place. In the 1940s the character of the bar began to change and it became more clearly a gay male bar. But it retained a special flavor. Allen Ginsberg described it as "the greatest gay bar in America . . . totally open, bohemian. . . . All the gay screaming queens would come, the heterosexual gray flannel suit types, longshoremen. All the poets went there." For over fifteen years, beginning in the late 1940s, its owner Sol Stoumen steadfastly engaged in a court fight against the state liquor board to stay open, spending over $38,000 to finance his protracted court battle.

During the 1950s, the Black Cat had a drag entertainer, José Sarria, who staged satirical operas on Sunday afternoons that drew an overflow crowd of two to three hundred. Sarria took a traditional, sometimes oppressive and self-deprecating, form of gay male humor—camp and drag—and transformed it into political theater. Outrageously dressed in female attire, he would perform Carmen, except that

Carmen was a homosexual hiding in the bushes of Union Square trying to avoid capture by the vice squad. For years, Sarria ended his show without satire. As George Mendenhall, a pre-Stonewall activist, recalled it, "José would make these political comments about our rights as homosexuals and at the end . . . of every concert, he would have everybody in the room stand, we would put our arms around each other and sing, 'God Save Us Nelly Queens.' It sounds silly, but if you lived at that time and had the oppression coming down from the police department and from society . . ., to be able to put your arms around other gay men and sing 'God Save Us Nelly Queens.' . . . We were not really saying, 'God Save Us Nelly Queens.' We were saying, 'We have our rights too.' "

In 1961, at the height of the police crackdown, Sarria took his political message out of the bars. He decided to run for city supervisor. Sarria had no chance of winning, but victory wasn't his goal. "I was trying to prove to my gay audience," he recalled, "that I had the right, being as notorious and gay as I was, to run for public office, because people in those days didn't believe you had rights." Sarria's operas made him the best-known gay man in San Francisco; his reputation extended to the entire bar-going population. Though he collected only six thousand votes, his candidacy was the hot topic in the bars that fall, forcing patrons to think about their lives and their sexual orientation in political terms.

Sarria's candidacy set in motion developments that fed a steadily growing stream of lesbian and gay political activity in San Francisco throughout the 1960s. During his campaign, a group of gay men began publishing a biweekly newspaper that they distributed in the bars. Financed by advertising from gay tavern owners, the League for Civil Education *News* used a muckraking style to expose gay oppression. Headlines such as "SFPD ATTACKS HOMOS" and "WE MUST FIGHT NOW!" fueled an ongoing discussion of police abuses among bar patrons. LCE *News* encouraged gays to vote as a bloc and sponsored registration drives. By 1963 candidates for public office were taking ads in the paper. In 1962 several gay bar owners formed the Tavern Guild as a defense organization to resist attacks from the state. In 1964 some members of the Tavern Guild and a few other friends founded the Society for Individual Rights. SIR was virtually alone among pre-Stonewall gay male homophile organizations in legitimating the social needs of homosexuals. In addition to voter registration, candidates' nights during election time, public picketing, and other "political" activity, SIR sponsored dances, bridge clubs, and picnics, provided VD testing, and opened a community center. Its meetings often attracted more than two hundred people, and by 1968 it had a membership of almost a thousand, making it far and away the largest male homophile organization in the country.

By the mid-1960s, lesbians and gay men in San Francisco were breaking out of the isolation that oppression imposed upon them. In 1964, Glide Memorial Methodist Church, whose social-action ministry in the Tenderloin forced it to confront the situation of young male hustlers, opened a dialogue with the city's homophile organizations. Lesbian and gay activists and ministers of several denominations formed the Council on Religion and the Homosexual. The ministers received a vivid display of gay oppression when they sponsored a New Year's Eve Dance for San Francisco's gay community. The SFPD was there to photograph people as they entered California Hall and to arrest several "chaperones" for "obstructing" police officers. The police came under heavy attack from the press, the ACLU took the case, and a municipal judge dismissed all charges and reprimanded the police. Thereafter, a segment of the city's Protestant clergy spoke out for gay rights and initiated discussions of homosexuality within their denominations. Phyllis Lyon of DOB was hired to run CRH's educational program. In 1965, Del Martin of DOB helped organize Citizens Alert, a twenty-four-hour hotline to respond to incidents of police brutality. In 1966, Mattachine and SIR, with the assistance of Glide, won OEO (Office of Economic Opportunity) funding for the Tenderloin area to work with male hustlers. Two openly gay men were hired for the project. That summer, DOB planned ten days of public forums at which city officials addressed themselves to gay concerns. Homophile groups cooperatively sponsored candidates' nights each year and local politicians began to court the gay vote. Some, like state legislator Willie Brown, enthusiastically took up gay concerns.

Unlike the Stonewall Riot of 1969, the impact of Sarria's symbolic candidacy remained confined to San Francisco. The city's situation was too unique, gay men and lesbians in the rest of the country still too isolated and invisible, for it to have anything more than a local effect. At the end of the 1960s, news of a gay riot in New York could spread rapidly through the networks of communication created by the mass movements of the decade. In 1961, with the exception of the Southern civil rights movement, those movements and those channels for disseminating information did not exist. And the absence of a nationwide gay movement placed limits in turn on how far gay politics in San Francisco could develop.

However, there were additional reasons why, on a local level, the discontent within the bars was channeled into reform politics. SIR and the Tavern Guild maintained a close working relationship (the two had an overlapping leadership), and SIR relied on the Guild for much of its funds and for publicity. Bar owners wanted police harassment of their businesses to end; once that goal had been achieved, as it largely had by about 1966, their interest in politics waned and their needs increasingly diverged from patrons who faced job discrimination and police harassment in other urban spaces. The dependence on gay entrepreneurs encouraged SIR's leaders not to rock the boat. Those gay men for whom the Beats' cultural protest and glorification of nonconformity had originally struck a responsive chord found little in SIR to claim their allegiance. Instead, the heirs of the Beats—the burgeoning hippie movement and counterculture in the Bay Area—offered them a more hospitable home. By the late 1960s gay politics in San Francisco had lost its dynamism.

Homophile politics in San Francisco remained within the limits of reformism during the 1960s and actively involved only a small fraction of the city's lesbian and gay male population. At most, 2,000 men and women had organizational affiliation and of these only a few dozen could be considered "hard-core" activists. Yet the movement had achieved a level of visibility unmatched in other cities, so that by the late 1960s mass-circulation magazines were referring to San Francisco as the gay capital of the United States. When the Stonewall Riot catalyzed a gay liberation movement, the basis existed for San Francisco's lesbian and gay male community to assume a leading role.

## THE GROWTH OF THE
## GAY LIBERATION MOVEMENT

The Stonewall Riot in New York in June 1969 was able to inspire a nationwide grass-roots liberation movement of gay men and lesbians because of the mass radical movements that preceded it. Black militants provided a model of an oppressed minority that rejected assimilation and aggressively transformed their "stigma" into a source of pride and strength. The New Left, antiwar movement, and student movement popularized a critique of American society and a confrontational style of political action. The counterculture encouraged the rejection of the values and lifestyle of the middle class, especially in its sexual mores. Above all, the women's liberation movement had provided a political analysis of sex roles and sexism.

Stonewall initiated a qualitatively different phase of gay and lesbian politics. Two aspects deserve emphasis. One is the notion of "coming out," which served both as a goal and a strategy. Coming out became a profoundly political act that an individual could take. It promised an immediate improvement in one's life, a huge step forward in shedding the self-hatred and internalized oppression imposed by a homophobic society. Coming out also became the key strategy for building a mass movement. When gay women and men came out, we crossed a critical dividing line. We relinquished our invisibility, made ourselves vulnerable to attack, and became personally invested in the success of the movement in a way that mere adherence to a political line could never accomplish. Visible lesbians and gay men, moreover, served as magnets that drew others to us.

Coming out quickly captured the imagination of tens of thousands, perhaps hundreds of thousands, of lesbians and gay men. A mass movement was born almost overnight. On the eve of Stonewall, after almost twenty years of homophile politics, fewer than fifty organizations existed. By 1973, there were more than eight hundred lesbian and gay male groups scattered across the country. The largest pre-Stonewall homophile demonstrations attracted only a few dozen people. In June 1970 five thousand women and men marched in New York to commemorate the Stonewall Rebellion. By the mid-1970s, the yearly marches in several cities were larger than any other political demonstrations since the decline of the civil rights and antiwar movements. Lesbians and gay men created publications and independent presses, record companies, coffeehouses, community centers, counseling services, health clinics, and professional associations.

A second critical feature of the post-Stonewall era was the emergence of a lesbian movement. Lesbians were but a small fraction of the tiny homophile movement. The almost simultaneous birth of women's liberation and gay liberation propelled large numbers of lesbians into liberation politics. Lesbians were active both in early gay liberation groups and in feminist organizations. By 1970 the experience of sexism in gay liberation groups and of heterosexism in the women's liberation movement inspired many lesbians to form organizations of their own, such as Radicalesbians in New York, the Furies Collective in Washington, D.C., and Gay Women's Liberation in San Francisco. Lesbian-feminism pushed the analysis of sexism and heterosexism beyond where either the women's or gay liberation movement ventured and so cogently related the two systems of oppression that sectors of the women's movement and gay movement had to incorporate lesbian-feminist analysis into their political practice.

Though gay liberation and women's liberation each played an important role in the emergence of a lesbian-feminist movement, in certain ways the latter exerted a special influence. The feminist movement provided the physical and psychic space for growing numbers of women to come out. As women explored their oppression together, it became easier to acknowledge their love for other women and to embrace "woman-identification." Many lesbians were already living independent, autonomous lives: unencumbered by primary sexual and emotional attachments to men, lesbians had the freedom to explore the farthest reaches of a feminist future. They also had the inclination and need to build and sustain a network of women-identified institutions and spaces—coffeehouses, clinics, shelters, record companies, presses, schools, and communes—that continually nourished the growth of a lesbian-feminist politics. As opponents of feminism were quick to realize, the women's movement was, in fact, a "breeding ground" for lesbians.

Only a minority of lesbians and gay men had organizational involvement in our liberation movements, but that minority decisively affected the lives of a much larger number. Through coming out, through the example of gay pride, through the vastly increased flow of information about lesbianism and gayness that an activist minority stimulated, and especially through the inhibitions on police harassment that our militancy imposed, lesbian and gay liberation transformed the self-image of even "apolitical" gays, and offered the hope of a better life to many who never attended a meeting or participated in a demonstration.

In concrete terms a better life often translated into a decision to move to one of the handful of large cities known to have a well-developed gay subculture. America in the 1970s saw what Gayle Rubin has called a massive "sexual migration" set in motion by the lesbian and gay movements. Here, San Francisco had a running start on every other city. Homophile groups were already getting attention from liberal politicians and had already limited police harassment of bars. Magazines played up San Francisco's reputation as a city that tolerated gays. The 1960s, moreover, established the Bay Area as an enclave of radical and lifestyle politics— from the Berkeley Free Speech Movement through draft resistance, the strike led by Third World students at San Francisco State College, and People's Park. The women's movement in the Bay Area, though not free of gay-straight conflict, was noticeably more hospitable to lesbians than elsewhere. While New York NOW, for instance, was purging lesbians from its ranks, San Francisco NOW was pushing for a lesbian rights resolution at the organization's 1971 national convention.

By the mid-1970s San Francisco had become, in comparison to the rest of the country, a liberated zone for lesbians and gay men. It had the largest number and widest variety of organizations and institutions. An enormous in-migration had created a new social phenomenon, residential areas that were visibly gay in composition: Duboce Triangle, Noe Valley, and the Upper Mission for lesbians; the Haight, Folsom, and above all the Castro for gay men. Geographic concentration offered the opportunity for local political power that invisibility precluded.

The explosive growth of the gay community and its political activism also made internal differences visible. For some gay men liberation meant freedom from harassment; for radical lesbians it meant overthrowing the patriarchy. Bay Area Gay Liberation participated in anti-imperialist coalitions while members of the Alice B. Toklas Democratic Club sought to climb within the Democratic Party hierarchy. The interests of gay entrepreneurs in the Castro clashed with those of their gay employees. Gay male real estate speculators displayed little concern for "brothers" who could not pay the skyrocketing rents. Gay men and women of color found themselves displaced by more privileged members of the community as gentrification spread to more and more neighborhoods. Sexual orientation created a kind of unity, but other aspects of identity brought to the surface conflicting needs and interests.

## GAY POLITICS IN THE LATE SEVENTIES

The second half of the 1970s witnessed a rapid coming of age of gays as a political force in San Francisco. In 1975 George Moscone, a liberal state senator, was elected mayor by a narrow margin of three thousand votes. In contrast to his predecessor and his opponent, Moscone had a pro-gay legislative record, having played a key role in securing passage of California's consenting adult law. Moscone credited gays with providing his margin of victory and included gays among the constituencies to be courted with political appointments. He picked Harvey Milk for the Board of Permit Appeals, lesbian activists Jo Daly and Phyllis Lyon for the Human Rights Commission, and Del Martin for the Commission On The Status Of Women, a tokenism that should not obscure how novel such tokens were. In November 1976 gay residential areas voted heavily for Proposition T, which mandated district elections for city supervisors. The following year Milk, a political outsider with few ties to the gay Democratic "establishment," won election from District 5, which included the Castro, Noe Valley, and the Haight. In June 1976 San Francisco surpassed New York in the size of its Gay Freedom Day march. The turnout of over ninety thousand alerted politicians to the potential significance of the gay vote.

The antigay backlash of the New Right provided the stimulus that, for a time, appeared to transform that potential into a force with real power. The Dade County repeal campaign in 1977 pointed to San Francisco as a concrete example of where gay rights would lead. Anita Bryant called San Francisco "a cesspool of sexual perversion gone rampant." "Don't let Miami become another San Francisco" was the theme of the antigay forces. The night of the Miami vote more than five thousand women and men marched through the city to Union Square where a lesbian shinnied up a flagpole to raise a red "Gay Revolution" banner. The anger of the crowd stunned "gay leaders" who had planned a silent, candlelight vigil on Castro Street. Two weeks later Robert Hillsborough was murdered by four youths who shouted "faggot, faggot" as they stabbed him fifteen times. Moscone ordered the flags at city hall lowered to half-mast and offered a reward for the killers' capture. A few days later, a staggering crowd of two hundred thousand women and men marched in San Francisco to mark the eighth anniversary of the Stonewall Riot. Over the next year, after each of the gay rights repeal votes—in St. Paul,

Wichita, and Eugene—the city's lesbians and gay men took to the streets. Their slogans revealed the depth of their anger: "civil rights or civil war."

California's lesbians and gay men, meanwhile, were faced with an antigay measure of their own, one that went beyond the repeal of civil rights guarantees. The day after the Miami vote, John Briggs, an ultraconservative state senator from Orange County with aspirations for higher office, announced plans to introduce legislation to prohibit gays from teaching in the public schools. When it became obvious that the legislation had no chance of passage, Briggs shifted tactics and mounted a campaign to have his proposal placed on the ballot as a statewide initiative. By early 1978 it was clear that California voters would have to decide in November whether lesbians and gay men, as well as anyone who publicly or privately advocated or encouraged homosexual conduct, should be dismissed from jobs in the public school system.

The Briggs initiative stimulated the most far-reaching and sustained gay organizing campaign in history. A bewildering array of organizations came into existence in every part of the state, with a wide range of political perspectives. Unlike the previous campaigns in other cities—low-key, respectable, "human rights" in emphasis—a major sector of the anti-Briggs effort decided to confront issues of homophobia and sexuality directly, to link the antigay initiative with Proposition 7, a measure to reinstitute the death penalty, and to discuss the Briggs initiative as one part of a New Right strategy to attack racial minorities, women, and workers. The San Francisco lesbian and gay communities were in the forefront of the more radical approach to the anti-Briggs campaign and throughout the summer and fall they sustained an extraordinary level of political activity, not only in San Francisco but throughout Northern California.

The mobilization of San Francisco's lesbians and gay men against Briggs secured other important gains and provided further evidence of growing gay power. The Prop 6 campaign forced most of the city's politicians to take a pro-gay stand, however tenuous and opportunistic. In March 1978, after years of effort, a comprehensive gay rights ordinance was passed by the Board of Supervisors. The board also voted a certificate of honor to Del Martin and Phyllis Lyon for their contribution to civic improvement (i.e., lesbian activism), and for twenty-five years of living together. The city allocated public funds for Gay Freedom Day activities; three hundred thousand people assembled for the rally at Civic Center. San Francisco's police chief, Charles Gain, announced a drive to recruit lesbians and gay men for the police force and urged gays already in the department to come out.

The anti-Briggs campaign also had a profound effect on the political career and image of Harvey Milk, San Francisco's gay supervisor. Milk was not the "leader" of the No on 6 effort, which was too diverse and decentralized to have a primary spokesperson. But as the state's only openly gay elected official and as a representative from the heavily gay District 5, Milk was uniquely visible. He debated Briggs throughout the state and received enormous media exposure; for many, Milk came to symbolize gay liberation.

The anti-Briggs campaign also gave Milk a degree of political leverage that most local politicians only dream of attaining. Beyond his statewide visibility, he was the elected representative of the largest, most mobilized constituency in San Francisco. Milk's record during his one year in office indicates that he matured as a political leader, became more than a gay spokesperson, and was moving beyond liberalism. He worked hard to cement a coalition among gays, racial minorities, and the elderly. He became a strong advocate of rent control and measures to restrict real estate speculation, he opposed the redevelopment plans being pushed by downtown corporate interests; and he introduced a resolution to have the South African consulate in San Francisco closed. During 1978 he helped to push Moscone away from mainstream liberalism and toward a populist-style coalition politics. By the time of the November election, Milk had become one of the most popular politicians in San Francisco and had achieved wide voter recognition throughout the state.

The November balloting brought a decisive victory to California's lesbians and gay men. Although early polls indicated extensive support for the Briggs initiative, by late September there was a noticeable shift in public opinion. Almost sixty per cent of the electorate voted no on Prop 6. In San Francisco the figure was seventy-five per cent, with only a handful of the city's nine hundred precincts supporting the measure. The California victory was enormously significant in checking the mood of gloom and despair that was infecting the lesbian and gay movement throughout the country. Locally, it stimulated celebrations and fueled a sense of growing, almost unstoppable, power. Then, less than three weeks later, Milk and Moscone were assassinated by former city supervisor Dan White.

The day after the murders, the *Chronicle* called them "politically motivated." The truth of that charge was apparent. White, a veteran, former cop and firefighter, was the most conservative member of the Board of Supervisors and notoriously antigay. His 1977 campaign included rhetorical attacks on "social deviates." He was the only supervisor to vote against the gay rights ordinance. He tried to block street closings for the Gay Day rally in 1978. He supported the Briggs initiative. White and Milk stood at opposite ends of the political spectrum represented on the Board of Supervisors. The assassination of Milk and Moscone effected a political coup in San Francisco. There were no progressive Democrats of comparable stature to replace them. Dianne Feinstein, closely allied to downtown business interests and a mentor of Dan White, became mayor.

The assassination made clear that gay power in San Francisco was fragile. The political momentum generated among lesbians and gay men in San Francisco by the antigay backlash, and the gains made in the city during 1977–78, had tended to obscure the extent of homophobia in San Francisco. When Sheriff Hongisto campaigned for gays in Miami, for instance, the deputy sheriffs' association sent a telegram of support to Anita Bryant. Police chief Charles Gain's drive to recruit lesbian and gay cops aroused the ire of the rank and file. A few days after the massive 1977 Gay Freedom Day march, five gay businesses on Castro Street were bombed. While the Board of Supervisors debated the gay rights ordinance, arsonists were setting fires in gay-owned stores in the south-of-Market Folsom area. Feinstein coupled her vote for the gay rights bill with a warning to the gay community to "set some standards." She introduced legislation, for the fifth time, to regulate adult bookstores and theaters, many of which catered to gay men. Throughout 1977 and 1978, street violence against lesbians and gay men was a pervasive problem. There was sporadic police harassment of gay male backroom bars.

After the assassination, the balance of forces in San Francisco shifted abruptly in a way that undermined the strength of the lesbian and gay community. A few days after becoming mayor, Feinstein warned the gay community that we were a minority in a heterosexual society and had to respect the sensibilities and standards of the majority. She coupled her exhortations with shrewd political maneuvering by waiting six weeks to appoint Milk's successor. Feinstein's gay supporters, the people she turned to for advice, were political enemies of Milk. Gay Democrats like Jim Foster, Rick Stokes, and Jo Daly were party loyalists whose vision of gay liberation was constricted by the desire to rise in the party hierarchy (Foster and Daly had been Carter delegates in 1976). Unlike Milk, they had little desire to build a gay politics independent of the party machinery. Feinstein could hardly choose an enemy of Milk for his supervisory post, but she could use her appointive power to try to upset the fragile political coalition that Milk had labored to build. The six-week delay allowed plenty of time for personal ambition and factional rivalry to surface. Milk's supporters, and the lesbian community more generally, rallied around Anne Kronenberg, Milk's campaign manager and closest aide. Instead, Feinstein appointed Harry Britt, another Milk aide and initially a backer of Kronenberg. His unilateral acceptance of the post antagonized many and weakened the trust between lesbian and gay male activists that the Briggs campaign had slowly built. Britt also initially lacked the stature and community base that Milk possessed, although since taking office he has built a strong following in the community, emerged as an important spokesperson on progressive issues, and won re-election twice.

Feinstein's crude political maneuvering was soon overshadowed by the harassment and violence directed at the lesbian and gay community. In December 1978, Feinstein's antiporn bill became law and the district attorney's office began an investigation and crackdown against gay male bookstores and theaters. The city's press ran lurid stories about these dens of iniquity with quotes from vice squad members describing gay male sex as "disgusting" and "degenerate." In January, police officers assaulted and arrested two women as they left Amelia's, a lesbian bar in the Upper Mission. In March, a group of drunk off-duty cops burst into Peg's Place, a lesbian bar in the Richmond, and indiscriminately attacked patrons. The police began harassing gay male leather bars in the Folsom area and hassling young gays on Polk Street whom some "respectable" gay leaders chose to label "street punks" rather than acknowledge as runaway gay youth. The plan of these attacks was clearly to leave the Castro, the heavily gay male area, alone, but attack the "periphery" of the gay subculture: lesbian rather than gay male bars, gay youth rather than adults, sadomasochists rather than ordinary gays, porn stores and theaters rather than "good gay" meeting places.

Police harassment was accompanied by the spread of street violence. Incidents were occurring virtually every night, on the edges of gay areas in the city, but the police were slow to respond and the press generally gave no coverage to them. Occasionally an attack was too flagrant to ignore: a lesbian and gay man who were terrorized by youths in their apartment; a gay man brutally beaten by teenagers on a bus while the driver and other passengers sat quietly. But, mostly, knowledge of the attacks spread by word of mouth, along with a growing, gnawing fear.

Then came the Dan White murder trial: an all-white, all-straight jury; a prosecutor who never mentioned the political antagonisms between White and Milk and therefore could not prove premeditation; a taped confession, taken by White's former softball coach, that made jurors weep in sympathy for the defendant; and prosecution witnesses, like Mayor Feinstein, who praised the moral character of the killer. Throughout the trial the local press was unusually sympathetic toward the assassin of the city's mayor and gay supervisor. Cops were reported to be wearing "Free Dan White" T-shirts; a local reporter told me that when the manslaughter verdict (the lightest possible conviction) was announced, "Oh Danny Boy" was played on the police radio.

The manslaughter verdict of May 21, 1979, sparked a riot, but did not cause the riot. The actions of the five to ten thousand gay men and women at City Hall that night were caused by six months of accumulating anger over police harassment and violence, street attacks, and an increasingly hostile city administration. The riot was the response of a community that had worked hard for its victories and then, after its greatest triumph, watched its dreams shattered by bullets from an assassin who represented everything that lesbians and gay men were fighting against.

Gay men and women at City Hall attacked property; later that night, after the rioting was over, the police smashed heads. Rank-and-file police, packed into squad cars and vans, and encouraged by their officers, arrived on Castro Street and produced a terrifying display of indiscriminate violence. They charged into the Elephant Walk, a popular bar, smashing windows and upsetting tables. Screaming "dirty cocksuckers" and "sick faggots," and "we lost the battle of City Hall; we won't lose this one," they attacked the bar's patrons. Others went marauding through the street, bloodying the faces of passersby. For two hours Castro Street was a virtual war zone with the police on the offensive.

## AFTER THE CITY HALL RIOT

The City Hall riot did not lead to a massive upsurge of national gay political activity in the way that the Stonewall Riot had ten years earlier. Nevertheless, it does serve as a signpost of sorts for the changes that occurred in the 1970s, in San Francisco and elsewhere, and for what the future holds.

First of all, the City Hall riot reveals a maturing and deepening of political consciousness. Stonewall was a spontaneous response by bar patrons to an immediate attack upon themselves by the police; the riot took place on gay turf. The rioters in San Francisco were reacting to a trial; they made the connection between the injustice they experience in their own lives and the workings of the judicial system, and then attacked the symbols of that system, not their own community institutions. That represents a major change from the time, not too long ago, when few gays perceived themselves as members of a group that was systematically oppressed. The largest group of demonstrators, moreover, were "clones," handsome, masculine-looking gay men who literally poured out of the bars and into the streets to go to City Hall. Once again, as with Sarria's campaign and the Stonewall Riot, the bars proved themselves to be repositories of political consciousness and places from which gay anger erupted. Activists who tend to dismiss the bar subculture as at best apolitical and at worst reactionary would do well to take notice.

Secondly, surrounding the City Hall riot was the grim reality of violence against gay men and lesbians, the legalized violence of the police and the extralegal violence of street crime. Simply to call the rising incidence a backlash can lead us to miss an important change. Violence against us is easier to commit now than in the past because lesbians and gay men are more visible than ever before. Visibility is a precondition of gay and lesbian politics, and it may be our most basic achievement in the 1970s, but it also means that every homophobe in America knows what we look like and where to find us.

The violence promises to get worse. Its intensification in San Francisco, where now gangs of youth attack gays on the street, has forced city hearings on the problem. But the violence is nationwide: lesbians beaten outside of bars in Boston and Washington, D.C.; a prominent activist in Houston killed by police; in Greenwich Village, the machine-gunning of gay bars, leaving two men dead and several wounded. These examples could be multiplied; only the most horrific receive mention in the press.

The street violence directed at gay men and lesbians is just one aspect of the larger problem of sexual violence which, in turn, is the most brutal form of a New Right effort to reconstruct traditional patriarchal gender roles and sexual relations. A few days after Reagan's election, Jerry Falwell of Moral Majority announced from the steps of the New Jersey Capitol a renewed campaign against abortion, homosexuality, and pornography. If we fail to link the fight against homophobia with the fight against sexism, we'll be missing the connections that the New Right understands only too well.

Finally, the size of the riot points to the huge growth of San Francisco's lesbian and gay community. Growth has also meant differentiation, diversity, and divisions. Gay communities around the country are coming to mirror the society at large with all of the conflicting interests that stem from differences of gender, race, and class.

One important development since the City Hall riot has been the upsurge in organizing among Third World gay men and lesbians—black, Hispanic, and Asian—who can serve as a bridge between oppressed communities. There has also been a noticeable move toward consciousness-raising around racism among some parts of the white lesbian and gay male community. This is especially significant because of the salience of the gentrification issue in San Francisco and many other cities. Third World as well as white working-class communities are being displaced by white, middle-class urban "pioneers," some of whom are gay. Housing needs, street crime, and city services could be a point of unity between a large segment of the white gay population and Third World city-dwellers rather than a source of conflict. The central city is an attractive, even necessary, place for gays to live, but many white gay men can no more afford the skyrocketing rents than can most Third World people and lesbians. The enemy is the same: corporations, banks, and real estate developers who help provoke and cash in on the changes in urban geography.

Coming out could be the linchpin of our strategy, as it was for most of the 1970s, when oppression seemed total and undifferentiated. Being gay was a lot to have in common. But one result of the gains achieved through coming out is that sexual orientation is not a sufficient basis of unity for our politics, for moving us toward liberation. A politics of visibility is necessary but not sufficient. We now need a strategy that goes beyond coming out.

# 5

# GAY HISTORY

## A NEW FIELD OF STUDY

---

*Although gay history is still a relatively new field of study, enough work has been done in the last fifteen years to make an assessment of it timely and useful. Reviewing the historical literature on male homosexuality made it obvious to me that interesting, exciting, and provocative writing has already appeared.*

*In appraising the current body of work, I was most struck by how the essentialist/constructionist debate (that is, is gay identity a historically universal phenomenon, or is it historically specific, a construction of particular societies and eras?) no longer seems useful as a way of moving our understanding of the past forward. We need to begin asking a new set of questions, and the concluding section of the essay suggests at least some of them. Shortly after finishing this piece, I read Eve Kosofsky Sedgwick's new book,* The Epistemology of the Closet *(Berkeley: University of California Press, 1990), in which she explicitly argues against having to choose between the two. Rather, she says, both perspectives may have something to tell us. The fact that these two opposing views have such a long history may in itself be an issue that needs elaboration.*

"Gay History": in 1970, this phrase was an oxymoron. Homosexuality had no history. It was a medical condition, a psychopathological state embodied in aberrant individuals. It had been and remained hidden, isolated, and marginal, a set of disconnected and fragmentary life stories. In addition, since the triumph of Chris-

tianity, Western attitudes toward homosexual behavior had been unremittingly
hostile, and state policy uniformly repressive. At best, then, the history of homosexuality might consist of forays into the civilization of the ancient Greeks and the
biographies of famous men whose sexual predilections remained contested.

Two decades later, gay history constitutes an emergent field of inquiry, with a
vibrant scholarship. We have monographs, articles, and collections of documents
covering material from the ancient world to the contemporary era. This literature
is opening up new understandings of sexuality as a force in history, of gender and
its social organization, and of state formation, the exercise of political power, and
the construction of authority.

What accounts for this profound shift? One source of change emanates from
the discipline of history. By the 1960s historians were moving beyond the study
of national politics, war, and diplomacy toward a more complex history of society.
The Annales School in France, the Cambridge Population Study Group in Britain,
and the growth of the New Social History in the United States led the discipline
to investigate broad social processes. In addition, social movements such as the
black emancipation struggle in the United States and a revived feminism throughout
the West encouraged the exploration of "history from the bottom up," a history
of the lives of ordinary people.

Of all these impulses, the growth of feminism was of most relevance for the
study of homosexuality. To write the history of women was to enter the "private
world." Topics such as marriage, fertility, and courtship opened the domain of
sexuality to historical scrutiny. More important, feminism transformed gender and
sexuality into political issues, into questions of power and control, resistance and
struggle. In identifying gender and sexuality as social constructs rather than
biological facts, feminism reconfigured our understanding of homosexuality. By
the early 1980s, at least in the United States, the study of gender and sexuality
had become the most dynamic area of historical writing.

Into this moment of intellectual ferment came the gay liberation movement. In
June 1969, when police in New York City raided a gay bar, the Stonewall Inn,
they provoked three nights of rioting by enraged homosexuals. Soon, radicalized
gay men and lesbians formed the Gay Liberation Front. The impulse quickly spread
from New York throughout the United States and much of the industrialized
West. As with feminism, one aspect of gay liberation involved contesting received
wisdom. In history and in other disciplines, the post-Stonewall era witnessed the
production of a new scholarship.

The growth of gay history and the shaping of its concerns cannot be separated
from the evolution of the gay movement. The oppression of homosexuals has
inhibited scholarly work; it makes the pursuit of certain kinds of knowledge

**97**

potentially risky and fraught with penalties for individual careers. Not surprisingly, then, the writing of gay history is occurring both inside and outside the academy. Self-trained scholars without university affiliations have produced some of the pioneering scholarship. At the same time, the progress of the gay movement has opened up space within the university to pursue gay scholarship.

This essay will review the English-language historical literature on male homosexuality published in the last fifteen years. I will discuss the key works that have defined the contours of the field, and the major themes emerging from this literature. I will conclude with some comments on issues needing attention and directions that research could profitably take.

## EARLY WORKS

Several books released between 1976 and 1980 helped establish the legitimacy of gay male history as a field of study. In 1976, Jonathan Katz published *Gay American History*, a massive collection of documents with commentary.[1] Katz, an independent scholar active in gay liberation, had set himself the task of proving that a history of homosexuality could be written. He succeeded: the collection was breathtaking in its scope, a remarkable exercise in historical excavation. Arranging his material by topic—trouble; treatment; passing women; Native Americans/Gay Americans; resistance; love—Katz demonstrated that newspapers, diaries, medical journals, vice commission reports, court records, government documents, and social science literature were rich repositories of raw material for the history of homosexuality.

As a pioneering work *Gay American History* was understandably short on analysis and theoretically unclear. At times, Katz disputed the idea of "homosexuality per se, an ahistorical, unchanging entity." According to Katz, there was "no such thing as homosexuality in general, only particular historical forms of homosexuality." Yet he also referred repeatedly to gays as a "people," suggesting a transhistorical identity.[2] What emerged from the documents was a story of victimization and resistance that alternately enraged and inspired the reader. Nonetheless, Katz's topical headings did help shape a research agenda as issues of oppression, resistance, and the medicalization of homosexuality figured prominently in the scholarship of the 1980s.

The following year, Jeffrey Weeks, a British historian and gay activist, published the first historical monograph on homosexuality, *Coming Out: Homosexual Politics in Britain from the Nineteenth Century to the Present*.[3] The story he told was a fragmentary one, of an emancipation effort that moved by fits and starts, patiently attempting to disseminate ideas about the need for law reform until, in the 1950s, it was finally placed on the British political agenda. Weeks looked at pioneers such as John Addington Symonds and Edward Carpenter, at the first reform organizations, at the 1957 Wolfenden Report, and at the impact of gay liberation in the 1970s. *Coming Out* was both an analysis and a critique of the sexual liberalism that had dominated homosexual politics in Britain. In it, Weeks himself "comes out" as a proponent of radical gay liberation.

Of greater significance than his study of politics was Weeks's theoretical framework. Elaborating ideas suggested a decade earlier by Mary McIntosh, a British sociologist, he drew a sharp distinction between "homosexual behaviour, which is universal, and a homosexual identity, which is historically specific—and a comparatively recent phenomenon in Britain."[4] Weeks saw the late nineteenth century as the critical moment for the articulation of a distinctive homosexual identity and the emergence of a modern gay subculture. He explained this profound shift in the organization and meaning of homosexual desire as a result of the reorganization of the family by a triumphant industrial capitalism. With gender roles "more clearly defined," and sexuality "more closely harnessed ideologically to the reproduction of the population," a deepening hostility to male homosexuality set in and was reflected in more severe legal penalties and the formulation of a medical model. All of this, he said, pointed to "a changing reality," not simply to "new labels for old realities."[5] In a few bold strokes, Weeks had established "social constructionism" as the dominant paradigm in the emerging field of gay history.

Following closely on the heels of *Coming Out* came the English translation of Michel Foucault's *La Volonté de Savoir*.[6] Like Weeks, Foucault identified the nineteenth century as the time when homosexual expression underwent a crucial transformation. In a much-quoted passage, he wrote: "The nineteenth-century homosexual became a personage, a past, a case history, a childhood, in addition to being a type of life, a life form, and a morphology. . . . The sodomite had been a temporary aberration; the homosexual was now a species."[7] Foucault invested this shift with great significance. For him, the study of sexuality was something more and other than a history of a particular sphere of life. Foucault saw sexuality not as "a stubborn drive," but rather "as an especially dense transfer point for relations of power."[8] In his hands the history of sexuality became nothing less than a history of the workings of power in the modern West, an entry point for understanding the operations of both power and the will to knowledge. Because of his immense stature in contemporary intellectual life, Foucault was able to move sexuality from the margins of historical scholarship closer to the center. He made research in the area respectable and imparted a new importance to the study of homosexuality. His provocative formulations also pointed scholars away from a simple study of repression to a far more complex exploration of power, authority, and resistance.

The last of the germinal studies is John Boswell's *Christianity, Social Tolerance, and Homosexuality*.[9] Boswell's book moved across 1,400 years of Western history. In it he rebutted "the common idea that religious belief—Christian or other—has been the *cause* of intolerance in regard to gay people."[10] Boswell located long periods of tolerance in Christian Europe during which a gay subculture openly flourished. Rather than blame the Church, he explained intolerance in part as a function of the decline of urban life and the rise of rural societies and in part as an effect of absolutist political rule. Challenging as it did some deeply cherished cultural beliefs, Boswell's book was widely reviewed in academic journals *and* in the popular press—and just as widely praised. It was published by a major university press and was far more commercially successful than most works of serious scholarship.

Boswell's theoretical framework differed dramatically from either Weeks's or Foucault's. He seemed to argue for a transhistorical gay identity. In his view, gay people "were dispersed throughout the general population everywhere in Europe; they constituted a substantial minority in every age."[11] For Boswell the question was whether the "gay minority" could be open and visible or whether it had to remain hidden; this in turn depended on the level of tolerance or intolerance. Homosexual identity was not socially constructed but a constant, continually reproduced from one era to the next.

As the earliest significant works in the field, these books generated much discussion, stimulated further research, suggested the kinds of sources that could be explored, and set the boundaries that still define the field. Much of what has been written since then has attempted or confirm or deny the arguments made by these authors, to deepen or modify their conclusions. Rather than discuss the scholarship of the 1980s work by work, I will organize my discussion around two recurrent themes in the literature: 1) the emergence of homosexual identities and subcultures; and 2) patterns of persecution and resistance.

## IDENTITIES AND SUBCULTURES

A great deal of writing has appeared exploring the emergence of gay identities and subcultures. Research on the ancient world, on early modern Europe, and on the United States has tended to confirm the social construction perspective that homosexual identity is not a transhistorical phenomenon but a historically specific creation. But there is not as yet a consensus as to precisely why, when, and how this happened.

The scholarship on the ancient world strengthens social constructionism by virtue of what it does not find. Kenneth J. Dover's *Greek Homosexuality* opened up the topic for contemporary investigators.[12] Rigorously empirical in his approach, Dover put to rest an earlier tradition of classical scholarship that bowdlerized texts and engaged in pious euphemism to avoid acknowledging the valued place that homosexual behavior occupied. He found that homosexual relations among the Greeks were typically pederastic, that homosexual desire was considered natural and unexceptional, that it was not forbidden by law, and that relationships between adult males and adolescent youths were praised and honored.

David Halperin, in *One Hundred Years of Homosexuality*, built upon the empirical findings of Dover and the theoretical formulations of Foucault.[13] He disputes the claims of scholars such as Boswell who argue that "gay people" were tolerated and their relationships accepted. As Halperin framed it, "reciprocal erotic desire among males is unknown" in classical Athens, and "no category of homosexuality . . . is indigenous to the ancient world."[14] Homosexuality was accepted *only* in the context of rigidly age-structured relationships, and the men engaging in them were expected to marry. Sex for the Greeks was a deeply polarizing experience. Male homosexual desire was embedded in a hierarchical structure, which resonated with political and social life. In Halperin's words, "the social body precedes the sexual body" in the ancient world, and modern scholars would do well to "decenter" sexuality when they study the Greeks.[15] For Halperin, there clearly were no homosexuals in classical Athens.

Halperin's interpretation of the Greek material allows for a reading of Boswell's book that is different from Boswell's own. Boswell himself had acknowledged that "the categories 'homosexual' and 'heterosexual' simply did not intrude on the consciousness of most Greeks or . . . Romans."[16] Does it then make sense to speak of "gay people" in the ancient world? The evidence in Boswell, Dover, and Halperin all points to a categorization of sexual expression that, if anything, revolved around concepts of "active" and "passive" rather than heterosexual and homosexual. From this angle, gender, age, and citizen status figure prominently in the construction of sexual desire and experience, while sexual object choice fades into insignificance. The Greeks and the Romans, however they integrated male homosexuality into their social world, were not ancestors of the modern homosexual.

Perhaps the most provocative work on the issue of identity is coming from historians of early modern Europe. These scholars are plagued thus far by a limited body of evidence—largely court records of criminal prosecutions, supplemented by novels, plays, and tracts produced by moral reform societies. Nonetheless, they have been able to chart, at least for England and the Dutch republic, a shift between the mid-seventeenth and mid-eighteenth century from discrete sodomitical acts to an inchoate sodomitical identity.[17]

Alan Bray, in *Homosexuality in Renaissance England*, has constructed the most elegant description of the change.[18] In the sixteenth and seventeenth centuries, homosexuality—or, more properly, sodomy—was conceived as part of a "symbolic universe" that included heresy and sorcery. Sodomy was a form of debauchery, a capacity for which everyone shared. It was not, Bray wrote, "a sexuality in its own right, but existed as a potential for confusion and disorder in one undivided sexuality."[19] As such, it called forth horrific denunciations. At the same time, Bray finds extensive evidence of casual homosexual behavior within the patriarchal relations of society—between master and servant, teacher and student, patron and prostitute. Bray explains the coexistence of these two contradictory phenomena— intense abhorrence alongside everyday behavior—by arguing that "the individual could simply avoid making the connection." Because homosexuality was mediated "by social relationships that did not take their form from homosexuality and were not exclusive to it, the barrier between heterosexual and homosexual behaviour . . . was in practice vague and imprecise."[20] In effect, no one imagined that what master and servant did in a bed could bear any similarity to the debauchery and disorder associated with Sodom and Gomorrah.

By the early eighteenth century, this picture had been radically redrawn. In London, and perhaps in other large market towns, "molly houses" had sprung up, drawing a clientele of men who engaged in homosexual activity. This was, according to Bray, part of a "specifically homosexual world, a society within a society," existing in its own right, and characterized by extravagant effeminacy and transvestism as well as rituals of belonging.[21] The older world of undefined, casual homosexual behavior continued to survive, but it would gradually fade in the coming generations.

The contrast between the social organization of homosexuality in the seventeenth and in the eighteenth century has been confirmed by others. Several historians of the Dutch republic have written of networks of sodomites in existence by the 1720s, with meeting places, social rituals, and a language of recognition. Some of the men had transient contacts, while others had affairs and long-lasting relationships. Participants in this rudimentary subculture in one city knew about meeting places in other parts of the country. By contrast, the infrequent prosecutions for sodomy in the seventeenth century reveal no accompanying separate social world.[22] Randolph Trumbach, in a series of articles about eighteenth-century London, has given further weight to the claims of new forms of homosexual expression arising alongside new definitions of masculinity and the redrawing of boundaries for acceptable male behavior. In particular, he has emphasized a shift from relationships structured by differences in age and status to those between peers.[23] Theo van der Meer has summarized the extent—and the limits—of the change by arguing that sodomy had shifted by the 1730s "from a casual act into a mode of behavior. Yet it was not considered to be a state of mind," as medical theorists in the nineteenth century would claim. Rather, it was conceived as "a permanent *state of sin*."[24]

Although the literature from the English and Dutch experience supports similar conclusions about the emergence of a homosexual identity and a rudimentary subculture, research from other parts of Europe is more ambiguous. Guido Ruggiero's study of sexuality in Venice argues that a subculture existed by the fifteenth century, although much of his evidence points to the kind of age-structured, hierarchical relationships that Bray describes in Renaissance England and Halperin discusses for the ancient world.[25] By contrast, William Monter's account of the Inquisition in sixteenth-century Spain uncovers many prosecutions for sodomy, but little indication of either a subculture or a sharply defined homosexual identity.[26] Meanwhile, in an exploration of attitudes toward homosexuality in eighteenth-century France, D. A. Coward argues that a "mood of sexual ambivalence dominated cultured society. . . . In the absence of strong taboos and interdictions," he wrote, "the very notion of sexual identity was blurred."[27] Until further research is done, it will remain difficult to draw firm conclusions from the Italian, Spanish, and French material.

Of all the national histories being investigated, that of the United States most clearly confirms the argument of Weeks and Foucault concerning the emergence of a distinctive gay identity. The peculiarities of North America development meant that only after the American Civil War did the market relations of industrial capitalism finally triumph; only in the late nineteenth century did the United States unmistakably become a nation of cities. These changes coincided with the professionalization of medicine, its seizure of sexuality as a specialized domain of knowledge, and its reconceptualization of homosexuality as a condition.

Jonathan Katz applied a social construction perspective to the United States in a second book, *Gay/Lesbian Almanac*.[28] This time, Katz organized his documentary material chronologically, in two sections prefaced by interpretive essays. The titles of each—"The Age of Sodomitical Sin, 1607–1740," and "The Invention of the Homosexual, 1880–1950"—highlight the core of his interpretation. In the former period, homosexual behavior existed as a discrete act, excoriated as sin and punished by a biblically-inspired law; in the latter, it had coalesced into a person, the homosexual. Although Katz did not definitively specify the cause for this change, his emphasis on medical documents in the years from 1880 to 1920 suggest a disposition to invest these new ideas with the power to shape a new social reality.

The privileging of the role of science in the articulation of a gay identity has come under criticism from a number of writers. George Chauncey, in a sensitive reading of trial records from an investigation into homosexuality in Newport, Rhode Island, after World War I, has convincingly demonstrated the existence of a working-class gay male subculture in which medical conceptualizations are strikingly absent.[29] Allan Bérubé's recent study, *Coming Out Under Fire*, persuasively argues that the medical model did not significantly influence social understanding of homosexuality until World War II, when the military incorporated psychiatric definitions into its regulations and screening policies. At the same time, Bérubé's evidence makes clear that a gay identity and subculture already existed before the war.[30] My own work points to the late nineteenth century as the period in which a modern gay identity coalesced and sees the appearance of the medical model as a *response* to changes in social experience. "These theories," I wrote, "did not represent scientific breakthroughs, elucidations of previously undiscovered areas of knowledge; rather, they were an ideological response to a new way of organizing one's personal life."[31] Like Bérubé, I identified the mid-twentieth century as the period in which the gay male subculture achieved stable, institutionalized form.

The argument for the articulation of a distinctive gay identity in the late nineteenth century is not without its critics. Two recent books by Charles Shively on Walt Whitman dispute the arguments discussed above.[32] Shively presents substantial evidence of Whitman's erotic inclinations toward working-class men and their reciprocation of his desires. Yet most of the men with whom Whitman was involved eventually married, and Whitman himself stubbornly resisted the notion of a distinctive homosexual sensibility. Certainly Whitman's life points to individuals who valued and cherished erotic passion between men. But it also suggests that desire in itself does not constitute an identity.

Theorizing about the emergence of a homosexual identity has not kept pace with the empirical research. Most of what has been argued focuses either on the reorganization of family life and gender roles, the rise of capitalist market relations, or some combination of the two. Trumbach explains the appearance of the "mollies" as an effect of what he calls the "unprecedented development of equality" between men and women in the eighteenth century.[33] Weeks ties modern gay identity to the restructuring of the family in the late nineteenth century, whereas I have attributed it to the spread of "free labor" under capitalism and the possibilities it opened up for individuals to organize their personal lives and relationships around homosexual desires.[34] Bray attributes the change in England to "a broader crisis in the relationship of society and the individual."[35]

## PERSECUTION AND RESISTANCE

Before the current wave of research, the explanation for the persecution of male homosexuality was simple and straightforward: the triumph of Christianity in the late Roman Empire brought with it an implacable antagonism to homosexual behavior rooted in Old Testament scriptures and reformulated by Paul. The rise of a powerful, centralized state apparatus in early modern Europe saw the incorporation of Church teaching into civil codes. In the nineteenth century, medical theories about homosexuality added another layer of hostility.

This interpretation has been challenged at a number of points. Boswell has argued that the Christian era witnessed wildly fluctuating levels of tolerance and intolerance. Bray posits a rhetoric of sodomy in Renaissance England so extreme that most homosexual behavior went literally unnoticed.[36] Studies of the eighteenth and nineteenth centuries find significant national distinctions, with Britain appearing as most repressive, France and Italy more tolerant, and the Dutch somewhere in between.[37] Even in Britain and the United States, a normative homosociality in the "Victorian era" left ample room for physical closeness and expressions of affection between men.[38] Finally, a number of writers have seen in the medicalization of homosexuality a contradictory legacy: it certainly became a vehicle for punishment and persecution; yet it also proved a force for tolerance and affirmation.[39]

Although the traditional view of unremitting hostility can no longer be sustained, no satisfying overarching explanation has been offered in its place to account for the fluctuation in attitudes, particularly with regard to the intensification of persecution in various eras. Boswell has proposed a rural/urban hypothesis: in societies of the former type, intolerance dominates, while the latter is more conducive to tolerance.[40] Yet, the thirteenth century, which Boswell identifies as the moment when intolerance became codified in Christian teaching, was a time of increasing urbanization in Europe. Moreover, the first half of the twentieth century, during which the West was thoroughly urbanized, very likely represents the pinnacle of persecution of male homosexuality.

Jeffrey Weeks has offered the notion of "moral panics": at times of extreme stress, some Western societies are likely to fasten upon sexual deviance as a symbol of disorder and to scapegoat the deviant as the cause of a nation's ills.[41] The concept is a useful one. My own work on the persecution of homosexuals in the United States during the McCarthy era certainly gives credence to it, as does the work of Arthur Gilbert on the intensification of hostility toward sodomy in England during the Napoleonic Wars.[42] Even so, the explanatory power of "moral panics" remains limited, failing as it does to identify why, precisely, male homosexuality should be seized upon at some times of stress and not at other times.

What remains, then, are a host of particularistic interpretations designed to illuminate various moments of persecution. Randolph Trumbach, for example, explains the hardening of the distinction between homosexual and heterosexual behavior in eighteenth-century Britain as a result of a growing egalitarianism in marriage.[43] Theo van der Meer has proposed that the sporadic outbursts of persecution in the Dutch republics of the same era were "a part of state formation processes" through which the state was confirmed in its right to exercise power over the bodies of its citizens.[44] Gilbert attributes the increase in prosecutions and executions for sodomy in Britain in the early nineteenth century to the social and political stresses engendered by the Napoleonic Wars. Associated as sodomy was with the Old Testament story of disaster and retribution, it became "a fairly easy matter to transpose Old Testament catastrophe into the contemporary London scene."[45] I have interpreted the persecutions of the Cold War years in the United States as a result of a crisis in normative gender roles spawned by the disruptions of the Depression and World War II.[46]

Whatever one concludes about the ultimate causes of persecution and oppression, when we turn to the area of resistance it is clear that something profound has occurred in much of the West in the last hundred years. Prior to then, one can find individual acts of resistance and affirmations of homosexual desire, as in the case of William Brown, arrested in London in 1726, who told his persecutors, "I think there is no crime in making what use I please of my own body."[47] One can also identify individual thinkers who were willing to break with the orthodox appraisal of homosexual behavior.[48] But, only since the late nineteenth century have social movements for homosexual emancipation taken shape. Their rapid spread in the last twenty years offers something distinctively new in Western history.

Because homosexual politics is one of the most accessible topics for historians to research and because gay history has such close ties to the contemporary gay movement, it is not surprising that a number of important studies have appeared. Some of this work has taken the form of biographical studies of proponents of homosexual emancipation.[49] We also have valuable accounts of gay politics in Germany, Britain, and the United States as well as a wide-ranging survey of movements throughout the West.[50]

The bare outlines of the story of resistance are clear. In the late nineteenth century in Germany, and spreading in the early twentieth century to such countries as Britain, the Netherlands, and France, a slow but steady stream of organized, self-conscious, collective resistance to oppression began to flow. Particularly in Germany and Britain, the early homosexual emancipation movement was peopled by professionals, often doctors, who sought to persuade elite opinion to eliminate legal penalties against homosexual acts. These early activists attempted to reshape medical theory to justify the goal of penal code reform, as in the case of Magnus Hirschfeld's and Edward Carpenter's "third sex" or "intermediate sex" theories, and Havelock Ellis's congenital explanation for homosexuality. The various national movements rarely tried to mobilize large numbers of homosexuals themselves to take up the cause, but by the 1920s important international networks of sex reformers had been created. The rise of totalitarianism in the 1930s—Nazism in Germany and Stalinism in the Soviet Union—brought these efforts almost to a halt, but after World War II, the stream of homosexual politics surfaced once again, particularly in the United States, Britain, and the Netherlands. The Stonewall Riot in New York City in June 1969 mark a historic rupture. Suddenly a mass, militant movement of homosexuals for their own liberation coursed rapidly through the industrialized West and many other nations as well.

A number of important themes have emerged from the literature on homosexual politics. Some of it points to the significance of the medical model in stimulating homosexual resistance. By transforming homosexuality into an identifying characteristic of individuals, medical theorizing invested it with greater significance and helped further a process by which sexuality came to define the person. It also created the opportunity for what Foucault described as a "reverse discourse": "homosexuality began to speak in its own behalf, to demand that its legitimacy or 'naturality' be acknowledged, often in the same vocabulary, using the same categories by which it was medically disqualified."[51]

At the same time, the possibilities of resistance were clearly circumscribed by the state of development of the gay subculture. In other words, the failure of pre–World War II reform efforts to mobilize large numbers of homosexuals tells us as much about the rudimentary nature of a collective gay experience as it does about the strategic choices that reformers made. The material conditions of gay life until the 1960s were such that most gay men had little opportunity to conceive of themselves as part of a collectivity, as members of an oppressed and mistreated group. The prosperity of the post–World War II decades and the flourishing of a consumer culture, particularly in the United States, opened up space for a gay urban subculture to take firm root and expand. Without this, a mass gay politics was unlikely to develop.[52]

The work on gay politics also makes clear the critical role of consciousness. Not only did the relatively isolated nature of homosexual life militate against the growth of a mass movement; so also did the ideological configuration of homosexuality as sin, crime, and disease. As I have argued about the United States, before activists could succeed in mobilizing a constituency, "first they had to create one."[53] The idea that homosexuals were a minority, that they were the targets of unjust treatment, had to be disseminated and at least somewhat internalized throughout the culture. And, in fact, it seems as if this was the signal achievement of reformers in the United States and Britain in the decades before Stonewall.

Finally, studies of homosexual politics raise questions of the distinction between radicalism and reformism and of the causes and nature of gay oppression. Is the mistreatment of gay men simply the result of old, outmoded laws and cultural beliefs which patient educational efforts will gradually dismantle? Or is it more deeply embedded in social and economic structures whose elimination requires more far-reaching changes? Is freedom for homosexuals a question of accepting a group of people different by virtue of their sexual "orientation," or does it demand the social and cultural reconstruction of human sexuality and gender roles? To answer these questions returns us to the other issues this article has explored, to questions of the origins of gay identity and the causes of gay oppression.

## CONCLUSIONS

The research that has been done in the 1980s allows one to offer tentative speculation about the contours of gay history beyond what the initial works proposed. Social constructionism has proven tremendously useful in opening new sets of questions about the past, particularly in its exploration of the creation of a distinctive homosexual identity. It does appear that the early modern period saw the beginnings of a fundamental reorganization of the meaning and experience of homosexual behavior. Rather than being but one manifestation of a kin-based patriarchal society in which homosexual activity occurred within a hierarchy of age and status, homosexuality gradually was transformed into an expression of individual desire. It became a way of organizing one's "personal life" in peer-based relationships in which sexual attraction and emotional compatibility figured prominently.

This important change seems related to the cluster of developments associated with the rise of capitalism: the spread of market relations with its attendant decline in kin-based economic structures; the rise of an ideological framework of "possessive individualism" with its stress on the male's ownership of his own body and its capacities;[54] the replacement of a divine cosmology with "a new faith in individual reason."[55] Yet, even as this fundamental reorientation in Western life made possible the articulation of a homosexual identity, it also encouraged the tightening of boundaries against sodomitical behavior. As choice rather than family strategy came to dominate the sphere of intimate relationships, prohibitions were constructed against the pursuit of a non-procreative sexuality. As competition in economic life subverted the autonomy on which a market society allegedly rested, sodomitical sex may have come symbolically to represent the last bastion of bodily autonomy for men.

By the late nineteenth century, capitalism had profoundly reorganized economic, social and political life in the West. The gradual accumulation of change meant that homosexual identity and social life were no longer rare, fragmentary, and discontinuous. The conceptual reorganization that medicine provided in the nineteenth century gave further substance to this evolutionary process and magnified the possibilities of resistance. With the substantial growth of urban subcultures in the twentieth century, homosexual emancipation movements could develop. The recent mass affirmation of homosexual desire, constituting as it does a significant break in patterns of sexual meaning, may very well portend, in words used by David Halperin, "deep seismic shifts in the structure of underlying social relations."[56]

The social construction perspective, which thus far has primarily focused on the issue of gay identity, is in danger of devolving into a search for the first homosexual. Rather than continue to ask when a distinctive homosexual identity emerged in the West, we might pose a different set of questions: How is homosexual desire negotiated? Given structures of kinship, economic relations, urban life, and state power, in what forms and contexts does homosexual activity take place? What are the outcomes of various forms of experience, various modes of interaction, and various contours of social life? Deeper investigation into patterns of persecution and resistance also needs to occur. As the expression of homosexual desire takes on new forms, does the meaning of hostility and persecution also change? Can the articulation of a homosexual identity in the early modern period and the rise of mass movements of affirmation in the contemporary era open up new understandings of Western society? Finally, the writing of gay male history has developed largely in the context of the history of sexuality. What if we situated it differently? What if we explored it from the vantage point of gender, of masculinity, in the way that much of lesbian history has been theorized from a base in women's history? Would new insights and conclusions emerge?

In comparison to what we knew a scant fifteen years ago about the history of male homosexuality, the wealth of writing already produced has advanced our knowledge considerably. In comparison to what one would like to know, gay history is still in its infancy. Laboring in this field promises to open new vistas of understanding about the past—and about the present.

## NOTES

1. Jonathan Katz, *Gay American History* (New York: Thomas Crowell, 1976).

2. Ibid., 447, 6, 284.

3. Jeffrey Weeks, *Coming Out: Homosexual Politics in Britain from the Nineteenth Century to the Present* (London: Quartet Books, 1977).

4. Ibid., 3. For McIntosh's path-breaking discussion see Mary McIntosh, "The Homosexual Role," *Social Problems* 16 (1968): 182–92.

5. Weeks, *Coming Out*, 6, 2.

6. Michel Foucault, *The History of Sexuality, vol. 1, An Introduction*, trans. Robert Hurley (New York: Pantheon, 1978).

7. Ibid., 43.

8. Ibid., 103.

9. John Boswell, *Christianity, Social Tolerance, and Homosexuality: Gay People in Western Europe from the Beginning of the Christian Era to the Fourteenth Century* (Chicago: University of Chicago Press, 1980).

10. Ibid., 6.

11. Ibid., 5.

12. Kenneth J. Dover, *Greek Homosexuality* (New York: Vintage Books, 1978).

13. David Halperin, *One Hundred Years of Homosexuality* (New York: Routledge, 1990).

14. Ibid., 21, 24. For another discussion of the Greeks which comes to similar conclusions see Robert Padgug, "Sexual Matters: On Conceptualizing Sexuality in History," *Radical History Review* 20 (Spring/Summer 1979): 3–23. Padgug's article has been reprinted, in somewhat different form, in Martin Duberman et al., *Hidden From History: Reclaiming the Gay and Lesbian Past* (New York: New American Library, 1989), 54–64.

15. Halperin, *One Hundred Years*, 38.

16. Boswell, *Christianity*, 59. Boswell has responded to the criticism of his "essentialism" in "Revolutions, Universals and Sexual Categories," *Salmagundi* no. 58–59 (Fall–Winter 1982–83): 89–113, reprinted in Duberman et al., *Hidden From History*, 17–36.

17. The literature on the early modern period is extensive enough to have generated some review essays of its own. See Randolph Trumbach, "Sodomitical Subcultures, Sodomitical Roles, and the Gender Revolution of the Eighteenth Century: The Recent Historiography," *Eighteenth-Century Life* 9 (1985): 109–121; G. S. Rousseau, "The Pursuit of Homosexuality in the Eighteenth Century: 'Utterly Confused Category' or Rich Repository," *Eighteenth-Century Life* 10 (1985–86): 132–68; and James M. Saslow, "Homosexuality in the Renaissance: Behavior, Identity, and Artistic Expression," in Duberman et al., *Hidden From History*, 90–105.

18. Alan Bray, *Homosexuality in Renaissance England* (London: Gay Men's Press, 1982).

19. Ibid., 21, 25.

20. Ibid., 67, 69.

21. Ibid., 85.

22. On the Dutch experience see Arend H. Huussen, Jr., "Sodomy in the Dutch Republic During the Eighteenth Century," in Duberman et al., *Hidden From History*, 141–149; and the articles by Dirk Jaap Noordam, Jan Oosterhoff, L. J. Boon, Arend H. Huussen, Jr., and Theo van der Meer in the *Journal of Homosexuality* 16, no. 1/2 (1988): 207–307. This special double issue of the *Journal of Homosexuality* was devoted to the subject of male homosexuality in Renaissance and Enlightenment Europe.

23. See Randolph Trumbach, "London's Sodomites: Homosexual Behavior and Western Culture in the Eighteenth Century," *Journal of Social History* 11 (1977): pp. 1–33; "Sodomitical Assaults, Gender Role, and Sexual Development in Eighteenth-Century London," *Journal of Homosexuality* 16, no. 1/2 (1988): 407–29; and "The Birth of the Queen: Sodomy and the Emergence of Gender Equality in Modern Culture, 1660–1750," in Duberman et al., *Hidden From History*, 129–40.

24. Theo van der Meer, "The Persecutions of Sodomites in Eighteenth-Century Amsterdam: Changing Perceptions of Sodomy," *Journal of Homosexuality* 16, no. 1/2 (1988): 296.

25. Guido Ruggiero, *The Boundaries of Eros: Sex Crime and Sexuality in Renaissance Venice* (New York: Oxford University Press, 1985).

26. William Monter, *Frontier of Heresy* (New York: Cambridge University Press, 1990).

27. D. A. Coward, "Attitudes to Homosexuality in Eighteenth-Century France," *Journal of European Studies* 10 (1980): 249–50.

28. Jonathan Ned Katz, *Gay/Lesbian Almanac* (New York: Harper & Row, 1983).

29. George Chauncey, Jr., "Christian Brotherhood or Sexual Perversion? Homosexual Identities and the Construction of Sexual Boundaries in the World War One Era," *Journal of Social History* 19 (1985): 189–211; reprinted in Duberman et al., *Hidden From History*, 294–317.

30. Allan Bérubé, *Coming Out Under Fire: The History of Gay Men and Women in World War II* (New York: Free Press, 1990).

31. John D'Emilio, "Capitalism and Gay Identity," in Ann Snitow et al., *Powers of Desire: The Politics of Sexuality* (New York: Monthly Review Press, 1983), 105. See also John D'Emilio, *Sexual Politics, Sexual Communities: The Making of a Homosexual Minority in the United States, 1940–1970* (Chicago: University of Chicago Press, 1983).

32. Charles Shively, ed., *Calamus Lovers: Walt Whitman's Working Class Camerados* (San Francisco: Gay Sunshine Press, 1987); and *Drum Beats: Walt Whitman's Civil War Boy Lovers* (San Francisco: Gay Sunshine Press, 1989).

33. Trumbach, "The Birth of the Queen," 140.

34. Weeks, *Coming Out*; and D'Emilio, "Capitalism and Gay Identity."

35. Bray, *Homosexuality in Renaissance England*, 113.

36. Ibid., 75.

37. For comparisons of various European countries see Louis Crompton, *Byron and Greek Love: Homophobia in Nineteenth-Century England* (Berkeley: University of California Press, 1985).

38. Eve Kosofsky Sedgwick, *Between Men: English Literature and Male Homosocial Desire* (New York: Columbia University Press, 1985); John W. Crowley, "Howells, Stoddard, and Male Homosocial Attachment in Victorian America," in Harry Brod, ed., *The Making of Masculinities: The New Men's Studies* (Boston: Allen and Unwin, 1987), 301–24; and John D'Emilio and Estelle B. Freedman, *Intimate Matters: A History of Sexuality in America* (New York: Harper & Row, 1988), 109–11, 121–30.

39. Bérubé, *Coming Out Under Fire*; D'Emilio, *Sexual Politics, Sexual Communities*; Foucault, *A History of Sexuality*; and Jeffrey Weeks, "Movements of Affirmation: Sexual Meanings and Homosexual Identities," in Kathy Peiss and Christina Simmons, eds., *Passion and Power: Sexuality in History* (Philadelphia: Temple University Press, 1989), 70–86.

40. Boswell, *Christianity, Social Tolerance, and Homosexuality*, 31–36.

41. Jeffrey Weeks, *Sex, Politics, and Society: The Regulation of Sexuality Since 1800* (London: Longmans, 1981), 14.

42. John D'Emilio, "The Homosexual Menace: The Politics of Sexuality in Cold War America," in Peiss and Simmons, eds., *Passion and Power*, 226–40; and Arthur Gilbert, "Sexual Deviance and Disaster During the Napoleonic Wars," *Albion* 9 (1977): 98–113.

43. Trumbach, "The Birth of the Queen."

44. Van der Meer, "The Persecutions of Sodomites," 298.

45. Gilbert, "Sexual Deviance and Disaster," 113.

46. D'Emilio, "The Homosexual Menace."

47. Bray, *Homosexuality in Renaissance England*, 114.

48. See, for example, the discussion of Jeremy Bentham in Crompton, *Byron and Greek Love*.

49. See Stuart Timmons, *The Trouble with Harry Hay: Founder of the Modern Gay Movement* (Boston: Alyson, 1990); Hubert Kennedy, *Ulrichs: The Life and Works of Karl Heinrich Ulrichs, Pioneer of the Modern Gay Movement* (Boston: Alyson, 1988); and Sheila Rowbotham and Jeffrey Weeks, *Socialism and the New Life: The Personal and Sexual Politics of Edward Carpenter and Havelock Ellis* (London: Pluto, 1977).

50. James D. Steakley, *The Homosexual Emancipation Movement in Germany* (New York: Arno, 1975); Jeffrey Weeks, *Coming Out*; John D'Emilio, *Sexual Politics, Sexual Communities*; and Barry D. Adam, *The Rise of a Lesbian and Gay Movement* (Boston: Twayne, 1987).

51. Foucault, *The History of Sexuality*, 101.

52. For a discussion of this process using San Francisco as a case study see John D'Emilio, "Gay Politics, Gay Community: San Francisco's Experience," *Socialist Review* 55 (January–February 1981): 77–104; reprinted in revised form in Duberman et al., *Hidden From History*, 456–73.

53. D'Emilio, *Sexual Politics, Sexual Communities*, 5.

54. See C. B. Macpherson, *The Political Theory of Possessive Individualism: Hobbes to Locke* (London: Oxford, 1962).

55. Saslow, "Homosexuality in the Renaissance," 104.

56. Halperin, *One Hundred Years of Homosexuality*, 49.

PART TWO

# REMAKING THE UNIVERSITY

# 6

# THE UNIVERSITIES AND
# THE GAY EXPERIENCE

---

*The historic first conference of the Gay Academic Union, held in New York City over Thanksgiving weekend in 1973, proved so exhilarating that the planners decided to preserve a record of the event by publishing the proceedings. Since publishers were not yet rushing to acquire manuscripts on gay topics, we did it ourselves. The essay that follows was the introduction to the volume; it was my first effort as a writer of things gay. Because I composed it so close in time to the events I describe, I think it can be viewed as a document. It captures fairly, I believe, the high spirits and intense passions that gay and lesbian activism generated in the early 1970s. Reading it now brings to life for me the heady atmosphere of those early meetings.*

*I also experience some measure of embarrassment in encountering these pages. The first section represents my thinking about the homophile movement at a point when I had barely begun my research. I was still working from the assumption that pre-Stonewall activism was of only minimal significance. It would take a lot of digging through the historical record before I would begin to understand the impact of the first generation of gay and lesbian politics.*

Gay liberation, the youngest of the movements for social change to emerge in the 1960s, exploded into life on a summer evening in June 1969. The New York City police had raided a gay bar, the Stonewall, a common enough event in the gay world. But on that night, the gays at the scene in Greenwich Village fought back.

With rocks, bottles, and other street weapons they forcefully challenged police intrusion into their way of life.

The Stonewall Riot, and the flurry of activity and organizing which quickly followed, caught both the gay world and straight society by surprise. A political movement appeared seemingly full grown yet without apparent roots. In fact, however, a homophile movement had existed for almost two decades before Stonewall, and the cultural, social, and political ferment of the 1960s had created a setting in which gay liberation might emerge and thrive. The current movement, and, indeed, the place of the Gay Academic Union within it, is understandable only within that context.

Among minorities gay women and men faced a unique set of problems in confronting an oppressive society: their identity as a group remained invisible and unknown, and the social taboos against homosexual behavior extended even to the public discussion of it. As long as such conditions prevailed, the requisites for a viable political movement were lacking.

These circumstances changed markedly during the 1940s and early 1950s, as homosexual behavior became a matter of public concern, no longer restricted in its discussion to the pages of medical and psychiatric journals. During World War II the army and navy instituted for the first time systematic psychiatric screening of inductees to weed out the mentally unfit; homosexual behavior and tendencies were, of course, categorized as undesirable. Although few members of the armed forces received exemptions or dismissals under this provision, gay men, and to an extent gay women, were made explicitly aware that their sexual preferences rendered them somehow unfit to serve their country.

Such open disapproval intensified as Cold War tensions led to the appearance of McCarthyism as a political force in America. The search for a scapegoat for our foreign policy failures pushed the more demagogic elements in national politics to an attack upon "sexual perverts" in government. Slanderous speeches on the floor of the Senate, congressional investigations into government hiring policies, security classifications, and the dismissal and blacklisting of foreign service officials by the score, highlighted the precariousness of being gay. The cloak of invisibility surrounding society's gay minority was slowly lifting, but at the cost of greater sanctions and a tightening circle of oppression.

Other social forces were, meanwhile, circumscribing the lives of lesbian women. After the disrupting effects of almost two decades of depression and war on family life, Americans in the postwar period were stampeding toward the security of marriage. The popular press, including women's magazines, extolled the virtues of childrearing and downgraded the importance, and even the appropriateness, of a career outside the home for women. Even though their participation in the labor force remained high, women worked more often than not to supplement family income rather than as a means to financial and personal freedom. As social disapproval of the independent career woman mounted, the lesbian woman whose preferences inclined her to a lifestyle independent of men found herself in an increasingly difficult position.

In this setting of blatant hostility and diminishing options, gay women and men began for the first time to organize. The early 1950s witnessed the tentative beginnings of three homophile organizations on the West Coast: Mattachine, Daughters of Bilitis, and One, Inc. The impulse behind their formation was not, to be sure, purely defensive, nor was it a sign of desperation. For in the midst of pervasive social condemnation, lesbian women and gay men at last possessed a weapon which had dramatically broken through the doors of silence and opened a pathway to change.

The Kinsey studies of male and female sexual behavior were both novel and startling: their method was unprecedented and their findings unanticipated. A team of highly trained natural and behavioral scientists, using the technique of face-to-face interviewing, had obtained the sexual histories of several thousand Americans from every geographic region and along the whole spectrum of economic and social status. The reports were widely discussed in both scholarly journals and the popular press; "Kinsey" became a household word. Kinsey's findings were significant in many respects, but nowhere more so than in the area of homosexual behavior among males and females. He found that both in incidence and as a percentage of total sexual outlet, sexual activity between members of the same gender was far more extensive than anyone had believed. In rating individuals along a heterosexual-homosexual continuum, Kinsey suggested a fluidity to human sexuality that defenders of traditional morality could only have considered shocking.

Armed with the knowledge that their sexual orientation was neither unusual nor, as Kinsey emphasized, unnatural, the first members of the early homophile organizations embarked upon their work. Societal attitudes militated against too public a course of action, but among themselves gays discussed their common problems and began verbalizing their hopes for social change. By the early 1960s DOB and Mattachine had spread to the East Coast, and in Washington, D.C., public acts of protest were being conducted by Mattachine members against federal employment policies. The growing number of gay groups formed a loose coalition, the North American Conference of Homophile Organizations. At annual conventions, NACHO representatives shared ideas, debated tactics, and formulated goals.

Growth was slow, however, and expectations remained limited; after almost two decades, the homophile movement's impact on both the larger society and the gay subculture was hardly discernible. The Stonewall Riot and the sudden burgeoning of gay liberation thus caught everyone by surprise. What had happened to push an invisible and fragmented minority (stigmatized, harassed, and also extremely vulnerable to attack) to persistently demand recognition and acceptance?

Gay liberation offers revealing insights into the dynamics of social change, into how the struggle of an oppressed group for recognition does not occur in a vacuum but is dependent upon other forces at work in society. The 1960s was one of the most tumultuous decades in America's history: social attitudes and cultural forms were sharply criticized and the political order attacked. Without revealing themselves, gay women and men participated in and were affected by these events. As antiwar activists and student radicals, they defied the police in the streets and on the campuses. As counterculture adherents they eagerly embraced lifestyles sharply at odds with the dominant mode. As Afro–Americans stigmatized by skin color, they transformed the mark of their oppression into a symbol of pride and self-assertion. And as feminists they challenged traditional sex roles and long-established notions of femininity and masculinity. Equality, justice, and the freedom to be different became rallying cries for those who felt alienated from the American mainstream. As the decade drew to a close, gay Americans joined the ranks of protest and expressed their demands for change.

That gay liberation was, to a certain extent, spawned by earlier protest movements is apparent in the rhetoric, style, and tactics of its early years. The Gay Liberation Front, the first of the militant organizations, attempted to reach decisions consensually, in New Left style, after full and open debate. "The personal is political" and "Gay is good" were articles of faith. GLF adopted the tactics of confrontation while also asserting solidarity with the struggles of other oppressed groups. Never national in its structure, autonomous GLF chapters were, nonetheless, formed on college campuses and in cities across the country.

The politics of GLF were too radical, however, for it to attract many segments of the gay community; it was not long before some of its members separated to form an organization of another sort. The Gay Activists Alliance, while also militant in its espousal of confrontation tactics, eschewed involvement with other political issues and movements. It was a one-issue organization, concerned solely with attaining full acceptance for gays in American society. GAA was also local in structure. Gays in a number of cities, though they adopted the name, remained independent.

In just a few short years GLF, GAA, and a host of other gay liberation groups accomplished much. Through their public acts of protest they ended the invisibility of the nation's largest unrecognized minority and threw before a public reluctant to be disabused of its prejudices a new image of gayness. For many in the gay community, the movement offered an opportunity to discard the mask of secrecy and shed the self-hatred generated by a hostile society. Gay women and men in large numbers were for the first time taking pride in being different.

Diversity was the movement's hallmark, a crucial factor in attracting adherents and stimulating political action on a variety of fronts. Yet diverse as the gay liberation and homophile organizations were, they by and large shared one important characteristic: their membership was composed of individuals acting publicly to win acceptance of their private lifestyle. The gay activist of whatever persuasion was working with others on the basis of a common sexual orientation.

Herein lies the significance of the Gay Academic Union. In a real sense GAU represents a new plateau in the gay movement—gay women and men struggling together around their place of work. (I do not mean to suggest here that GAU is either the first or the only organization of this sort; merely that it is but one example of a trend discernible in several occupational areas.) If the gay activist experiences a sense of liberation through the public avowal of gayness, imagine the heightened exhilaration felt when the espousal of one's gay identity takes place within the context of one's life work, when private self and public role come together, and the relevance and connectedness of one to the other is asserted and acted upon.

Exhilaration is, perhaps, too weak a word. It only faintly expresses the shared feelings of those who attended the initial GAU meetings. The organization came into being almost by accident; the first meeting was not really a meeting at all. On a Saturday afternoon late in March 1973, seven men and one woman—college faculty, graduate students, a writer, and a director, all gay—gathered informally in a Manhattan apartment. We were mostly strangers to each other. We were all interested in discussing problems encountered in doing research. We came from a variety of academic disciplines. Some of us had done research in what might broadly be construed as gay studies while others were virtually untutored. Our conversation ranged widely. We talked in highly personal terms of the difficulties of being gay in a university setting, how we coped with being in the closet, if that was the case, or what sort of reaction coming out had engendered. A couple of people had taught or were preparing to teach gay-oriented courses and the rest of us listened with interest to their classroom experiences and the hassles involved in obtaining administration approval for such courses. Perhaps most enlightening, however, was the discovery that our academic training, regardless of discipline or particular research interests, allowed each of us to contribute something of substance, some insight, to the discussion. Ideas bounced about the room; we fed off each other intellectually. Several hours of stimulating talk—the afternoon passed quickly that Saturday—had created a quite tangible sense of kinship among us.

We had encountered a large measure of commonality in our personal experiences and aspirations and an exciting complementarity in our professional skills.

We resolved to meet again in two weeks, to continue from where we had unwillingly left off. At the second gathering our numbers had doubled. Informally we had passed on to our gay academic friends a description of the first meeting that awakened interest and appealed to deeply felt needs. Indeed, throughout the spring and summer, as our biweekly sessions continued, new faces kept appearing. By the fourth meeting there was a pervasive awareness that as gay teachers, scholars, and writers, we could contribute to the gay movement and to our own liberation by organizing in a formal way.

Something very special happened that summer as the Gay Academic Union slowly took shape. My life, and the lives of many of the other active participants, changed fundamentally. We did not merely create another gay activist organization. Slowly, and at times painfully, we raised our consciousness as gays as we grappled with the inevitable political issues involved in forming GAU.

The spirit of those first months was not entirely fortuitous. It owed much to the setting in which we met, to our previous background in the gay movement, and of course to the fact that we were academics. Gathering in the apartments of members, we avoided the rigidified atmosphere of sterile meeting halls with their straight-backed chairs. We spread ourselves in circular fashion around a living room, sprawling on the floor, sitting on window sills, leaning against walls. The physical arrangement militated against anyone being thrust, willingly or not, into a position of leadership. Few of us, moreover, had had any previous experience in gay politics. We were novices without a fixed and unbending political stance, articulating and working out for the first time the politics of being gay. Our shared ignorance saved us from one deadly peril. We ranged in status from first-year graduate students to chaired professors and department chairpersons. Surely it was an ideal setting in which to pull rank, yet that never happened. An abiding respect for the opinions of others suffused our sessions. We listened patiently, for we recognized, I think, that in our untutored state we all had something to learn.

And, of course, we were academics. The verbal nit-picking for which we are famous at last served us well. No statement went unquestioned; no idea escaped merciless scrutiny. GAU's statement of purpose which, when read today, seems a model of clarity and simplicity, took six weeks of prolonged discussion before it was finally approved. We debated the relative merits of the terms "homosexual" and "gay." We agonized over whether explicitly to include bisexuals in it; whether concerned heterosexuals should be made welcome; what precisely would constitute "new approaches" to the study of the gay experience; whether gay studies was, really, a valid concept.

122

In retrospect the earnestness with which some of these questions were considered appears somewhat excessive, but the entire process was invaluable. For the painstaking, often tedious, debate which characterized our meetings led not merely to the careful articulation of personal positions but also to a deeply felt sharing, a sense of cooperative effort, of collective accomplishment. We learned a lot about ourselves and a lot about each other. We came to trust one another as friends of long standing.

Nowhere was this process more fully played out than in the debates over sexism, feminism, and whether GAU could accommodate meaningfully the needs of both lesbian women and gay men. The questions were hardly new ones. One could easily write the history of the homophile or gay liberation movement as a story of male and female separatism. Few, if any, gay organizations have witnessed the equal participation of women and men. Gay men clearly share here more with their heterosexual counterparts than they care to admit. Raised as men in a male-dominated culture, they have incorporated the sexist attitudes which perpetuate the caste-like status of women in America. Rarely do gay men understand that the lesbian's oppression stems as much from her womanhood as from her gayness; rarely do they couple their expectations for lesbian cooperation in the gay movement with a commitment to women-related issues; rarely do gay men appreciate the interconnectedness of the feminist struggle against traditional sex roles and rigid gender identification and the gay male's fight for acceptance. Of all the political issues debated in GAU, feminism aroused the most passion.

From the start GAU was overwhelmingly male in membership; until August, there were never more than three women at any meeting. While proclaiming our intention to create an organization for men and women, we (the men) found ingenuous explanations for the persistent and rather glaring absence of women: women were underrepresented in the academic community; most lesbian academics were probably committing their energy to the women's movement; word-of-mouth recruitment of new members, a temporary phenomenon until we were better organized, perpetuated the numerical preponderance of males. Our rationalizations contained just the degree of plausibility to allow us to retain our illusions. But we could not banish the problem entirely. At virtually every meeting the women in GAU challenged the chauvinism of the men. And some of the men were finally confronting a most unpleasant fact: the few women who did attend a meeting rarely returned beyond a second time.

In mid-August we at last decided to devote an entire meeting to the problem of sexism among gay men and how to assure the equal participation of women in GAU. The session began with testimony from a man and a woman, the one describing the subtle ways in which his own male behavior often proved oppressive of women, the other describing the particular problems she faced as a lesbian woman. We then broke into small groups randomly chosen to discuss the issues and to devise concrete proposals for the general meeting to debate. The outcome was revealing. For while each of the groups expressed the hope that women would come to feel welcome in GAU, only one, in which three of the six participants were women, had specific recommendations. (To this day I do not know whether the statistically improbable concentration of women in one group was fortuitous or whether, as I suspect, it reflected the shrewdness which the underdog must cultivate to survive.) Their resolutions were provocative: (1) that our statement of purpose be amended to include as our first goal "to oppose all forms of discrimination against all women in academia" and (2) that regardless of their numerical inferiority, women in GAU should have fifty percent of the voting power.

Debate on the first proposal took place that night. It was heated and impassioned, and carried us beyond midnight. Many of the men reacted as if their lifeblood were being tapped. GAU was being transformed, they charged, from a gay to a feminist organization. What relevance did many women's issues have to gay oppression? Why should gays support the feminist movement when many women's groups were so hostile to gays? The women, with the support of some men, responded patiently and persuasively. The two movements were intimately connected, they argued. As long as women were relegated to a second-class position in society, the root cause of the gay male's oppression—sexism—would remain. As long as the notion persisted that women were inferior to men, then gay men, whose love for other men was branded "womanly" or "effeminate" by the dominant culture, would remain oppressed.

The women presented their case well. It took several hours, but when the resolution came to a vote, enough of the men had been persuaded of its cogency for it to pass by a substantial majority. Exhaustion ruled out debate on the second recommendation; it was deferred to the following meeting.

The next meeting almost ruptured GAU irreparably. The proposal was defeated. It was too stark an assault upon the almost reflexive allegiance to democratic structures; it was asking too much to expect that forty men would diminish their voting power to equal that of six women. In its stead a compromise was adopted, acceptable to the women, which created a much-needed steering committee, empowered to plan the agenda for meetings and to make interim decisions, with equal male and female representation. Although the final outcome was satisfying, however, the tenor of the debate was appalling. Quite a few of the men in GAU had already accepted, intellectually, the women's position. But sexism goes beyond intellect. For our commitment to feminist goals to have substance, we (the men) had to get in touch with those attitudes and feelings so deeply bred that they are scarcely noticed. The women could not do it for us; it had to come from ourselves.

During the evening's debate some of the men, through the flagrant sexism of their remarks, unwittingly held up a mirror in which others could glimpse themselves. It was impossible not to squirm with embarrassment at statements like "Some of my best friends are women, but I'm not going to let them take over my organization," or "I've marched for feminist causes, but this is a gay organization." It was a humbling experience! Shocked out of their sexist complacency, a large group of men in GAU were now prepared to make an earnest effort in support of the women's view. They also realized that in this sensitive area men had to be willing, at times, to surrender their prerogative of independent judgment and admit that others were wiser than they.

GAU had taken a major step in the right direction. But the problem of membership remained. As long as recruitment came informally by word-of-mouth, the numerical preponderance of men would continue and with it the danger of slipping into old ways. We expected a solution to come from a conference being planned for Thanksgiving weekend. It was advertised widely in newspapers and periodicals and publicized through gay and feminist organizations. What would be the response?

A conference! The decision to hold one had been made simultaneously with the determination to form the Gay Academic Union. We were all veterans of academic conventions, those tedious assemblages where dry scholarship is disseminated among dried-out people. How appropriate for us to take this worn-out form and remake it into a celebration of gayness! The conference would be our coming out.

Planning began early in July; Thanksgiving weekend was the time chosen. We had but four months in which to find a place, sketch out a program, select speakers. The work was done by an open committee of volunteers, forever expanding as our tasks increased, meeting more frequently as November approached. In many ways the conference committee mirrored GAU as a whole. The same spirit permeated our meetings; a similar patience characterized our debates; every decision was painstakingly made.

We easily agreed that a university was the most suitable setting. After being rebutted by a number of major schools in New York, we obtained the facilities of the City University's John Jay College of Criminal Justice (a precious irony). Other questions required more discussion: Should heterosexual scholars be invited to participate? Do we aim for celebrities to enhance our media appeal? Should we rely only upon our own membership for speakers?

We dismissed the idea of inviting anyone who was not gay to participate. Although there were straight scholars in a number of fields whose work lacked the biases of a heterosexual value system, we felt strongly that it was important for us, as gays, to delineate our own critique of the prevailing wisdom and suggest our own alternatives. Rejected, too, was the celebrity path. It ran contrary to the implicit respect in which we held each other for us to grovel in search of media scholars to legitimize our endeavor. No. We would plan our program first and then select those individuals, whether renowned or not, most capable of meeting our needs. In some cases we were to draw upon our own membership; in others, we had to search elsewhere.

GAU's purposes reflected both personal and professional concerns: combatting discrimination, mutual support in coming out, encouraging unbiased scholarship and the teaching of gay studies. A conference program mixing sessions of the whole and small discussion groups evolved which integrated all of these goals. The first day's panel was entitled "Scholarship and the Gay Experience." Our intention was to focus on the ways in which scholarly activity had contributed to the oppression of gays and to suggest alternative avenues of thought. We were not looking for meticulously footnoted research papers; rather we sought speakers who would cover a generous chunk of intellectual territory. The sciences, religion, education, literature, and the social sciences were the scope of the panel. Following it we scheduled informal workshops led by GAU members along disciplinary lines in which gays of similar interests might meet and talk.

We deliberately oriented the first sessions around "scholarly" concerns. Attendance at the conference for many, we reasoned, would be their first public act as gays, and we ought, therefore, to usher them in on familiar ground. We hoped to offer an atmosphere conducive enough to relaxed interaction so that by the following day personal concerns would be discussed freely. "Coming Out in the University," the second day's panel, was to be an experience of a different sort. Here we asked speakers to talk more directly about their gayness; about their decisions to come out, or the need to keep passing; about the reaction of students and colleagues, both positive and negative; about the changes which coming out effected in their lives. We assembled a panel whose members ranged from undergraduate to full professor and whose institutional affiliations ran the gamut from prestigious urban universities to rural colleges. Again, after the panel we scheduled smaller group discussions where each of us could talk about coming out.

The mood of the conference committee oscillated. Overcome with enthusiasm at times, we projected hordes of gay academics pouring out of the closet and into our conference. How would we accommodate the crowds of eager scholars? Or we quaked at the prospect of panelists speaking to an empty auditorium. Neither extreme materialized. We attracted a group of about three hundred, a perfect fit for the facilities we had available. And the conference was, by all standards, a resounding success. The ebullient spirit which made GAU and planned the conference was infectious. Three hundred gay academics, women and men, working together, sharing ideas, feeling good, and proud to be gay.

\* \* \*

Here is the statement of purpose that GAU adopted in the summer of 1973 after extensive debate:

> "As gay men and women and as scholars, we believe we must work for liberation as a means for change in our lives and in the communities in which we find ourselves. We choose to do this collectively for we know that no individual, alone, can liberate herself or himself from society's oppression.
>
> "The work of gay liberation in the scholarly and teaching community centers around five tasks which we now undertake:
>
> 1. to oppose all forms of discrimination against all women within academia;
> 2. to oppose all forms of discrimination against gay people within academia;
> 3. to support individual academics in the process of coming out;
> 4. to promote new approaches to the study of the gay experience;
> 5. to encourage the teaching of gay studies throughout the American educational system.
>
> "We assert the interconnection between personal liberation and social change. We seek simultaneously to foster our self-awareness as individuals and, by applying our professional skills, to become the agency for a critical examination of the gay experience that will challenge those generalizations supporting the current oppression. We are people with a variety of life experiences and institutional affiliations, and we represent a diversity of academic disciplines. Our hope is that by pooling our experiences and sharing our expertise, we will be able to begin the arduous job of challenging the sexist myths that now dominate public discourse and influence private association."

# 7

# THE ISSUE OF SEXUAL PREFERENCE ON COLLEGE CAMPUSES

## RETROSPECT AND PROSPECT

*In 1983, Oberlin College celebrated its 150th anniversary as the first coeducational institution of higher education in the United States. As part of the festivities, it planned a two-day conference with panels and symposia on a range of issues relating to coeducation and to issues of social justice and higher education. The essay which follows is a written version of the talk which I gave at the event. It offers a judicious assessment of where things stood in the early 1980s for gay men and lesbians in higher education.*

*My being asked to participate in the conference was, in itself, one small sign of change in the academy. Oberlin, of course, is not a typical college. It is home to a long, proud tradition of activism and leadership on social issues, exemplified by the monument to the Underground Railroad located in the center of the town. Nonetheless, the willingness of the conference organizers to address issues of homosexuality in the context of equal access to education indicated to me that a space that had not existed ten years earlier was beginning to open.*

*The essay ends with a call to come out. I do not believe that coming out is a magic talisman that will bring liberation. I also understand that for some individuals in certain situations coming out can be foolhardy. Yet I am as convinced now as I was then that more of us can take the plunge successfully and that it is only our fears which hold us back.*

Reprinted with permission from *Educating Men and Women Together: Coeducation in a Changing World*, ed. Carol Lasser (Urbana, Ill.: University of Illinois Press, 1987), 142–151.

To explore the recent history of the sexual preference issue on college campuses is a redundancy; sexual preference as an issue—that is, as something that involves controversy, contention, or debate—has only a recent history. It was as recently as 1967 that the first gay student group was formed on a college campus, and only 1973 when lesbian and gay male faculty, graduate students, and university staff formed the Gay Academic Union.

Discussions of the issue must take account of the critical differences between sexual preference and two other social categories, gender and race, often examined in relation to oppression and inequality. First of all, the body of historical experience is vastly different. We have more than a century of institutional experience to draw upon in looking at issues of gender and racial inequality. That translates into the time to have tried a variety of approaches under changing social conditions, to have refined our strategic perspective, and to be able to assess successes and failures. Gay men and lesbians lack this historical tradition. The first gay rights organization was formed in Los Angeles in 1950, the first lesbian organization in San Francisco in 1955, the first gay student group was chartered at Columbia in 1967, and the first faculty group came into existence in New York City in 1973. One result of the relative poverty of this historical experience is that the agenda for achieving equality remains in many ways unformulated and underdeveloped.

A second critical difference, related to the first yet also distinct, concerns the comparative status of the issue of inequality based on gender, race, and sexual preference. Gender and racial oppression remain pervasive in America; they are systemic and institutionalized. Yet there is also a large body of formal opinion, cultural belief, and law that supports equality in principle and provides some tools for moving toward equality in practice. This is not yet true for lesbians and gay men. Almost half of the states retain criminal penalties for homosexual behavior; only one state, Wisconsin, has added sexual preference to its civil rights laws; and court decisions, while strong in some areas, are weak or nonexistent in others. Courts that routinely deny lesbians custody of their children, for instance, are unlikely to be staunch defenders of the right of gay women and men to teach America's youth.

Finally, equality on the basis of sexual preference is at its heart a question of coming out. Equal access has been a critical issue for racial minorities and for women, but gay men and lesbians are already well represented in the university community. For us, a primary mark of equality is not entry to the university but whether, once there, we can come out on campus and still remain on campus.

These differences, and their impact on the situation of gay men and lesbians in the academy, can best be explored by first reviewing briefly the history and then describing the current status of three areas of concern: students, faculty, and scholarship.

## STUDENTS

Students have taken the lead in creating a visible gay and lesbian presence in the university community. The first organizational expression of gay political consciousness on a college campus came in 1967, when students at Columbia University formed the Student Homophile League. It says something about the state of American society then that all of the students felt compelled to use pseudonyms. The *New York Times* carried a front-page story about the group, but the nature of its coverage suggests that the *Times* did not consider the event a blow for human freedom.[1]

The gay liberation phase of the homosexual freedom movement began during the summer of 1969 in the wake of the Stonewall Riot in New York City. The police raid of a Greenwich Village gay bar, the Stonewall Inn, provoked three nights of rioting and led to the rapid proliferation of militant gay organizations. Gay liberation quickly attached itself to the larger radical impulse called "the Movement"—the combination of black power, antiwar activity, countercultural protest, and feminism that occupied American youth in the 1960s. Because so much of the political protest of those years was student-based, it was natural that gay liberation would grow on campuses. Lesbian and gay male students benefitted from the radicalism of their peers who welcomed additions to their ranks. Gay student groups also could take advantage of the relatively weakened condition of university administrators who were reeling from years of demonstrations, student strikes, and building occupations by black and white student radicals. By 1974, only five years after the birth of gay liberation, almost 175 gay student groups were in existence. Today, in 1985, despite the decline in student activism, the number of such organizations is estimated at 300.[2]

The formation of these groups has not always been easy. In 1970, students at New York University in Greenwich Village had to occupy a university building for a week in order to get university approval for a gay dance. Over the years, gay student organizations have had to fight court battles to overturn the decisions of recalcitrant administrators who had refused them recognition. In New Hampshire, Oklahoma, and Florida, the right of gay students to associate has become a statewide political issue. Moreover, on many campuses, the appearance of a gay student group has provoked harassment and attempts at intimidation from some heterosexual students.

The rationale behind administrators' opposition to gay student groups has been fairly consistent—these groups will encourage activity that violates the criminal law. Almost without exception, however, the courts have sustained the right of gay students to associate. In California, Georgia, New Hampshire, Virginia, Missouri, and South Carolina, to name just a few states that have seen litigation over this issue, judges have reversed the actions of university administrators. These cases have been won because the issue involved a clear violation of First Amendment rights of freedom of speech and assembly—not because courts evinced any particular sympathy for homosexual behavior.[3]

The spread of gay student groups and their victories in court are important indicators of progress. These organizations provide critical peer support for young women and men at a difficult stage in their coming out. They also provide an opportunity to break down stereotypes among the majority student population. In many ways, they serve as a training ground for lesbian and gay youth who will later become proud advocates of gay equality in society at large. Of course, this is precisely why administrators and politicians find these groups objectionable. And it is also why the rights of gay students are so important to defend.

Although the status of gay student groups provides the best evidence of positive change over the last fifteen years, the current situation also illustrates the relative impoverishment of the historical tradition. If we were on the verge of achieving meaningful equality for lesbians and gay men within academia, the question of recogniton would have been settled long ago, and there would be gay student groups not simply on a large minority of the nation's campuses, but in every college and university in America. Instead of having to fight for their right to meet in a student lounge, gay students would be working through another, lengthier agenda: the provision of counseling services whose personnel are respectful of a student's sexual choices and encourage self-acceptance; scientific, rather than moralistic, information on sexually transmitted diseases, including AIDS; dormitory counselors who know how to deal with the homophobia of heterosexual students, and university administrators who are prepared to take strong disciplinary action in cases of harassment; curriculum development in the humanities, the social sciences, and the natural sciences resulting in a college education that informs lesbians and gay men about the complexity, variety, and significance of human sexual expression; the guarantee that the activism of gay undergraduates will not later be used against them by university administrators in ways that compromise or restrict their future options. Progress in all of these areas remains rare and exceptional.

## FACULTY

When we turn our attention to faculty, we face a situation that is more complex and shows less evidence of progress. Gay liberation could spread easily among students in the early 1970s because of the widespread antiestablishment politics that existed among the young. Moreover, each new entering class of first-year students benefits from the social changes that gay liberation has provoked. Younger men and women are coming of age with models of lesbian and gay pride in the media. They have not internalized to the same extent the fear, the terror, and the habits of discretion that previous generations of lesbians and homosexuals absorbed. Among older tenured faculty, the culture of silence that was once unquestionably necessary for survival remains difficult to break. Among nontenured faculty, the poor state of the job market makes the cost of coming out too high. Staying in the closet is the price that one has to pay for an academic career.

It should come as no surprise, then, that gay male and lesbian faculty have been slower to organize than students and have done so with less success. In 1973, a small group of men and women formed the Gay Academic Union in New York City. In its early years GAU grew rapidly. Its first conference drew 300 people. In 1974 it attracted more than 600, and the following year, 1,200. Chapters have appeared in many parts of the country. But since the mid-1970s, as the extent of the academic job crisis has become clear, and the political climate has grown more conservative, the numbers have started to decline. And even the numbers that do exist distort one's perception of reality. GAU has always attracted a large number of men and women who are not academics, but who are looking for an alternative to the bars as a way of meeting their educational peers; a disproportionate number of psychologists and therapists who are self-employed; and large numbers of gay men and lesbians who are doing intellectual work outside the academic community.[4]

The reason for the absence of substantial numbers of openly gay faculty members on most university campuses is simple. Discrimination in hiring and promotion is pervasive, even if it is also most often subtle and covert. I know of only one case where a court has supported the suit of a gay faculty member who was fired, and that was because the case involved First Amendment issues.[5]

The most revealing evidence about discrimination comes from a 1982 report of the Task Force on Homosexuality of the American Sociological Association.[6] The Task Force sent a questionnaire to department heads around the country and received replies from 640 sociology departments. Only 7 percent reported that awarding degrees to gay or lesbian students would pose a problem. But 63 percent said that hiring a known homosexual would pose serious difficulties, and 84 percent held serious reservations about hiring a gay activist. Forty-eight percent reported barriers in promotion, and 65 percent foresaw problems in promoting activists. Together these 640 department heads reported only thirty-nine lesbian or gay colleagues who are open about their sexuality, and only another forty-five whose sexual preference is known to a small circle. This, mind you, comes from a profession that in 1969 passed a resolution opposing discrimination against lesbians and gay men in employment.

The situation of faculty also offers the clearest articulation of the contrast between what gay men and lesbians face in the university. Let me speak here impressionistically and from personal knowledge. I know of quite a number of gay male historians who have come out publicly either through their research and writing, or through their work as activists in the profession. I know of far fewer lesbian historians who have done the same, even though my personal acquaintanceship is probably just as great among lesbians as among gay men. The feminist resurgence of the 1960s and 1970s and the growth of women's studies programs have created what at times seems like a parallel structure in the academy. An organization like the National Women's Studies Association provides lesbians with a larger sea in which to swim. It is a place where it is possible for lesbians to find both personal and intellectual support. Yet it is also clear that the precarious position of women within the university structure and of women's studies programs does not allow that personal support to translate into the safety and strength to come out. Women whose scholarship focuses on women's studies are being denied tenure. Under these circumstances, it is risky for lesbian academics to come out in their disciplines.

Still, even in the area of faculty, one has to acknowledge the progress that has been made. In 1970 there was not one openly gay or lesbian college professor in America. To be exposed as a homosexual once meant the certain end of one's career. In the last ten years, gay caucuses have formed in most of the professional associations and are especially active in the Modern Language Association, the American Historical Association, and the American Sociological Association. Some faculty members have come out and have survived.

## SCHOLARSHIP

The final area I would like to touch upon is scholarship. If one were to check the card catalog of a major university library and count the books on homosexuality and lesbianism that were published before 1970, the pickings would be very slim. Most of what one would find would be medical literature that reinforced some of the most pernicious stereotypes about gay men and women. Except for some books written in a confessional mode, there were only a few that represented serious intellectual effort: for example, Donald Webster Cory's *The Homosexual in America* and *The Lesbian in America*; Dr. Martin Hoffman's *The Gay World*, which is a study of the male homosexual subculture in San Francisco; and Jeannette Foster's *Sex Variant Women* in *Literature*, an impressive work of scholarship that Foster had to publish herself.[7]

One of the great achievements of the gay liberation movement has been the explosion of books and articles written by and about lesbians and gay men. There are bookstores in the nation's larger cities that carry only material about the lesbian and gay experience, and mail-order houses that distribute such literature to customers in every corner of the country. There are small independent publishing firms, such as Alyson Publishers and Naiad Press, whose focus is gay or lesbian literature.

Scholars are slowly contributing to this stream of words. In the last few years a number of impressively researched and intellectually significant books have appeared: Dover's history of Greek homosexuality and Boswell's history of the Middle Ages; Faderman's literary study of romantic attachments between women since the Renaissance, and Robert K. Martin's monograph on male homosexual poetry in America; a lesbian studies reader that Margaret Cruikshank has edited; my own book on the homosexual rights movement in the United States, and a sociological study by Susan Krieger of a contemporary lesbian community. The journal *Signs* published a special issue on lesbianism.[8] These books and others like them, as well as a much larger number of articles, are gradually filling in the contours of a neglected aspect of human experience. They also are making it increasingly possible to integrate material about homosexuality into standard courses in a number of disciplines, as well as to construct separate gay and lesbian studies courses.

Although progress in the area of scholarly production is clear, it is worth noting that we are still at the level of tokenism, and not simply because it takes a long time to research and write a book. The same pressures that keep gay and lesbian faculty members in the closet also discourage them, as well as graduate students, from doing work on homosexuality. The study of sociologists that I referred to earlier also had something to say about this: half of the gay sociologists who were interviewed reported obstacles to doing research on the topic and advice that it would hurt their careers. (Sociology, remember, is a discipline with a subfield—deviance theory—that makes the study of homosexuality natural.) In American history, my own book is still the only monograph on homosexuality. There are many excellent topics for dissertations that would make major contributions to our understanding of the American experience, but these dissertations are not being written.

Gay men and lesbians are skilled at turning adversity to their own advantage, and the area of scholarship is no exception. One result of the obstacles to research within the academic community is that many are doing the work anyway and making it a resource for the gay community. Lesbian and gay history projects in Boston, San Francisco, Chicago, Buffalo, and elsewhere are doing an excellent job of researching gay history, and sharing that information within the community through public forums, slide shows, pamphlets, and small-press books. Magazines such as *Conditions*, *Sinister Wisdom*, and *Gay Sunshine* have published articles that put mainstream scholarly journals to shame. Even gay newspapers carry the work of community-based, grass-roots scholars. But creation of successful alternatives should not make us ignore the barriers within the academic community. The university has resources—the libraries, the research money, the legitimacy that wins fellowship support—that lesbian and gay male intellectuals need.

## CONCLUSION

Students, faculty, and scholarship. Each of these areas provides evidence of real, positive change over the last fifteen years. Those who remember gay life before 1970 can only think of the changes as nothing short of miraculous. Yet if we look ahead toward the future, toward a vision of equality, it is obvious that the longer part of the road is still to be traveled.

Until now, gay and lesbian students have contributed the most to the quest for equality. It is admirable, and not surprising, that they have done so, but they should not have to carry this responsibility forever.

The expansion of scholarly production is a critical piece of any strategy for equality. Information, education, and ideas are powerful levers for social change, and as we have more information, we will be progressively empowered to act in the world.

But scholarship requires scholars, and that brings me back to faculty, which I consider the weakest link in the chain. Faculty members simply have to come out. Coming out, of course, must be an individual's decision. It needs to be done carefully and thoughtfully, and with a strong support network to sustain the individual. Coming out also involves risk, more in some situations than in others. But much of the danger we perceive does not in fact represent an objective external reality, but our own internalized fears. We need to step through that fear.

In posing this challenge, I especially want to direct it at other white men like myself. We are the ones in this society with the most options. We do not face the added barriers of racial and gender oppression. If we have tenure, of course, we have a degree of security that few Americans enjoy. But even if we do not, we have room to maneuver. Our education has made us socially mobile and opened opportunities. For us, coming out is simply not an overwhelming threat to our survival.

The ideals of our profession demand it from us. The teachers we all remember best, and the ones whom we cherish the most, are those who modeled integrity in the classroom and in their lives, those for whom the search for justice and truth did not represent empty words. We will be failing our students and ourselves if we do not take up this challenge. But if we do seize the challenge, when the time comes to look back and assess our lives, we will be proud of our choice.

## NOTES

1. *New York Times*, 3 May 1967.

2. On gay student groups see J. Lee Lehman, ed., *Gays on Campus* (Washington, D.C.: National Student Association, 1975); *Chronicle of Higher Education, 20 October 1982, 9–10, Newsweek* 5 April 1982, 75–77. The current estimate of 300 gay student groups comes from *The Advocate*, 419, 30 April 1985, 12–13. For the context in which these first groups developed, see Dennis Altman, *Homosexual Oppression and Liberation* (New York: Avon Books, 1971); John D'Emilio, *Sexual Politics, Sexual Communities: The Making of a Homosexual Minority in the United States, 1940–1970* (Chicago: University of Chicago Press, 1983); and Donn Teal, *The Gay Militants* (New York: Stein and Day, 1971).

3. The most comprehensive assessment of court cases related to homosexual rights, including those concerning universities, is Rhonda J. Rivera, "Our Straight-Laced Judges: The Legal Position of Homosexual Persons in the United States," *Hastings Law Journal* 30 (March 1979): 799–956. For more recent assessments of court rulings concerning gay student groups see W. R. Stanley, "The Rights of Gay Student Organizations," *Journal of College and University Law* 10 (Winter 1983/84): 397–418, and A. Gibbs, "Colleges and Gay Student Organizations: An Update," *NASPA Journal* 22 (Summer 1984): 38–41. On 1 April 1985, the Supreme Court sustained a lower court ruling upholding the right of a gay student group to receive recognition at Texas A&M University. See *New York Times*, 2 April 1985, 15.

4. On the founding of the Gay Academic Union, see *The Universities and the Gay Experience: Proceedings of a Conference Sponsored by the Women and Men of the Gay Academic Union*, November 23–24, 1973 (New York, 1974).

5. *Aumiller v. University of Delaware*, 434 F. Supp. 1273.

6. For a summary of the study see *Footnotes* (a publication of the American Sociological Association), December 1982, 1.

7. Donald Webster Cory, *The Homosexual in America* (New York: Greenberg, 1951), and *The Lesbian in America* (New York: Citadel Press, 1964); Martin Hoffman, *The Gay World* (New York: Basic Books, 1968); Jeannette Foster, *Sex Variant Women in Literature* (New York: Vantage Press, 1956).

8. K. J. Dover, *Greek Homosexuality* (New York: Vintage Books, 1980); John Boswell, *Christianity, Social Tolerance and Homosexuality* (Chicago: University of Chicago Press, 1980); Lillian Faderman, *Surpassing the Love of Men* (New York: William Morrow, 1981); Robert K. Martin, *The Homosexual Tradition in American Poetry* (Austin: University of Texas Press, 1979); Margaret Cruikshank, *Lesbian Studies* (Old Westbury, N.Y.: Feminist Press, 1982); John D'Emilio, *Sexual Politics, Sexual Communities*; and Susan Krieger, *The Mirror Dance* (Philadelphia: Temple University Press, 1983). The special issue of *Signs* is Vol. 9, Summer 1984.

# 8

# NOT A SIMPLE MATTER

## GAY HISTORY AND GAY HISTORIANS

———————

*In 1989 the* Journal of American History, *published by the Organization of American Historians, featured a roundtable on the topic "What has Changed and Not Changed in American Historical Practice?" In the words of David Thelen, the journals' editor, "We conceived this round table as a conversation about ways the organized profession of American history has responded to the challenges that people with different identities, commitments, and agendas have brought to research and teaching in American history." The jumping-off point for the conversation was an article by Jonathan Wiener (to which I refer in my essay) on the profession's hostile reaction to the work of radical historians in the 1960s and the process by which those radicals and their work came to win acceptance among the larger body of historians. The editors invited a number of other historians to respond either to Wiener's article or to the larger issue of how the profession controls access to or sets the agenda for the writing of history.*

*It was something of a milestone, I think, for a gay historian to be asked to participate in so public a forum (the* Journal of American History *is the most important professional journal for work in U.S. history). The opportunity weighed heavily on me. As the opening paragraphs suggest, writing this essay tapped into a mood of discouragement and pessimism that does not usually characterize my work. In most situations one can choose to see the proverbial glass as half empty or half full. I am normally drawn to the latter view but, in this case, all I could see was the empty half. For whatever reason, this became the moment to express the tensions and frustrations and exhaustion that had accumulated from working as an openly gay man in a mainstream profession.*

Reprinted with permission from the *Journal of American History*, 76 (1989): 435–442.

Almost since the moment I agreed to write this, a line from a television commercial has been ringing in my head: "Never let them see you sweat!" Since I have avoided putting pen to paper for months, I have had plenty of opportunity to reflect upon why this is so. The issue is not one of anxiety about self-revelation, about "coming out." I have done that again and again. Remove from my vita the items that mark me as gay or that might lead someone to draw that conclusion, and not much would be left. Nor is it a matter of fearing to express personal grievance in the pages of an important professional journal, for my own grievances are few. I was hired by a department whose eyes were open to my work and my identity; I now have tenure; and my university has been supportive of my scholarly endeavors. Mine is a gay success story.

Something else is at stake. As I have played with various ideas about how to structure this essay and about what to include in it (indeed, whenever I have even remembered that I am committed to writing it), I have found myself engulfed by emotions normally alien to me. "Sane," "cheerful," "optimistic," "energetic," and "hopeful" are the words friends and colleagues usually use to describe me. But to contemplate the subject at hand, to think—really to think—about gay history and gay historians in relation to the profession is to tap an interior well of pessimism, discouragement, despair, and exhaustion that shocks as well as frightens me.

The task of adequately addressing in a few pages the issues posed by this roundtable also seems daunting. Twenty years after the birth of gay liberation, sixteen years after a group of faculty and graduate students formed the Gay Academic Union (GAU), and a decade after gay men and lesbians began meeting in what became the Committee on Lesbian and Gay History of the American Historical Association, our issues, our agenda, and our achievements are only beginning to reach beyond the circles we have created.[1] When I search for anchors to which I can attach my discussion so that it will seem familiar to readers, I am struck more by the differences than the commonalities. Radicalism is a perspective that can be brought to the study of any historical topic; race has been a central thread in the experience of the United States; women have held up half of the American sky. By contrast, gayness has been relatively marginal and marginalized for much of the American experience. (Ironically, the dominant paradigm in gay history—social constructionism—tends to reinforce this by arguing that gayness and lesbianism did not emerge as social identities until near the end of the nineteenth century.) Then, too, radicals, people of color, and women have had to battle for entrance into the profession, and the latter two groups are still grossly underrepresented. But, for gay men at least, the problem is neither access nor entry but rather coming out and staying in. And since work on gay or lesbian topics is commonly treated as a de facto statement of identity, the task of producing gay history involves more than simple matters of research and writing.

I started graduate school in 1971, not to enter a profession, but to change the world. I had been a bit player—maybe only an extra—in campus and antiwar protests in the 1960s. Two years of struggle over the draft and with my draft board ended with a lucky draw in the lottery. Out of school, I happened upon William Appleman William's *The Great Evasion*. No other book had ever so stimulated my intellectual juices. It made me want to understand my country's history, and I spent the next several months devouring the books that Jon Wiener has written about.[2] At Columbia University the graduate students seemed to be either radicals or interested in the new social history, or both. I wrote a master's essay on corporate liberal planning during World War II. My being gay was a social fact rather than a political identity, and "gay history" was a term not yet invented. One student in the department professed an interest in "sexual history" but few of us took it seriously.

The early gay liberation movement in New York was swirling around me at the time, and in retrospect, it seems to have been inevitable that I was drawn into it. In the spring of 1973, I had the good fortune to attend an informal meeting of New York City faculty and graduate students to talk about being gay in the university. The feeling in the room was electric, as personal and professional identity seemed to merge for each of us for the first time. We sustained that intensity over the following months as we shaped the GAU, planned its first conference, and watched in amazement as several hundred gay men and lesbians responded to our call.[3]

As Betty Friedan remarked in another context, "It changed my life."[4] On a personal level, it led me to begin coming out to my peers in graduate school, one by one. (I realize now that the ease of doing so came, in no small part, from the fact that it was a radical cohort of students.) Professionally, it meant that the time having arrived to choose a dissertation topic, I decided to write on some aspect of homosexuality in American history.

In some ways it was a very easy decision to make. The level of emotional and intellectual sustenance that the GAU provided was extraordinary; I have never, before or since, enjoyed attending so many meetings. Martin Duberman had come out in print in *Black Mountain* and was beginning his own research into the history of sexuality. Jonathan Katz's research had already resulted in a documentary play, *Coming Out!*, and he was continuing the work that would eventually lead to the publication of the path-breaking *Gay American History*. Faculty and graduate students from a variety of disciplines were daily giving meaning to the concept of a community of scholars as we eagerly shared every new bit of information that we found.[5]

In other ways, however, it was not so easy, and I began to sweat. For one, I was choosing an area of research for which there was no context, no literature, no definition of issues, and no sources that had ever been tapped. Were I writing about the coming of the Civil War or the New Deal, I would have absorbed the contours of my subject even before I first entered an archives. Was this an act of faith or of foolishness? Then, too, the decision forced me to begin a process of strategizing about my choices, or my career, that has now become second nature. For my dissertation adviser I chose William Leuchtenburg. I had worked with him before, respected him, and knew that he respected me. But I was also reasoning that with his stature in the department, I had to convince only him of the merit of my topic. If he approved it, no one else's objections would matter much. (Another member of the department, grasping a file cabinet for support when I told him of my topic, asked if I realized what this would mean for my career.) As it turned out, it was one of the wisest decisions I've ever made, because working with Leuchtenburg made me a real historian. Much of my ability as a writer of history I owe to the training I received under his direction.

I want to say something about this issue of strategizing. On one level, it's a very good thing to have to think with care about one's choices, to be circumspect about decisions, to ruminate about the implications of one's prospective actions. If there are any "advantages" to finding oneself in an oppressed group, maybe that is it. Because I don't take for granted entry, or acceptance, because I don't assume ownership or a voice in setting the agenda of something as highfalutin as a "profession," I feel compelled to weigh what I do with care, all the time. But it is also at times exhausting, and sometimes I wish I could discard the habit and simply act on impulse. The habit, however, runs deep.

Having said that, however, I should also acknowledge a subterranean emotional stream, not seen as such by me at the time, that represented nothing so thoughtful as a "strategy." There was something almost defiant in my decision to pursue gay history. I was testing the waters. If I couldn't do that kind of research, then I didn't want "in." It seemed easy to adopt that stance. The gay movement was creating an alternative source of identity and community; I was part of an enterprise that seemed much more significant than academic history; and, in many ways, it was far more congenial to see myself as a cultural worker in a liberation movement than as an aspiring young professional. What that set in motion for me was a rigid emotional stance in which I defined myself in part by what I had decided I was most definitely not—a professional historian. I would no more have thought of going to a meeting of the American Historical Association or the Organization of American Historians than I would have considered working on Wall Street.

The one exception to that detachment was women's history, a field exploding with new and exciting scholarship in the mid-1970s. The understandings of the historical construction of gender that feminist historians were developing seemed central to my own enterprise; they were also, not surprisingly, producing most of the interesting work in the field of sexuality. Lesbianism was not yet emerging as a historical topic in its own right within the field of women's history, and lesbian historians, in fact, had to campaign mightily to make sure that the issue received its due at the Berkshire Conferences. Even so, there were moments of great excitement in the 1970s. I remember, for instance, when Carroll Smith-Rosenberg spoke in an informal workshop at the Berkshire Conference held at Radcliffe College, discussing the work that would later be published as "The Female World of Love and Ritual."[6] The packed audience knew it was listening to something that would have a decisive impact on the shape of an emerging lesbian history.

Still, such moments were unusual, even at the Berks. Throughout the 1970s as I did my research and began to write, I looked outside the academy and the profession for intellectual sustenance and challenge. Katz's *Gay American History* was stimulating a grass-roots effort within the lesbian and gay movement to uncover our history. By the end of the decade, local history projects were springing up around the country—in San Francisco, New York, Buffalo, Boston, Chicago, and elsewhere. Alongside them were a number of community-based archives collecting the raw materials to construct a gay and lesbian history. The most successful, the Lesbian Herstory Archives in New York, traced its roots to the early GAU.

These projects deserve a chronicler of their own. They generated enormous interest and commitment, and an esprit among participants. Composed mostly of self-trained historians, with only a smattering of academically trained members, they provoked research every bit as solid as what the profession produces and led to projects that were certainly more accessible to a lay audience. Much of their work appeared over the years in publications of the gay community, beyond the ken of the profession: *Body Politic, Gay Community News*, the *Advocate, Sinister Wisdom*, and elsewhere. One characteristic product was the slide show. I remember when Allan Bérubé first showed "Lesbian Masquerade," a slide lecture about women who passed as men in early San Francisco.[7] The standing-room-only audience of almost four hundred laughed, cheered, and cried its way through a presentation that lasted two hours. Such events were replicated around the country. There was magic in these rooms as audience and author celebrated the product.

To understand this reaction requires the recognition that, at least in the 1970s and 1980s, the doing of gay and lesbian history has been more than a form of intellectual labor (as it probably will be for some time hence). It was transforming, for both the doer and the receiver, and in the social context of those decades, inherently political. The politics of it was independent of the particular conclusions one drew. Rather, for my generation and for cohorts both older and younger, the absence of self-affirming words and images and the cultural denial of our very existence made any kind of history a profound, subversive revelation. The obvious strokes that we received from the community also made it possible to continue the work under difficult material conditions that the academic historian normally doesn't face—no institutional affiliation, difficulties getting access to libraries and archives, no teacher's salary to support summer research and writing, and virtual exclusion from grants and fellowships. There's a price that one pays for being outside the profession.

By 1980 some of those costs were beginning to wear on me. I generally had no money. The jobs that I did have, usually part-time or short-term and in what loosely could be called community organizing, had their satisfactions, but they also pulled me away from history, which was my passion. I also had to acknowledge the ways that my own oppositional stance toward the profession had become counterproductive—indeed, had become an expression of internalized gay oppression, a microcosm of what Barry Adam, a gay sociologist, has described as "the survival of domination."[8] My opposition was producing marginalization, precisely the role into which an oppressive society thrusts gay people. Rather than push for entry into the profession, I was colluding in my own exclusion. And it was hurting me. I wasn't completing my dissertation, or my "book," as I thought of it, because to do so would force me to face head-on the possibility that I might be excluded from the profession because of my work or my identity.

What I've just described came as a bolt from the sky and provoked just as sudden a decision. After dawdling on the dissertation for six years, I finished a first draft in four months, rewrote it twice over the next six months, received a book contract from the University of Chicago Press, and defended the dissertation. I also applied for jobs, and eventually I was hired at the institution where I still teach and now have tenure.

With jobs still scarce and many younger historians working as adjuncts or in revolving-door positions, it may seem insensitive for me to complain about my job search. Yet it has always struck me as odd that with a book accepted by a major university press, a degree from an Ivy League school, recommendations from historians of stature, and applications out to about fifty schools over a period of 2½ years, I was considered a serious candidate at only one institution.

This emphasis on autobiography reflects the progress of gay history: there was simply too little work completed in the 1970s to be able to discuss it as a field.

Now by the end of the 1980s, the situation has begun to change. Exciting and valuable scholarship is in print, and more is on the way.

The work that keeps wanting to assert itself is "breakthrough"—the 1980s has been our breakthrough decade. Even as I write this, however, I am wondering whether it confirms the marginal status of gay scholarship. The current corpus in American history consists only of several monographs, collections of essays and documents, and perhaps as many articles. One could read it all during a single summer and still take a leisurely vacation. Some of those works have been produced by nonacademic historians, and others have come from outside the discipline of history; the work-in-progress that I know of continues the pattern of scholarship produced from outside the academy and outside the discipline.[9]

Limited as the body of scholarship is, it already is telling us something of importance about the twentieth-century United States. Understanding what has been called the "morbidification" of female relationships seems to me essential for explaining what happened to feminism after suffrage, the new configuration of gender roles in the mid-twentieth century, and the restructuring of American sexual norms after World War I. With the diffusion of Freudianism in the 1920s, intense female relationships came under suspicion. The bonding that had sustained not only a female social world but female reform organizations as well yielded to a new ethic of heterosocial intimacy. I think it is difficult to explain fully the social and cultural history of the 1920s without reference to this essentially new lesbian taboo. Similarly, work that has been done on the United States in the Cold War era, not only on homosexuality but also on marriage, the family, and sexuality, makes it clear to me that gay history—particularly the intensification of oppression that occurred in the late 1940s and 1950s—is a critical piece of the fabric of the era. The enforcement of political conformity through the McCarthy-era red scare found its parallel in personal life through the specter of the homosexual menace. In fact, the number of lives affected by arrests, indictments, and firings of suspected homosexuals far exceeds those touched by anti-Communism. Recognizing the congruence between political structures and sexual systems makes possible a much more nuanced and ultimately plausible interpretation of the depth of the Cold War consensus. Finally, it is hard for me to imagine how anyone can teach contemporary American history without dealing extensively with the politicization of sexual identity, and the manipulation of the gay issue in political and social discourse. I wish I could be a fly on the ceiling of classrooms throughout the United States to see whether the new scholarship and new interpretations are yet influencing the way that United States history gets taught.[10]

The issue of what we teach is significant because it is one of the important ways that the historians of today shape the agenda of the profession in the next generation. The content of our courses defines for students what history is and can be. It communicates to graduate students which subject matter is legitimate and affects their choice of dissertation topics. Graduate students are vulnerable; they look to us for legitimation. Silence in the classroom and around the seminar table about homosexuality sends a loud and powerful message.

What we teach is not the only issue. There is also the question of discrimination. Unfortunately, we have no hard evidence about patterns of discrimination in the profession or about the attitudes that might inhibit gay scholarship and visibility. The only careful documentation that I know of comes from sociology. Responses from the heads of 640 sociology departments early in the 1980s revealed that 63 percent held reservations about hiring a known homosexual and 84 percent about hiring a gay activist. Almost half reported barriers in promotion, and the figure jumped to two-thirds in the case of activists. Of the gay sociologists surveyed, half told of obstacles placed in the way of their doing research on homosexuality and of advice that it would hurt their careers.[11]

Perhaps the figures would look different for history departments. Maybe historians are more accepting of diversity; maybe the 1980s has brought more tolerance of gays and lesbians. But I doubt it. It is useful to remember that the American Sociological Association passed an antidiscrimination resolution in 1969, and that sociologists have long made a place for research on such subjects as sexuality, "deviance," and subcultures. Yet prejudicial attitudes and practices remain endemic among them.

For myself, I have a few reference points that tell me that discriminatory attitudes and policies, whether covert or overt, are alive and well. For instance, I know of only two graduate students in history who are writing dissertations on aspects of homosexuality in American history, despite the fact that many promising topics await researchers. A number of graduate students and junior faculty mask their interest in gay history by choosing safer topics in social history that will touch upon it—crime, delinquency, "vice," the history of medicine, sexuality. My own experience of applying for grants has proved interesting. Whenever the proposal has been specifically gay, I have been turned down; if I present my work as the history of sexuality, I have a good record of success.

I don't see great evidence of change on the horizon, though a roundtable such as this helps. With grit and determination, with careful strategizing, some few younger historians will succeed in expanding a bit the boundaries of the discipline to include gay history. My own situation demonstrates that it is possible; I encourage those of you reading this essay to persist, and I offer you my assistance. Yet I also know that many more will be deterred, and that fact saddens me.

As for me, past experience and my sense of what the immediate future holds lead me to expect that I will continue to work a double shift—as an academic historian in a university department and as an activist and a community-connected scholar. It would be nice to feel confident that someday I could simply teach my classes, write my books, and rest.

## NOTES

1.  For discussions of gay and lesbian history, see Lisa Duggan, "History's Gay Ghetto: The Contradictions of Growth in Lesbian and Gay History," in *Presenting the Past: Essays on History and the Public,* eds. Susan Porter Benson et al. (Philadelphia: Temple University Press, 1986), 281–92; and Martin Bauml Duberman, "Reclaiming the Gay Past," *Reviews in American History* 16 (December 1988): 515–25.

2.  Jonathan M. Weiner, "Radical Historians and the Crisis in Amerian History, 1959–1980," *Journal of American History* 76 (1989): 399–434.

3.  *The Universities and the Gay Experience: Proceedings of the Conference Sponsored by the Gay Academic Union* (New York, 1974). The conference was held Nov. 23–24, 1973.

4.  Betty Friedan, *It Changed My Life: Writings on the Women's Movement* (New York: Random House, 1976).

5.  Martin Duberman, *Black Mountain: An Exploration in Community* (New York: Dutton, 1972); Jonathan Katz, *Coming Out!* (New York: Arno Press, 1975); Jonathan Katz, *Gay American History: Lesbians and Gay Men in the U.S.A.: A Documentary* (New York: Crowell, 1976).

6.  Carroll Smith-Rosenberg, "The Female World of Love and Ritual: Relations Between Women in Nineteenth-Century America," *Signs* 1 (Autumn 1975): 1–29.

7.  A revised version of this presentation has been produced as a slide-tape by the San Francisco Lesbian and Gay History Project: *She Even Chewed Tobacco,* produced by Liz Stevens and Estelle Freedman, original research by Allan Bérubé (San Francisco, 1983).

8.  Barry Adam, *The Survival of Domination* (New York: Elsevier, 1978).

9.  Important works include Jonathan Ned Katz, *Gay/Lesbian Almanac: A New Documentary* (New York: Harper & Row, 1983); John D'Emilio, *Sexual Politics, Sexual Communities: The Making of a Homosexual Minority in the United States, 1940–1970* (Chicago: University of Chicago Press, 1983); Lillian Faderman, *Surpassing the Love of Men: Romantic Friendships and Love Between Women from the Renaissance to the Present* (New York: Morrow, 1981); Walter L. Williams, *The Spirit and the Flesh: Sexual Diversity in American Indian Culture* (Boston: Beacon Press, 1986); Martin Bauml Duberman, *About Time: Exploring the Gay Past* (New York: Gay Presses of New York City, 1986); Leila J. Rupp, " 'Imagine My

Surprise': Women's Relationships in Historical Perspective," *Frontiers* 5 (Fall 1980): 61–70; Madeline Davis and Elizabeth Lapovsky Kennedy, "Oral History and the Study of Sexuality in the Lesbian Community: Buffalo, New York, 1940–1960," *Feminist Studies* 12 (Spring 1986): 7–26; George Chauncey, Jr., "Christian Brotherhood or Sexual Perversion? Homosexual Identities and the Construction of Sexual Boundaries in the World War One Era," *Journal of Social History* 19 (Winter 1985): 189–211; and George Chauncey, Jr., "From Sexual Inversion to Homosexuality: Medicine and the Changing Conceptualization of Female Deviance," *Salmagundi* no. 58–59 (Fall–Winter 1982–83), 114–46. Important work-in-progress includes a monograph on gay men and lesbians in the military during World War II, by Allan Bérubé, a study of the Buffalo lesbian community, by Madeline Davis and Elizabeth Kennedy; a study of the lesbian community in Cherry Grove, New York, by Esther Newton; and a history of the gay male subculture in New York City, by George Chauncey, Jr. Chauncey, Duberman, and Martha Vicinus are editing an anthology to be published in late 1989 by New American Library, New York, titled *Hidden from History: Reclaiming the Gay and Lesbian Past.*

10. On the 1920s, see Estelle Freedman, "Separatism as Strategy: Female Institution Building and American Feminism, 1870–1930," *Feminist Studies* 5 (Fall 1979): 512–29; Christina Simmons, "Companionate Marriage and the Lesbian Threat," *Frontiers* 4 (Fall 1979): 54–59; and Carroll Smith-Rosenberg, *Disorderly Conduct: Visions of Gender in Victorian America* (New York: Knopf, 1985), 245–96. On the Cold War era, see John D'Emilio, "The Homosexual Menace: The Politics of Sexuality in Cold War America," in *Passion and Power: Sexuality in History,* eds. Kathy Peiss and Christina Simmons (Philadelphia: Temple University Press, 1989), 226–40; Barbara Ehrenreich, *The Hearts of Men: American Dreams and the Flight from Commitment* (Garden City, N.Y.: Anchor Press, 1983), 14–28; Estelle Freedman, " 'Uncontrolled Desires': The Response to the Sexual Psychopath, 1920–1960," *Journal of American History* 74 (June 1987): 83–106; and Elaine Tyler May, *Homeward Bound: American Families in the Cold War Era* (New York: Basic Books, 1988).

11. A summary of the study may be found in a publication of the American Sociological Association, "Task Group on Homosexuality Report Published," *ASA Footnotes* 10 (December 1982): 1.

# 9

# THE CAMPUS
# ENVIRONMENT FOR
# GAY AND LESBIAN LIFE

───────────

*Shortly after the previous essay was published, I was contacted by the editor of* Academe, *the bulletin of the American Association of University Professors, to contribute to a special issue being planned on the topic "The University and Private Life." Commissioned articles included discussions of dual-career couples, the ethical issues involved in faculty-student sexual relationships, problems of chemical dependency among professors, and the need for access to child care. I was asked to discuss the campus environment for gay men and lesbians.*

*As I thought about what to write, I realized that the question I wanted to answer was "What would make the university a hospitable place for lesbians and gay men?" Answering that question forced me to move beyond simply the concerns of faculty, since we are only a small—and privileged—segment of the campus population. In sketching the contents, I was aided immensely by the upsurge in campus activism among gays and lesbians which occurred in the late 1980s; I was also helped by my involvement with the National Gay and Lesbian Task Force, whose campus organizing project has done much to nurture this campus-based movement. What follows, then, is a modest outline of a "gay agenda" for our campuses, more extensive than what I had suggested in my Oberlin lecture seven years earlier (See chapter 7.)*

Reprinted with permission from *Academe*, January–February 1990, 16–19.

The theme of this issue of *Academe* confirms the profound influence of feminism on contemporary life. Just over twenty years ago, a new generation of feminists coined the phrase, "The personal is political." Although the slogan has carried different meanings for those who use it, one implication has been to challenge our notions of private and public. Feminists have argued, and rightly so, that defining women's sphere and women's concerns as "private" has effectively excluded women from full and equal participation in the "public realm." As more and more women in the 1970s and 1980s fought for entry into academic life, higher education institutions increasingly have had to deal with a host of issues that were once safely tucked away in the private domain.

In the pre-feminist era, however, colleges and universities addressed privacy only in the breach with respect to matters of sexual identity. Consider the following examples:

—In 1959, at a small midwestern college, a student told her faculty adviser that one of her friends was a homosexual. The adviser informed a dean, who called in the student in question and pressured him into naming others. Within twenty-four hours, three students had been expelled; a week later, one of them hung himself.

—About the same time, a faculty member at a Big Ten school was arrested in mid-semester on a morals charge (at that time, all homosexual expression was subject to criminal penalties). The police alerted the administration, and the professor was summarily told to leave the campus. He never appeared before his classes again.

—At an elite college in the Northeast, male students in the 1960s were in the habit of training a telescope on the windows of the women's dormitories. In one instance, they spied two female students erotically engaged. The women—not the men—were disciplined.

—At a women's college in New England, where accusations of lesbianism were periodically leveled against roommates in the 1960s, the standard solution was to separate the accused by housing them in different dorms.

I could list many more such examples. They came to me not through research but through the gay and lesbian academic grapevine. Stories like these are the substance of an oral tradition by which gay academics who came of age before the 1970s warned one another of the dangers they faced and socialized their younger peers into necessary habits of caution and discretion.

The point, I trust, is clear. For gay men and lesbians, the past is a history of privacy invaded, of an academy that enforced, maintained, and reproduced a particular moral order—a moral order aggressively antagonistic toward homosexual expression.

Since 1969, when the Stonewall Riot in New York City ushered in the gay liberation movement, activists across the country have challenged that order. We have formed organizations by the thousands, lobbied legislatures, initiated public education campaigns, engaged in civil disobedience, and promoted self-help efforts. We have attempted to emancipate gays and lesbians from the laws, policies, scientific theories, and cultural attitudes that have consigned us to an inferior position in society.

When one considers that the political climate for most of the last twenty years has been conservative, and that this new conservatism has taken shape largely through an appeal to "traditional" notions of family, sexuality, and gender roles, the successes of the gay movement appear rather impressive. Half the states have repealed their sodomy laws. Many of the nation's largest cities have enacted some form of gay civil rights ordinance, and a number of states are seriously debating the issue. The American Psychiatric Association has removed homosexuality from its list of mental disorders. Several religious denominations are revising their positions on the morality of homosexual relationships. And lesbian and gay organizations around the country are better financed and more stable now than at any point in their past.

Those of us associated with institutions of higher education have contributed to this movement and have benefitted from it as well. Because the birth of gay liberation was so closely tied to the social movements of the 1960s, student groups have been part of the gay political and social landscape from the beginning. Currently, more than four hundred of these groups exist, in community colleges and research universities, in public institutions and private ones. Braving the ostracism and harassment that visibility sometimes brings, these young women and men have often had to battle for recognition and funding. In the process, their struggles have created a substantial body of judicial opinion that protects gay student groups as an expression of First Amendment rights of speech and assembly.

Faculty members, too, have organized. Initially forming separate organizations, such as the Gay Academic Union, they have increasingly turned to their professional associations as venues for action. Most social science and humanities disciplines now have lesbian and gay caucuses that publish newsletters, review current literature, and sponsor well-attended sessions at annual meetings. A vibrant new scholarship has emerged in the last decade that is substantial enough to spark a movement for gay studies programs in institutions as diverse as San Francisco City College, Yale University, and the City University of New York.

If one's reference point is university life a generation ago, one can say that things are getting better for gay faculty, students, administrators, and staff. Grit, courage, and determination have opened up some space in which it is possible to live, breath, and work openly. Our situation no longer appears uniformly grim.

Nevertheless, being openly gay on campus still goes against the grain. Despite the changes in American society in the last two decades, gay people are still swimming in a largely oppressive sea. Most campuses do not have gay student groups. Most gay faculty members and administrators have not come out. Even on campuses that have proven responsive to gay and lesbian concerns, progress has often come through the work of a mere handful of individuals who have chosen to be visible. And, although I do not have statistics to measure this precisely, I know that there are still many, many campuses in the United States where no lesbian or gay man feels safe enough to come out. From a gay vantage point, something is still wrong in the academy.

Oppression in its many forms is still alive, and the university is not immune to it. Indeed, as the gay population has become a better-organized and stronger force in the 1980s, we have also become easier to target. In recent years, harassment, violence, and other hate-motivated acts against lesbians and gay men have surfaced with alarming frequency on campuses across the country. Institutions such as the University of Kansas and the University of Chicago, to name just two, have witnessed campaigns of terror against their gay members. At Pennsylvania State University, a report on tolerance found that bias-motivated incidents most frequently targeted gay people.

Unlike many other groups—women and African–Americans, for instance—in which one's identity is clear for the world to see, most gay men and lesbians have the option to remain invisible. I cannot fault individuals who choose that path: the costs of visibility often can be high. Yet the fear that compels most gay people to remain hidden exacts a price of its own. It leads us to doubt our own self-worth and dignity. It encourages us to remain isolated and detached from our colleagues and peers, as too much familiarity can lead to exposure. And it often results in habitual patterns of mistrust and defensiveness because anyone, potentially, may cause our downfall. Hence, speaking about gay oppression involves not only addressing injustice in the abstract but also acknowledging the emotional toll it levies on particular individuals and the institutions of which they are a part.

For reasons that I cannot quite fathom, I still expect the academy to embrace higher standards of civility, decency, and justice than the society around it. Having been granted the extraordinary privilege of thinking critically as a way of life, we should be astute enough to recognize when a group of people is being systematically mistreated. We have the intelligence to devise solutions to problems that appear in our community. I expect us also to have the courage to lead rather than to follow.

Although gay oppression has deep roots in American society, the actions that would combat it effectively on campuses are not especially difficult to devise and formulate. What sort of policies would make a difference? What would a gay-positive institution look like?

One set of policies would place institutions of higher education firmly on the side of equal treatment. Gay faculty, administrators, staff, and students need to know that their school is committed to fairness, to treating us on the basis of our abilities. At a minimum that would mean:

—A nondiscrimination policy, formally enacted, openly announced, and in print wherever the institution proclaims its policy with regard to race, gender, and religion. Such a policy would apply to hiring, promotion, tenure, admissions, and financial aid. Because of the history of discrimination in this country, it is not enough for an administration to claim that it subscribes to the principle of fairness for everyone. Sexual orientation, sexual preference, sexual identity, or whatever term one chooses to adopt, needs to be explicitly acknowledged.

—Spousal benefits for the partners of gay men and lesbians, at every level of institutional life and for every service that is normally provided to husbands and wives. These benefits include health insurance, library privileges, access to the gym and other recreational facilities, listings in school directories if spouses are customarily listed, and access to married students' housing for gay and lesbian couples.

—An approach to gay student groups that is identical to that for all other groups with regard to recognition procedures, funding, and access to facilities. Administrators who place obstructions in the way of these groups are doing a costly disservice to their institutions, since courts have uniformly sustained the rights of gay students to organize.

Subscribing to the above policies would simply place lesbians and gays in a de jure position of parity. Implementing these measures would go a long way toward alleviating the fears that we live with, integrating us fully into the life of the campus, and letting us know that we are valued and "welcomed."

The university's responsibility toward its gay members goes well beyond these elementary procedures of fairness, however. Administrators will need to take an active stance to counteract the misinformation about gays and lesbians that many members of the university community have, the cultural prejudices that are still endemic in the United States, and the growing problem of hate-motivated incidents. The following areas need attention:

1. One of the prime locations where harassment occurs is in residence halls. Dormitory directors and their assistants need to be sensitized about gay issues and trained in how to respond quickly and firmly to instances of oppressive behavior and harassment. In an age when heterosexual undergraduates routinely hold hands, walk arm-in-arm, and engage in other simple displays of affection, lesbian and gay students need to know that they will not have their rooms ransacked, or their physical safety endangered, for doing the same. They also need reassurances that campus activism on gay issues will not come back to haunt them when they return to their dorms each night.

2. Student affairs programming is an important tool in fostering toleration, understanding, and enthusiasm for differences in culture and identity. Resources should be made available to sponsor special gay awareness week events, as well as to integrate gay films, public lectures, and other events and activities into the regular programming.

3. Late adolescence is an especially stressful time for gay men and lesbians. These may be the years when they become sexually active, form their first relationships, and grapple with issues of identity. School counseling services need personnel who are sensitive to these issues and who can foster self-acceptance and self-esteem rather than reinforce self-hatred.

4. Because the issues and situations affecting lesbians and gay men range widely across the structure of large and medium-sized campuses, hiring an "ombudsperson" for gay and lesbian concerns makes good institutional sense. Someone who can think expansively about these issues, provide a resource where needed, and intervene decisively in emergencies can move a whole campus forward.

5. When hate-motivated incidents occur—and the evidence of the last few years suggests that they happen with greater frequency than we care to admit—the highest officers of the university need to exercise their full authority in condemning the attacks and correcting the underlying problems which encourage such incidents. Bias-motivated incidents are

awful, but they also offer a unique opportunity for raising consciousness and for shifting the climate of opinion on a campus.

6. An institution that prohibits discrimination against gays ought not to countenance the presence on campus of institutions and organizations that engage in such discrimination. The government intelligence agencies and the military are the most egregious perpetrators of anti-gay bias. Recent actions by the military against its gay and lesbian personnel amount to a form of terrorism. Military recruiters and ROTC programs ought to be banned from American campuses until the armed forces change their policies.

7. Last, but not least, is the issue of research. The 1980s have witnessed an efflorescence of scholarship on gay and lesbian issues in several disciplines. Yet many topics go begging for researchers because faculty members know that prejudiced department heads and tenure committees will label such work trivial and insignificant. Gay scholarship, opening as it does a new window on human experience, must be encouraged.

On sunny mornings, I am optimistic that the 1990s will see a dramatic improvement in the quality of life for gay men and lesbians in higher education: the body of scholarship is growing and pressure for gay studies programs will mount; academics in many disciplines have created stable and permanent caucuses which will strengthen our networks; regional associations of gay student groups are forming to reinforce those groups already established on individual campuses. In addition, the National Gay and Lesbian Task Force in Washington, D.C., recently initiated a campus-organizing project so that gay men and lesbians on each campus no longer have to reinvent the wheel.

Of equal importance, perhaps, some administrators are moving beyond the most elementary issues of visibility and recognition. They are addressing the key areas of equal treatment and deep-rooted prejudice. Such a stance—on every campus—is long overdue.

# 10

## INAUGURATING THE
## FIRST LESBIAN AND GAY
## STUDIES DEPARTMENT

### SAN FRANCISCO CITY COLLEGE

---

*This short speech, which I delivered at the opening of a conference in October 1989 to celebrate the establishment of the first lesbian and gay studies department in the United States, needs little introduction. It was an historic occasion, and I felt privileged to be a part of it. As I mention in my remarks, the event blended personal, professional, and political concerns in a way that few situations could.*

As a teacher, I have grown accustomed to speaking before groups of people. The rush of lectures comes so fast in the course of a semester that I have often joked that with twenty-four hours notice, I could pull together a fifty-minute talk on virtually anything.

I promise you that this talk won't last fifty minutes. And I did get a lot more than a day's notice. Yet it has been a very hard one to prepare. As my thoughts have turned to it over the last few weeks, I have found myself searching for just the right phrase, and struggling to fashion the perfect comments on this important occasion.

At some point I realized that this inaugural event is heavily weighted with meaning for me. It brings together, in a way that no other event could, significant personal, professional, and political concerns of mine. I want to structure my remarks around those three themes—the personal, the professional, and the political.

Jack Collins, whose commitment and hard work have been so important in pulling this first lesbian and gay studies department together, shares a very long history with me. We first met in 1962, when we were freshmen at a New York City high school run by the Jesuits. Our friendship was cemented on the school's fall outing to Bear Mountain, when we were sophomores. It rained that day and, while most of our peers were running around in the mud playing football or hiking up the mountainside, we stayed in the local soda shoppe and told each other all of the dirty jokes we knew, laughing till our sides were hurting. We didn't share with one another—perhaps because we didn't yet know—that we were gay, but we bonded like brothers and shared an intense four years of high school.

We also went to college together. Columbia, between 1966 and 1970, was an exciting place to be. These were the years when the white student movement and the antiwar movement were at their height; Columbia, especially in 1968, seemed at times to be the nerve center of college protest. (Among other things, the first gay student group in the nation formed there while we were undergraduates, though neither one of us was prepared to participate in it.) I don't see how anyone could have been at Columbia then and not be completely changed by the experience; I still think of those years as the time when my social and political consciousness formed. Above all, it was then—watching how college administrators lied about what the university was doing in the community and with the government; reading mainstream papers like the *New York Times* and knowing that they were misreporting events that I had witnessed—that I first found myself developing a critical stance toward the university as an institution and toward "the system" as a whole.

Jack and I participated in these events together. We marched and demonstrated and ran around like crazies in the streets; we struggled with our draft board and with our consciences. We also came out to one another, one Friday night in my dorm room, after we both had had a little too much to drink. At the time I don't think that either of us made an explicit connection between our gayness and the ease with which we shed our conservative Catholic upbringing and were radicalized by events. Yet to some degree I am sure that our emerging sexual identities had something to do with it. We *were* outsiders—the bane of gay oppression and the boon of gay sensibility—and that fact made the critique of society that young radicals were propounding plausible to us.

After college Jack came to California, and I stayed in New York. We remained in touch, though not intimate in the way we had been for years. And now, after many twists and turns in each of our lives, we find ourselves together again—Jack as chair of this pioneering program, and me as a logical choice for an inaugural speaker. It is both amazing and thrilling to me that our lives are still so entwined, that our paths can cross on a terrain that is new and unexplored, yet also bears the traces of our history.

The inauguration of this program also resonates deeply with my professional life since my own career parallels the growth of gay studies. Between the time when Jack and I were in college together and the moment in graduate school when it was time to choose my dissertation topic, something momentous occurred: the Stonewall Riot and the birth of gay liberation. Stonewall and its aftermath transformed life for many of us. In fact, the lives of all gay men and lesbians in this country, whether or not they've ever marched for gay freedom or joined a political organization, are different because of Stonewall.

I was lucky enough to be among the group of people who founded the Gay Academic Union in New York City in 1973. That chance circumstance set my life on a path that I am still traveling. GAU offered a tremendous amount of support for thinking the unthinkable. Confronted with the need to find a dissertation topic—a fateful moment in the life of a graduate student!—I decided to do something on gay history, without quite knowing what that meant.

Throughout those years in the 1970s when I was doing the research and then the writing, my intellectual and emotional sustenance came from outside the university. It was the gay movement and the gay community to which I turned for encouragement and support, particularly to the developing network of grass-roots lesbian and gay historians. It kept me going when not much was happening in the academy itself.

By the early 1980s, when it was time to either look for an academic job or find some other way to earn a living, gay and lesbian scholarship was beginning to take shape. It was not completely outlandish to be doing gay history, but it wasn't normative either. I managed to get hired, and eventually to get tenure. I don't work in a gay-hostile environment, but neither is it gay-positive: my campus doesn't have a gay faculty or staff or student group, and we don't have gay and lesbian studies courses.

Now, at the end of the 1980s, enough research and writing has been done in a number of disciplines to make it possible to think seriously about gay and lesbian studies as a distinct field of knowledge. It is gratifying to me to know that my work has helped make this possible. I am also acutely aware of how important it is to me that programs such as this one succeed, and that others like it are established. Your efforts here will make my life and my work easier back in North Carolina. In other words, I need you.

Finally, there is the political significance of this occasion. I will confess a twinge of uneasiness about using that word. "Politics," we all know, is not supposed to intrude upon the world of higher education. Instead, we are supposed to be energetically engaged in the pursuit of objective knowledge, neutral in its stance toward political questions, detached from the world of self-interest and private prejudice.

I don't buy that, and I hope you don't either. If there is any lesson of the 1960s that remains engraved in my consciousness, it is that there most definitely is a "politics of knowledge." The research we do, the questions we ask, the results that we publish, and the courses that we teach all reflect a view of the world, of our society, and of human nature. Our social characteristics, our values, and the vantage point from which we gaze at society shape the conclusions we reach. And the ideas that we put forward in print or in the classroom help to reproduce, or to modify, or to subvert, the order of things. That makes the work of the university political.

There is a politics involved in gay studies. It is not politics in the conventional way in which that word is used. It is also not a politics of correct or incorrect research. The last thing we, as gay men and lesbians, need is a new form of thought control: we've been subjected to that for generations. But we are involved in an effort to reshape a worldview and an intellectual tradition that has ignored, debased, and attacked same-sex relationships and that has, in the process, impoverished our understanding of human experience and human possibilities. Our attempt to correct that bias is profoundly political.

Gay studies is political in another sense: without a gay movement, there would be no gay scholarship, no gay studies. It is no accident that San Francisco City College is the site of the first lesbian and gay studies department in the country. The city that even in the 1960s was being called the "gay capital" of the United States and that, since Stonewall, has seen the most extensive organizing, the most highly developed community infrastructure, and the most vibrant lesbian and gay culture—of course this would be the place to take this profoundly significant step first. We should be proud—and not surprised—that a community college rather than an elite institution is leading the way.

What should a program such as this be about? What should it look like? These are the questions that this conference will be addressing over the next few days, and hopefully some concrete proposals will emerge. But to answer these questions well, we need to operate from a clearly articulated perspective about education, and about institutions of higher education. Let me tell you mine.

Colleges and universities are important institutions. Large numbers of young people and adults pass through them. Universities also shape the public school system. Elementary and secondary school teachers are taught, trained, and certified through them. Textbooks are often written by college educators. Colleges and universities often occupy a place of influence in the life of communities around the nation. In other words, we are not dealing with ivory towers unconnected to "real life." Institutions of higher education shape values, impart (or withhold) information, and define and describe social, cultural, and political reality.

For me, the purpose of education generally, and of higher education in particular, is to offer and refine an accurate description of reality—a description of what is, of how things came to be, and of how to make change. It should allow us to imagine and envision what we want our lives and our society to look like. By having a gay studies program, we are making a statement about values, about society, and about our vision of the future.

In establishing these programs we can take different roads. We can see them as our own feudal manors, as a fief that has been granted, or extracted, from a lord—and then go about busily fortifying it against hostile marauders.

I hope that's not what happens here. Yes, these programs will become a home base, a safe place for gay and lesbian students, faculty, and staff. But they also need to extend a welcome to others. They need to be reaching ever outward. A program such as this must not only nurture gay studies and scholarship. It must also be a force for reshaping the institution of which it is a part, and the society in which we live.

In the Jesuit high school where Jack and I first met, the classics played a central role in the curriculum. I can't claim to remember much Latin, but I do know that the word educate has as its root the Latin verb *ducare*, to lead. If we can hold on to an expansive vision of what gay studies programs can accomplish, then they will be educational ventures in the truest sense of the word—"leading us out," out of ignorance, prejudice, and injustice.

# 11

# GAY AND LESBIAN STUDIES

## NEW KID ON THE BLOCK?

---

*As the 1990s began, gay and lesbian studies no longer seemed a pipe dream. Scholars in many disciplines had created a visible gay and lesbian presence; academic and trade publishers were looking to publish our work; the number of conferences in which gay and lesbian research found a forum was growing; and new courses were appearing on many college campuses. We are poised, I think, to make important inroads in the academic world. My greatest concern at this point is that the austerity that is now hitting state governments and the non-profit sector—because of twelve years of Republican-administered tax policies and income redistribution upward—will make fiscal obstacles the excuse that is used to delay the implementation of lesbian and gay studies programs.*

*One sign of the progress that is being made is the year-long lecture series on gay and lesbian studies that Penn State sponsored during the 1989–1990 academic year. I was asked to give the last of the talks, and I used it not as an occasion to present my own research but to assess the state of this new field of study. The lecture presented some historical background, developed at greater length some of my comments on the "politics of knowledge" which I alluded to in my speech at San Francisco City College, and addressed tactical and strategic issues surrounding implementation.*

*In no sense does the following essay encompass all of the institutional initiatives and all of the splendid work being done by researchers around the country. That would require much more than an hour-long lecture.*

Historians love to tell stories—real-life stories of the past—and invest them with "meaning." So let me begin this talk with a few:

—In 1974 I made the decision to write my dissertation on a gay topic. There was, at that time, nothing that was recognized as gay history and, to my knowledge, no one had ever written a history dissertation on the subject of homosexuality. But I was a young gay activist and, with the support of lots of friends who were making equally significant personal choices about coming out, I'd decided to take my stand. After obsessing about it for weeks, I summoned up my courage and, with palms sweating and my heart beating fast, walked into my adviser's office and said: "Professor Leuchtenberg, I've decided to write my dissertation on the history of homosexuality in the United States." Without skipping a beat, he looked at me and responded: "John, I think that's a fine idea, but you'll need to narrow your topic." The meaning: shrewd and incisive historian that he was, he recognized that there was a gay history waiting to be uncovered, and it would be too rich, too broad, and too complex to be encompassed by one scholar, or one research project.

—A few years ago, I offered my history of sexuality course in the evening, in order to make it available to adult students who worked during the day. One of those who took it was a high school teacher who had gone to college in the mid-1960s. At some point in the semester I gave a lecture on the career of Margaret Sanger, the birth control agitator, and prefaced the lecture, as I always do, with the comment that in my opinion Sanger was one of a handful of individuals who had decisively influenced twentieth-century American life. Halfway through the discussion that followed, Linda suddenly erupted in anger. "How is it," she demanded to know, "that I could have gotten through college with *no one* ever even mentioning Sanger's name to me? Why did I hear nothing about this?" Her question was rhetorical, and we both knew the answer: we get our view of the world as much by omission as by anything else. And the omissions can tell us a lot about what is wrong with our society.

—I had to miss a class in order to come here for this talk. The students in my course on the United States in the 1960s wanted to know why, and so I told them: I had been invited to give a talk at Penn State in a series on gay studies. What would it be about, they wanted to know? I gave them a quick run through, and told them the title: "Gay Studies: New Kid on the Block?" A number of them started to laugh, and I began to wonder if I had tapped into a well of unexplored homophobia, when one of them asked, "Are they gay?" "Who?" "Them!" "Who's them?" "New Kids on the Block!"

The meaning? A generational divide has opened between the students of today and my generation. And, just as I haven't kept up with the popular culture of today, the experience of my generation is in danger of being lost unless it is consciously passed along. In terms of my talk tonight, that means that when I address the issue of gay studies, I am assuming—as many others who passed through universities in the 1960s would also assume—that there is a "politics of knowledge" and a politics of higher education.

In looking at the state of gay and lesbian studies in the United States today, I want to do a number of things. First, I will set the stage by exploring what I mean by a "politics of knowledge." Second, I will provide a bit of what I consider to be the essential context for understanding the growth of this field—namely, the gay and lesbian emancipation movement of the last generation. Without this movement, we would not be here tonight talking about gay studies. Third, I will sketch a broad overview of gay and lesbian organizing within higher education in order to assess where we are, what's been accomplished, and what we can build upon in the 1990s. Then I want to turn to issues of strategy and problems in implementation. And, finally, I will address the question of what lesbian and gay studies have to teach us by looking at a couple of examples from my own field.

## THE POLITICS OF KNOWLEDGE

One of the signal achievements of the campus turmoil of the 1960s was the recognition that universities are not ivory towers where individuals engage in the disinterested, dispassionate, and detached pursuit of knowledge and truth. Rather, universities are intimately connected to the society of which they are a part. They are capable of producing change, to be sure, but they can also reflect, and reproduce, the dominant values, beliefs, habits, and inequalities of their society. Everything we do—the research questions we formulate; the research process itself; where we publish our results; the courses we decide, or are told, to teach; the books and articles we assign—represents choices that individuals make. These choices reflect a particular view of the world, of our society, and of how things ought to be.

This became most immediately and sharply clear around the issue of the war in Southeast Asia. One of the rallying cries of campus activities in the 1960s was "university complicity." Student radicals used their research skills to uncover all sorts of ties between the campus and the "war machine." There were lucrative research contracts and research institutes dependent for their survival on the largesse of the Pentagon. Members of the boards of trustees were executives of major corporations that were profiting from the war, while university administrators often sat on the boards of these same corporations. The CIA came to campus to recruit; ROTC programs trained the officers who led the troops in Vietnam; and the universities were tied to the Selective Service System through a complex system of draft deferments which privileged college students.

Years of protest against the war, against university complicity in "The System" as it was, had the effect of destabilizing university administrations. For a time, the authority of administrators was delegitimized. This created an opening for two social movements of the era—the black movement and the women's movement— to begin reshaping the intellectual life of the universities. On a host of campuses, black studies programs (and other racial/ethnic programs) and women's studies programs were institutionalized in the late 1960s and early 1970s. They faced problems—they were rarely adequately funded and, as the political climate grew more conservative, many had to fight for survival—but they also accomplished something profound. What seemed avant-garde and extreme twenty years ago now appears self-evident: namely, that race and gender can serve as the organizing principle for intellectual work, that viewing society through the prism of these social categories can teach us something we didn't know before.

These programs, and the scholars whose work revolves around these issues, have had an enormous impact. The debates of the late 1980s about the "canon" and about the content of the liberal arts curriculum are a direct result. By the mid-1980s enough work had been done in a variety of disciplines to reshape knowledge, and the defenders of the intellectual status quo felt threatened and compelled to respond.

These conservative attacks on intellectual change, from William Bennett, Allan Bloom, Lynne Cheney, and others, are often expressed in terms of a fear of losing our way as a culture, a fear of faddish tampering with universals. But they ignore the fact that the intellectual traditions and structures that they defend as traditional and enduring are themselves the product of change. Disciplinary boundaries that are regarded as sacred are themselves of recent creation. And a program such as American Studies never comes under fire from conservative critics, even though it was a political creature if ever there was one—a product of the Cold War, an effort to provide ideological, intellectual backing to America's postwar global chauvinism.

Why am I saying all this in a talk on the state of gay studies? Because I want to emphasize that our understanding of "what is knowledge," and "what is important knowledge," is not cast in stone, but is always in flux, always changing. And changes comes not simply because scholars accumulate knowledge, but because social pressures, movements of the disenfranchised, create demands for new knowledge and for the reorganization and reconceptualization of what we already know. If gay and lesbian studies is pushing its way on to the agenda of higher education in the 1990s, it is because another disenfranchised group is creating pressures for change.

## THE ESSENTIAL CONTEXT: A LESBIAN
## AND GAY EMANCIPATION MOVEMENT

Although some lesbians and gay men have been organizing for freedom since the post–World War II era, it is only in the last twenty years that the movement has been large and unruly enough to attract much notice. The mythic event that set the wheels of a mass movement in motion occurred in New York City near the end of June 1969. When the police raided a gay bar, the Stonewall Inn, patrons fought back and a weekend of rioting erupted. The riot galvanized radical young gays and lesbians around the country and, before long, a gay liberation movement became an established feature of the nation's social and political landscape.

Pre-Stonewall lesbian and gay life was not solely a story of oppression and victimization, but oppression was certainly a defining element. The teachings of Christianity and Judaism, the theories of scientists, the criminalization of homosexual acts, pervasive police harassment, discriminatory government policies, and cruel, demeaning stereotypes: all of these and more conspired to keep gays and lesbians at the margins of American society, invisible and determinedly protective of their anonymity. While "the closet" guaranteed some measure of safety, it also allowed prejudice and punishment to continue unchecked.

Stonewall was the spark that ignited a powder keg of gay anger and resistance. By 1973, just four years later, almost a thousand lesbian and gay organizations had been created; today, there are many thousands of groups giving voice to this community's aspirations. These organizations come in all sizes and shapes: national, state, and local; political, religious, cultural, service, recreational, and commercial; organizations based on gender, ethnic, and racial identity; and organizations based on occupational and professional affiliation. In the last twenty years, the movement has achieved major gains: sodomy laws repealed in half the states; civil rights statutes enacted in several score of cities, including many of the largest; changes in the medical classification of homosexuality and debates in many religious denominations about church teachings; and the elimination of the federal civil service ban on the employment of gay men and lesbians.

I would summarize the growth of the movement in this way: in the 1970s, gays and lesbians struggled to achieve visibility and to create communities. The organizations they established were the building blocks of both of these goals. In the 1980s, a community infrastructure has been institutionalized in many places, and the goal has shifted to gaining access to power—political, cultural, and social. The AIDS epidemic has accelerated this shift in that it has added an element of urgency to organizing efforts, brought many more people into the movement, expanded the resources available to organizations, and pushed the movement toward coalition politics. Here is a dramatic marker of the change that has occurred in less than a generation: in 1970, when an anniversary march was held in New York City to commemorate the Stonewall Riot, about 5,000 people turned out. In 1987, when gay men, lesbians, and their supporters gathered in Washington, D.C., to demand civil rights and action to stem the AIDS epidemic, the crowd was estimated in excess of half a million. *That* is change.

Without this movement, we would not be discussing the state of lesbian and gay studies and their prospects for the 1990s. The movement has opened a space within all the institutions of American society in which it is possible to "think gay." Events on and off campus are intimately related to one another. The pursuit of lesbian and gay scholarship is facilitated by progress toward equality in other contexts. And the campuses of the United States have been the site of much movement activity.

## WHERE WE ARE NOW

What has happened in terms of intellectual activity in the 1970s and 1980s? I won't pretend to offer a comprehensive picture. I don't know when or where the first gay studies course was offered; I don't know how many are being offered now. Instead, I want to offer bits and pieces of the larger mosaic, and provide some moments and measures of change.

Let me begin with personal experience. In 1973 I had the good fortune to be part of the group of men and women who founded the Gay Academic Union in New York City. To my knowledge, this was the first formal organization of gay and lesbian faculty in the United States. As we worked together, we would all share the bits of information we had that might contribute to gay and lesbian studies, but at the time the very concept still seemed a utopian dream. The card catalogs of university libraries, such as Columbia's, where I was a student, didn't offer much help beyond some works claiming the designation of science, but which were in fact repositories of cultural prejudice.

When we planned our first conference, for Thanksgiving weekend of 1973, we wondered whether many of our still closeted brothers and sisters would come. We also struggled to put together a conference program. For a two-day conference, we scheduled only a single panel on scholarship, with each of the four speakers to cover one broad area of knowledge: science, religion, literature, and social science. So little was as yet known that we reasonably expected someone to encompass a field in a thirty-minute presentation!

Three hundred men and women came to that first conference; our third one, in 1975, drew over a thousand. By that time, the proceedings had grown from one panel to at least a couple of dozen. We had obviously tapped into a great need and had unleashed, with the help of the larger lesbian and gay movement around us,· tremendous intellectual energy.

From the mid-1970s to the early 1980s, activity began percolating all over the place. The lines of influence from GAU were many, and they came to intersect with other independently conceived initiatives. Lesbian and gay caucuses began to form in many of the disciplinary associations, particularly in the humanities and the social sciences. These fledgling groups of activist scholars worked to achieve recognition, to call attention to the problem of discrimination and win resolutions condemning it, and to expand the network of members within their respective professions by enticing colleagues to come out. They began to organize sessions at the annual meetings of professional associations, where work-in-progress was presented and intellectual issues discussed.

In history, sociology, anthropology, literature, psychology, and probably some other fields as well, this process was well underway by the early 1980s. These efforts met with varying degrees of success. The most progress has been made in the field of literature. The annual meetings of the Modern Language Association are replete with sessions on lesbian and gay topics. The lesbian and gay caucus publishes its own newsletter three times a year, with upwards of forty pages in each one, packed with abstracts, research notes, book reviews, and bibliography. Literature is also the field where some of the most provocative theorizing of gay issues is being done.

Meanwhile, a great deal of intellectual work was being conducted outside the academy, in community-based institutions and projects. This occurred out of both necessity and choice: necessity, because the university was not, for the most part, an especially hospitable place either for gay research or gay people; and choice, because many of these intellectual laborers had a stronger commitment to the community and to the movement than they did to elite mainstream institutions, and they shaped their work accordingly. Though these grass-roots endeavors had little access to the privileges which the academic world offers, they also were free from the constraints of tenure decisions and disciplinary fashions. Researchers could set their own agenda.

A number of important initiatives occurred between the early 1970s and early 1980s. In New York City, a group of women formed the Lesbian Herstory Archives. Over the last fifteen years, it has accumulated a rich collection of material about lesbian life and culture, has played host to numerous researchers, and has spread the gospel of lesbian history far and wide. Other community-based archives have formed in a number of cities. One of them, the Bay Area Lesbian and Gay Historical Society, has now initiated a microfilming project of all lesbian and gay periodicals published in the San Francisco area. In the wake of Jonathan Katz's *Gay American History* (1976), researcher/activists in San Francisco, Boston, Buffalo, New York, Chicago, and perhaps other cities as well, formed local history projects. They produced slide shows that entertained and educated community members and sustained a supportive context in which individuals could pursue their own research interests. Some of that work is now bearing fruit. Allan Bérubé's new book, *Coming Out Under Fire: The History of Gay Men and Women in World War II*, and Elizabeth Kennedy and Madeline Davis's forthcoming community study of lesbians in twentieth-century Buffalo, had their genesis in local history projects. Finally, many of the periodicals that emerged from the gay and lesbian liberation movement—*Body Politic, Conditions, Sinister Wisdom, Out/Look,* and others—have opened their pages to the work of community-based scholars.

I cannot emphasize enough how important this community and movement support is to the nurture of lesbian and gay studies. Even though I have an academic job, my work was cultivated in this nonacademic context, and it continues to energize me. It also keeps lesbian and gay studies "honest." It reminds us that intellectual work is about living, breathing human beings and the issues that shape their lives; it helps to break down the class-based distinction between intellectual activity and the rest of life.

One other development of these years is worth mentioning: the founding of the *Journal of Homosexuality* in 1976 under the editorship of John DeCecco. Based at a nonelite school (San Francisco State University) in the gay capital of the nation, the journal has served an important function in legitimizing and encouraging research. Over the years, special issues on such topics as sex roles, youth, literary visions, and alcoholism, and in such disciplines as religious studies, anthropology, and history, have catalyzed research and mobilized interest in critically important areas.

By the early 1980s enough networking had been done, enough men and women had come out of the closet, and enough scholarly work was in progress that the foundations for a lesbian and gay studies movement could be laid. Here are some signs of change:

—In 1980, the University of Chicago Press published John Boswell's *Christianity, Social Tolerance, and Homosexuality*. A massive work of scholarly research, it surveyed 1,400 years of Western history and challenged deeply-cherished beliefs about the Western cultural tradition. Most of all, it was commercially successful, attracting much more attention than dense works of scholarship normally do. Nothing succeeds like success, and Boswell's book represented a breakthrough. Chicago's gamble was royally vindicated; other university presses that had rejected the manuscript kicked themselves. As the decade wore on, it became easier and easier to find university presses willing to publish gay and lesbian books. A young lesbian or gay scholar may have difficulty finding a job, but she or he is increasingly likely to have a dissertation published. Chicago has now published a number of gay books; Columbia University Press has created a gay series; Routledge has a very strong list of lesbian and gay scholarship; and many other university presses are pouncing upon potential manuscripts. The winds of intellectual fashion may shift at any time, but at the moment a large window of opportunity has opened.

—One of the banes of the first efforts to study lesbian and gay topics was the paucity of readily accessible research materials. Much of the archival work that I did for my study of the pre-Stonewall movement, for instance, occurred in the garages, basements, and living rooms of individuals. The homophobia responsible for this is at least starting to dissolve. Besides the community-based archives which now exist, some major research institutions are making a commitment to gather and process gay-related material. Cornell University has just acquired a major human sexuality collection with a heavy gay content; it has also hired an archivist to develop the collection further. The New York Public Library is also taking steps toward building a gay collection. In addition, as more and more scholarship is produced, the next generation of researchers will be able to build on the archival sources discovered and the data collected by those who came before them.

—The settings in which lesbian and gay scholarship can be shared are proliferating. I have already mentioned the sessions that now regularly occur at the annual meetings of discipline-based professional associations. To those can be added the gatherings of the National Women's Studies Association and the Berkshire Conference on Women's History, in which a "parallel track" lesbian studies conference could be said to exist. Gay and lesbian scholars are also creating settings of their own, as successors to the Gay Academic Union conferences of the 1970s. Historians held three hugely successful international gatherings in the 1980s. Over the last four years, a major gay and lesbian studies conference has been held at Yale and, this year, at Harvard. And the University of California at Santa Cruz, a hotbed of lesbian and gay research, has also begun holding "Queer Studies" conferences.

—The first tentative steps have been taken toward initiating programs and research centers. Last year, City College of San Francisco established the first gay and lesbian studies department in the United States. Because City College is a feeder institution whose graduates go on to study at various branches of the state system, this program will in time lead to pressures for other campuses in California to follow suit. The City University of New York and Yale are in the process of setting up research centers. Cornell's human sexuality collection will probably create a demand there for some kind of academic program. Rutgers University recently completed a comprehensive study of the campus environment for lesbians and gay men. Out of that will undoubtedly come a movement for curriculum change.

All of these developments would have seemed unthinkable twenty years ago. They are the product of much hard work and patient organizing. We have reason to believe that the movement in the direction of lesbian and gay studies will continue to grow. And, finally, remember that I am giving you bits and pieces only. What I have presented to you is the tip of the iceberg. I haven't even begun to approach the vast array of courses that are taught and being developed on campuses across the country.

Can we place all of this into some kind of framework to help us understand better the development of gay studies? I would say that for the most part, the 1970s was a decade characterized by organization and networking. The 1980s have witnessed the production and sharing of knowledge. I expect that the 1990s will be the time when we see significant movement toward the institutionalization of lesbian and gay studies in higher education. And, undergirding all of this progress has been the coming-out process. Every one of us who has come out makes it easier for others to follow; the more of us who come out, the greater will be our opportunities.

## IMPLEMENTATION AND STRATEGY

Here I want to raise some issues and pose some questions. The issues will get resolved and the questions answered in the course of doing the work of institutionalizing lesbian and gay studies.

First of all, let's remember that a curriculum does not develop in a vacuum. A gay studies program is but one piece of a much larger puzzle: making the campus a hospitable, welcoming place for its lesbian and gay members. Universities will be most likely to move forward on curriculum issues if they have also made progress in other critical areas: adoption of nondiscrimination policies in hiring, promotion, admission, and the like; the extension of partnership benefits, in areas such as insurance and housing, to the spouses of gay faculty, staff, and graduate students; recognition of student groups and support for programming relevant to gay and lesbian students; vigorous administrative response to hate-motivated incidents, which occur all too frequently on campuses. It also seems self-evident, at least to me, that campuses which have begun to grapple in a serious way with issues of gender, race, and ethnicity—in other words with the broad spectrum of concerns that fall under the rubric of diversity, or multiculturalism—are the most likely candidates to make progress on gay and lesbian concerns too.

So, gay studies needs to be conceptualized within a larger framework of campus organizing for justice. And, for it to work, one needs to involve not only faculty, but staff, administrators, and students—both graduate and undergraduate.

The building blocks of gay studies, as of any program or discipline, are individual courses, and course development is a first priority. But beyond that, a whole host of implementation issues will arise: should we strive to establish an interdisciplinary "program," or a separate "department"? Do we want a minor or a major? Are we talking about undergraduate education, or graduate training as well? Should a gay studies program have hiring authority, or will faculty be jointly appointed, with a department as a home base?

The answers to these questions will be rooted in the distinctive histories of particular institutions: How have other programs, such as women's studies or Chicano studies, been developed on a campus? How have previous programs fared? Are there pitfalls to avoid based on what has happened to other innovative academic endeavors?

It seems to me that the least that can be said is that we should push ourselves to think big, and then be prepared to scale back implementation according to the resources available. It is also true, I think, that the kind of academic programs that we're talking about are, at their best, valuable for the cross-fertilization of ideas that they encourage, and for the reconceptualization of experience and knowledge that they provoke. That means that we should be working to scramble the traditional lines of division between fields of knowledge: new issues don't necessarily require new methodologies, but innovation should be seen as a valuable asset.

One danger that gay studies must avoid is the "divide and conquer" syndrome. It is quite likely that the 1990s will be a time of serious financial austerity in higher education, especially at state-financed institutions. The tax policies of the Reagan years, federal cutbacks in social welfare programs, and huge federal budget deficits have all combined to squeeze the public sector and nonprofit institutions. The states are now starting to feel the pinch. Maybe the end of the Cold War will release large amounts of money for areas such as education, but that remains to be seen. I suspect the old "military-industrial complex," to borrow a phrase from Eisenhower, will resist mightily. In any case, this is not a good economic time for adding new programs on a campus; even many existing ones may face the axe. Advocates of gay and lesbian studies must be careful not to be manipulated into competing with women's studies or black studies for scarce resources. We need to work cooperatively, to be as innovative in our campus politicking as we are in our intellectual work.

Another important strategic issue involves the choice between mainstreaming and ghettoization. I suppose the very way I've phrased the problem displays my prejudice: mainstreaming of gay and lesbian issues is my goal. I would like to see the time come when so much research has been done, and our ways of thinking so thoroughly revised, that the gay and lesbian experience, the varieties of same-sex intimacy, and the role of sexuality in social life are all fully integrated into the curriculum.

But that is a long-term goal. While we can get there bit by bit, through the willingness of individual faculty to incorporate new knowledge and new perspectives into their teaching, the sweeping change that I'm advocating will only come about through collective endeavor. Autonomous gay studies programs are essential for that to happen. Without them, we won't have the critical mass of intellectual workers or the "free" intellectual space to do the work that will make curriculum reform someday feasible.

What worries me—and why I raise the issue of ghettoization—is the subtle way that separate academic programs can reinforce key elements of gay and lesbian internalized oppression. Isolation and social marginalization have been so central to the way we have been oppressed that we easily adopt that pose even when we don't need to. Because of our oppression, our desire for "home" and "family" is so strong that we become deeply, desperately attached to the homes and fictive families that we are able to create for ourselves. As we establish gay studies programs over the next decade, I think we will have to remind ourselves that the goal is not a program for its own sake, as a retreat from an oppressive society or institution, but rather a program that can serve as a means toward social transformation. And that will require ongoing engagement with our campus and our professions.

Finally, gay studies will find itself confronting one problem to whose solution the experience of ethnic and gender studies offers no clues—the issue of visibility, of the closet, of coming out. Although there is no inherent reason why only a gay man or lesbian would teach a gay studies course or do lesbian-related research, and no inherent reason why only gay and lesbian students would enroll in such courses, the fact is that these choices are often interpreted as a *de facto* declaration of identity. And, in a world where gay oppression is not a figment of our imagination, this can function as a serious obstacle to building a viable program. Who will enroll in these courses if students fear the consequences of a transcript that includes an "Introduction to Gay Studies" or "Lesbian Literature?" And, without enrollments, how can a program be built?

Solving this critical problem takes us back to points I made earlier. The growth of lesbian and gay studies is intimately tied to the progress of the larger gay movement; gay studies programs are only one part of a larger campus agenda for gays and lesbians. Gay studies will move forward only if we are heading toward meaningful equality in the rest of society and only if our campus is becoming a hospitable place for us. And so we return once again to the "politics of knowledge." Without ongoing political struggle to eliminate every vestige of homophobia and gay oppression, we will not see the development of gay studies. By the same token, the growth of gay studies is a form of political engagement.

## WHAT WE CAN LEARN

Everything I have said tonight would be pointless if gay and lesbian studies had nothing to teach us. But, happily, the work that has already been done in a variety of disciplines is opening up to us a deeper understanding of old concerns as well as raising new issues and problems to consider. Let me give two examples from my own field of U.S. history.

For a long time historians have debated two related historiographical issues: What happened to feminism after suffrage was achieved in 1920? And, what happened to the broader reform impulse called Progressivism, of which suffrage was a part?

The common wisdom about feminism was that it collapsed after suffrage because of a combination of success and strategic mistakes. The adoption of the Nineteenth Amendment granting women the right to vote was a major victory, the culmination of three generations of agitation. But, at the same time, because suffragists had made such broad claims about what the vote could accomplish, feminism no longer had a raison d'être after suffrage: women only had to use the ballot, and their other goals would be achieved. Feminism also faltered because of the conservatism of the 1920s, which likewise passed as the chief explanation for the decline of Progressivism. After two decades of growing strength, Progressivism ran aground during World War I; the conservative reaction which followed the war finally killed it.

The work of other historians has challenged these conclusions. Many would dispute the claim that either feminism or Progressivism died after 1920. Recent work on women's history in the 1920s and 1930s demonstrates that women continued to make gains in the areas of politics, education, and the professions. New organizations, such as the League of Women Voters, replaced those which had campaigned for the vote. And Progressivism, too, is seen as continuing. Some reforms were enacted in the 1920s, especially on the state level, and when the New Deal opened new opportunities for significant social welfare innovation, activists from the Progressive era were there to take advantage of this second chance.

Valuable as these interpretations are as a corrective to the voices which see the demise of feminism and Progressive reform, they still fail to grapple with the fact that something did change after World War I. Reformers were no longer on the offensive; they felt themselves beleaguered, struggling against the tide. And feminism, too, was no longer the dynamic movement that it had been in the years before suffrage.

Recent work by several women historians—Lillian Faderman, Estelle Freedman, Christina Simmons, and Carroll Smith-Rosenberg—is providing us with a much more subtle and plausible explanation for change. Nineteenth-century feminism emerged out of a Victorian world in which female bonding and female relationships were normative. Middle-class white women grew up in an essentially separate female sphere that validated female moral superiority and that expected close attachments to develop between women. This social experience nurtured a feminist politics by encouraging the building of female institutions—women's clubs, settlement houses, and women's colleges, as well as organizations like the Women's Christian Temperance Union. Mainstream ideology had the paradoxical effect of sanctioning the relationships and the institutions that some women would use to effect significant social change. The feminist movement and its campaign for suffrage were able to build upon this base, which also served to launch women upon the social crusades that were at the heart of Progressivism.

By the eve of World War I, American culture was retreating from the constraints of Victorian respectability. The Freudian reaction to Victorian morality challenged nineteenth-century assumptions about female purity and moral superiority; instead, women were said to be driven by the same kinds of lust and erotic drives as men. The 1920s witnessed something of a celebration of heterosociability and heterosexuality. The modern flapper smoked, drank, flirted, and petted.

Along with this came an articulation of a lesbian taboo. The normative female attachments which had sustained both feminism and Progressive reform now fell under a cloud of suspicion. Female bonding, in Lillian Faderman's terms, became "morbidified." The social basis for feminist politics was badly shaken as definitions of sexual deviance were extended to include the homosocial world of middle-class women. A sensitivity to the female bonding at the heart of much social reform in the early twentieth century and an understanding of the creation of a lesbian taboo after World War I can take us a long way toward resolving significant historical problems.

My second example comes from Cold War America. Historians have generated a truly vast literature on the origins and significance of the Cold War as well as on its domestic counterpart, the rabid anti-Communism of the post–World War II era. The interpretive twists and turns of the historical writing on these subjects are too complex to summarize easily, but I think it is fair to claim that most historians would agree on the following: anti-Communism became the animating force in American foreign policy; and fear of Communist subversion at home cast a pall over political life. There was a decided shift to the right in domestic politics, a narrowing of the spectrum of debate, and a suppression of political dissent.

I have never found this description of postwar America fully satisfying or complete. It doesn't adequately explain for me the depth of the consensus that existed in the 1950s, the widespread conformity in public and private life, and the retreat from political engagement which, except for the black population, seemed to characterize most of the country in these years. The contrast with the 1930s and immediate postwar years, when labor, leftists, and social justice liberals fought hard and vigorously for progressive change, and with the 1960s, another turbulent era in the nation's life, is too great to be explained simply by repression, or by exhaustion after years of depression and war.

We can make better sense of postwar America by turning to the sphere of personal life and noticing the articulation between it and politics. My own work on the McCarthy era has uncovered the massive mobilization to contain an alleged "homosexual menace." Government agencies, political leaders, the press and local police forces combined to expose, vilify, and harass homosexuals—all in the name of national security. The mobilization was clearly irrational, in the sense that gays did not pose any kind of threat to national security, yet it spread across the country with amazing force.

I have argued that the preoccupation with a "homosexual menace" grew out of a deep-seated anxiety about gender roles and family stability in the wake of fifteen years of depression and war. Projecting these fears onto an invisible sexual threat offered a safe form of expression. It also reinforced the drive toward a conforming privatization of American life. The baby boom, suburbanization, the resurgence of an ideology of domesticity and dichotomized gender roles—all of these features of postwar culture, though certainly driven in part by other social impulses, served to create moral order where chaos threatened, and to demonstrate probity rather than deviance. The homosexual menace functioned much as the accusation of Communism. Almost anyone could fall under suspicion, and only vigorous demonstrations of heterosexuality might save one's reputation. When this element of personal life, along with other aspects of the history of sexuality and gender in these years, is added to our portrait of postwar America, it becomes easier to appreciate the conservatism and conformity of the era.

Scholars in other disciplines could no doubt provide you with many other examples of the insights and revelations that attention to gay and lesbian issues can provide. We will only find our knowledge of past and present, of the individual and society, enriched by these explorations if we create a climate on campus, and in society, in which we all have the freedom to ask new kinds of questions and to search for the answers. In the long run, gay and lesbian studies will be good for everyone.

# 12

# GRADUATION DAY

---

*Every once in a while, something happens that, with startling clarity, reminds one of the fact of change. The graduation party that I describe below, which occurred in May 1988, was one of those occasions for me. It also reminded me that teaching is important work, and that what we model for our students can make a very big difference.*

*In rereading this short essay, which I wrote a few months after the event, I thought of a "theoretical issue" which the party raised for me. As an activist and as a student of social movements, I tend to focus most often on the conscious, deliberate efforts at social change made by people who band together with the intention of reshaping society. These collective efforts, I am convinced, are absolutely critical if we ever want to live in a world in which justice, dignity, respect, and the flowering of human possibilities are the stuff of everyday life rather than a distant dream. But the actions of individuals like Doug—who simply go about living their lives in a different way—also make a difference. They open up new possibilities that activists can then exploit to push the quest for freedom from oppression further along and to take it on new, unimagined paths. There is a younger generation of lesbians and gay men who are living differently because of what the Stonewall generation wrought, and who are creating a whole new ground on which activism can take place.*

Long ago I was attracted to the study of history for the comfort it gave me as a gay teenager. In a world which seemed to have no room for who I was, I found it reassuring to look across the sweep of centuries and know that change occurred.

If empires came and went, if dynasties rose and fell, then perhaps there would be a day when a decent life would be possible for people like me.

I still study history. I even research it and write it. It continues to provide me with hope and inspiration. The slow, plodding quality of daily life makes it difficult at times to grasp the fact of change as the essential reality of human life and society. History offers me a constant antidote to the weight of the present.

Sometimes, though, I don't have to turn to other lives and other eras to appreciate change. My own experience can be enough. Last spring, I attended a college graduation party for one of my students. The change I saw was dramatic.

I graduated from college in 1970. Gay liberation was about to celebrate its first birthday, but it would be two or three more years before I took a step in that direction. Meanwhile, I had made an accommodation of sorts with my gayness, one that allowed me to survive. I had told a very small number of friends that I was gay, I had found Greenwich Village, and I had even managed for a while to have a relationship.

But the stresses were great. The turmoil and secrecy opened a chasm in my relationship with my parents. They knew something was happening, but I couldn't talk to them and instead regularly exploded at their well-meaning efforts to make contact. During those years, the parents of a high school friend became a surrogate mother and father to me. I visited often, played with their younger children, ate many dinners with them, and talked freely—about everything except my sexuality. Still, their caring and my connection to them kept me afloat at a difficult time.

Three weeks after graduation, I fell madly, passionately, and completely in love. Virtually every moment not spent at work was filled by my lover. The relationship was so total that it seemed impossible not to talk about it with everyone. Yet it seemed just as impossible to come out. I resolved that tension by simply disappearing from the lives of nongay people I knew, including my surrogate parents. I remember convincing myself that they would not want me in their home if they knew I was gay. It was a heavy price to pay for love.

The card that arrived this April inviting me to Doug's graduation included a handwritten note from his mother: "You have had a profound impact on our son's life. We're looking forward to meeting you."

I had met Doug when he was a freshman. Two of his dorm friends were taking my course on the history of sexuality and had introduced us. Some few weeks later he stopped by my office to ask if we could talk. Over lunch, he asked many, many questions, told me about his own wrestling with his sexual identity, and asked for advice. I told Doug that only he could decide what made sense for him, but that I could testify that it was possible to have a full, satisfying, and vibrant life as a gay man.

**177**

We had many conversations in the succeeding years. He took my sexuality course. He also began showing up at gay events in town. By the end of the semester he had come out in class.

I was the only faculty member invited to the graduation party. On the surface it looked like any other: lots of family, spanning generations, and some of Doug's friends. But slowly I took closer stock of the scene. Doug was there with his male lover. Some of his friends were in mixed-gender couples; others were same sex. The dancing that went on reflected the variety of relationships. It was a celebratory occasion, and Doug's parents, grandparents, aunts, uncles, cousins, and siblings seemed thoroughly accepting of his gayness—not abstractly, but in the concrete form of his lover and his friends.

It's exhilarating to know that the lives of at least some young gay men and lesbians are so dramatically different from my experience of two decades ago. It's even more exciting to realize that I have played a modest role in pushing these changes along.

I suspect that throughout the United States, hidden from public view, equally profound changes are occurring in the lives of countless numbers of people. It is not only a story of gay lives, but one that also includes our families, friends, neighbors, and coworkers. The many, many instances of coming out, whether in front of television cameras, in the classroom, or in a restaurant over dinner, are reweaving the social fabric. They are winning us allies, creating a permanent change in attitudes, and raising an "army" which, though still invisible to the Falwells and the Helmses, is marching alongside us.

# PART THREE

# LIVING POLITICS

———————

# 13

# MAKING AND UNMAKING MINORITIES

## THE TENSIONS BETWEEN GAY HISTORY AND POLITICS

---

*The findings of many gay and lesbian historians and the agenda of the gay movement are often at odds. This essay in particular uses gay history to challenge the "gay minority" perspective that shapes much of the movement's strategy. It was given at a one-day symposium on the topic "Sexuality and the Law," held at New York University Law School in 1986. The event was an exciting one in that it brought together grass-roots activists, lawyers, and scholars to address movement issues.*

*The paper I presented was motivated in part by a concern, growing since the mid-1970s, that gay activism was abandoning the radical perspective of gay liberation and framing its enterprise ever more narrowly. Gone, especially, was the critique of sexual categories that was very much at the heart of gay liberation. The issue is not whether to seek equality under the law, but whether that is all we seek. A gay rights and gay minority perspective almost guarantees that we will settle for minor modifications of the status quo.*

Reprinted from the *Review of Law and Social Change*, 14 (1986): 915–922.

Since 1969, when the Stonewall Riot in Greenwich Village gave birth to the current phase of gay and lesbian political struggles in the United States, the gay and lesbian movement has evolved from one emphasizing gay liberation to one emphasizing gay rights.[1] Within that shift in terminology lies a major alteration in social analysis, political strategy, and ultimate goals. In its gay liberation phase, the lesbian and gay movement employed a language of political radicalism. It saw itself as one piece of a much larger political impulse that strove for a complete reorganization of institutions, values, and the structure of power in American life. Gay liberation sought to achieve its aims by organizing masses of gay men and lesbians whose political activity would occur largely outside courts and legislatures. These activists viewed accepted categories of homosexuality and heterosexuality as oppressive social constructs. The movement perceived human sexuality as diffuse and poly-morphous in nature, and potentially destructive of rigid social hierarchies.[2]

Over the last fifteen years, the movement has become exceedingly diverse. Today, gay and lesbian organizations include a host of constituencies—men and women, black, Hispanic, Asian and white, young and old, entrepreneurs, middle-class professionals, and unionized workers. Homosexuals have formed political clubs, churches, synagogues, health centers, and theater companies. Although no unified vision or political strategy animates these constituencies, we can say that as Stonewall has receded into the past, the movement as a whole has become less politically and socially radical. Its portrayal by the media, the statements of many movement leaders, and the program of action of individuals and organizations convey an image of the gay movement as one in quest of equal rights. That evolution, from gay liberation to gay rights, places the political and social struggles of lesbians and gay men in a familiar, well-established equal rights framework, deeply rooted in American history.[3] This history has provided gay men and lesbians with several models of struggles employed by minorities in search of equality. Blacks, women, ethnic groups, and religious minorities seek this equality through social movements, legislative agendas, and litigation. Recommending an analogous course of action for gay men and lesbians may be tempting.

Although I would not dispute the value of either judicial or legislative protections that guarantee due process, equal protection, and equal access, I would suggest that the "traditional" minority group model raises certain problems when applied to gay men and lesbians.[4] These difficulties emerge most clearly if one approaches the question from an historical perspective. Over the last decade, historians have done pioneering research that goes far beyond the uncovering of gay heroes. Historians have advanced toward a reconceptualization of the nature of human sexuality, and are creating theories with implications for both lawyers and social activists. My goal, therefore, is to interpret the work of gay and lesbian historians for an audience that may be unfamiliar with it.[5]

I shall begin with my own book, which is a history of the gay and lesbian movement in its formative stages—the two decades between the founding of the Mattachine Society in Los Angeles in 1950, and the Stonewall Riot in 1969.[6] The book's subtitle, "The Making of a Homosexual Minority in the United States," goes to the heart of this new conceptualization. During this period, a gay and lesbian minority emerged as a definable social group with a self-conscious sense of itself as different from the majority. This minority did not always exist; it lacks a historical presence in American society.[7]

Central to this argument is a view of human sexuality as exceedingly malleable. Sex is more than a configuration of bodies in space; it takes its definition from the values and structures of particular cultures, and from the consciousness of individuals within a society. Sexuality consists of acts with meanings. Although the acts may have a universal existence, the meanings may vary considerably. And it is through meaning, through an understanding of behavior which culture provides, that patterns of behavior take on social significance.[8]

This view of human sexuality as socially constructed has led many historians, on the basis of the evidence uncovered thus far, to conclude that sexual identity— in particular, a social world divided into homosexuals and heterosexuals—is a fairly recent historical invention. To phrase it more baldly, the reason a gay political movement did not exist before the post–World War II era was not because gay men and lesbians were slower to recognize injustice than were blacks or women, nor because the oppression was so severe that protest was too dangerous. Rather, the explanation lies in the fact that until the modern era, a gay and lesbian "minority" did not exist.[9] Many contemporary Americans take for granted that sexual orientation is a fixed category that indicates an essential difference in human beings. Yet, in the mid-eighteenth century, or even mid-nineteenth century, American society did not label people as heterosexuals or homosexuals.

Jonathan Katz's book, *Gay/Lesbian Almanac*, illustrates this conceptual distinction.[10] Katz divides his book into two parts: "The Age of Sodomitical Sin, 1607–1740," and "The Invention of the Homosexual, 1880–1950."[11] By examining in detail two eras separated by more than a century, Katz highlights the sharply distinctive sexual characteristics of each. In the former period, sodomy and sodomitical behavior were punished and excoriated as sin and crime.[12] Clerics and magistrates were preoccupied with certain proscribed behaviors, with discrete sexual acts. Sodomy was but one of many sexual activities prosecuted under the law. Others were adultery, fornication, rape, buggery, and public lewdness.[13] Sodomy was not a category that demarcated one type of individual from another. Instead, it represented a capacity for sin inherent in everyone.[14]

Katz describes a profoundly different social reality during the years 1880–1950. In medical writing, in literature, and in the testimony of men and women themselves, one finds an effort to redefine the meaning and the experience of homosexual behavior into a distinctive identity.[15] Sex becomes the distinguishing characteristic that describes the essential nature of some men and women. No

LIVING POLITICS

longer simply an act, homosexual behavior instead serves as a marker of identity.[16]
That identity encompasses personality, emotional state, sexual desire, and even,
according to some, physical characteristics.[17] The homosexual can exist apart from
any sexual activity: if one feels that one is a homosexual, that is sufficient.
Colonial Americans would have found such assertions incomprehensible. To them, a
sodomite was someone who had committed the sin of sodomy.[18]

The distinction between homosexual acts and homosexual identity represents
more than playing with words. The concepts describe two profoundly different
forms of homosexual expression, rooted in different social contexts. The process
of creating a sexual identity involves a complex dialectic between external labeling
and self-definition. In the century since the 1880s, the medical profession, courts,
legislatures, government agencies, the mass media, educational institutions, and
religious bodies have articulated a system that both describes and controls the
social category they helped to create. In tandem with this categorization process,
men and women have elaborated complex, diverse ways of living based upon their
sexual desires. They have adopted distinctive styles of dress, have evolved an argot
of their own, and have carved out social spaces—private friendship networks,
public cruising areas, bars, bathhouses, clubs, and most recently, political organizations—that have allowed this sexual identity to take shape. Along the way,
communities of mutual interest and experience have evolved. This reinforcing
process of social labeling and individual self-definition has created a homosexual
minority in the last half-century.[19]

Although there seems to be a fair consensus among gay and lesbian historians
that a homosexual minority has come into being in the modern era,[20] fewer of these
historians agree about precisely why this phenomenon occurred. One hypothesis is
that the emergence of American industrial capitalism in the late nineteenth century
provided an opportunity for individual autonomy that was a precondition for the
development of a gay identity.[21]

Throughout the United States diverse gay and lesbian identities and communities
developed. These communities emerged among female faculty of women's colleges,
among the single working women and prostitutes of boardinghouse districts in
large cities, among entertainers in Harlem, and along the fringes of bohemian
communities in places such as New York City's Greenwich Village. As time went
on, they interacted with one another and were all subject to the external forces
of social control in ways that may not have homogenized them, but that did
nonetheless create commonalities among them: blacks and whites crossed paths in
the clubs and cabarets of Harlem; college-educated social workers and prison
administrators encountered prostitutes and other working-class lesbians in the

courts and in penal institutions. Distinctive subcultures were forming, but the lines between them were sometimes blurred.

Before moving on to suggest some of the implications that this historical analysis has for contemporary legal and political strategies, let me add one more word about history. What many historians are saying about sexuality departs from common folk belief in another significant way. Popular wisdom might summarize the history of sex as follows: first, there were moralistic Puritans, then repressed Victorians, followed by liberated moderns. Individuals, the story goes, have become sexually freer since the 1920s.

In contrast, historical writers have argued that this repression/freedom model misses the essential nature of the last two centuries of change in Western attitudes toward sex. Sexual activity has gradually, though not completely, been detached from a reproductive, gender-based matrix, and has been reconstituted as an entity in itself. Sexuality has been elevated in importance; it has become, for heterosexual and homosexual alike, a marker of personal identity. Our happiness and our sense of self-worth often revolve around our sexuality, and the emotional relationships that attach to it. Perhaps this elevated importance of sexuality is a sign of freedom. But, it has also amplified the possibilities for public intervention in personal life and for new methods of social control.[22]

From this perspective, it is perhaps easier to understand why public conflicts over sexuality have become so significant in the last century. From the seventeenth through the mid-nineteenth century, one searches in vain for a politics of sexuality in America. As long as social and economic conditions kept sexual expression deeply embedded in a procreative, family-centered context, neither motive nor opportunity existed for social battles to rage around sexual issues. Since the Civil War, however, sex has generated political controversy of growing intensity and scope. Issues such as obscenity, birth control, prostitution, homosexuality, and abortion have proven capable of mobilizing vast numbers of Americans.[23] In this century, sexual issues have situated themselves nearer to the center of political concerns. At times, the leading edge of sexual politics seems to represent "freedom," while at other times the forces of "repression" appear to have the upper hand. Yet, both sides are united in the magnified importance that they attach to sexuality. If we have more sexual freedom than the Victorians had, that freedom is at best double-edged.

Are there ways in which this historical interpretation can clarify political strategies and tactics, especially in relation to the law? My comments about the present will not be as neat as my historical analysis. But let me at least describe some of the tensions and problems that arise when we place history alongside contemporary politics.

Take, for instance, the possibility of moving the courts to rule that gay men and lesbians deserve judicial intervention to guarantee equal protection under the law, that is, that we are a minority subject to discrimination. To achieve this, one would at least have to demonstrate convincingly a history of discrimination. This task is feasible if we restrict ourselves to the last generation. Unquestionably, gay men and lesbians have been subject since the 1940s to pervasive, systematic discrimination in many spheres of public life.[24] The military moved from simply court-martialing and discharging personnel who engaged in proscribed sexual behavior to excluding a whole class of men and women, regardless of their sexual activities, on the basis of their sexual inclinations—in other words, on the basis of their sexual identities.[25] The federal government banned the employment of gay men and lesbians, and many state governments and private employers followed suit.[26] Urban police forces arbitrarily conducted mass arrests at gay bars; probably tens of thousands of men and women were arrested every year.[27]

For the pre–World War II generations, however, there is little courtroom-ready evidence of discrimination. Homosexuality was a far less visible phenomenon. Society did not so clearly categorize on the basis of sexual orientation. The laws and public policies of a later time had not yet taken shape. Unlike blacks, against whom discriminatory laws stretch back to the seventeenth century, the "gay minority" has captured legislative attention only recently. A minority must exist before it can be oppressed, but a socially defined, self-conscious homosexual minority simply does not exist very far back in the nation's past. In addition, some discriminatory practices, such as the ban on civil service employment, have already been abolished. Given this historical record and the recent Supreme Court decision in *Bowers v. Hardwick*,[28] what is the likelihood federal courts will consider gay men and lesbians in need of protection?

As another example, consider a key item of a gay rights agenda—the modification of municipal, state, and federal civil rights statutes to include sexual preference. Clearly it is desirable to prohibit discrimination in housing, employment, and other areas of life. Yet central to the oppression of lesbians and gay men, and to society's ability to shape and enforce it, are the homosexual and heterosexual categories themselves. The identity and the oppression are bound together. Is it not deeply ironic and troubling that a strategy which relies on civil rights laws is a strategy which strengthens the categories that allow a system of oppression to continue? Is it possible that other approaches—litigation based on the freedoms of speech and assembly or legislative proposals that blur gender-based distinctions—might be both more successful and more consistent with the history we have uncovered?

Whatever the legislative goals we choose to pursue, however, I am certain of two things. First, the issue that gay men and lesbians are facing is not simply one of a minority struggling for civil rights or equality. The issue is sex and its place in society and individual lives. The call for minority rights is simply one way of framing part of this larger issue—an issue that taps into the deepest layers of human and social irrationality. Secondly, whatever our short-term goals, we need to frame arguments for them consistent with the core of historians' discovery that sex is a malleable social construct. In this way we will achieve an educative goal beyond our immediate aim.

Let me illustrate this second point with a personal experience. About three years ago, I found myself in a debate concerning gay rights. On one side were a congressman and a retired navy admiral; a representative of a prominent national gay rights organization and I were on the other side. The congressman made statements to the effect that homosexuals are willful, perverse sinners violating biblical law. In response, my partner declared that all the best medical evidence demonstrated conclusively that there was no choice involved, and that sexual identity is determined long before puberty.

Now, there was nothing new or startling about that statement. It is an argument made frequently in courts and legislatures, and articulated by many of our most committed activists and allies. But I heard it more clearly during this debate than I ever had before. It is a sincerely held viewpoint that squares well with the gut-level feelings of most of us. It also seems to promise political benefits; surely you will not punish us for something we cannot help.

This statement, however, ignores several valid arguments. Magnus Hirschfeld and other German activists used a variant of this argument earlier in the century when they claimed that homosexuality was not a willful perversion, but a congenital condition.[29] The argument did not deter Nazi persecution. Second, at a psychological level, there is something dreadfully wrong about basing a political movement on individual and collective helplessness. Do we really expect to bid for real power from a position of "I can't help it"? And third, what if the argument is simply not true?

A fatal weakness attends any gay political movement which defines itself as a fixed minority in quest of equal protection based on its minority status.[30] To do so implies acceptance of a sexual paradigm that itself shapes and strengthens the oppression we are battling. To argue that our identity, our sexuality, is in effect an accident of birth or of early conditioning is to embrace a sexual ideology that negates the choices we have made. So long as we accept these preset terms we have lost much of our freedom of choice. Fifteen years ago we supposed the terms of gay oppression to be that gay was bad, sick, and criminal. So the movement

LIVING POLITICS

proclaimed that gay is good. Now it is clear that the terms of that proclamation are the acceptance of the mutually exclusive categories of heterosexuality and homosexuality.

All of us have made sexual choices throughout our lives. This phenomenon exists for heterosexuals and homosexuals alike. Because the hegemonic models of sexuality offer only two possible self-definitions, we have retrospectively interpreted our activities as the unambiguous manifestation of our one true being. Francis Matthiessen, as a young gay man in the 1920s, illustrates this process in a comment he made after reading Havelock Ellis: "How clearly," he said, "I can now see every act and friendship of my boyhood interpreted from my proper sexual temperament."[31] Many of us have likewise experienced a moment when we said, "This is who I am"—and in the process homogenized and flattened the complexity of our lives.

A century ago, certain American men and women were making radical personal choices, pursuing untrodden paths of sexual desire. The paths they marked became the outlines both of new sexual definitions and of new oppressions. In many ways, we are still traveling those same paths. It is time to carve out new personal and political paths, and to lay claim to the possibility of choice, to embark on new journeys of sexual definition. In doing so, we will challenge not merely the particular inequalities which a minority faces, but also the meaning, the structure, and the place of sexuality in our society for everyone. A multifaceted movement which takes on that task, in its own community and in society, will provide lawyers and lobbyists with a social and political context that can radically reshape our legal and legislative strategies.

### NOTES

1. The complex reasons for that transformation are beyond the scope of this paper.

2. See Donn Teal, *The Gay Militants* (New York: Stein and Day, 1971); Karla Jay and Allen Young, eds., *Out of the Closets: Voices of Gay Liberation* (New York: Douglas, 1972); Dennis Altman, *Homosexual: Oppression and Liberation* (New York: Outerbridge & Dienstfrey, 1971); and Toby Marotta, *The Politics of Homosexuality* (Boston: Houghton Mifflin, 1981).

3. This tradition is manifested in American equal protection jurisprudence. For a description of this tradition, see Laurence Tribe, *American Constitutional Law* (Mineola, N.Y.: Foundation Press, 1978), 991–1136.

4. When a minority group pursues equal rights by identifying itself as a minority, it may, to some extent, defeat its objectives. To accept an identity as a fixed minority may reinforce the very oppression that we seek to dispel. For a description of equal rights models, see Tribe, *American Constitutional Law*.

5. See Jonathan Katz, *Gay American History* (New York: Crowell, 1976), and *Gay/Lesbian Almanac* (New York: Harper & Row, 1983); Jeffrey Weeks, *Coming Out: Homosexual Politics in Britain from the Nineteenth Century to the Present* (New York: Quartet Books, 1977); and James Steakley, *The Homosexual Emancipation Movement in Germany* (New York: Arno Press, 1975).

6. John D'Emilio, *Sexual Politics, Sexual Communities: The Making of a Homosexual Minority in the United States, 1940–1970* (Chicago: University of Chicago Press, 1983).

7. Ibid.

8. See Weeks, *Coming Out*; Kenneth Plummer, ed., *The Making of the Modern Homosexual* (London: Hutchinson, 1981); John Gagnon and William Simon, *Sexual Conduct: The Social Sources of Human Sexuality* (Chicago: Aldine, 1973); and Robert Padgug, "Sexual Matters: On Conceptualizing Sexuality in History," *Radical History Review* 20 (Spring/Summer 1979): 3–23.

9. See note 8.

10. Katz, *Gay/Lesbian Almanac*.

11. Ibid.

12. Ibid., 23–65.

13. Ibid., 66–133.

14. See generally D'Emilio, *Sexual Politics, Sexual Communities;* Weeks, *Coming Out*; see also Katz, *Gay/Lesbian Almanac*.

15. Katz, *Gay/Lesbian Almanac*, 137–74.

16. Ibid.

17. Ibid., 175–653.

18. See note 14.

19. See John D'Emilio, "Capitalism and Gay Identity," in *Powers of Desire: The Politics of Sexuality*, eds. Ann Snitow, Christine Stansell, and Sharon Thompson (New York: Monthly Review Press, 1983), 100–113.

20. See note 14.

21. See, for example, Lillian Faderman, *Surpassing the Love of Men* (New York: Morrow, 1981); Eric Garber, "T'Aint Nobody's Bizness: Homosexuality in 1920's Harlem," in *Black Men/White Men: A Gay Anthology*, ed. Michael J. Smith (San Francisco: Gay Sunshine Press, 1983), 7–16; and George Chauncey, Jr., "Christian Brotherhood or Sexual Perversion: Homosexual Identities and the Construction of Sexual Boundaries in the World War One Era," *Journal of Social History* 19 (Winter 1985): 189–211.

22.   See Michel Foucault, *The History of Sexuality*, trans. Robert Hurley (New York: Pantheon, 1978); Jeffrey Weeks, *Sex, Politics, and Society: The Regulation of Sexuality Since 1800* (London: Longmans, 1981).

23.   See, for example, Linda Gordon, *Woman's Body, Woman's Right: A Social History of Birth Control in America* (New York: Grossman, 1976); James Mohr, *Abortion in America: The Origins and Evolution of National Policy, 1800–1900* (New York: Oxford University Press, 1978); Judith Walkowitz, *Prostitution and Victorian Society: Women, Class and the State* (Cambridge: Cambridge University Press, 1980); and Kristin Luker, *Abortion and the Politics of Motherhood* (Berkeley: University of California Press, 1984).

24.   See D'Emilio, *Sexual Politics, Sexual Communities*, ch. 3.

25.   Ibid.

26.   Ibid.

27.   Ibid.

28.   106 S. Ct. 2841 (1986) (Georgia's criminalization of consensual sodomy held constitutional.)

29.   See generally Steakley, *The Homosexual Emancipation Movement in Germany*.

30.   See note 3.

31.   Louis Hyde, ed., *Rat and the Devil: The Journal Letters of F. O. Matthiessen and Russell Cheney* (Hamden, Conn.: Archon, 1978), 47.

# 14

# THE SUPREME COURT AND THE SODOMY STATUTES

## WHERE DO WE GO FROM HERE?

————————

*The 1986 Supreme Court decision in* Bowers v. Hardwick, *in which a narrow majority of the justices upheld the constitutionality of Georgia's sodomy statute, was an important moment in the evolution of the gay and lesbian movement. Many Americans were shocked and angered by the denial of basic privacy rights implied in the decision. The ruling also brought home the necessity of political activism to many gays and lesbians who previously had not been involved in the movement.*

*Far fewer individuals are aware that ten years earlier, in 1976, the Supreme Court had done essentially the same thing when it voted, 6 to 3, to let stand a lower court ruling sustaining Virginia's sodomy law. That decision motivated the following essay in which I discuss the pitfalls of relying on litigation and lobbying as the chief tactics for achieving equality and call on gay radicals to take the lead in building a mass movement for social change.*
Reprinted from *Gay Community News* (1976).

When I first heard about the Supreme Court decision upholding the constitutionality of the sodomy statutes, my immediate reaction was "So what? Who ever expected freedom to come from the hands of nine somber men dressed in black robes?" But a little bit of reflection has led me to conclude that the court's ruling may very well be a watershed for the gay movement, an event of major importance in the history of our struggle for liberation.

191

The short-term impact of the decision is, of course, unquestionably negative. Most immediately, it means that the gay movement must marshal the energy to mount thirty-six different statewide campaigns for the repeal of the remaining sodomy statutes. The Supreme Court's ruling will also strengthen the opposition to a wide range of demands by gay people. Lawyers attacking the military's ban against gays in the armed forces, for instance, will now have to contend with the argument that their clients, by acknowledging their homosexuality, have implicitly admitted that they are breaking the laws whose constitutionality has been upheld. Municipal and state legislators will be more reluctant to pass laws protecting the civil rights of gay people who are "criminals." The government and private employers can now more easily justify job discrimination against gay men and women. The courts can argue with added force that children should be taken away from lesbian mothers to protect them from the influence of criminal households. And the police, who in recent years have somewhat curbed their harassment of gay men, may take the Supreme Court's decision as a signal to renew and intensify their intimidating attacks against us.

These negative implications are real; the Supreme Court's decision is a major setback. But gay people also have the power to transform this defeat into an asset, *if* we use it as an opportunity to take stock of our goals and to reevaluate in an open and self-critical way our movement's strategy and its tactics.

In the last three or four years, the gay movement, especially its male sector, has increasingly narrowed its focus toward court cases and legislative lobbying efforts. Such a strategy has posed two serious dangers for the movement. It has tended, first of all, to make gay activism the property of a few well-trained professionals such as lawyers, and to restrict the movement to those who can devote a large measure of their time to lobbying campaigns that need careful direction and a full-time commitment. It thus has removed the gay movement from the lives of most gay people, who do not have the time or the skill for these highly specialized tasks. Second, and more seriously, the primacy of a courtroom-legislature strategy implicitly assumes a certain analysis of the nature of gay oppression which often passes unnoticed at the same time that it exerts an influence on how we continue to define our goals. This "invisible" analysis goes something like this: gay oppression is a holdover from a less-enlightened past; it survives today through the force of outmoded laws; if we can change the laws, gay oppression will wither away; thus, the most important task is to work within the system, to win over the men of power to our side.

That's somewhat of an oversimplification, of course. Some of the organizations pushing the approach based on civil rights laws and court cases, such as the

National Gay Task Force, are also doing other valuable work. But others, like David Goodstein and the *Advocate*, have gone so far as to say that the movement can achieve its goals only through the work of a few "respectable" professionals. The important point, though, is that as a whole the movement has been defining its goals and developing its tactics in a narrower and narrower way. The danger is that when that way fails, as it did in last week's Supreme Court decision, we are left without anything to fall back on.

The decision to uphold the constitutionality of the sodomy laws contains within it answers about how the gay movement can avoid the dead end toward which our recent strategy was leading us. The opinion of the lower court calls into question the simplistic notion that gay oppression is simply the result of a few outmoded laws and that our oppression will end when the laws are changed. In fact, the laws simply reflect the norms of the society; they enforce the values of a social order that comprehends all aspects of life. The lower court argued that the previous court rulings on the constitutional right to privacy involved marriage, the sanctity of the home, and family life—none of which are applicable to gay people! It rationalized the prohibition of homosexual behavior as a means of encouraging heterosexual marriage, and quoted from the Bible to support the contention that homosexuality is a form of moral delinquency not to be condoned. The Supreme Court supported this ruling without comment.

Marriage, the sanctity of the home, family life, the moral nature of heterosexuality—these are what our laws protect and this is where our oppression originates. As I read about the ruling I recalled the theme which lesbian-feminist Charlotte Bunch has been developing in her speeches and in her writings.[1] The goal of the gay movement, Bunch argues, must be to end the institutionalization of heterosexuality.

That's quite a task! It means more than the end of the sodomy laws and more than the protection of our civil rights. It means attacking all of the ways and all of the areas in which heterosexuality receives favored status. That includes marriage and tax laws; it includes the content of children's books and the curriculum of our schools at every educational level. It requires us to fight against the dichotomization of sex roles that define women only in terms of a role within a heterosexual family. It means the end of childrearing practices and environments in which children absorb a model of heterosexual intimacy as normal and gender hierarchy as natural.

These goals imply something other than raising the status of gay men and women to one of equality with heterosexual men and women. It implies a transformation of the society that confers differing statuses on men and women, on gays and straights. It suggests that gay liberation will succeed only to the degree to which it has a transforming effect on the lives of *all* of us. Gay liberation is not for gays only.

Such comprehensive goals require a strategy that is *inclusive*. By that I mean a strategy that does not define a single form of political action as *the one best way*. An inclusive strategy recognizes that the enormity of our oppression demands many kinds of political activity, and it encourages every gay person to participate in the way most appropriate to his or her circumstances. The Lambda Legal Defense Fund and the National Gay Task Force should continue to fight in the courts and in the legislative halls of our state capitols. Dignity should continue to exert pressure on the Catholic Church hierarchy to change its position on gayness. Meetings should be held with members of the psychiatric profession to guarantee constructive mental health care for gay people. The Gay Media Coalition should maintain a dialogue with the media, supporting positive programs and articles about gay people, and voicing our dissatisfaction with negative stereotypes. The Gay Academic Union should continue to provide a forum for the presentation of scholarly research on homosexuality and lesbianism. Conservative and liberal gays who do this kind of work within the system are making an important and necessary contribution to spreading a gay consciousness throughout the society, and are therefore helping to transform our society.

But the social transformation that will bring us liberation also requires the input of radicals, those of us who are opposed to "the system." We must continue to attack, to delegitimize and to demystify those institutions that are oppressive. We should openly and disrespectfully challenge (as the Gay Socialist Action Project did last week in New York City) the authority of medical "experts" such as Bieber, Socarides, and their psychoanalyst colleagues, who try to define for us standards of health and sickness that should be self-determined. We should expose the ways in which the political parties betray the legitimate interests of all exploited and oppressed peoples, including gay men and lesbians. We should create as much alternative space as possible for our gay brothers and sisters so that there is some measure of freedom from the pervasiveness of oppression, and a place where all of us can rest and receive support and strength in our continuing struggle. We must build and staff the coffeehouses and community centers that will liberate us from the crassly exploitative, well-lighted discos of gay entrepreneurs. And most of all, as radicals, we should be ready at all times to talk to and reason with gay people who are still committed to working within the system, analyzing in a persuasive manner the reasons why reform-oriented tactics won't take us all the way to liberation, and why in the long run we cannot end gay oppression without political activity that aims at the roots of our social organization.

If we rely solely on the courts, we allow those in power to deny us our freedom. The narrow strategy that the gay movement has been pursuing makes our liberation contingent upon the good will and approval of someone else. The Supreme Court's ruling has given us impressive evidence of how precarious such a strategy is. If, in its place, we encourage and support the self-activity of *all* gay people, at whatever level of time and commitment they find comfortable; if we can come to comprehend the enormity of our oppression and consequently the many, many ways in which it needs to be fought, we will have created a movement with mass participation that cannot be demoralized or defeated by the fiat of nine men. We will have exerted a transforming effect not only on our own lives, but on the lives of everyone in America.

**NOTES**

1.  Bunch's essays from this period are collected in Charlotte Bunch, *Passionate Politics: Feminist Theory in Action* (New York: St. Martin's Press, 1987).

# 15

# SATURDAY NIGHT

---

*For many gay radicals in the 1970s, "the movement" meant more than engaging in political activism; it was also about living our lives differently. That could take many forms, such as in the imperative to come out of the closet and to begin to integrate one's gay identity into the rest of one's life. It also meant building community by creating institutions that bonded us and that began to meet the many needs—social, cultural, spiritual, emotional, recreational—that we all have.*

*Beginning in 1976, I was a creator and participant in one small effort in that direction. Every Saturday night, for almost a decade, my apartment was the setting for an open house for gay men in New York. By the time it was well-established, upwards of fifty men would arrive every week for an evening of food and casual socializing. For me, these weekly gatherings were the glue holding my gay world together and attaching me to a vibrant community of men who cared deeply about one another.*

*The following essay was written after our open house had been going on for more than four years.* Reprinted from *Gay Community News* (August 9, 1980).

I want to tell you about an experiment I've been involved in for several years. Over four years ago, my roommate, Tony, and I were sitting in our living room on a Saturday afternoon trying to decide what to do that night. You know the syndrome: Saturday night, when *everyone* is supposed to do something exciting and have a great time. If you don't, you're likely to wake up on Sunday morning feeling weird and lonely, a social failure. We ticked off our options: dancing, the bars, a movie, the theater, the baths, a concert, dinner at a good restaurant. None of them hit the mark. We both realized that what we most wanted was to spend a quiet evening at home, socializing with some of our gay male friends. But it was too late for that. By late afternoon, everyone would have plans for the evening. Why, they were probably already ironing their T-shirts and jeans!

The idea struck, though, and Tony said, "What if we called our friends and said that we would be home *every* Saturday night; that we would make a big pot of food (spaghetti, chili, stew, rice and beans—something cheap that can stretch) and a salad; that our friends could drop by without calling, any Saturday, and they could bring their friends; and that they should bring something—drink, bread, fruit, dessert. Would it work?" Well, we tried it. We made the phone calls. Some of our friends were excited. Others, disbelieving, asked us to repeat what we had just said. Saturday night rolled around, and we cooked. The doorbell rang, Tony and I opened it, and a puzzled face peered in questioningly: "You're really here?"

About fifteen gay men came that first night. It was just like Tony and I had imagined it—a very pleasant, happy, relaxed evening with lots of friends. The evening ended and, as people were leaving, they asked, "You'll really be here next Saturday, too?" Yes. "I don't have to call in advance?" No. "Can I bring a friend?" Sure.

And so our Saturday night "open house" began in 1976. Some nights there were only eight or ten guests; at other times, as many as fifty arrived. There were friends, and friends of friends, and friends of friends of friends. Men would come who had only heard about it, and who risked walking into a room full of strangers, just for the possibility of a pleasant evening with other gay men. The crowd would change a lot from week to week, but that was part of the excitement: we never knew what the evening would be like. Some of our friends came every week; others showed only occasionally. Lots of new friendships formed; old friendships became tighter. One close friend now comes around with his lover: he met David on a Saturday night four years ago. Sometimes two men who are strangers to each other lock eyes and everyone can feel the erotic energy passing between them; hours later, the two go home together. Men who are taking their first, tentative steps into gay life find their way to our home. I think to myself: I wish something like this had fallen my way fourteen years ago when I was coming out.

Mostly the evenings are a kind of free-form socializing with men walking in and out of rooms, from one group or conversation to another. But other things happen too. The zap of Irving Bieber, Charles Socarides, et al. at the New York Academy of Medicine, I'm proud to say, was planned in my living room on a Saturday evening. Another time, we had a birthday party with cake and candles to celebrate the founding of the Mattachine Society in Los Angeles in November 1950; Jonathan Katz and I did a reading of the early documents. We have birthday parties for each other, too. The night before the Gay Pride March we all leave together, en masse, and dance our asses off in the Village. A *Body Politic* member came one evening to tell us about their trial; an activist from California spoke, in 1978, about the anti-Briggs work on the West Coast. Men who remember the 1950s start singing melodies from old Broadway shows. Sometimes everyone arrives with a big dessert and we spend the night stuffing our faces and getting high on sugar.

So far I've talked about our Saturday nights just in terms of men. But women attended too. Much of the time the gatherings are all-male; sometimes there are a couple of women; occasionally there are lots of lesbians. The latter situation usually occurs when several of us decide together to call our lesbian friends, extend an invitation, and suggest that they bring their friends. When that happens, the evenings work fine, but it's also true that women who come once, unlike men who are brought by friends, don't return. Why, I've wondered. Maybe we're sexist slobs. The fact is, though, that this group of men is by and large about as feminist and antisexist as any group of men one is likely to encounter.

There's a different reason, I think, why our gatherings remain predominantly male. Lesbians also need alternatives to the Duchess and the Sahara (New York City lesbian bars), but they need *lesbian* alternatives. A woman brought to our house for the first time is coming to a gay male household. She knows that to return on her own is to choose to spend her evening in a gay male environment. It's not *her* alternative anymore than it would be *mine*, if I were brought to an open house run by lesbians. The few women who do attend regularly aren't coming to an "alternative." They're coming to spend an evening with their close gay male friends.

After eighteen months of our weekly open house, Tony and I moved into a larger apartment, in the same neighborhood, with David, a friend who was a Saturday night regular. Now there were three of us. Still, after a while, it became a burden. We had to be home every week, and cooking—and cleaning the next morning—for thirty to forty people is a big job. Maybe it was time to call it quits. We talked about it with friends who sympathized but who were also horrified at the thought of a wonderful "institution" coming to an end. So we decided that a good solution would be to solicit pairs of volunteers to cook. That worked for a fall and winter, but then, except for a couple of diehards who kept volunteering, the work was mostly falling on the three of us again. So, we called a special emergency meeting of the dozen or so regulars and shouted, "Help!"

The outcome was perfect. We now have a collective of nine men who take charge of cooking and cleaning. We still solicit volunteers, but if no one raises a hand, the responsibility doesn't automatically fall on me, Tony, and David. In the last six months, I've only had to cook twice. Why, I don't even have to be there! I can actually go out on the town on a Saturday night if that's what I want to do.

Roughly every six months or so, we have an evening to evaluate how it's all going, to discuss what's going well, what isn't working, how we can change things to make the evenings more enjoyable. "I wish it were more sexual," one friend says. "I see this as an alternative to the bars, a place where the atmosphere won't be dripping with cruising vibes, but if I *never* go home with anyone, what kind of alternative is it?"

"Right," says another. "Sometimes I leave here and end up going to the baths. I wish I could meet someone here."

"What do you mean?" a third friends chimes in. "I think it's *too* cruisy. I want a gay space where I can hang loose and relax, and not think about scoring."

"Oh, I don't know," says someone else. "I do all right. I've met some sexy men here whom I've gone home with later."

"Maybe it's us. It's hard to break the dichotomy between socializing with friends and cruising with strangers. Saturday nights are almost like a laboratory. We're learning and experimenting with different ways of being gay."

Any one of those statements could have come from me. Most of the time, I go to bed by myself on Saturday night. Sometimes, I sink into the mattress, relaxed and mellow, a bit stoned, flushed with satisfaction at the wonderful, warm, ever-expanding circle of gay male friends I have. Sometimes I go to bed alone, horny and frustrated, angry at myself for not being more assertive and coming on to a new man who excited me. Twice, I've even had very sweet "affairettes" with men who made their way to my home.

Frustration now and then is a small price to pay for the wonder of our open house. We've had visitors from six continents (no gay penguins from Antartica yet) and many, many countries. Friends from far away give our names and address to their friends who are visiting New York: it's a nice resource to have when you're coming to a big, strange, and sometimes scary city. And the diversity of men is extraordinary. On any given Saturday night, one may find a street transvestite in the same room with an Ivy League college professor; a nineteen-year old from Gay Youth and men in their fifties who joke about founding the gay gray panthers; heavy-duty politicos and men who have never been to a demonstration; men with thirty years of experience in gay life and others for whom our open house is the first time they've ever sat in a room with a *group* of homosexuals. As I said, it's a wonder, and it works. In almost five years, there have been only four guests whose behavior was so disruptive that we haven't wanted them to return.

Visitors from other cities sometimes say they'd like to start a similar thing. It occurred to me that you, reading this, might want to do the same, so here are a few observations about the elements that I think have contributed to its success.

First, Tony, David, and I like having people around, lots of people. If we didn't the whole thing would have collapsed a long time ago.

Second, we don't play "host." We don't worry about fancy meals, good china, and silverware (most of our dishes were given to me by an aunt who collected them from boxes of detergent). These are not piss-elegant gatherings. The whole atmosphere is very informal, casual, and effortless.

Third, you need space. Tony and I started in a big, five-room apartment; now we have a seven-room place.

Fourth, there's the absolute regularity and dependability of it. No one has to call in advance because everyone *knows* we will be there. You don't have to plan ahead, but can make a spontaneous decision that afternoon. If we shifted locations, or even did it on alternate Saturday nights, it wouldn't work.

Fifth, we've had a lot of help from our friends.

Sixth, I think it's important that we don't live in a gay neighborhood. Yes, you can decide on the spur of the moment to attend an open house, but it's still a decision, a thoughtful choice of how to spend the evening, because most of our friends don't live in our neighborhood and have to travel to get here. I don't think it would work if we lived on Christopher Street and people could just pop in between stops at Boots & Saddles and Kellers.

Finally, I don't think it's an accident that Tony and I, who started it, and most of the core group who sustain our open house, are socialists. We aren't satisfied just to have the institutions and spaces provided for gay men by a capitalist society. Our vision of the future, which certainly nourishes me and my commitment to our Saturday night gathering, is not just made up of "political" changes in the narrow sense, but of changes across the whole range of social institutions, including how human beings relate to one another.

I can't resist the temptation to close this with a message, a little bit of editorializing. Gay men come under a lot of attack in our society. I don't mean the attacks from John Briggs, Anita Bryant, and their ilk. I mean the attacks from our friends—from heterosexual allies, from some lesbians, and from lots of gay men who rant and rave about our "shallow" lives, our "promiscuous" behavior, our "anonymous" sex, our sexual "objectification" of each other. (Those are not the words I would choose to use anymore.) One gay male writer in *Gay Community News* not too long ago, for instance, lashed out at those of us who "wear our cocks on our sleeves."

Now, I suppose I could take our Saturday nights and use them as proof of how "good" some of us are, as evidence of how hard we're trying. But for me, and I'm only speaking for myself, doing that would miss the whole point. If you took a photograph of Christopher Street on a warm summer evening, you could use the picture, filled as it would be with handsome, attractive men, to prove that we're cruising our lives away. *I* might be in the picture; so might David, or Tony, or any one of the men who come to our Saturday gatherings.

But a photo is the wrong frame of reference. It can't possibly capture the variety of our experience, not because gay men are so different from one another (though that of course is true), but because *each one* of our lives contains so much variety. I enjoy our open house because I also have the baths at my disposal. And I can enjoy the baths as much as I do in part because I also have a weekly open house as another option. Each of us deserves, not a snapshot, but a moving picture with lots of scenes and thousands of frames to capture the full richness and variety of our lives. And we ought to value all of it.

# 16

# WOMEN AGAINST PORNOGRAPHY

## FEMINIST FRONTIER OR
## SOCIAL PURITY CRUSADE?

---

*Late in the 1970s, as an outgrowth of organizing efforts against violence against women, many feminists took up the issue of pornography. Supreme Court decisions restricting the scope of obscenity statutes as well as the larger cultural shift described as "the sexual revolution" had brought pornography out of an underground, shadowy world and into the light of day. Some feminists, enraged by the level of violence directed at women and seeing pornographic representations that seemed to dehumanize and objectify women, targeted pornography as a key causal agent of violence. In 1979, an organization called Women Against Pornography opened a storefront in New York City and began to campaign against porn. The New York group was just one of many that spread across the country at the end of the decade.*

*WAP offered a tour of Times Square as part of its effort to mobilize public sentiment against pornography. Several of us who were members of a study group on the history of sexuality took the tour together early in 1980. That experience motivated the essay which follows.*

*As the essay suggests, my response to WAP and to pornography was shaped by my experience as a gay man. Both terms are significant. As someone gay, I knew that gay life often took shape in pornographic zones, making that space precious for me. As a man, I also knew that in our culture the meaning and significance of pornography are deeply gendered: porn simply doesn't carry for me the aura of danger and disrespect that it does for many women. That fact is both virtue and defect. It allows me to view pornography from a different vantage point even as it might obscure other angles of vision.*

*Since this essay was written, the "sex wars" erupted among feminists. Some feminists took their organizing efforts beyond consciousness raising and education and sought passage of laws restricting the sale and distribution of pornography. Other feminists, heterosexual and lesbian both, dissented and instead tried to open a larger space within feminism in which issues of sexuality could be explored.* An abridged version of this article appeared in Christopher Street (May 1980).

I have a long history of association with Times Square. In 1963, at age fifteen, I went with friends to see my first Broadway play. I also saw my first homosexuals: three young men, thin as toothpicks, with long teased hair, mascara, rouge and powder on their faces, their fingers fluttering in front of them. I was terrified. I also began going to Broadway plays regularly.

The next year, I read James Baldwin's novel, *Another Country*, which confirmed for me that homosexuals were indeed to be found on Times Square. Since there was a limit to how many Broadway plays I could see, and since I had to explain my whereabouts to my parents, I became a weekly visitor at the public library on 42nd Street. I would race in, grab a few books from the shelves, and rush over to Seventh Avenue. I probably read more books during those years than at any time since.

In August 1965, after one of those trips to the library, I stood pretending to look in a shop window on 42nd Street, aware of the men passing by. One of them, unshaven (only bums, Beatniks, and Fidel Castro had hair on their faces in those days), stopped next to me and stared. Eight seconds later, I had a roaring hard-on and, with the summer temperature in the eighties, no coat to hide the protrusion from the eyes of others. I quickly looked away. I heard him mutter, "You know you want it, kid!" I was terrified.

Since I was slightly more fearful of being discovered on the streets with an erection than of being killed in a stranger's apartment, I went to his place in a nearby SRO (single-room occupancy) hotel. He told me he was a graduate of Brooklyn Prep, a Jesuit high school. Since I, too, went to a Jesuit high school, I felt a little bit better. We took our clothes off and unmade the bed. My memory of the experience, distorted perhaps by time, is that his body was extraordinarily handsome, tanned, hairy, thin, and muscular. As I think back, I'm sure he wanted to fuck me: I was on my back, he raised my legs in the air several times. Of course, I had no idea that men fucked, had no idea of anything men did together, other than kiss and touch each other. Every new touch or movement brought fear into my eyes. He must have seen it and understood, because he didn't fuck me. Instead, there was much kissing, touching, stroking, and licking of my body, head to toe, and a blow job that made me scream.

I often think about this man, to me an unkempt, menacing stranger on a street that represented all that was bad, illicit, sordid, and threatening, and thank him for his gentleness and intuitive appreciation of my vulnerability.

Over the years, the trips to Times Square decreased in frequency. I came out, discovered the Village, found a lover, fell into the gay liberation movement, went to the baths, had lots of sex, and lots of gay male friends. Who needed Times Square? There were cleaner, safer, more respectable places to find sex. Times Square wasn't *me*; it was *them*.

Sometime in the mid-1970s I went back to Times Square for "political" reasons. A pornographic film called *Snuff* was about to open, and the feminist grapevine claimed that a woman was actually dismembered, snuffed out, to make the film "real." No one ever confirmed that, but it was clear to me that even if simulated, killing a woman in order to arouse sexual desire in a male heterosexual audience was intolerable. I was part of an ad hoc group of men who supported the women leading the demonstrations. We leafleted in front of the offices of the distributor, rapping with people on the street, urging them to write in protest to the theater chain, and to the district attorney's office. I can remember how careful we were in defining the issue to passersby: No, we weren't opposed to the film because it was about sex; we objected to violence, and to the association of sex and violence. We were against the marketing of violence against women.

More recently, I returned to Times Square. Women Against Pornography, one of the newer feminist organizations in New York, has opened a storefront on Ninth Avenue and 42nd Street. They offer a forty-minute slide show of pornographic and mass media images of women and then take their audience on a tour of 42nd Street's bookstores and sex palaces.

I went because I have become increasingly concerned, confused, and angry by the issues of pornography and violence, *and* by what I've been reading about and by Women Against Pornography. I went because I find myself fuming against WAP constantly, arguing about it, condemning it in discussions with friends. I knew that in good conscience I should not do this with information gathered from second-hand sources. I had to see the show for myself, go on the tour, hear their rap, and find out what my old hunting ground was like these days.

About twenty of us were assembled in WAP's storefront on the night I took the tour—fifteen women (including three WAP members) and five men, all white, most in our twenties and thirties. I went with three friends, all of us members of a study group on the history of sex—one a gay man, another a lesbian, the third a straight woman. Two other women whom we knew, both members of a socialist-feminist group, also happened to be there that night.

WAP asks for a $5 contribution from everyone taking the tour. I didn't like the idea, but I put my money in the coffee can and sat down. The first thing I noticed was the huge chart on the wall, documenting how much money WAP has in its coffers and where it has come from. WAP has raised at least $5,000 in each of the last three months. The chart has an easy-to-read code to let you know who has given how much. There are names of women I know, women with whom I've shared political work. Of the handful of large contributors, three were Con Edison, Off-Track Betting, and the League of New York Theaters and Producers. I hadn't known they were such ardent supporters of feminism.

A short talk preceded the slide show. "We are doing this to show you what pornography is really like. Pornography is about violence against women. It's about brutality, humiliation, degradation, exploitation. It's about power and domination. It has nothing to do with sex. Erotica is about sex. We're about pornography. We're not against sex." Clear enough.

"The show includes some of the worst hard-core porn we could find. The images are disgusting; they incite violence against women; they're responsible for the rising tide of rape, wife-battering, and child abuse. Child porn is an increasingly popular genre. Do you know how common gonorrhea is among young girls? Pornography is having its effect!

"We've also interspersed slides of newspaper and magazine ads, record album covers, and billboards, that will show you how pornographic images have filtered into the media. This creates a climate where sexual violence against women is a pervasive presence, tolerated, encouraged, even considered chic."

The first slide is of a huge billboard from about three years ago, displayed on Sunset Boulevard, for the Rolling Stones' album, "Black and Blue All Over." It pictures a woman standing, legs apart, bruises all over her body, with the Stones grouped suggestively between her thighs. A WAP member tells us—and I remember the story—that when the billboard went up, Los Angeles feminists organized Women Against Violence Against Women, conducted leafleting, demonstrations, and zaps, and in a short time the billboard was taken down. More than that, she says that Warner Communications has reached a settlement with WAVAW and has promised not to use violent images to sell its merchandise. A great victory for the women's movement, she concludes. I nod in agreement. The billboard makes me angry. It enrages me that corporate America should market its goods through visual devices that legitimize violating women. It *is* a victory. It raises morale and raises consciousness. I would like us to achieve more of them.

Of the forty-odd slides in the presentation, a few disgusted me, made me sick and furious, and provoked a visceral reaction. Several were from *Hustler*, published by Larry Flynt (surely one of the most miserable cretins on the social scene). One was a cover showing a women being fed into a meat grinder, and coming out the other end as juicy, blood-red chopped beef. Two others showed women as main courses for dinner—a woman's naked body splattered with "ketchup" atop a hamburger role; another, her naked ass up, hands appearing between her thighs, resting on a bed of rice, a red sauce spread over her. The images made me want to kill. I wanted to burn copies of *Hustler* in Times Square. I wanted to bring back the Luddites and have them smash the presses.

There were others: a construction worker with a jackhammer, drilling into a woman's vagina (You don't actually see that, but there are two legs flung high in the air. It doesn't take much imagination to fill in the rest); a naked woman, smiling, thighs open, spreading her labia with two fingers, and holding a sharp knife to her genitals; another woman standing, all her limbs in splints, her body and head wrapped in bandages.

Several slides showed record album covers, reminiscent of the Rolling Stones' billboard. One was for the Pure Food and Drug Act and proffered a woman's ass, stamped "Choice Cut." Zap 'em, I thought.

But most of the show, the vast majority of the slides, and the rap that went with it, left me alternately yawning and outraged at the puerile level of the "analysis." Men and women fucking. So what? Women in poses of bondage, so obviously simulated and contrived that I wondered how great an effort was required to make this material suitable for fantasy.

Then, their clinchers. Child porn flashed on the screen: a man fucking a young girl in the ass.

"Wait a minute," says one of the women in the audience. "That's no child! She's got the same body I do. I'm twenty."

"The pictures are deceptive," the WAP member snaps back. "Kiddie porn like this encourages men to molest young girls. A man sees a picture like this of a girl being raped, and it becomes permissible for him to do the same."

"Wait a minute," says my friend, a woman who has written about rape and has been active in the antirape movement. "What makes you say this is rape?" The woman is not tied, nor held down by the man. Their clothes are off, and they're lying on a bed with the covers drawn back, clean white sheets showing.

"She's underage, isn't she? That's statutory rape, isn't it? That makes it rape, doesn't it? Besides, she's being fucked in the ass which is humiliating, degrading and painful. It's rape!"

Humiliating? Painful? Do we now unite behind the missionary position? Are we advocating a Spic 'n Span model of human sexual behavior?

With the next slide, it was my turn to speak up. The image showed an

Alexander's ad, probably from the *Daily News*, with two young girls aged ten or so, in sweaters and pleated skirts, for $8.99, smiling, standing in poses that I supposed could be considered seductive.

"Here you see how the image of girls as sexual objects, to be used and exploited, filters into advertising."

"I'm confused," I say. "I thought you told us at the beginning that pornography was about violence and had nothing to do with sex, and that's why you're against it. And that erotica is about sex, and that's okay. There is *nothing* violent about that slide. I'm not even sure it's erotic."

"The connection is there. It's all part of the same thing. You can't really separate the two."

"Wait a minute," I continue. "Are you saying there's a causal connection between the spread of pornography in the 1970s and ads like this? I've been seeing similar ads for at least twenty years in the *News*. Besides, these ads are aimed at women, not men. They're meant to persuade *mothers* to buy clothes for their daughters. I don't understand what this slide has to do with pornography or with violence against women."

"We think there's a connection," she responds.

It continued to get worse. Like little children, we were told what we were seeing and what it meant. Time and again, there was little if any correspondence between what the WAP leaders told us and what I saw on the screen. Repeatedly, one or another member of the audience questioned the official line, only to get a rigid, unbending response. Zap 'em, I thought. This time I meant our hosts.


The time for our tour had arrived. We divided into two groups of ten, each with a guide, to make ourselves less conspicuous. Fat chance! My friends and I huddled together, maneuvering our way into the same group. We would make three stops: two sex emporiums and a bookstore.

We arrived at 42nd Street and Eighth Avenue, at the entrance to the first pleasure palace, flashing lights announcing nude girls and live sex shows inside. Our guide gives us instructions. She's bristling with anger and indignation as she warns us of the dangers inside. "We'll go in together. Stay in pairs. Don't get separated. Don't go downstairs. Watch out! Be careful."

We enter en masse and stride down a long corridor with carnival-colored lights flashing around us, rows of doorways on either side that lead into tiny 3' by 3' booths where for a quarter you can see the cheap flick advertised on each entrance. At the end is a barker, making his rap. It reminds me of the Danbury County Fair.

"Get your tokens here! Twenty-five cents each! We've got what you're looking for! Take your pick! See our flicks!

"Live sex shows downstairs! Lesbians making love! See what turns the pretty ladies on! What do they do? How do they do it? See for yourselves! Downstairs!"

We've reached the barker and already our guide has become entangled in a confrontation. The two are shouting at each other. Will we be allowed to stay? I'm starting to cringe. I can't resist the analogy with Carry Nation, swinging her axe, smashing the windows and bottles in saloons across America. These are dens of iniquity and we're facing the devil. There can be no compromise with evil, no time for reason. This is the enemy—the barker, his sidekicks, the patrons.

I decide that I can't go through with it. I'll take the tour, yes, but I will detach myself from the group, entering each place a few moments after everyone else, staying a couple of minutes longer, so that I'm free to wander around, sample the wares, blend in (?) with the rest of the patrons.

I spent more money than I had intended. I shopped carefully, taking my cues from the titles and pictures at each booth's entrance, looking for the most offensive, the most violent, the most abusive. "Bust Her Cunt Open" and "Child Bride" seemed among the most likely candidates.

I was surprised by what I saw. The cheaply made films were all rather innocuous. Hard-core sex, that is, fucking on a bed, was preceded by making out on a sofa. My couple started with their clothes on, casually but neatly dressed, smiles on their faces, touching, kissing, fondling one another. They undressed each other slowly, almost sensuously. No clothes ripped off, no women flung onto beds and held down. In another, a nurse enters a hospital ward carrying a tray of food. A male patient has a shit-eating grin on his face. She approaches the bed, puts down the tray, pulls back the sheet. He has an erection. She smiles. As for the child porn, the "girl," as in the slide show, was a young woman, perhaps in her late teens, maybe even older. My random sample uncovered no violence, only sex. Erotica, not pornography.

In fairness, of course, I only saw a tiny part of what was available. Each of the places we toured had dozens of booths and I only had time for four films. One of the women on the tour did see a bondage film, with a woman stretched on a rack. I suspect there were many others like it that none of us happened to see.

I looked at the customers. I was struck by how oblivious they all seemed to the presence of a group of white, middle-class women on their turf. They appeared intent, preoccupied with the business at hand. A wide variety of men was there, but mostly I focused on how ordinary they seemed, like salesmen from the Bronx, bookkeepers from Brooklyn, social workers, teachers, unemployed youths. The kind of men you see on the subways during rush hour reading the *Daily News*, the young working-class guys who hang out in my neighborhood on street corners. The enemy? Menacing?

Several offered me drugs—THC, smoke, acid—good and cheap. Another, as I was about to enter a booth, put his hand on my arm and said, "No—don't bother," and pointed to the one three doors down. "That one's really hot!" One guy comes up to me on the street.

"Grass?"

"No thanks."

"Where you from? Canada?"

"No. Here."

"Where? Buffalo?"

"No. New York. The Bronx."

"Yeah? Where?"

"Parkchester."

"Hey! I'm from Gun Hill Road."

"No kidding."

We arrived at the bookstore. I couldn't believe it: piles and piles of magazines on top of cheap wooden tables, in the middle, on the sides, in the back, the front of the store. Thousands of them, tens of thousands. I didn't know there were *that* many. My eye spots a sign, "Bondage Section," above a rack of thin paperbacks, and I head straight for it. It was pretty hard for me to take. I looked at one, set in a Nazi concentration camp, and another, in a prison, with a woman being gang-raped. I was angry. Concentration camps were no joke, the sexual fantasies lived by the ss guards nothing one should ever imitate. Ditto for gang rape and prisons. I remember the late 1960s, when I was still closeted, and recall my involvement in campus radical activities and the antiwar movement. I remember how careful I was never to put myself in a situation that would lead to arrest and jail. I *knew* what would happen to me in prison—gang rape. It happens to women in other places, lots of places. For a moment, I stop caring about the distinction between fantasy and reality. These books are real. If there are male psyches turned on by concentration camps, they'll have to excite their fantasies without the props of books—material objects—conceived, written, produced, and distributed in the real world, the one that I live in.

I turn away and go to the piles of magazines. I'm back to the ordinary stuff, pictures of cock, ass, cunt, tits, sucking, and fucking. I can't help thinking there must be an awful lot of sexual deprivation if this actually turns someone on. The pictures are so boring that I start reading the text that accompanies them: "The Kinsey study of male sexual behavior discovered that American men have a wide variety of outlets for their sexual needs. Though heterosexual outlets are the most common and the most acceptable, a surprisingly large portion of American males turn to the less acceptable but also enjoyable homosexual outlet."

We buzzed among ourselves as we headed back to the storefront. For most, the tour wasn't what they had expected. The aura of danger, menace, mystery that surrounded Times Square had dissolved. It was no longer scary. A little weird perhaps, incomprehensible maybe, innocuous even, but certainly not threatening. If nothing else, WAP was accomplishing one good thing.

At the office we arranged the chairs in a circle, consciousness-raising style, to share our reactions to the slide show and the tour. One of the guides suggested we just go around the circle, one at a time. She picks someone to start, my friend, the feminist anthropologist. "Well, it really demystified Times Square for me. It all seemed so ordinary, so insignificant. I saw almost nothing that I would call violence. Just a lot of material for fantasy. Actually, I was disappointed. I thought I'd find it erotic.

"The slide show really bothered me. You're throwing together a lot of very different things that have different sexual meanings and you're calling it all violence when in fact it . . ."

She hardly had the chance to finish when one of the WAP members launched into the party line, arguing, dismissing, and invalidating my friend's perceptions. I wondered how many other tours there had been where disagreement was squelched by the sharp responses of WAP "experts." I intervened: "I think it would be good if we went around the circle first and gave everybody a chance to speak before we have discussion. And *not* comment on what people say. That way it will be safer for all of us to put out what we really think, whatever it is."

That night the deck was stacked. The first six people to speak were the members of my study group and our two feminist acquaintances. Though each of us had unique emotional responses to what we observed, we all expressed discomfort with the obvious disjuncture between what we had seen on Times Square and WAP's absolutist claim that pornography equals violence. Many of us also took issue with the slide show. Here, one would have expected the worst since WAP members could choose whatever they wanted. But much of it wasn't violent either. Worse, they were lumping together a variety of phenomena, blurring distinctions (especially their loudly touted one between pornography/violence and erotica/sex), assuming causal connections, ignoring the difference between fantasy and reality. Almost two-thirds of the group came back from the tour with serious reservations about WAP, and with questions that cried out for answers. In the discussion that followed, our tour leaders were not open to the reservations; their answers to our questions did not inspire confidence.

Coming on the heels of the tour and the slide show, their responses convinced me that Woman Against Pornography is at best misguided and at worst downright dangerous. The only thing that keeps me from settling on the latter is that WAP's act is so untogether, the contradictions so manifest, that I believe it will collapse of its own weight. I cannot believe there are that many feminists whose second thought will allow them to support WAP.

"Pornography equals violence equals pornography." The equation gets repeated ad nauseam. When you confront WAP with the evidence of your own eyes, that you saw very little violence, members deny your claims. Pornography is violent, leads to violence. Inexorably, like the headwaters of the Mississippi flowing southward toward the Gulf, every image, every word, leads irresistibly to the same outcome—violence against women.

"A *social* definition of pornography exists in America," one of my women friends tells our guide. "WAP may claim that pornography is about violence and that's why you oppose it, but tens of millions of Americans who hate pornography think differently. For them, pornography means sex." The response: "I guess we have a lot of educational work to do."

WAP travels to towns and suburbs in the tristate area. They present their slides, tell their audience that pornography exists in their own backyard, in bookstores and supermarkets, and that they should *do* something about it. Then they leave. What kind of educational work is this? Will WAP return when *Gay American History, Rubyfruit Jungle*, and *Dancer from the Dance* disappear from the shelves?

Across America there is a growing backlash against the women's movement and against gay liberation. Abortion, the ERA, and gay rights are biting the dust. WAP claims that it would never form coalitions with right-wing groups or solicit their support. I believe WAP is sincere in saying this. I also believe that in this case sincerity doesn't count for much. Regardless of its professed intentions, WAP plays into the hands of the right.

Times Square is a cheap target. The weight of city government, the power of the banks, corporations, and real estate interests in New York, are devoted to cleaning up Times Square. That includes the *New York Times* with its own large property holdings that would skyrocket in value if the area were porn-free. No wonder that the *Times* gives more sympathetic and substantial coverage to WAP's march of 5,000 against pornography than it does to the lesbian and gay rights march of 100,000 in Washington, D.C.

"Pornography is a $4 billion industry," WAP informs us. "It's big business." The figures does not impress me. In an economy that measures gross national product in the trillions, four billion is peanuts, a fraction of one percent. It's nineteenth-century competitive capitalism.

The big money lies elsewhere, with NBC and CBS, with United Artists and Warner Communications and MCA. On television, in the movies, on record covers, and in songs can be found the images and words that daily reach the majority of the American people. It is far more insidious than pornography, since the mass media pose as real life. The shield of fantasy is removed.

Why isn't WAP out there targeting those products of corporate America? Why aren't they picketing the theaters showing *Time after Time*, a quaint Hollywood film with a nifty idea—H.G. Wells chasing Jack the Ripper through time in Wells's own time machine, landing in San Francisco in 1979. On the screen are women, white and black, in offices, discos, on the street, punished for being sexual, slashed from neck to thigh, strangled, mutilated, dismembered. *Time after Time* has a PG rating.

Last summer, the gay male community of New York did target one of those products in the making, the film *Cruising*. The issue behind the protests was not sex, but violence. The city's daily press didn't like the demonstrators. They babbled on about the First Amendment and censorship while we talked about our lives being on the line. I wonder how the press would change its tune toward Women Against Pornography if WAP's focus shifted from Times Square to the first-run movie houses on the fashionable East Side, or corporate offices on the Avenue of the Americas.

What's in a name? In this case, plenty. There are other feminist groups concerned about violence, with names like Women Against Violence Against Women. The name defines the issue. It allows members, and potential recruits, at least to be clear about the problem (if not the solution), and to develop strategies that focus on the real menace—not pornography, but violence against women.

Women Against Pornography is about sex, not violence. We live in a society that's antisex to its core. It's also sex-obsessed. At the center of each of us is a hard rock of sex-negative attitudes so much a part of us that it escapes our notice. WAP may claim to be about violence, but what I saw and heard in its office convinced me that what's been unleashed in the women who are involved is the hatred and fear of sex that we've all internalized.

I am angry, angry because I am witnessing another "clean up Times Square" effort, an antisex movement, a new social purity campaign, masquerading under the guise of something that's been profoundly important in my life—feminism.

America has had social purity campaigns before. Purity advocates of the Victorian era had many targets, and included in their ranks feminists and antifeminists. The feminist wing of the movement, motivated by anger over how the "double standard" victimized women, wanted to make men conform to the higher morality of the female sex. History does not record many lasting achievements for them. Another purity advocate, Anthony Comstock, fared much better. He won passage of a comprehensive federal antiobscenity statute that is still the law of the land. He also instigated the arrest of Victoria Woodhull and Tennessee Claflin, two champions of women's rights and proponents of free love who deplored the double standard but who, unlike the more conservative feminists of the era, fought for a thoroughly revised sexual morality for *both* sexes. WAP would do well to reflect upon this bit of our past.

There is a relationship in our society between sex and violence. There is, too, a relationship between pornography and violence. And, also, a relationship between violence and almost every other phenomenon in our culture—sports, childrearing, political activism, the school system, street life.

I don't know exactly what the relationship is, but I do know it is not simple. It is not a one-to-one relationship, not one of direct causality. The relationship is subtle and complex, not simple.

One of the complexities that can't be ignored is that the relationship between sex and violence is experienced differently by different groups of people. As a man, my experience is not the same as a woman's. I could detach myself from the tour group to explore Times Square on my own. The male patrons of the area didn't hassle me. I was one of them. Women can't do that. I also don't suffer from the constant sexual harassment, the aggressiveness of heterosexual males, the presumption that my body is available to be taken, the ever-present fear of sexual assault. If I did, I might also have the same emotional response to pornography that the members of WAP have.

However, I'm also a *gay* man, which distinguishes my experience from that of women in another way. One of the benefits of our oppression, one of the results of being a "sexual outlaw," as John Rechy has described our status, is that I've had a range of sexual experiences, a freedom to explore sex, that most men and women will never have. Sex doesn't scare me; it isn't the great unknown. I've learned—through doing—that much of what our culture calls bad, degrading, humiliating, dehumanizing, isn't that at all. In fact, it can be fun!

Violence is a serious problem. Women experience it all the time, as a threat and as something all too real. Much of the violence *is* sexual; we must do something about it.

Violence is also real within the gay male community. Much of it is external, perpetrated on *us*, by *them*. But much of it we do to ourselves. We do often violate each other's bodies, in the name of sex, in the service of what turns us on. It bothers me a lot. I would like us to do something about it.

I would like us to talk more among ourselves about sex, beyond trading stories of what we did on Saturday night, beyond saying that gay is good, not bad. We, too, have that hard rock of sex-negative attitudes inside us, no matter how many cocks we've sucked, or asses we've fucked, no matter how relaxed we are when we lie on our stomachs in the baths, our anuses twitching with expectation, no matter how liberated we've each become or how much we've changed over the years. It affects us all the time, affects our fantasies, our feelings, our sexual behavior. We need to question it all, to scrutinize ourselves, imagine together a future and a sexuality that we're proud to call our own.

I don't know what that sexuality will look like. I have no idea of the variety of sexual behavior we will someday embrace when we live in a sex-positive society. I don't know whose visions to trust. I am suspicious of anything that smacks of a "healthy" sexuality. But one thing I do know. I will have more confidence in those who have explored what American culture calls pornographic, who have dabbled in the kinky, the dirty, the sexual fringe, and who can laugh with joy and delight as they talk about it, than I will have in those whose backs become stiff when they talk about Times Square.

Despite my recent reunion with my old hunting ground, I doubt that Times Square and I will renew our former intimate relationship. It's not where my action is. I do, however, continue to patronize establishments that most of America would wish to expunge. My sex life, according to the definitions of many, is pornographic. Occasionally, in the evenings, I wend my way down Amsterdam Avenue to 74th Street and enter a small store called "It's a Man's World." The windows and door are painted yellow to shield the interior from the eyes of passersby. Inside the 12' by 12' shop, with its glass display cases and magazine racks, one can buy dildos, vibrators, bottles of amyl, tubes of lubricant, cheap pulp paperbacks, and the *Advocate*.

I plop $1.50 on the counter and head for the turnstile that leads to the back. It's dark here. There's a juke box, filled with the latest disco hits, and five wooden cubicles, large enough for two men standing. Each one has a porn film. In an open one a fortyish man stands, lips parted slightly, beckoning to me. He's sexy, but I'm not warmed up yet. I go into an empty booth to see a film. Two college buddies have spent the afternoon studying. One goes to take a shower before an evening date. The other sneaks in and soon the two of them—blond, with taut muscles and washboard stomachs—are having sex in the shower, alternately fucking and sucking each other.

I've seen a lot of these flicks. None of them have ever been violent, that is, there's been no coercive use of physical force for the purpose of getting sex. Many of them do involve what might be called aggressive sexuality, one man concentrating the full power of his physical strength on another man's body on the way toward orgasm.

Behind a curtain is another room. It's even darker here, and at a distance of more than a few feet you can't make out the faces of the men. There are cigarette butts all over the floor. Under my foot, I can feel something sticky, the not-yet-dry cum of one of the patrons. The late November chill doesn't penetrate here. The air is hot, stifling. There is little movement. Fifteen or so men stand around, silently, a few with thumbs in the pockets of their jeans, their fingers tapping their thighs, or stroking their crotches.

I weave through them slowly. In one corner a man is on his knees. Another man is grasping his skull, holding it steady, and thrusting his cock rapidly, rudely, into the open mouth. I remember seeing sex like this in some of the films; probably these guys have seen the same film. I also remember going to Doctor Greenstein's when I was three. He held me down, threw my head back, and shoved a wooden tongue depressor down my throat. I screamed, kicked him in the groin, and almost puked. He hit me. My mother punched him. Cocks shoved into mouths remind me of Doctor Greenstein. They don't turn me on.

I move on. Along another wall are two men, shirts open, pants down below their knees, making out. I inch closer. Neither is conventionally handsome, one of them I wouldn't cruise on the street or in a bar. No doubt they've seen the same porn movies as the rest of us, thrusting cocks and all. But they're doing something different. It's sensuous. Deep, long kisses. Bodies swaying rhythmically to the voice of Jane Oliver crooning "He's so fine. Wish he were mine." Hands tracing the curves of soft buns.

I look for a while. Tentatively, I stroke the back of one man's neck, with two fingers. I run my hand through the other's hair. Neither pushes me away. My hand slides down a neck, past a shoulder, to a chest. Thumb and forefinger find a nipple and squeeze. "Ahhh!" I squeeze a little harder.

I'm no longer an outsider. Bodies shift position to incorporate me. We huddle, football style, arms around each other's shoulders, heads close, tongues and mouths meeting. Saliva drips to the floor. My pants come down. We touch and stroke all over. We bite and suck. We're making noises.

A circle of men has formed around us. They're watching us intently. This is hot. But no one moves in, no one touches us. Our energy is high, but it's a closed system. Intuitively, the others respect our space.

How long can we continue without cuming? Our threesome goes on for over an hour. One set of patrons has left, a new shift has arrived. We start to laugh. "Let's go," one of us says. We take a cab to 93rd Street, to one of our apartments, and play for several hours until all of us reach orgasm. From porn shop to bed, the rhythm was unbroken.

# 17

# THE NAMES PROJECT QUILT

## A PEOPLE'S MEMORIAL

———————————

*No one who went to Washington over the Columbus Day weekend for the national march for lesbian and gay freedom will ever forget the event. For seventy-two hours the District of Columbia was transformed into one huge gay urban space as hundreds of thousands of us converged on the city. There were endless meetings in which activists networked, and several memorable public events: a mass wedding for lesbian and gay couples outside the National Cathedral; a "Town Meeting" on sex and politics sponsored by the National Gay and Lesbian Task Force and packed to the rafters; the civil disobedience in front of the Supreme Court to protest the* Hardwick *decision; and the march itself, which drew over half a million people.*

*Of all the events of that weekend, the unveiling of the Names Project Quilt, a memorial to those who had died from* AIDS, *touched me most deeply. What follows is a letter that I wrote to a friend several months after the event, when the publication of a book about the quilt had reminded me of its emotional power. The friend to whom I wrote is a heterosexual man, a labor organizer from the 1930s and 1940s, with whom I have been "in dialogue" for several years about gay issues.*

Dear Harvey,

I meant to write to you about the Names Project Quilt when I saw it in Washington, D.C., last October at the march in support of gay rights. Now, the project has published a book about the quilt which I've bought and have been using to work through some of the accumulated grief from this epidemic. It's the finest, most inspiring, and most exciting activist endeavor that I've encountered in years—the sort of thing that gives one renewed hope and faith in people and their ability to respond creatively to the most awesome challenges.

The Names Project was the brainchild of a San Francisco gay activist. I met Cleve about ten years ago, at an especially critical moment in the life of the San Francisco gay community (Harvey Milk had been assassinated and there had been riots in the city when his killer received the lightest possible sentence from a jury). I was impressed by a very special quality that Cleve had. He knew how to reach people *exactly* where they were, and move them forward. He did this in conversation on a one-to-one level, but he could also do this with large groups, even a whole community. Cleve could take the frustration, or the despair, or the cynicism of a group, reach inside, and turn it into positive, constructive, committed energy directed toward liberation work.

The Names Project is one more example of that quality, except that this time it's operating at a national level, involving tens of thousands of people from all walks of life, from every group in the population. (It has reached even larger numbers.) Cleve had seen his circle of friends and, indeed, the whole San Francisco gay male community, more than decimated by the AIDS epidemic. The hopefulness of the 1970s, when gay men and lesbians throughout the United States were moving effectively against oppression, seemed to be evaporating as people were caught in a tight web of grief, terror, despair, and self-destructive frustration because of the endless number of deaths and the mounting caseloads of ill people. The Names Project was a way to grieve publicly and collectively, to affirm the value of the lives of those who had died, and to call attention to the severity of the epidemic. People were invited to make a quilt, three feet by six feet, for someone they knew who had died. And all the individual quilts would be sewn together into one giant memorial, to be displayed on the mall in Washington the weekend of the gay rights march. By the time of the march there were three thousand panels, enough to cover two football fields.

The ceremony, if that's the right word, at which the quilt was laid out was memorable. A huge rectangular canvas frame was spread out between the Capitol and the Washington Monument. It was crisscrossed with paths of canvas, creating large squares of grass big enough to hold thirty-two individual quilts stitched together. Precisely at dawn, there began a simple reading of names, eight at a time: as each group of eight names was spoken, volunteers unwrapped a panel of eight quilts. Three hours later, when all the names had been read, this magnificently varied work of people's art, of collective caring and commemoration, was spread out under the morning sun.

I was there for much of the reading of names. At any given moment, there were probably two thousand people there, listening and watching. Several times I heard the names of men whom I'd known, and cried. Others around me were holding one another, crying when a familiar name was read, or because the respectful crowd provided the safety to grieve openly about losses they'd experienced. When the quilt was completely laid out, there were a few moments of silence, and then we were all allowed to walk through the canvas paths, searching for familiar names, stopping to admire the love and creativity that went into the making of each panel. The crying intensified. At any one moment, probably several hundred people were having one of the most deeply cathartic healing experiences of their lives. I was awestruck at how profound a memorial this was, at the wisdom behind the idea. Instead of individual, silent, pent-up grief, the quilt had made it possible for grief to be shared, released, and finished with in a collective fashion— and for the lives of those who had died to be remembered with dignity and respect. A few hours later, half a million people marched against gay oppression and for a more vigorous government response to the AIDS epidemic.

Since then, a few thousand additional panels have been made. The idea has obviously tapped into some deeply felt emotions. The book that's just been published tells the story behind the Names Project and many of its panels, and also is liberally illustrated. Some of the panels are exquisitely beautiful, complex works of art, revealing on fabric the personality and history of one person's life. Others get their power from the utter simplicity, even starkness, of their design. One of them, which seems to strike a powerful lode of old feelings in me, is a black piece of fabric with a name in bold white letters, and an image of swirling galaxies. An arrow points to the very center and the phrase "you are here" hangs above it. I cry every time I see the image. One of the quilts was made by the staff of a university library. A colleague had died of AIDS, and the day after his death, every member of the staff received a yellow rose and a personal note from their deceased coworker. For weeks after, they gathered over lunch in a conference room, making the quilt, sharing memories, and achieving a level of intimacy and openness that must be unusual for any workplace. Imagine how fine a place it must be in which to work.

Many of the stories are inspiring. There is instance after instance of friends, families, lovers, neighbors, and coworkers pulling together to care for the sick, trying to make the last days of life and an impending death as decent as possible. There is nothing good about this epidemic, but the response that it is generating is heroic, and is bringing out the best in many people. There are also stories that reveal how heavy the stigma of AIDS is, and how deeply entrenched gay oppression and homophobia are. One panel was made by a young woman for her gay father.

She'd written her father's name on it, but the rest of the family objected. So, she blocked it out and simply spray-painted the phrase "Love you, Daddy," across the panel.

Reading the book seems to generate endless hours of emotional release. There is enough hope and heroism in its pages that I don't seem to need to have a counselor with me. The book is enough. Some of the grief is for friends who've died of AIDS, but there's more to it than that. The hours and hours of crying that I've done have given me a new, still-evolving perspective on death. I'm pretty sure there is some grieving that needs to be done over a loved one's death, but how much depends a lot on the relationship. If the relationship was in good shape, the grieving will be sharp and heavy and sustained, but clearly finite. But if there were issues left unresolved, if the relationship was off in some important ways, the crying feels as if it's a bottomless pit. I have a new appreciation for the importance of not leaving things unsaid, of expressing my loving and caring openly, in the here and now, when someone is alive to enjoy it.

The Names Project has also given me a much clearer understanding of why I write the kind of history I do—social history, a history of ordinary lives and of their efforts to change their world, rather than the history of the rich and powerful. The quilts are creating a permanent record of "ordinary" Americans. We all deserve that kind of memorial, that sliver of immortality. Every life is precious, and the Names Project demonstrates it so dramatically: a disease that carries the weight of so much stigma and oppression cannot compromise this simple truth.

# 18

# YOU CAN'T BUILD A MOVEMENT ON ANGER

---

*In contrast to the constructive, healing way in which the Names Project Quilt has allowed us to feel our grief and then move on from it, the "War Conference" which was held outside of Washington, D.C., in February 1988 was drenched in a politics of rage. In the opening paragraph of this essay I describe the outcome of the conference in vague and generalized positive terms, more out of an unwillingness at the time to trash fellow activists in print than out of my experience of the event. The gathering, hastily organized to plan a strategy for the "war" that was being waged against us, was an unpleasant experience, and was saved from being a complete disaster only because of the informal networking that went on in the course of the weekend.*

*The War Conference crystallized for me half-formed thoughts I had been having for a long time about the play of feelings and emotions in social movements—the gay movement as well as others. We are without question feeling and emotion-laden beings. Some of those feelings are high-spirited and should be enjoyed for all they are worth. Others are painful and potentially debilitating. These, too, need to be felt, but then left behind, so that we can go on with our lives. To use our pain as the foundation for thinking and strategizing about social change and social justice will only create a movement grounded in distress rather than based on visionary possibilities.*

*A number of gay and lesbian newspapers across the country asked to reprint this piece after it first appeared in* Gay Community News *of Boston. It spoke, I suspect, to what many of us had been thinking.*

Reprinted from *Gay Community News* (June 19, 1988).

At the "War Conference" that was held last February near Washington, D.C., two hundred lesbian and gay leaders from around the country put our heads together to assess the state of our movement and look to the future. The conference has been criticized, and rightly so, for its inadequate outreach to people of color and to women. Still, whenever that many sharp, experienced, and committed activists get together, good things are bound to happen. The energy level was high, the tone was by and large cooperative and optimistic, and lots of fine thinking was done.

· There was a motif that kept recurring through the weekend, and that's stayed with me since then. The motif wasn't new or startling, but I heard it in a new way. Again and again, in the midst of working groups or strategy sessions, someone would say, "But where's our anger? They're out there killing us—through disease, violence, or neglect—and we're sitting here talking politely about strategy and thinking of 'nice' things to do. Where's our anger? Where's our rage?" As I said, it's not a brand new idea. It's been said many times before, including by me. But this time when I heard it, and as I've thought about it since, I realized that I couldn't disagree more. I'm convinced that political strategies based on anger—or any other kind of emotion—are recipes for failure.

My reasons for saying this may become clearer if we think for a minute about some of the feelings other than rage that are common to our lives. Take grief and sadness, for instance. For the last few years, tidal waves of grief have swept over our communities as lovers, friends, neighbors, coworkers, and acquaintances have died of AIDS. Grief has become a pervasive part of our lives. We are learning all sorts of creative ways to acknowledge and express it, from bereavement groups and community memorial services to the Names Project, and we need to keep doing this in order not to sink under the weight of our own sadness. But do we want to base our movement on it? Do we want to develop a political strategy based on grief to end our oppression? Of what use would such a strategy, distorted by the paralyzing despair that death engenders, be? Not very useful, I suspect.

What about fear and terror? Terror entered my life the moment I became aware that I was gay, and it has remained a more or less prominent feature of my consciousness ever since. Fear, as a teenager, that I'd be arrested, blackmailed, or in some way publicly humiliated or exposed. Fear, in college and right after, that somehow my life would be ruined if word got out. Despite the fact that I have been publicly visible for the last fifteen years, I still experience fear when I come out in new situations, or when I take the time to notice just how visible I am. Where would I be if I let gay terror serve as my guide for action? How much progress would the movement have made if we let it be shaped by the numbing fear that life in a violently oppressive society generates?

At first glance, anger appears different. It's healthy. It's not an emotion based on victimization, but a sign of life, strength, and a determination to fight back, right? I'm not so sure. I think rage is as much a sign of how much we've been hurt as is grief and terror. Were there not wrongs done to us and those we love, we'd have nothing to be angry about. And just as sadness and fear are not reliable guides to political strategizing, neither is anger.

The experience of the black movement in the 1960s and the feminist movement in the 1970s has a lot to tell us about the political dangers of mobilizing around rage. In the early 1960s, blacks built an extraordinarily broad-based movement. Sit-ins, freedom rides, mass marches, community-wide mobilizations, national boycotts, court litigation, and legislative lobbying made racial justice, for a time, the central issue in American life. Careful, thoughtful, reasoned strategizing lay behind it all.

The resistance was intense. Especially in the Deep South, blacks faced police brutality, Klan night-riders, beatings, bombings, and shootings. Eventually, the violence reshaped the movement as some black activists began to mobilize on the basis of rage.

That may have been emotionally satisfying for some, but it was also politically suicidal. Militants in SNCC (the Student Nonviolent Coordinating Committee) and the Black Panthers found themselves cut off from the rest of the movement. The rhetoric of rage alienated many former supporters and paralyzed others. Angry, impassioned calls to pick up the gun in self-defense lost for the movement the mantle of moral superiority that had been so potent a force in the early 1960s. Violence directed at the movement mounted, but now, instead of provoking public outrage, it could be justified as necessary for restoring order. Strategies and tactics that evolved out of unthinking rage helped cripple a movement that only a few years before had been on the offensive.

Rage also reshaped the women's movement in the late 1970s. After the initial upsurge of feminism, many women took on issues of sexual violence—rape, battering, abuse, incest. Laws were changed, public consciousness raised, and institutions such as shelters were created. But, dealing with the survivors of sexual violence day after day took its toll. Many feminists active in the antiviolence movement were living in a state of constant rage. And it began to affect their thinking about issues and strategy. From a campaign against violence came the feminist campaigns against pornography, with an overarching, simplistic analysis that defined porn as the source of the problem. The antiporn wars gave sustenance to the Christian New Right, spawned internecine warfare among feminists, and created its own kind of political casualties.

To me the lessons seem clear. A politics of rage weakens and destroys its proponents and their cause more effectively than it weakens and destroys an oppressive system. Movements for social justice cannot be based on painful emotion, whether it be grief, terror, or rage. Yes, we have to feel these things. The feelings have real causes. And, yes, we need to find ways to support one another through it all. But a movement that mobilizes a constituency on the basis of pain will end up feeling its way to despair, disillusionment, and, ultimately, failure. I would much prefer that we think our way to success.

# 19

# A GENERATION OF PROGRESS

---

*History can be presented in many different ways and put to many different uses. I was asked to give the opening keynote address at NGLTF's 1988 Creating Change Conference a few months after I wrote the previous essay on anger. Because issues about the relationship between emotions and social movements were on my mind, I decided to give a speech that would take my knowledge of the movement's history and shape it to appeal to the best in my audience. In reminding us in clear unambiguous terms of how much we had accomplished, I intended to generate feelings of pride, confidence, and hope—a frame of mind that I believe necessary if we expect to keep moving forward.*

Let me begin by acknowledging that we are living through complex, confusing, and contradictory times:

> —Six hundred thousand lesbians, gay men, and supporters march on Washington and engage in massive civil disobedience in front of the Supreme Court and, that same week, the Senate almost unanimously passes the homophobic Helms Amendment;

—Congress appropriates record funds to fight AIDS but, at the last minute, deletes provisions to protect confidentiality;

—Our community supports political action committees that are better organized and better funded than ever before, yet the election results are very likely giving us all nightmares;

—Four years from now we may very well have a Supreme Court that will be rewriting the Constitution, but not to our liking.

If I didn't at least acknowledge this difficult, bewildering political climate, you'd be right in labeling me a fool. But having said this, I would like to put the evidence of gloom and doom aside, and spend the rest of my time reminding us of what we have accomplished.

I make this choice for a reason. I do not think there is any danger that we will forget what we are up against. But I think we can easily forget how well we're doing. We need to remember our successes.

I find myself increasingly disturbed by a tendency which has grown throughout the 1980s to evaluate the state of the gay and lesbian movement negatively—to look at the Reagan years, the New Right, the AIDS epidemic, the defeat of the ERA, the *Hardwick* decision, the questioning of the sexual revolution, as incontrovertible evidence of defeat, of loss, of disarray, of failure.

That's not how I see things. Perhaps because I am a historian as well as an activist, I can't separate my sense of the present from my knowledge of the past. And so this morning, I want to review the progress, the change, the achievements, that a generation of gay and lesbian activists have wrought. I will review progress in four areas, using two special moments in gay political history as my markers of change. One of these will be familiar to all of you—1969, the year of the Stonewall Riot in New York City, the birth of gay liberation. The other is probably less familiar—1950, the year of the founding of the Mattachine Society in Los Angeles, which initiated an unbroken line of gay activism in the United States.

## CONSCIOUSNESS AND SELF-AFFIRMATION

One area of enormous progress has been in gay and lesbian consciousness, in our sense of ourselves and our identity, and in the resources available for self-affirmation.

225

In 1950, the resources for affirming gay and lesbian experience were minuscule. There was the Kinsey report on male sexual behavior: a huge tome, with charts, graphs, and tables, that received enormous play in the media. In seemingly nonjudgmental language, surrounded by the authority of science, Kinsey said that millions of American men—from every class, region, educational level, and religious background—engaged in homosexual behavior. To Kinsey there was nothing unnatural or inherently pathological about it. In fact, he suggested that were it not for the prohibitions against homosexual behavior, there would probably be more of it in American society.

There were a few novels: classics such as *The Well of Loneliness*, which a generation of lesbians had read, which gave a name to feelings, and which conjured up images that might be used to shape one's own experience.

But, in everyday life, the organs of heterosexual culture were either silent or else they presented a message that was overwhelmingly negative in its content. This was the era when the holy trinity of sin, sickness, and criminality reigned supreme, when the heterosexual majority possessed a seemingly unbreakable monopoly of control over the images of us that did filter into American society. It is hard today to imagine just how complete the silence was, and it is sobering to reflect upon how corrosive to one's self-image that could be.

Between 1950 and 1969, the homophile movement began to challenge the silence. Small and fragile though these pioneer gay and lesbian organizations were, they knew how important the printed word was, and so they devoted scarce resources to publishing magazines: *Mattachine Review*, the *Ladder*, *ONE* magazine. The press runs were small, but the circulation was much larger, as precious copies were passed from hand to hand. These magazines made a tremendous difference, as the letters to the editor reveal. When you have so little, one issue can be a lifeline.

In the 1960s, a little more space opened up. It became fashionable for magazines, newspapers, and television to do an occasional feature on gay life. The content tended to be negative; the participants were often presented in shadows, or seated behind potted palms (I've often heard the story, perhaps apocryphal, of a Los Angeles show in which the men and women appeared with paper bags over their heads!), but they nonetheless served as road maps to the geography of the gay world. Passing mention of Greenwich Village, or North Beach, or Hollywood, might easily impel a young reader to move to where there were others.

The movement was also becoming newsworthy by the mid-1960s. A few brave souls held small demonstrations or set up picket lines in Washington, Philadelphia, and New York. To see something like that on the evening news in 1965 could change a gay man's or lesbian's life.

Finally, there were major breakthroughs in the realm of literature. The obscenity decisions of the Warren Court were making it easier to write about homosexuality and get into print. The genre of lesbian pulp novels exploded: upwards of a hundred were being published yearly, available in your local drugstore. In mainstream literature, too, gay and lesbian characters were making more frequent appearances. I remember my own experience, as a fifteen-year-old adolescent in 1964, reading James Baldwin's novel *Another Country*. There was a moment of exhilarating—and also terrifying—recognition as I was finally able to put a name to the feelings I had.

The resources for naming who we were, for finding something, anything, to grasp so that we could remain afloat, *were* growing in the 1960s. There was a maze that younger gay men and lesbians could thread their way through, till they found the prize at the center.

Since Stonewall, there has been a veritable explosion of things gay. Collectively we have created a vigorous lesbian and gay culture. We have our own newspapers, magazines, publishing houses, music companies, theater groups, and film collectives.

In the early 1960s, an industrious reader might very well be able to consume virtually everything of value that was published in a year. Today, that's impossible. It would be exhausting to plough through even a specific genre: gay male spiritual autobiographies; lesbian detective fiction; the psychology of couple relationships.

We have made change in the larger society, too. The early gay liberation movement recognized the power of the media; some of its first demonstrations after Stonewall were directed against institutions such as the *Village Voice*, the *San Francisco Examiner*, and *Harper's*. Now in the late 1980s, we have decisively cracked open the world of journalism and print, made some gains in broadcast, and fewer in film.

Admittedly, we do not yet control the content of what is written or projected about us. There is much that is still insufficient, and much that is negative and offensive. But today one has to work very, very hard *not* to find positive, self-affirming images. In Greensboro, North Carolina, a medium-sized city in the South, there is a gay and lesbian bookstore. In Thomasville, North Carolina—a very small town—a student of mine happened upon a copy of my book on the gay movement in the public library!

The point is: we have succeeded in broadcasting the message loudly and clearly that we are good, fine, intelligent, creative, excellent human beings, living viable, rewarding, and constructive lives. We have ended the silence that engulfed our lives, and we have broken the monopoly of control which *they* had over the discourse about *us*.

## ORGANIZATION AND COMMUNITY-
## BUILDING

A second area of enormous change has been in the growth and spread of gay and lesbian organizations.

Historians will probably keep finding evidence of efforts to form organizations in the past. But 1950 will always remain a critical year: it marked the founding of the Mattachine Society in Los Angeles, and from that moment on there has been an unbroken, continuous history of gay and lesbian political organizing in the United States.

The organizations of the 1950s—the Mattachine Society, the Daughters of Bilitis, ONE Inc.—were weak, fragile, and tenuous. They survived because of the stamina and commitment of a handful of people. They operated in an environment where they wondered whether it was even legal to meet. But they hung on, and the organizational impulse gradually spread.

On the eve of Stonewall, in 1969, after almost twenty years of organizing, there were still only about fifty gay groups. Most of them were in California and the Northeast, with a sprinkling of groups in the Midwest. They remained small. They had little influence outside of New York and San Francisco. Combined, they had perhaps two to three thousand members, and fewer than a couple of hundred of committed people.

Then came Stonewall, and the organizational landscape changed quickly and dramatically. By 1974, there were upwards of a thousand lesbian and gay organizations. Today, there are many, many thousands. The last two decades have witnessed an extraordinary, almost miraculous proliferation of organizations. These groups express the strength of our communities, help to expand our communities' reach, and deepen the bonds between us.

We have around us an incredible richness and variety of organization: political action groups, Democratic and Republican clubs, health organizations, newspapers and magazines, cultural institutions, community centers, businesses of many sorts, student groups, churches and synagogues, crisis hot lines, social service organizations, sport leagues, and many more. Gay men and lesbians are increasingly forming caucuses and interest groups within mainstream institutions: in religious denominations, in the professions, and in unions.

A pattern of organizational formation developed in the years after Stonewall. A city might start with an allegedly "all-purpose" gay liberation group which claimed to speak for everyone, but that often was white, male, and middle-class in its style, membership, and outlook. Very quickly it would spawn countless other groups, sometimes representing a particular focus or purpose—gay teachers, for instance—or sometimes representing a constituency, or identity, whose needs were not being addressed. This occurred for lesbians especially in the early 1970s. By the late 1970s, gay and lesbian people of color were taking the initiative to form organizations of their own. A national conference held in Washington in October 1979 was especially important in facilitating the spread of organizations within communities of color. In the 1980s, we can see more and more constituencies doing the same, such as youth, seniors, and people with physical disabilities.

The 1970s and 1980s have seen a great geographic spread. There isn't a state in the nation without some form of gay or lesbian organization. The spread has been uneven, but the organizational impulse has permeated the country. In the year since the March on Washington, this has been especially true in the South.

Not only are there more organizations of every imaginable sort, but there has also been in the 1980s a change in the structure, functioning, and stability of the groups we've created. Our national organizations are in better shape, and are working together instead of at cross-purposes. There are now quite a number of statewide coalitions—some fledgling and barely alive, but others well grounded and well functioning. More and more organizations have paid staff. They are becoming permanent institutions, with highly skilled staffers who move in the world of policy-making and service delivery with greater and greater sophistication.

Some of this change has been in response to AIDS: the epidemic has tapped into money that wasn't available before; AIDS-service organizations are becoming behemoths. But the change has extended beyond AIDS and is benefitting a wide range of organizations, including political action committees, lobbying and litigation groups, and local community centers.

What does all this organization-building mean? Among other things it means that we have built a visible community where before we were an underground subculture hidden from view. In the process, we have changed what it means to be a gay man or lesbian. The old buzzwords—sad, lonely, marginal, sick—don't ring true anymore.

Organization also means power. We have been, and still are, creating a power base for ourselves. We are boldly and dramatically ending the invisibility which allowed stereotypes, prejudice, and misinformation to thrive.

## WINNING ALLIES

A third critical area of progress is that we are winning allies for ourselves.

In 1950, gay men and lesbians could find no expressions of organizational support. There were a mere handful of individuals, like Alfred Kinsey, who might speak out against the prejudices of society, but beyond that there was nothing. It was the middle of the Cold War, the era of the second red scare, when a portrait of the homosexual as a menace to security was being constructed. Even organizations that we might expect to stand on principle and defend the unpopular—like the ACLU—were unwilling to take a stand on our behalf.

In the 1950s and 1960s, there were some small, tentative signs of change. A primary goal of the homophile movement in the 1950s was to win the support of respected professionals. Activists often sought this assistance for the wrong reasons—in the accommodationist fifties, they believed that only "the experts" could speak with authority about our lives—but, on a local level, they found clergy, lawyers, doctors, and therapists who were willing to provide services for gays in trouble, and to go to bat for individuals when the need arose.

In the 1960s, a changing political climate and a more aggressive cohort of activists pushed further. They successfully lobbied the ACLU, which came out against the constitutionality of the sodomy laws and against employment discrimination based solely on sexual orientation. A Council on Religion and the Homosexual opened dialogue between representatives of some mainline Protestant denominations and the gay community. The Quakers spoke out on our behalf, and influential medical professionals, with ties to the homophile movement, began to lobby against the classification of homosexuality as a disease.

Since 1969, the change has been dramatic. Admittedly, it sometimes *feels* as if we are still isolated, as if we have to do it all ourselves because no one else really cares or understands, but objectively that is simply not true. We have built for ourselves a strong, and growing, cadre of allies.

The examples are legion. Above all, perhaps, there has been the women's movement in general, and the National Organization of Women in particular. The alliance is not perfect, there are strains and tensions on both sides and areas of disagreement and misunderstanding, but basically there is a large, organized constituency that speaks out against injustice directed at us. On the state level, NOW affiliates often are critical in providing lobbying assistance and a public profile for lesbian and gay issues: this is especially true in states where the gay movement is still weak. And, besides, the work of the women's movement, whether gay-focused or not, redounds to our benefit. Any progress that is made toward gender equality is progress against the sex-role stereotyping that oppresses gay men and lesbians.

Many other examples can be listed: the ACLU, which is now pouring enormous resources, at the national and state level, into gay and lesbian causes. It has taken on a large number of cases, on a variety of issues. It is the first nongay organization that I know of to have taken a position in favor of the legalization of gay marriages. There is PFLAG—Parents and Friends of Lesbians and Gays—mobilizing heterosexuals for us. There is Jesse Jackson's Rainbow Coalition, the American Public Health Association, the American Psychological Association, the Unitarians, the American Bar Association, and many, many more. All of these have signed on to at least part of our movement's agenda. Church leaders, elected officials, prominent social critics, newspaper editorial writers—many can be counted on to speak or write boldly about the injustice of the oppression we confront.

The fact is we are winning allies for ourselves in every corner of society. And as we do so, and continue to win more, we are lessening our isolation and social marginality and weakening the forces of oppression.

## DISMANTLING THE STRUCTURE OF INSTITUTIONALIZED OPPRESSION

A final area of progress might be called the dismantling of the structure of institutionalized oppression.

In the 1950s, our situation was actually getting worse. Besides the sodomy statutes which existed in every state, police were aggressively using solicitation, disorderly conduct, and vagrancy laws to harass, arrest, and prosecute us. The federal government was enacting new, and more extensive disabilities—the military was discharging men and women for "being gay," regardless of their behavior while in service; Eisenhower prohibited our employment in any and all government jobs; the FBI was actively collecting names and compiling files. Christian teaching on homosexuality reflected a consensus that had held since the thirteenth century. The sickness model shaped the medical and mental health profession's approach to us, and the model was expanding its reach through state sexual psychopath laws enacted during the sex panic of the late 1940s and early 1950s. Obscenity laws were still being used to censor and seize gay materials.

By 1969, only minor changes had occurred. The movement was too weak to effect institutional change. Supreme Court rulings had considerably narrowed the scope of the obscenity statutes; a few cases challenging employment discrimination were wending their way through the courts; in a handful of states, gay bars had won protection from arbitrary police raids; in New York and San Francisco, the movement had managed to curtail some of the worst excesses of police harassment. But beyond that, the level of day-to-day oppression was distressingly high.

Today, even though the greater part of our work is still ahead of us, much has been accomplished. Sodomy laws have been repealed in half the states, removing the stigma of criminality from our sexuality. Our constitutional right of freedom of speech and assembly has been affirmed by the courts again and again. We have seen the beginnings of civil rights legislation at the municipal level—several dozen cities, including many of the largest, have passed laws prohibiting discrimination in housing, employment, and public accommodations. Wisconsin has done the same, and a number of other states are close to following suit. Federal job discrimination has been sharply restricted, extending now only to the military and the intelligence agencies. The American Psychiatric Association has removed homosexuality from its list of mental illnesses. Debates about the morality of homosexuality and about the role of gay men and lesbians in congregations and the ministry have opened up in a number of denominations. And, above all perhaps, there is a much, much lower level of police harassment in most parts of the country.

This is an extraordinary achievement for so short a time. Our daily lives are profoundly different because of this. We *are* succeeding, despite—maybe even because of—a vocal, well-organized opposition.

The rest of this conference is about the future, about creating more change, about learning skills, sharing experiences, and thinking about strategy. As we do this work, I hope we will all remember the successes and the achievements we can already claim.

I want to close with a couple of final observations, one that I owe to the intuitive wisdom of my students, and the other that comes from the generation of activists that preceded me.

Lots of my classroom time is spent discussing issues of social change and movements for liberation, particularly those of the last generation. I try to shake the hold that the "great man" theory of history still has on my students. I talk about organization, collective action, the commitment and cooperation of masses of ordinary people working together to change a society.

They resist me all the way. On exam essays, they remember and focus upon individuals: on Rosa Parks, who refused to give up her seat on a Montgomery bus; on four college students who sat at the lunch counter at a Woolworth's two miles from where I teach; on a previously unknown and undistinguished woman writer named Betty Friedan who blew the lid off gender relations with a book called *The Feminine Mystique*; on Leonard Matlovich, on the cover of *Time*, challenging the military's ban on gay soldiers.

I think they're trying to tell *me* something. They are telling me that the individual matters, that the individual commitment to resist injustice, to take a stand, and to set things right, is critical and important.

We—you and I—are those individuals. The commitments we have made and will continue to make, the actions we have taken and will continue to take, are the very stuff of history.

Finally, there's the insight of our elders. In the mid-1970s, I interviewed several dozen of the men and women who had been active in the pre-Stonewall homophile movement. Many of them had been passed by and were no longer involved in gay politics; each of them had a unique story to tell. But in interview after interview, at some point or another a phrase recurred: "Never in my wildest dreams did I think I would live to see so much change."

Wouldn't it be fine, wouldn't it be splendid if, as this century comes to a close we could look back on our accomplishments and say, "Never in my wildest dreams did I expect to succeed so magnificently!"

It is not too much to expect of each other.

# 20

# AFTER STONEWALL

---

*The previous essay on the movement's progress, while "true," tells only half of the story. History at its most sophisticated and complex is rarely a straight-line narrative of victories and successes. Mistakes get made, hopes are dashed, and the best-laid plans often come to naught.*

*This final essay, written in the winter and spring of 1991, represents an initial attempt to come to grips with the history of post-Stonewall activism. It was motivated by my own need to make sense of the last twenty years, by my annoyance at the lack of scholarly attention to what I believe is a critically important phenomenon in the recent history of the United States, and by a concern that our precious history of struggle remains unknown to a new generation of committed young activists. I make no claims to comprehensiveness (how could one essay encompass such a rich collective effort?) nor would I stake my reputation as a historian on the interpretation it offers. My research on the post-Stonewall movement is still in the early stages, and my analysis and conclusions are subject to revision. Nonetheless, it seems worthwhile to present these ideas now in order to foster further debate and analysis and to encourage more research. We need a host of historians and sociologists willing to explore this most valuable part of our past.*

When I began my research on the pre-Stonewall lesbian and gay movement, I saw my work as a form of political intervention. As a young historian who was also an activist in New York in the mid-1970s, I was struck by the tension between the rhetoric of the movement and my own knowledge as a student of social movements. As our rhetoric would have it, gay life before Stonewall was characterized by silence, invisibility, and isolation. Before Stonewall, there was no history of lesbians and gay men struggling for freedom; indeed, before Stonewall, there was no gay history other than a chronicle of unrelieved oppression. But mass movements for social change do not spring full-blown into existence, like Athena from the forehead of Zeus. Movements have roots; they have origins. Surely, I reasoned, *something* of significance must have occurred before that night of outrage in Greenwich Village to explain why a spontaneous riot could have birthed a mass grass-roots movement.

The book that grew out of my research, *Sexual Politics, Sexual Communities*, demonstrated the importance of the pre-Stonewall "homophile" movement. Through the efforts of a brave band of pioneering activists, the idea that homosexuals were a mistreated minority, rather than sinful, criminal, or sick creatures, was infiltrating society and slowly altering the way that gay men and lesbians thought about themselves. In effecting this subtle change in consciousness, activists had prepared the seedbed in which gay liberation would flower in the 1970s. *Sexual Politics, Sexual Communities* was an extraordinarily rewarding book to write. Not only did I retrieve an important piece of our history, but because the movement was small in those decades, I had the satisfying sense that I had been able to tell the whole story.

When I finished the book, I assumed that I was leaving the topic of gay and lesbian politics behind, and would move on to other historical issues. The post-Stonewall movement was too huge to be able to do it justice. Also, as an activist, I felt too deeply enmeshed in it to maintain enough distance to view the movement critically. But, in the last year or so, I have found myself reconsidering that decision and being drawn irresistibly toward studying the post-Stonewall movement.

A couple of circumstances account for this shift. My own activism ebbs and flows according to the stage of my research and writing. In the last three years activism has superseded scholarship as a focus of my energy and, through my work with the National Gay and Lesbian Task Force, I have had the privilege of being in contact with large numbers of grass-roots activists from around the country. But I can never shed my historian skin, and it saddens me how little our history, particularly our political history of emancipatory struggle, has been woven into the fabric of our work. Especially in the last year or so, as ACT UP chapters have experienced searing conflicts about structure, goals, and the like, and as Queer Nation has given shape to a new generation's activism, I have been struck by how loudly the past echoes in the present. The dilemmas we face today are not new.

Yet, because we have not done a very good job of keeping alive our history of political resistance, we often seem to act as if we were inventing the alphabet of movement building.

Another motive for examining post-Stonewall history grows out of my reading in the last few months. This past year, while on leave from teaching, I have had the time to dip into the sociological literature on social movements. Since the late 1960s, there has been an efflorescence of scholarly interest in mass movements and collective action.[1] Social scientists have engaged in much productive theorizing and developed useful insights about what makes movements tick, how they grow, why they fail, what works, and what does not. The scholarly literature was born, in many cases, out of a passionate commitment to social justice. Yet as I read more and more of this material, I became increasingly perturbed by the singular lack of reference to one of the largest, most vital movements of the last twenty years—ours. The gay and lesbian movement is appallingly under-studied.[2]

This lack of attention is a shame because the gay movement offers a set of interesting puzzles and issues. Resolving them might affect both the direction of social scientific theorizing and our understanding of the recent history of the United States. For instance:

—The last ten to fifteen years have been exceedingly difficult ones for social movements of what might broadly be called "the left." Among feminists, civil rights activists, and others, there is a widespread sense of retrenchment, of losing ground, of being under siege. By contrast, the gay and lesbian movement grew steadily through the 1980s and is now more vigorous and dynamic than ever before. This vitality is all the more remarkable in the light of an inhospitable political environment in which a resurgent conservatism has built its strength in part by pointedly targeting homosexuals. What accounts for this vitality? How has a gay and lesbian movement managed to flourish in such unlikely circumstances?

—The gay and lesbian movement also offers us evidence of something arrestingly new in Western culture, the mass public affirmation of homosexual desire. Nothing like it has existed in the West for at least fifteen hundred years. One would think that it portends some sort of striking shift in society and culture and that, by studying it, social scientists might learn something profound about contemporary life. What accounts for this decisive rupture? What can it tell us about ourselves and our society?

—We are living through an era in the United States, one that stretches back to the mid-1960s and the rise of the Black Power movement, in which issues of *identity* have come to define much of both oppositional and mainstream politics. Although this is not entirely new (conflict between Catholic and Protestant in the nineteenth century comes to mind as an earlier instance of identity politics), I would argue that the current multiplication of identities and the centrality of identity as an organizing framework for social and political mobilization are novel. Moreover, the gay and lesbian movement is a place where an extraordinarily wide range of identities converge. Will we perhaps learn something crucial about the politics of identity by examining this particular social movement? Can we unravel some issues about identity and social change that so far may have eluded theorists?

—Finally, the gay and lesbian movement offers interesting interpretive challenges because of the way sexual identity takes shape. One is neither born nor socialized into it at an early age. The identity has to be discovered and accepted. One can choose not to accept it, or one can choose to hide it. At the very least, this suggests that the history of lesbian and gay politics is as much the history of the creation and elaboration of a self-conscious community and culture as it is the story of a social movement. Penetrating the analytical mysteries of the movement will involve exploring the continuing dialectic between the history of the movement and the history of the community. The structure of the community marks the terrain on which the movement can operate, and the actions of the movement are continually reshaping the life of the community.

I am not yet far enough along in my research to be able to address directly these larger issues.[3] Instead, I offer this essay with a far more modest goal in mind, namely, to tell in broad outline the story of the movement over the last twenty or so years. I will set the stage by briefly describing the accomplishments of activists in the 1950s and 1960s. I will then move on to examine Stonewall and the eruption of a gay liberation movement at the end of the 1960s. I will analyze two of the many paths that activism traveled in the 1970s; the two paths I will look at were primarily defined by gender differences. I then will discuss a series of challenges that arose toward the end of the 1970s. And, finally, I will suggest some of the ways that the response to the AIDS epidemic has reshaped and redirected the gay and lesbian movement.

## THE HOMOPHILE YEARS[4]

A movement first formed in the post–World War II decade, at a critical moment in our history, a moment of tension and conflict. As Allan Bérubé has ably shown in his book *Coming Out Under Fire: The History of Gay Men and Women in World War Two*, the 1940s opened a larger cultural and social space in which to be gay.[5] The war years led to a sharpened sense of sexual identity, dramatically expanded the opportunities for a collective life to develop, and saw a significant growth in the urban subculture of gay men and lesbians. Yet just as the wartime generation was shaping this new world, the political currents associated with the Cold War and McCarthyism widened the dangers associated with gay life. The homosexual emerged from the shadows, but in the image of a menace to the nation. Various branches and agencies of the national government in Washington investigated, exposed, excluded, harassed, purged, and spied upon gay Americans. Irrational witch-hunts swept through communities. Across the country, urban police forces harassed gays and lesbians with impunity.

World War II, the Cold War, and McCarthyism provided the context in which a gay freedom struggle initially formed and did its work. In the course of the 1950s and 1960s, the politics of the movement underwent many twists and turns, and throughout this era the movement itself remained small and relatively marginal to the social forces shaping the life of the nation. Nonetheless, by the end of the 1960s, there existed a core of activists who spoke in crisply articulate ways of injustice, projected a firm sense of moral righteousness in presenting their cause, and put themselves squarely on the line as proponents of an unpopular cause. By the time of Stonewall, some limited but important gains had been made:

—The Supreme Court had affirmed the right to publish gay and lesbian magazines;

—The first employment discrimination cases had been won in federal court;

—In a number of states, court rulings had given gay bars a more secure existence, and in cities like New York and San Francisco, the movement had placed constraints on police harassment of the subculture;

—A dialogue had opened with segments of the scientific community about the classification of homosexuality as mental illness, and with the religious community about the categorization of homosexuality as sin;

—Because of the shift to direct action tactics of public protest, the movement was now achieving some occasional media visibility;

—The organizational impulse had spread from its place of origin in Southern California and, on the eve of Stonewall, about fifty lesbian and gay movement organizations existed;

—Finally, through the persistent work of activists, the idea that gays and lesbians were a mistreated, persecuted minority had begun to infiltrate American society and the gay subculture.

The birth of gay liberation has so overshadowed this earlier activism that it has been easy to overlook the continuities between the pre- and post-Stonewall eras. The slogan "Gay is good," an empowering rejection of cultural norms, was adopted by homophile activists a year before Stonewall. In Southern California, Troy Perry had formed the first Metropolitan Community Church, and the *Advocate* was being hawked in gay bars in Los Angeles. Gays and lesbians staged "visibility actions," to borrow a term from Queer Nation in the 1990s, outside the California State Fair; activists "came out" in the press and on television. In many ways, the movement was straining to reach new heights.

As the 1960s ended, the homophile movement could accurately be described as a reform movement solidly implanted in the American liberal tradition. It had isolated a problem, the mistreatment of homosexuals, and identified the configuration of laws, policies, and beliefs that sustained a caste-like status for gay women and men. It proposed a solution: decriminalization of homosexual acts, equal treatment and equal rights under the law, and the dissemination of accurate, "unbiased" information about homosexuality. Activists had formed organizations, were mobilizing support, and were petitioning through a variety of means for the redress of grievances.

The problem was not an absence of gay politics. Rather, pre-Stonewall activists were employing ordinary means to attack an extraordinary situation. The hostility to homosexuality was so deeply embedded in American society and culture, and the penalties attached to exposure were so great in the 1950s and 1960s, that few gay men and lesbians were willing to affiliate with the movement. The enticements of the closet were far more alluring than anything activists could offer. Oppression posed a seemingly insuperable barrier to recruitment.

It was this problem—how to challenge the regime of the closet—that the Stonewall Riot and its aftermath appeared to solve. The Stonewall generation of gay liberationists crashed through the recruitment barrier and landed in a wide sunlit space that, for many, proved far more attractive than the closet.

## STONEWALL AND THE EMERGENCE OF RADICAL GAY LIBERATION[6]

The Stonewall Riot has come to assume mythic proportions among gay men and lesbians. The image of drag queens rioting in the streets and engaging in

239

combat with the helmeted officers of New York City's tactical police inverted the stereotype of meek, limp-wristed fairies. It was a wonderful moment of explosive rage in which a few transvestites and young gay men of color reshaped gay life forever.

The story of the Stonewall Riot has been told many times. Here I want to explore more closely its genesis. It would be a mistake, I think, to describe it, as is so often done, as a spontaneous outpouring of anger that changed the course of history. Yes, the riot was unplanned, impulsive, and unrehearsed—three common meanings of "spontaneous"—but it was also rooted in a specific context that shaped the experience and consciousness of the participants. To wrench the riot from its moorings in time and place impoverishes our understanding of it.

On the most immediate level, a memorial service for Judy Garland had taken place earlier in the day, just a few miles uptown on the West Side. Garland was *the* cultural icon for gay men of the 1950s and 1960s. Through her music, her movies, and her life, a generation of gay men bonded with each other. Her death was a shared tragedy, a loss that rippled through the gay world and that crossed class and race boundaries. Something precious had been taken away, and one can imagine that sensibility coursing through the psyches of those at the Stonewall as the police attempted to seize another symbol of community.

The raid on the Stonewall provoked outrage for another reason. By 1969, bar raids were no longer commonplace in New York City. A few years earlier, the homophile movement had successfully pressed the liberal Lindsay administration to rein in the police. Though harassment did not stop entirely—some forms of public cruising still made one especially vulnerable to arrest—the bars were for the most part left alone, and they flourished. With less harassment, bars had longer lifespans, patrons could become "regulars" and form stronger ties to one another, and particular bars might become community centers of sorts. But 1969 was also an election year in municipal politics. That spring, police raids recommenced. When the cops arrived at the Stonewall, they were invading a space that patrons had come to see as rightfully theirs.

Finally, the outburst took place in a larger nongay context. Put most simply, a riot was not an unusual event in 1969. Martha Shelley, who was an antiwar activist and former officer of the Daughters of Bilitis, and who would become a key activist in early gay and lesbian liberation, was in the Village with a friend the night of the raid on the Stonewall. She remembered approaching Sheridan Square and noticing all the turmoil. Rather than investigate, she simply looked at her friend and said, "Oh, another riot," and continued on her way.[7]

The unruly social practices that the 1960s had made into a norm had to have béen absorbed by the patrons of the Stonewall. Young gay men of color as many of them were, they could not have been immune to the rhetoric and politics of groups such as the Black Panthers and the Young Lords, whose cachet ran especially high among young, dispossessed African–Americans and Puerto Ricans in New York. The Stonewall Riot may very well have been the first of its kind in history, but when the patrons confronted the police they were extending to gay turf familiar modes of action.

The larger political context also explains the aftermath of Stonewall. In the days and weeks that followed, lesbians and gay men in New York City kept talking. Before long, some of them had coalesced into a new organization, the Gay Liberation Front, fundamentally different from its homophile predecessors. A radical mass movement was aborning.

How could this happen? In the 1960s, many strands of radicalism were exerting their influence on a generation of young Americans. And, in one way or another, every major movement of the decade spoke to the condition of gays and lesbians. The civil rights movement had proven that ordinary folk, people brutally oppressed and without access to the resources of money and influence that typically defined power in our society, could shake the nation. Its metamorphosis into a militant nationalist politics in the late 1960s only made the parallels more striking. Black Power, Black Is Beautiful: the conjoining of words that in the lexicon of American English were always meant to be separate. Could gay come to embody power, too? Might gay be as good as black was now beautiful?

The white student movement and the antiwar movement also spoke to young gays. Children of privilege were challenging the system, engaging with ferocious abandon in pitched battles with armed police and, in some cases, with troops. The counterculture—that diffuse cultural impulse reflected in music, styles of hair and dress, and drug use, which contrasted being "true to one's self" and "doing your own thing" with the obscene materialism of consumer capitalism—scoffed at the hypocrisy of middle-class sexual mores. Finally, feminism, only recently reborn when the Stonewall Riot occurred, was articulating a new language of gender and sexuality that was transforming personal tribulation into political grievance. In this setting, how could a gay liberation movement *not* be born?

I said that the movements of the 1960s "spoke to" young lesbians and gays. That is not quite accurate. That phrase implies that they were not in the stream of radical protest, when in fact many participated with vigor. Just as women's liberation exploded into existence because a generation of young women had already been radicalized in other movements, so too could gay liberation erupt onto the landscape because many of us were part of the turmoil of the decade. Once those queens rioted outside the Stonewall, the political connections were unmistakable.

In contrast to the reform orientation of homophile politics, the phase of gay and lesbian activism that Stonewall initiated was radical. A number of characteristics marked it in this way. The name these new activists took, the Gay Liberation Front, was the queer version of the National Liberation Front in Vietnam, whose flag was often brandished in demonstrations of the late 1960s. GLFers identified the problem they were attacking—the mistreatment of gay men and lesbians—not as a narrow, discrete issue, but as systemic. Echoing the rhetoric of the radicalism around them, the founding document of GLF in New York denounced the "dirty, vile, fucked-up capitalist conspiracy" which it placed at the heart of the matter.[8]

GLFers began to construct a rudimentary analysis of gay *oppression*. It was not a matter of simple prejudice, misinformation, or outmoded beliefs. Rather, the oppression of homosexuals was woven into the fabric of sexism. Institutionalized heterosexuality reinforced a patriarchal nuclear family that socialized men and women into narrow roles and placed homosexuality beyond the pale. These gender dichotomies also reinforced other divisions based on race and class, and thus allowed an imperial American capitalism to exploit the population and make war around the globe.

Finally, the liberation of lesbians and gay men would come not by waging a separate, self-contained struggle but by making common cause with "all the oppressed: the Vietnamese struggle, the Third World, the blacks, the workers."[9] Many of GLF's early actions were not gay events at all, but rather displays of commitment to a much larger project of political change. With eye-catching banners designed for everyone to see, they appeared at rallies in support of the Black Panther Party and at the massive antiwar mobilizations held in Washington and in other cities around the country.

The men and women of GLF made these choices for reasons that were not simply "political." As Toby Marotta has pointed out in his study of gay and lesbian politics in New York, most of these radicals were young. Many of them were still struggling to come to terms with their sexual identity, and they lacked roots in the traditional gay world. Instead, much of their time was spent in the milieu of "the Movement." The New Left and countercultural values about community and human relationships that they had imbibed made them recoil from the subculture of Mafia-run bars, seedy bathhouses, butch-femme roles, and anonymous sex. The people they knew and the people with whom they felt an affinity were to be found among the ranks of radicalized youth at antiwar, Black Panther, and campus demonstrations. Where better, then, to propagate the message of gay liberation than among the already radical, in an environment that felt to them like home?

Their instincts proved accurate. Over the next year or two, as GLFers appeared at Movement events, word of this new liberation struggle spread very rapidly. The process was closely akin to what Sara Evans has described in her study of the origins of women's liberation.[10] The networks that the black, student, and antiwar movements provided allowed the first wave of radical feminists to reach hordes of politicized young women in short order. Similarly, these new lesbian and gay radicals could also tap the Movement in order to find converts. GLFs, or kindred groups, formed in city after city and on many college campuses; the speed with which gay liberation spread seemed to accelerate with each passing month.[11]

When it came to planning a strategy to achieve the liberation of homosexuals, GLFers stumbled. One option was to align with the Movement and thus add to the forces of radical change. But, since most GLFers were already enmeshed in that world, simply changing banners would hardly expand the number of radicals in America. Another was to convince radical leaders that gays and lesbians were oppressed, and therefore an integral part of the struggle, so that when the revolution came, it would liberate homosexuals as well. Although this strategy did win new allies, no revolutionary clouds appeared on the horizon. As for destroying sex roles and "smashing the nuclear family," how was a movement to do that?

The inability of radical gay liberationists to devise a strategy commensurate with their political vision should not lead us to dismiss the significance of this political impulse. Across the country, for the three or four years after Stonewall, this new breed of radicals participated in an almost continuous round of flashy, dramatic public demonstrations. Their most common targets were the media, the police, and the medical profession, all of whom were seriously implicated in the maintenance of gay oppression. GLFers rioted in the streets, and spoke in high school civics classes. In everything they did and everywhere they went, they sought to create visibility, to give substance to a new image of lesbians and gays.

The achievements of radical gay liberation were great, even if they are not best measured by reference to changes in institutional practices, public policies, or legal codes. GLF and similar groups operated on the terrain of culture and everyday life, and here their accomplishments were profound. Let me suggest three:

1.  Radical GLFers fashioned a new language and style of homosexuality. The accent was on pride and affirmation; they were blatant, outrageous, and flamboyant. Discarding notions of sickness and sin, they represented homosexuality as a revolutionary path toward freedom, as a step out of the constricted, stultifying gender roles of middle-class America. They engaged in public displays of affection, violated gender conventions, and gloried in the discomfort they deliberately provoked in others.

243

2. These radicals unleashed a mania for organization. On the eve of Stonewall, some fifty gay and lesbian movement groups existed; by the end of 1973, there were upwards of a thousand. These organizations published newspapers, sponsored speakers' bureaus, planned dances, staffed crisis lines, and engaged in many other kinds of activities as well, some overtly political, others more broadly social or cultural. But whatever their purpose or goal, the impulse to join together, which radical gay liberation so visibly embodied, proved irresistible. The organizational results were the essential building blocks of both a movement and a community.

3. Most significantly of all, radical gay liberation transformed the meaning of "coming out." Before Stonewall, the phrase had signified the acknowledgment of one's sexuality to others in the gay world; after Stonewall, it meant the public affirmation of homosexual identity. This revised form of coming out became, I believe, the quintessential expression of sixties cultural radicalism. It was "doing your own thing" with a vengeance; it embodied the insight that "The personal is political" as no other single act could.

It was also a tactical stroke of great genius. Here was a decision that any gay person could make. The results were personally transformative, and the consequences socially significant. People who came out were relinquishing the one protection that gays had against stigmatization. They therefore required new forms of self-defense, which is precisely what a gay liberation movement was. Once out of the closet, a gay man or lesbian was heavily invested in the success of the movement. Coming out created an army of permanent recruits.

These young radicals were ideally, perhaps even uniquely, suited to scout what must have felt like unknown territory. Because they were already converts to a radical critique of American society, the usual penalties that kept gays and lesbians in line failed to intimidate them. To declare one's homosexuality disqualified one from the draft, but GLF men were already opposed to the war. Lesbians and gays were excluded from federal civil service jobs and many other kinds of employment, but these counterculturalists believed in dropping out of a materialistic, straight rat race. Flaunting one's homosexuality might subject one to arrest, but in the New Left, getting arrested was a mark of commitment. They called the system's bluff in a way that most gay men and lesbians of the time would not. And, although it took a cohort of young radicals to challenge the regime of the closet, their example proved irresistible to others.

The new generation of gay liberationists saved the Stonewall Riot from being simply "an event." They fleshed out the implications of the riot, and ensured that they would become the symbol of a new militance. GLF broke through the barriers that had constrained the reform-oriented homophile movement. It transformed forever the shape of lesbian and gay activism in this country. It was radicalism, theirs and the times, that made these achievements possible.

By the mid-1970s, the version of gay politics which I have been describing as "radical gay liberation" was clearly in retreat. Many GLFs had died, and were being replaced by other kinds of gay and lesbian organizations. Radical gay liberation had ceased to be the leading edge, or the defining tendency, of the movement.

This rapid dissolution of radical gay liberation in the face of the powerful influence that GLF exerted on the lives of gay men and lesbians requires explanation. Certainly one reason is that the soil that fertilized GLF, the radicalism of the 1960s, was drying up rapidly. The belief that a revolution was imminent and that gays and lesbians should get on board, was fast losing whatever momentary plausibility it had. By the early 1970s, the nation was entering a long period of political conservatism and economic retrenchment. With every new proclamation of revolutionary intentions, radicals compromised their credibility.

Another serious problem was organizational. GLF was, quite frankly, chaotic. It was more of an impulse, or a mood, than an organization. Its distrust of leadership and its lack of structure made things infuriatingly difficult to get done. Small subsets of like-minded people could unite behind a short-term project or a particular action, but GLF was not well suited for the long march through institutions that a sustained movement would have to undertake. As time went on, the endless talking and the empty rhetoric generated impatience and estranged more and more recruits until most GLFs simply faded away.

Finally, GLF ran aground on the rocks of identity politics. It had been born just at the moment when identity had pressed to the foreground in the configuration of social movements in this country. This attention to identity, both as the organizing framework for oppression and as the basis for collective mobilization, simultaneously expanded and fractured the forces campaigning for change. As people came to see the many ways they were targeted because of who they were, their newly discovered anger brought many into grass-roots social activism.

But the politics of identity also proved to be a centrifugal force pulling that world apart. In the case of GLF, it worked in two conflicting ways. For many white lesbians and for people of color, GLF offered too little: it could not adequately address their needs as individuals who experienced not only gay oppression, but also sexism, or racism, or both. For many white gay men, GLF demanded too much. Just as they were awakening to a political consciousness of their oppression and beginning to fashion an agenda for action, GLF was calling for a commitment to fight all forms of oppression. The insistence on solidarity with the struggles of others too easily sounded like self-abnegation.

No single form of movement politics rose to preeminence in place of radical gay liberation; instead, the gay and lesbian freedom struggle spun out in many different directions. Here and there, the GLF impulse remained alive, though it was far overshadowed by the multiplicity of new political tendencies. I want to follow two of those tendencies as they developed in the 1970s: a gay rights movement, largely male in composition and reformist in its political orientation; and lesbian-feminism, an initially radical movement that became increasingly utopian with the passage of time.

## THE GENDERED SEVENTIES, I
## A GAY RIGHTS MOVEMENT[12]

By the beginning of the 1970s, gay activism—most particularly its white, middle-class male variant—was quickly reconfiguring itself. Already in December 1969, some GLF members in New York, disgruntled by the agenda and the procedures of the organization, had seceded to form the Gay Activists Alliance. This development was not unique to New York, not a product of its fractious politics. Rather, in city after city, a similar process took place, reflected in a change of nomenclature from liberation to activist. As the 1970s wore on, many gay communities new to the movement skipped the GLF phase entirely and launched their organizations in the gay activist mold.

Peering in from the outside, one would have initially been hard-pressed to notice the differences between radical gay liberation and what I'm choosing to call gay rights. Gay rights activists retained a central emphasis on coming out; they engaged in militant, angry protests; they adopted the language of pride and self-affirmation that radical gay liberation constructed.

Nonetheless, there were differences beyond the not-insignificant change in name. The newer gay activist groups tended to share a number of characteristics that sharply separated them from the radical GLF impulse. For one, they were single-issue organizations, completely gay-focused in their concerns. Their agendas might be large—civil rights legislation, media responsiveness, social activities, publishing, hot lines, and the like—but everything was defined by its overriding gay content. They also were *organizations*, with clearly specified structures and processes. Constitutions were written, bylaws adopted, officers elected, committees formed, meetings held, and membership requirements specified. Votes were taken and meetings conduced by *Robert's Rules of Order*. Gay activist groups also occupied a relationship to the political system different from that of GLF. Rather than try to destroy the old in order to build something new, they saw themselves as unjustly excluded from full participation in American society and wanted recognition and a place inside. This perspective helped to shape an agenda that diverged from that of GLF. Thus a GAA would work for changes in municipal civil rights codes to include sexual orientation; the groups sought the endorsement of elected officials and candidates for political office.

The shift to a single-issue politics encouraged the further proliferation of organizations. It made sense for new groups to form in order to reflect a particular need or to focus on a particular issue within the framework of gay rights. Gay and lesbian Episcopalians formed Integrity, an organization devoted to winning acceptance within their church. Gay and lesbian academics created the Gay Academic Union to fight for visibility and an end to discrimination within higher education. These examples could be multiplied.

What the complex of changes meant is that by the middle of the 1970s the bulk of gay male activism—and some lesbian activism as well—had returned to the reform-oriented perspective of the pre-Stonewall homophile movement. Rather than a struggle for liberation, the movement had become, once again, a quest for "rights." Rather than trying to reconstruct American society and its institutions from top to bottom, the movement sought gay inclusion into the system as it stood, with only the adjustments necessary to ensure equal treatment. Once again, the gay movement was riding the track of liberal reform: it had identified a particular problem, proposed a limited solution, formed organizations to work for change, and employed a range of tactics to win redress of grievances.

Reformist though it was, the gay rights movement of the mid-1970s did not mimic homophile politics. Reform-oriented activists could not erase—indeed, were not interested in erasing—the entire legacy of lesbian and gay liberation. Certain key changes effected by gay liberation were enthusiastically incorporated into the outlook, the style, and the program of these newer groups. Among these, the imperative to come out publicly, with all that implied about pride, self-affirmation, and the rejection of mainstream cultural views of homosexuality, stands out. Many gay activists remained as bold and brazen as their GLF predecessors had been. They expected and demanded acceptance for who they were, without apology.

The assimilation of pride into the very marrow of the movement also meant that, even as reformers campaigned for inclusion, activists were willing to absorb unruly tactics into their repertoire of methods to achieve their goals. GAA in New

York City, for instance, can be credited with perfecting the "zap." When Mayor John Lindsay proved unwilling to support unequivocally the gay rights bill before the City Council, GAA felt no compunction about declaring "total war" against Lindsay. For a time, wherever he went in the city, Lindsay faced angry gays who disrupted cultural events, chained themselves to offices, and threw themselves in front of TV cameras to embarrass the mayor. A gay rights perspective did not necessarily translate into a suit-and-tie, dress-and-stockings style of political mobilization. Finally, whether fighting for rights or fighting for liberation, the gay and lesbian movement was forever transformed by the huge infusion of numbers wrought by Stonewall and radical gay liberation.

Taken together, the living legacies of gay liberation served to mask troubling contradictions that inhered in single-issue politics. The movement had grown larger in size, yet its political framework, and hence its possibilities, had contracted. The goals of activists had narrowed, yet activists in the mid-1970s almost uniformly displayed an élan that made them feel as if they were mounting the barricades. Activists increasingly engaged in routinized and mundane organizational tasks, yet they believed they were remaking the world.

My own experience in New York City in the Gay Academic Union between 1973 and 1975 illustrates what I mean.[13] During these years an ever-expanding group of gay men and lesbians associated with colleges and universities came together to translate the new post-Stonewall zeitgeist into an agenda for higher education. Some of the participants might be described as mainstream liberals or even conservatives; others of us positioned ourselves as radicals. Some already had a background in the movement; many, like me, were new to it. No other experience in my life up to that point matched the intensity of those endless meetings and monstrously large conferences. And, to judge by the commitment and excitement of the people around me, most of the others felt the same way. We believed, as I said, that we were remaking the world, yet our program—an end to discrimination; encouraging academics to come out; support for gay research and the teaching of gay studies—was a textbook example of a reform agenda.

What accounts, then, for the disparity between our goals and the way many of us, including the radicals, interpreted what we were doing? How could so modest a program, in the grand scheme of things, provoke among us such an inflated sense of its meaning? The answer lies, I think, in the magic of coming out. No matter what one's personal or political aspirations were—to be a chaired professor at Harvard, to win a seat on the New York Stock Exchange, or to build a revolutionary socialist state—coming out in the 1970s profoundly reshaped one's life. The anxiety one experienced in anticipating it, the exhilaration of surviving it, and the cheers and strokes from peers in the movement after the fact, made it a step of profound significance. For a gay man or lesbian of that time, I don't think that it was possible to experience anything of comparable intensity. In a psychological sense it was an act of "revolutionary" import. No manner of political analysis could convince someone who had come out that he or she wasn't turning the world inside out and upside down. Only later, as the movement matured, would it become clear that coming out was a first step only. An openly gay banker is still a banker.

Critical though this analysis of a gay reform perspective sounds, it is also true that reformers were able to provoke important, ground-breaking change. Unlike GLFers, who were long on rhetoric and had a flair for the dramatic action, reformers began to target in a sustained way the range of institutions implicated in lesbian and gay oppression. In late 1973, they won a major victory when the American Psychiatric Association voted to eliminate homosexuality from its list of mental disorders. In 1975, the federal Civil Service Commission dropped its ban on the employment of gays and lesbians.

Activists began to burrow their way into the churches of America, demanding a reconsideration of Christian teaching and calling for the ordination of openly gay and lesbian ministers. The National Council of Churches issued a strong statement condemning discrimination against homosexuals. In some denominations, such as the United Church of Christ and the Episcopal Church, insurgents brought forward test cases of the ban on ordination.

Some elements of the print media, particularly in those cities where the movement was most in evidence, began to cover its activities, breaking the invisibility and the silence that hampered its growth. Through sustained lobbying by the National Gay Task Force, a gay rights bill was introduced into Congress in 1975. By 1976, seventeen states had repealed their sodomy statutes, and thirty-six cities, including some of the largest, had enacted legislation banning discrimination.

Activists also worked to draw others into the movement enterprise. Lesbians won a statement of support at the annual conference of the National Organization for Women in 1971; four years later, NOW committed itself programmatically to supporting lesbian rights. Ties with organizations such as the American Civil Liberties Union, which even before Stonewall had backed some test cases for the homophile movement, grew stronger, and gay activists in a number of states could count on the legal resources and skill of ACLU lawyers. In 1977, as activities for International Women's Year geared up, lesbian staffers and board members of the National Gay Task Force fashioned a major campaign to promote lesbian visibility and to make lesbian rights a key issue embraced by feminists around the country. At thirty of the state conferences held in the summer of 1977, lesbian rights resolutions were adopted, and at the national conference in Houston, a high-water mark of feminist solidarity in the 1970s, a sexual preference resolution was accepted by an overwhelming margin.[14]

One other change of great import occurred during these years: in cities where a visible movement coalesced, law enforcement practices shifted dramatically. Throughout the 1950s and 1960s, police harassment of the subculture—not only in public spaces where gay men had sex, but in gay male bathhouses, in lesbian and gay bars, and even in the privacy of homes—was like a cancer raging out of control. Even if an individual managed to elude arrest, he or she would know of others less fortunate—men and women taken away in vans, forced to appear in night court, and sometimes confronted by the next day's newspaper revealing their names, addresses, and places of employment. The effects were devastating. To whatever joys or satisfactions the collective gay world brought, police persecution inevitably fused emotions of terror, humiliation, and shame.

Police harassment certainly hadn't disappeared by the mid-1970s, but the pattern had altered and new boundaries were drawn. In many large cities change came in two forms: 1) a major reduction in the sheer quantity of incidents, so that harassment was no longer ubiquitous; and 2) something of a "hands off" policy toward the less public manifestations of gay male life (bathhouses rather than public sex) and toward the gay neighborhoods that partook of middle-class "respectability" (the Castro and Greenwich Village rather than the Tenderloin and Times Square). In other words, the benefits of the movement were unevenly distributed.

This renegotiation of relations between the police and a newly mobilized community had important effects. When the police did overstep the new boundaries that the movement had drawn, their actions stimulated resistance and could be used effectively by activists to mobilize support. For middle-class white gay men especially, the change in law enforcement practices also meant that the texture of daily experience was thoroughly reshaped. Institutions of a public commercialized subculture proliferated. The pre-Stonewall pattern of control by the criminal underworld was replaced by legitimate small-time entrepreneurs, typically gay themselves, venturing into a new world of economic opportunity. Bars, bathhouses, sex clubs, restaurants, and discos seemed to appear everywhere, sustaining a thick network of social connections.[15]

This world bore little resemblance to what only recently had seemed the divine order of things. A vignette from my own experience in New York: I was taken to a gay bar for the first time in 1968. We descended a few steps below street level to enter. There was a small window with blackened glass, and a thick wooden door. The inside looked and felt like a dank, unfinished basement. It was dark, some men were dancing near the back, and the smell of tobacco, beer, and men's cologne combined in less than sweet ways. I didn't return. Six years later the bar of preference for me and my friends was the Roadhouse. Located on a busy corner of Hudson Street in the West Village, it was light and airy, with a large plate glass window occupying most of one wall and a door that, in late spring and summer, was always open. On Sundays, the management offered a simple buffet-style dinner at a nominal price. The crowd of men moved easily between bar and street; the line dividing inside from out dissolved. Knots of men engaging in jovial conversation stood on the street, some with plates of food, some with a beer in one hand and the·other resting on the shoulder, or curled around the waist, of a friend.

Most of the men who participated in this public world of sociability and sexual exchange were not activists. They did not belong to movement organizations. But they were the beneficiaries of what the movement had already wrought. The message of gay pride wafted through the air; it altered the way they lived and the way they understood their lives and identity. Gay male activists also enthusiastically participated in this world, at the same time that they—we—experienced no end of frustration with the seemingly apolitical stance of these "new" gay men. Though it was not apparent at the time, the commercialized subculture was, however, the seedbed for a consciousness that would be susceptible to political mobilization.

Ironically, the absence of overt politicization can be attributed in part to the success, in its own narrow terms, of reformist politics. Reformers fought for the right to be gay, free from harassment and punishment. Since the sexual subculture had been the location where gay men most acutely experienced both their gayness and their vulnerability, the fading police presence seemed incontrovertible evidence that they were free. As far as they could tell, gay liberation had succeeded. They could be open about their "lifestyle" on the streets of the burgeoning gay neighborhoods suddenly visible in large American cities after the mid-1970s. Activist harangues about the persistence of job discrimination, about media invisibility, about the role of the churches and the military in excluding homosexuals from equal participation in American life, seemed like the ravings of grim politicos who just didn't know how to have fun.

## THE GENDERED SEVENTIES, II
## LESBIAN-FEMINISM[16]

I have described the gay rights movement as male in its composition and emphasis, and I believe this is accurate as a generalized statement of its orientation. Yet it is also true that throughout the 1970s lesbians were a part of it. Lesbians who framed their identity primarily through their homosexuality, lesbians whose personal ties to gay men were stronger than their ties to heterosexual women, and those who were more attracted to the reform politics of gay rights, all struggled to make a home for themselves in a male-dominated movement. It wasn't easy. The new consciousness of sexism in interpersonal relationships, spawned by feminism, meant that everyday encounters with men bristled with tension. And most gay men's lack of understanding of institutionalized sexism forced lesbians repeatedly to fight for political formulations and action agendas that recognized their needs. Gender-mixed organizations in the 1970s were a minefield in which a single misstep could shatter the enterprise. They worked best in those rare situations where gender parity was incorporated into organizational structure, where sufficient numbers of women were involved to counter isolation, and where the organization's potential seemed promising enough to warrant continuing participation. In the seventies, such organizations were rare.

The main action of lesbian politics in the decade took place not in mixed organizations but in autonomous lesbian-feminist groups. In the early 1970s, a separate lesbian-feminist movement coalesced and declared itself heir of the "revolutionary" politics of the 1960s. Initially radical in its aspirations and self-conception, it would become in time ever more utopian as separatism traveled the long distance from political tactic to social vision.

The lesbian-feminist movement owed its existence to the convergence of two clusters of activists: lesbians with experience in women's liberation, and women with experience in gay liberation. Of the two movements, women's liberation proved most critical in birthing lesbian-feminism. Feminism was constructing a framework for interpreting the dissatisfaction women experienced in GLF, while the rhetoric of sisterhood was inducing many previously heterosexual women in the radical wing of the feminist movement to come out as lesbians. The sense of betrayal that these new lesbians experienced in feeling silenced and dismissed by those who had only recently been their comrades would propel them into a lesbian-feminist movement of their own; once there, a feminist consciousness would draw sharp lines between them and the men of the gay rights movement.

As a collective movement, lesbian-feminism embarked on two distinct projects. The first was an effort to fashion an ideology of lesbianism and its political significance free of the corrosive implications of the dominant rhetoric. The second was organizational, the building of institutions and the creation of lesbian-only spaces where a culture and a community could flourish.

In constructing a new discourse of lesbianism, these young radicals had several goals. One was to overcome what has been described as the "historical denial of lesbianism."[17] Within the traditional domains of science, religion, and law, lesbianism appeared as little more than a footnote to theories and discussions that revolved around male homosexuality. Another was to counter the new rhetoric of gay liberation, which often framed its purpose in terms of a model of sexual freedom shaped by male experience. Finally, radical lesbians sought to contest the views of feminists who, at best, relegated lesbianism to the private sphere and, at worst, dismissed it as evidence of male conditioning, as a preoccupation with sex from which feminists were trying to disentangle themselves.

A radically new formulation of lesbianism made its debut in May 1970 in New York City at the Congress to Unite Women, a conference of women's liberationists from the East Coast. A consciousness-raising group initiated by Rita Mae Brown and bringing together lesbians from the women's movement and the gay movement organized a "lavender menace" zap of the gathering. There they presented a carefully crafted document, "The Woman-Identified Woman," which would rapidly achieve canonical status among lesbian activists in the 1970s.

The opening lines of the essay staked out the ground on which radical lesbians would make their claims. "What is a lesbian?" it began. "A lesbian is the rage of all women condensed to the point of explosion." Here was a formulation that, as Alice Echols has pointed out, stripped lesbianism of its sexual content, and in which lesbianism was defined as the very essence of female anger.[18] To be a lesbian was to make a political statement about gender. The authors identified lesbians as the vanguard of the feminist revolution. Over the next few years, the most often-repeated assertion of lesbian-feminists would be that feminism was impossible without lesbianism. The two were so conflated that to be one was necessarily to be the other; conversely, the failure to identify as a lesbian was to have one's feminist loyalties disputed.

Lesbian-feminists also elaborated a political critique of heterosexuality. No longer simply a statement of behavior, or an expression of deep-rooted drives, it became an institution through which male supremacy was enforced and through which some women achieved limited privileges. As Charlotte Bunch, one of the key figures in this emergent movement, argued, virtually every institution that feminists had identified as oppressive to women was also premised on the naturalness of women's ties to men through marriage.[19] The failure to question the assumption of heterosexuality would forever inhibit women's quest for autonomy.

Although the analysis of heterosexism would eventually be picked up and incorporated into feminist and gay politics, the definition of lesbianism as a political vanguard always remained highly charged. With heterosexual feminists, the assertion of a vanguard role led to emotionally scarring combat and the rupture of the women's liberation movement in many cities as the "gay-straight split" became an impassable divide. Within gay liberation organizations the insistence that lesbians always put women first left no ground for common action: men, as much as male supremacy, were defined as the enemy.

Among a new generation of lesbians, however, the "Woman-Identified Woman" quickly came to define their lives and served to plot their course of action. Since all institutions were corrupted by patriarchal assumptions, to counter the invisibility of lesbians they applied themselves to creating an institutional world of their own. The 1970s witnessed an extraordinarily vital drive to build a self-sufficient lesbian community. Lesbians set up crisis lines and community centers. They founded magazines and newspapers, established publishing companies to print the steady flow of novels, poetry, and nonfiction that lesbian-feminists were composing, and bookstores to sell them. Theater groups performed the work of lesbian writers, record companies and concert producers ensured that lesbian musicians would reach an audience of eager listeners, and film collectives gave visual representation to lesbian lives. Lesbians formed archives and libraries to gather and preserve their culture; they bought land in common for rural separatist retreats; they opened food co-ops and restaurants and coffeehouses and self-defense schools and shelters for battered women. Groups of women created collectives to teach skills ranging from carpentry and plumbing to auto mechanics. In a few short years, a thriving lesbian-feminist community flowered around the country. The energy, creativity, and sheer will that went into sustaining it at times made Amazon Nation seem closer to literal truth than to metaphor.

Liberating as this new lesbian world was, in time it generated problems and tensions of its own. One concerned the balance between institution-building and political action. Hard as lesbian-feminists tried, they were never able to formulate a distinctively *lesbian* political agenda. With the exception of the rights of lesbian mothers, it proved impossible to identify a goal that wasn't either feminist (that is, about gender) or gay (that is, about sexual orientation). And since their ideology kept lesbian-feminists from working in coalition with men and insisted on their vanguard status within feminism, many found themselves withdrawing into a separate institutional world as much through inexorable political logic as out of choice. Community-building, in other words, had eclipsed political engagement.

This narrowing of vision did not go unchallenged. Some radical lesbians commented on the substitution of "community" for "movement" in the lesbian-feminist lexicon. "Somewhere along the way," declared one, "we stopped calling ourselves a movement and now call ourselves a community. . . . Communities may be groovy things to belong to . . . but communities don't make a revolution."[20] Charlotte Bunch, one of the fashioners of lesbian-separatist ideology, had by the mid-1970s moved away from a separatist politics because it had left her "too isolated." Instead of defining separatism as a permanent condition, she came to see it as a "dynamic strategy to be moved in and out of."[21] Bunch was not alone in this analysis. Some lesbian activists, having nurtured their identity and having internalized a lesbian-feminist analysis of heterosexism, plunged into other social movements, such as the campaigns against nuclear power and the nuclear arms race. For them, the lesbian community was a place to return to in order to find sustenance.

A second set of tensions was spawned by the continuing effort to shape a new lesbian identity. As the energies of many lesbian-feminists focused ever more intently on building a separate community, the power of the woman-identified-woman model accomplished a strange sleight of hand. Women's music, women's culture, the women's community, the women's coffeehouse: "lesbian" was becoming as invisible in the representation of this new universe as it was in the world at large. Did this betray, as some critics suggested, an uneasiness with the stigma attached to the label? Was it a tactical effort to weaken the heterosexual-homosexual division among women, to welcome all women into this inchoate community? Or did it signal the triumph of a lesbian-feminist ideology that erased, without a trace, the distinction between woman and lesbian?

Whatever the complex of motives, the conviction that lesbianism was fundamentally a matter of political consciousness was hardening for many into dogma. As it did so, it proved a source of stress to the very survival of the community. The patriarchy was powerful; consciousness was malleable. A lifetime of socialization, the fragility of female autonomy in a sexist society, and the threat of male violence meant not only that most women faced insuperable obstacles before they could achieve woman-identification, but also that this consciousness, once attained, was precarious. It had to be protected and defended. Thus at the very source of the lesbian-feminist movement were the elements that would lead it from a radical political stance into a utopian, perfectionist impulse. For many, separatism became not a tactic, not a temporary oasis, not a means of elaborating an ideology untainted by sexist and homophobic assumptions, not a prelude to a politics of engagement, but a way of life.

Dogma breeds both heresy and inquisition. To counter the external threats to this unstable identity and to protect this slippery consciousness led some to specify ever more precisely the elusive content of "lesbian." But the drive toward correctness, in lifestyle, political commitment, relationships, and sexuality, generated conflict. The "separatist wars" of the mid-1970s found not only separatists and nonseparatists clashing over what constituted true women-identification but also separatists themselves fighting to determine who best embodied separatist philosophy. Even in locales where separatism was not the dominant tendency, it seemed to shape the political dialogue: one had to defend or justify one's choices in relation to the purest expression of the idea. In this fragile, newly created, and beleaguered community, deviance was as dangerous as in the world at large.

## CHALLENGES

By the second half of the 1970s, each of these gendered movements was confronted by a paradox. On one hand, each had accomplished a lot. The gay rights movement could congratulate itself for the significant institutional changes it had effected in a mere handful of years. Life was clearly better than it had been in the previous decade. There was less discrimination and harassment, greater visibility, and a much larger and more congenial gay world. Lesbian-feminists had succeeded in building a multiplicity of institutions in which lesbians could flourish. In particular, the movement had created a range of woman-identified cultural products that affirmed the choice these women had made to focus their energy on women.

On the other hand, each of these political impulses was defining itself in ways that sharply limited its capacity for recruiting an expanding constituency. For the gay rights movement, a huge gulf had opened between activists and the men who populated the urban subculture. Activists had defined the goal of the movement as the freedom to be gay. They had accomplished enough for white middle-class gay men in the cities to experience unprecedented freedom. The movement, in other words, was succeeding according to its own lights. Moreover, as gay rights advocates became more and more wedded to working within institutions, and as institutions proved just flexible enough to initiate dialogue and adjust some of their practices, activists fell back on techniques—lobbying, negotiation, and the like—that made their work invisible to the men of the subculture. Movement participants might cry "false consciousness," but it was a consciousness they had helped to shape through their political rhetoric and tactics.

Meanwhile, as the leading edge of lesbian feminism became ever more identified with a separatist philosophy, it too progressively narrowed its appeal. Reform-minded women were put off by what they considered the glorification of marginality. Many of them struggled to work within largely male gay rights groups or within mainstream feminist organizations; others built lesbian reform organizations committed to working in coalition with both the gay movement and the women's movement. Some lesbians with allegiance to a broad radical vision of social transformation dispersed into a range of other political causes where they provided tough, incisive leadership. Women who were "old gay" identified, who had an allegiance to the traditional lesbian and gay world of the pre-Stonewall era and for whom lesbianism was a sexual identity, not simply an expression of feminism, were alienated by the prescriptive lifestyle politics of separatists. Finally, the relentless celebration of sameness, the emphasis on femaleness as the overarching definition of self, kept away lesbians with conflicting loyalties. Especially among women whose identity bound them to racial and ethnic home communities, lesbian separatism demanded choices they were unwilling to make. Like gay rights activists, separatists might attribute the failure of all women to flock to their banner as a sign of false consciousness, as evidence of an identity corrupted by the patriarchy. But such an explanation only dramatized the inability of separatists to speak to the needs of most lesbians.

Both movements also tended drastically to misapprehend their strength. The fact is that by the end of the 1960s, the oppression of homosexuals was increasingly out of step with contemporary culture. With the "sexual revolution" of the sixties, two generations of change had coalesced into a substantially new sexual order. In a society in which heterosexuality was only tenuously attached to procreative intent, and in which sexual pleasure was championed in the media of mass and popular culture, the prohibitions on homosexual expression seemed increasingly anachronistic. This profound cultural shift seemed to accelerate in the 1970s. As the birth rate plummeted and the age of marriage rose, as divorce rates skyrocketed and cohabitation among heterosexuals spread, as the number of households diverging from the nuclear family ideal grew dramatically, the boundaries separating gay and lesbian experience from that of heterosexuals blurred.

Moreover, the upheavals of the 1960s had, for a brief historical moment, seriously weakened those very institutions that enforced gay oppression. Years of urban riots and antiwar agitation left municipal authorities shaken; one can imagine them easily abandoning age-worn policies of harassing gay meeting places, once those policies were vigorously challenged. The psychiatric profession, buffeted by ideological assaults ranging from the work of Thomas Szasz to that of R. D. Laing, meekly reversed generations of pronouncements about the pathology of homosexuality.[22] Religion, too, was in ferment, with liberation theology and issues of social justice displacing doctrine and ritual in the concerns of many churches.

I am not suggesting that the gains associated with gay liberation in the 1970s came through the beneficence of a responsive system. Without a social movement agitating for change, without collective action persistently applying pressure on a range of institutions, and without masses of gay people willing to force the issue by coming out, the pace of progress in the seventies might well have resembled the snail-like inching forward of the homophile movement in the 1960s. But the achievements of gay liberation and its successor movements owed at least as much to the broad crisis of authority that existed by the end of the 1960s as they did to the power of the movement. To be sure, in absolute terms the movement was larger and stronger. But our opponents were also temporarily enfeebled. By the latter part of the 1970s the crisis was over; its passing would make new demands of gay and lesbian politics.

Misapprehension played itself out in another way. At the time, most activists of each of these gendered movements were acutely aware of how different the trajectories of gay and lesbian life were. Depending on conviction or experience, one might evaluate these differences in any one of a variety of ways. I know that I, and some of my gay male friends, tended to look with envy at the solidarity, the sense of community, and the commitment to radical transformation that we associated with lesbian-feminism, including its separatist form. Later I would learn that many lesbian-feminists were fascinated and, to some degree, attracted by the richness of our sexual subculture. But most would have agreed that the points of convergence between gay men and lesbians were few and far between.

As I look retrospectively at these two political impulses, I am now struck by their surprisingly similar outcomes. Take, for instance, what may very well be the quintessential product of each: the elaborate, glitzy, high-tech gay male discos found in many cities, and the self-sufficient, rural communes of lesbian separatists. Here were men, in a public space, spending money, focused on themselves, and searching for sex. And here were women, in a private retreat, financially marginal, focused on group process, and nurturing loving relationships. For all our talk about a brave new world of sexual freedom, or the building of an Amazon Nation, what I now see is how thoroughly enmeshed such institutions remained in gender conventions. A cynic might argue that, unencumbered by the constraints imposed by the "opposite sex," stereotypical gender roles reached their full flowering. A more accurate view, I believe, would acknowledge that some scrambling of gender characteristics did occur, while still conceding that gender dichotomies continued to be reproduced by those who claimed little allegiance to them.

During the flush times of new freedoms in the early and mid-1970s, it was possible to brush aside uncertainties and revel in the adventure of remaking our worlds. But as the decade neared its end, challenges erupted on a variety of fronts. These challenges exposed both strengths and weaknesses in the gendered movements that replaced radical gay liberation.

The first of these challenges came in the form of the New Right's crusade against homosexuality, a crusade that testified to the gains the movement had achieved.[23] After 1977, activists faced not the garden-variety homophobia that had come to seem familiar, but a more truculent, militant variety. Two disparate forces—a religious fundamentalism only recently politicized, and an aggressive new conservatism burrowing into the Republican Party and looking for a winning strategy—began to make common cause. Sharing a revulsion at the effects of the upheavals of the 1960s and fashioning a rhetoric of moral renewal and national resuscitation, they formed a potent coalition that shaped the politics of the 1980s.

The New Right initially targeted the gay movement in Dade County, Florida. In January 1977 the county commissioners, with little public debate or fanfare, added sexual orientation to the local civil rights ordinance. Fundamentalists countered very quickly, forming as their vehicle an organization with the emotionally explosive name of "Save Our Children" and with the popular singer Anita Bryant as its spokesperson. Bryant's involvement guaranteed that the repeal campaign would draw national media attention—the first such sustained exposure for issues of gay rights—and New Right luminaries such as Jerry Falwell made repeated appearances in south Florida. Activists attempted to respond, but their efforts at reasoned presentation of the issues and the sparse resources they could muster on their behalf proved sorely inadequate. When voters cast their ballot in June, the gay rights clause was overwhelmingly defeated.

The Dade County drive was the first of several referenda and initiative campaigns that were waged over the next eighteen months. In St. Paul, in Wichita, and in Eugene, Oregon, voters resoundingly rejected gay rights. In Seattle and in California, the gay community emerged victorious. The California campaign against the Briggs initiative was especially significant because of its statewide scope. In particular, it offered a favorable portent of things to come as many gay men and lesbians for the first time found themselves working together against a common enemy. But even this victory turned sour when Harvey Milk, the openly gay supervisor in San Francisco, was assassinated three weeks after the November balloting.

The rise of the New Right sent tremors of fear through the gay and lesbian community across the country. Its press increasingly offered analogies with McCarthy's America and Nazi Germany. The movement seemed to lack the financial resources, the numbers, the influence, and the political sophistication to counter the threat. The placid politics of gay rights lobbying was helpless before the emotional onslaught of fundamentalist rhetoric. The single-issue orientation of gay rights activists made effective coalitions difficult to construct, or even to conceive; the separate community-building strategy of lesbian-feminism left little room for fierce political engagement. A collective crisis of faith seemed to paralyze the movement. The dazed leadership of national organizations expended more energy in internecine warfare and mutual recrimination than in attending to the crisis at hand.

A second challenge came in the form of the collapse of the lesbian-separatist utopia. In part this could be blamed on the changing economic times. High inflation in the Carter years and high unemployment in the early Reagan years pressed marginal institutions to the wall. Organizations fully dependent on volunteer labor struggled to survive, and the accumulated stress of years of subsistence living took their toll on women who, by virtue of their class position and educational background, in fact had other options. Downward mobility became less and less liberating and more and more painful.

But the shattering of utopian dreams stemmed from internal tensions as well. Toward the end of the 1970s, the effort to enforce standards of "political correctness" turned toward sexual issues. Some radical feminists, enraged by images of sexual violence, campaigned for restrictions on the distribution and sale of pornography. Using emotionally volatile slogans—"Pornography is the theory; rape is the practice"—they seemed to be making common cause with the New Right. In fact, they were encouraging an assault on elements of the sexual revolution that, by permitting discussion of previously forbidden topics, had opened a space for the representation of lesbian and gay life.[24]

The pornography issue sparked an acrimonious debate within the lesbian community—and among feminists more generally—about a broad spectrum of sexual matters. As some lesbians expressed reservations about the pornography crusade, they found their "credentials" as lesbian-feminists questioned. Soon lesbian-feminists with roots in the pre-Stonewall world, such as Joan Nestle, began to deconstruct the rhetorical strategem of "The Woman-Identified Woman," which had conflated lesbianism with feminism and eliminated the erotic component of lesbian identity.[25] Discussions of butch-femme roles, a style of sexual interaction that had predominated in pre-Stonewall bar life, of sexual fantasy, and of sadomasochism coursed through the lesbian-feminist community. At the 1982 Scholar and the Feminist Conference, "Towards a Politics of Sexuality," held at Barnard College, the tensions exploded into view as some of the lesbians present were attacked publicly because of their sexuality.[26]

The eruption of the "sex wars," as these controversies came to be known, exposed divisions within the lesbian community. In the long run, the woman-identified-woman model of lesbianism, so powerful in creating a lesbian-feminist movement, lost its hegemony, slowly to be replaced by a more fluid discourse that acknowledged and affirmed sexual differences. In the short run, however, the emotionally searing conflicts soured the utopian dreams of the 1970s.

A third challenge emanated from the autonomous organizing efforts of lesbians and gays of color, which by the end of the 1970s had reached a critical mass.[27] One characteristic that gay rights and lesbian separatism shared was that each, in some sense, was a "single identity" movement. In the former case, sexual "orientation" was the focal point for organizing; in the latter, it was gender. Neither left much room for a broader, more complex vision of social change; neither easily tolerated competing claims or loyalties.

Separate organizing by people of color began within a year or so after Stonewall. In some GLFs, Third World caucuses formed; in a few cities, distinct groups were started. Like GLF, these early organizations were deeply affected by the changing political climate. The demoralization that by the early 1970s infected communities of color hastened their decline. As government repression hit radical organizations with special force, many groups collapsed under the pressure.

In the ensuing years, some people managed to navigate the currents of a gendered politics. Some women of color could be found in lesbian-feminist organizations, including the most separatist-oriented, although evidence abounds from this era of tensions around race. A few individuals—I think of Betty Powell and Mel Boozer, for instance, both of whom worked with the National Gay Task Force in the 1970s and early 1980s—maintained a presence in the gay rights movement. Others joined forces in organizations that were explicitly interracial in their focus, such as Black and White Men Together, which had chapters in many cities by the end of the 1970s. But increasingly the preferred option was to establish a political space of their own. Organizations such as Salsa Soul Sisters in New York, the collective that published the magazine *Azalea*, and the multi-chaptered National Coalition of Black Gays sought to define a political agenda and to create a collective identity true to their own experience.

A major step forward came in 1979, when a call was issued for a national conference of Third World gays, to be held in Washington in October. Initiated by African–American groups, which at that point were the most solidly established, the conference provided the opportunity for intensive mobilizing in an effort to gather a large, nationally representative body of people. The significance of the conference was magnified when other grass-roots activists called for a national march on Washington the same weekend. The march guaranteed that large numbers of white lesbians and gay men would learn of the work and the demands of people of color.

Autonomous organization-building would continue and, indeed, accelerate in the 1980s, but after 1979 activists of color self-consciously confronted white organizations with ever greater insistence. (During these years a similar process was under way within the women's movement.) They demanded inclusion in both representation and setting of agendas. Their demands rested on an analysis of oppression and identity fundamentally different from that of the gendered politics of the 1970s. Rather than the single-issue orientation of the gay rights movement, or the vanguard cry of "We are the most oppressed" emanating from some lesbian separatists, lesbians and gays of color argued for what Barbara Smith has called "the simultaneity of oppression." The many layers of identity inscribed in each person made individuals the target of multiple vectors of oppression. White activists were challenged to expand their vision to include whole human beings instead of just slices of the self.

By the early 1980s the clamor for recognition and inclusiveness had become ever present. There were few significant movement gatherings where the demands of people of color were not raised. Although the response of white organizations was limited, the level of discomfort was rising dramatically.

We can never know what response this combination of challenges might have generated: Would it have led in the 1980s to dynamic growth, strategic innovation, and increased effectiveness? Or would it have led to fracturing, demoralization, and disarray? Local community studies may someday tell us a variety of conflicting stories. Certainly the massive organizing that occurred in California around the Briggs initiative evinced creative, constructive possibilities. But, at this stage of my own research, I am more impressed by the signs of danger. The New Right, not the gay and lesbian movement, was setting the terms of the debate. Lesbian-feminists were engaged in bruising, destructive battles with one another. White activists and activists of color were locked in what Torie Osborn has called "the guilt-rage dance."

I have said that "we can never know" what might have happened. The reason is probably obvious to many readers. As the 1980s began, yet another challenge, life-threatening in nature, made its appearance. The AIDS epidemic mapped the terrain on which resolutions of these other challenges would get worked through.


## THE IMPACT OF AIDS[28]


It is not my task here to recount the history of the AIDS epidemic. AIDS has already found a number of able chroniclers and, as the epidemic goes on and reaches ever more deeply into American life, it will produce many more. But I do want to look at the ways that the virus, which struck the gay male community with special force, has thoroughly reshaped lesbian and gay politics. Through the imperative of mounting an effective response to the epidemic, the movement has achieved a level of sophistication, influence, and permanence that activists of the 1970s could only dream about.

Among white middle-class gay men, AIDS has bridged the gulf that divided the movement from the subculture. The epidemic elucidated, in a manner that movement rhetoric could not, the continuing strength of gay oppression. Men with a firm sense of gay identity, but who had eschewed activism, were forced to acknowledge that only a deeply rooted, systemic homophobia could explain the callous, even murderous, neglect by the government and the mass media of an epidemic that was killing them and their loved ones. Many had to admit how marginal and despised they were, despite the class or race or gender privileges they enjoyed. The epidemic provoked some extraordinary transformations: who would have predicted that Wall Street stockbrokers would become street militants and advocates of massive civil disobedience?

The impact on the movement has likewise been profound. The dense and extensive social networks that developed in the 1970s but that remained resistant to political mobilization now could be tapped. The movement gained access to new reservoirs of money, of skills, and of recruits. Much of this, of course, went toward building AIDS service and advocacy organizations, but much of it was also directed toward the broader agenda of gay politics.

For gays and lesbians of color, the epidemic sounded a clarion call to escalate their organizing efforts. From the beginning of the epidemic, African–American and Latino communities were disproportionately struck by the disease. Not only gay and bisexual men, but intravenous drug users, their sexual partners, and their children were at risk. Because drug users lacked the organizational infrastructure of the gay community, and because they and their communities were resource-poor, they were not easily able to mount a response of their own. And because of the homophobia within communities of color, the established leadership was often unwilling to concede the severity of the problem in their midst.

Gay and lesbian activists of color thus found themselves in a strategically unique position. In relation to gay-focused AIDS organizations, their demands for entry, access, and power took on added urgency. Without exaggerating or romanticizing the openness of AIDS organizations, the fact is that many of them proved more responsive to calls for inclusion than gay organizations had previously been. In relation to their racial and ethnic communities, gays and lesbians of color were among the first to perceive the significance of the epidemic; through it, they have been able to initiate—or extend—a dialogue about homophobia and gay oppression. And, as the epidemic spread and funds were pried loose from government agencies to target minority communities, it was often gays and lesbians who had the experience and the willingness to staff these new organizations. The result has been a dramatic increase in the level of organization and visibility of gays of color.

Two examples can illustrate the scope of change. In February 1990, I helped facilitate a leadership retreat for paid executive directors of gay and lesbian organizations. The planners had made a commitment to assemble a diverse group, but our criteria for invitations were leading to a very white list. By expanding our reach to include gay directors of AIDS organizations, we ended up with 29 participants, of whom forty percent were of color. The AIDS service bureaucracy has become a vehicle for placing gays and lesbians of color in formal leadership roles.

Later that year another retreat was designed for activist leaders in New York City. Here the specifications for attendance were broad enough to make it relatively easy to have half the attendees be white and half be of color. The participants included an assistant to the mayor, two city commissioners, a deputy commissioner, and an elected Democratic Party district leader; all five were people of color. It is difficult to imagine a similar scenario from ten, or even five, years ago.

As the 1990s begin, the turn toward racial and ethnic inclusion is growing. Conferences are less likely to be virtually all-white gatherings; some of the national gay and lesbian organizations are acting on firm commitments to diversify staffs and boards; and in some cities, the movement is taking on rainbow hues.

For many white lesbians, the AIDS epidemic propelled them into political work with gay men. Two of the more widely remarked gay-related phenomena of the 1980s were the depth of lesbian involvement in the fight against AIDS and the assumption by lesbians of key leadership roles in what had been male-dominated organizations. Too often the explanations for this change have been framed in ways that cynically impugn its significance or that make it sound like a temporary accommodation during a crisis. Lesbians have flocked to AIDS work, the story goes, because they embody qualities of generosity, self-sacrifice, or nurturance—in other words, for the stereotypically female reason of putting the needs of others first. Or lesbians are now leading the movement because gay men are dying off—our variation on the heterosexual theme of women's skills being valued in wartime.

I don't buy these explanations as sufficient to account for the seismic shift in gender relations that has occurred in the movement. Something deeper and more complex is going on. There is, it seems to me, both a political and a cultural component to the rapprochement between women and men. Politically, lesbian-feminism offered sharper analytical tools for comprehending the full significance of the AIDS epidemic from its earliest years. The confrontation with sexism that was at the heart of feminism made most lesbian activists—whether separatist, reformist, or somewhere in between—acutely conscious of the systemic nature of oppression. Few had ever bought the notion, common in gay rights politics, that minor adjustments in law and public policy would bring freedom. Health issues, moreover, had been a key component of feminist organizing since the late 1960s. Much consciousness raising had been done, for instance, around fights to expose the dangers of the birth-control pill and the IUD. One result of these and other battles was that lesbians were less likely than gay men initially were to frame the epidemic as a simple issue of medicine and public health.

That this understanding of the politics of health might play itself out in the choices of lesbian activists was brought home to me in a particular conversation of a few years ago. Katy Taylor was working as an investigator in the AIDS discrimination unit of the New York City Human Rights Commission. Her previous history of activism stretched back to the civil rights and antiwar movements; in the 1970s, she had focused on union organizing among women and on issues of sexual violence. She had never before worked with gay men, or on gay-related issues. When I asked Taylor why in 1983 she had chosen, when AIDS was still barely spoken about outside big-city gay male circles, to apply for the job, her answer was direct: "I didn't just apply for the job—I pursued it. Because of the work I had done," she said, "I *knew* that AIDS was going to bring together all of the issues I cared about. Right away I could see that AIDS was about class, and race, and sexuality, and homophobia, and gender—it was about everything. And I wanted to be there." I suspect that many other lesbian-feminists thought in similar ways.

Once the lesbian presence was established in the world of AIDS service and politics, it struck a deep vein of gratitude among gay men. But the bonds that have developed between men and women could become strong and sturdy because of changes in the sexual culture of *both genders*. The modifications of gay male sexuality that the epidemic provoked—the new emphasis on dating, on intimacy, on relationships—were occurring at the very moment that the sex wars had incited explorations of sexuality within the lesbian community. In other words, the gender gap that had yawned so widely in the 1970s was narrowing. A new culture of sexuality was taking shape, in which some men and women could meet on ground that, if not common, was at least in the same neighborhood.

Finally, the AIDS epidemic helped dissolve the political marginalization and social isolation that had hampered the movement's ability to counter the New Right. AIDS forced many mainstream institutions into sustained negotiation with the gay and lesbian community. As the epidemic spread, churches, mental health professionals, the medical and public health establishment, the social and human service bureaucracies, corporations, municipal, state, and federal officials, congressional staffers, and many more eventually had no choice but to deal with AIDS. When gays had approached these institutions for a cause that smacked of sexual freedom, it was relatively easy to turn the other way. When these same activists arrived wearing the hat of AIDS service provider or educator and addressing a menace to the public health of the nation, at least some doors opened. And doors that opened because of AIDS remained access points for dealing later on with a range of other lesbian and gay issues. The relationships that formed, the bonds of respect that were forged, and the knowledge of how institutions worked and how decisions were made became valuable resources for the gay community.

The AIDS epidemic may not have been the sole motivator of change in the 1980s, but it certainly shaped the field on which other challenges and problems were played out. Through it, the gay and lesbian movement has been so thoroughly reconstructed that it scarcely resembles the creature of a decade ago. Some of the differences between 1980 and 1990 are as follows:

1.  Many groups have access to vastly expanded resources and have become permanent fixtures. In 1980, there were few gay and lesbian organizations whose future seemed assured. Most depended on volunteer labor. Their funding base was insecure and the life cycle of most was short.

    The situation of New York City gives some sense of the scope of change. In 1981, on the eve of the epidemic, the city where the Stonewall Riot occurred and with the largest population of gay men and lesbians in the country, sustained fewer than a dozen activists in paid staff positions. In 1990, if one includes AIDS organizations with a gay focus and AIDS workers who are gay-identified, the number is pushing two hundred.

    The growth is not simply confined to AIDS organizations. The resource pie has grown. The budgets of many gay and lesbian groups in cities across the country have expanded. These groups have become sophisticated in the use of fund-raising techniques pioneered by the New Right in the 1970s. Incorporation and boards of directors give some measure of stability. Activists with years of grass-roots experience behind them are now able to have "careers" in the movement, instead of retreating to private pursuits when the burden of volunteerism becomes too great. Experience and sophistication are accumulating within the ranks of the movement, replacing the revolving-door pattern characteristic of volunteer-based efforts.

2.  The 1980s have witnessed the reinvigoration of grass-roots local activism and the spread of the movement to parts of the country that had barely been touched by it in the 1970s.

    Maybe these changes would have occurred without AIDS, but I'm not persuaded. The conservatism of the Reagan years and the vitriolic campaigns of the New Right were inhibiting the spread of activism beyond large metropolitan areas, especially in parts of the country where political conservatism and religious fundamentalism were strongest. But, whereas many people might have been reluctant to fight for gay liberation, they were unwilling to turn their backs on the casualties of the epidemic. AIDS added altruism, compassion, and kindness to the bag of possible motivations for activism, and it overcame constraints against mobilization.

Participation in AIDS service work, which was often the initial path toward involvement, could not easily remain sequestered in an apolitical world. AIDS service organizations found their efforts threatened by state legislative proposals to make HIV status reportable and to forbid the use of tax dollars for certain kinds of educational material, and by other, more draconian measures. Service providers also needed levels of funding that only municipal, state, or federal officials could provide. Caretaking work, especially when it stretched for months or years, provoked anger, reshaped consciousness, and forged unexpected commitments. In short, the lines dividing service and politics blurred. So, too, did the boundaries between AIDS organizing and gay and lesbian organizing.

The 1987 March on Washington to demand a national response to AIDS and attention to lesbian and gay rights marked a critical moment in this process. In 1979, the first national march had attracted perhaps 100,000; eight years later the crowd surpassed half a million. The turnout was a sign of the density of organizational networks and community ties. And in some states, like my own of North Carolina, where ad hoc groups had coalesced to bring people to Washington (a "safe" activity that did not threaten exposure at home), the weekend in Washington proved uncontainable. The display of the Names Project Quilt, the massive wedding ceremony at the National Cathedral, and the impressive parade of contingents from every state in the nation, struck a chord of self-respect so deep that it could not be ignored. People returned to their home communities transformed, ready to do what seemed unimaginable a few days before.

3. AIDS has stimulated a return to tactics of direct action and civil disobedience on a scale not seen since the early 1970s.

Most closely associated with ACT UP, direct action has been reincorporated among the spectrum of tactics considered permissible even by the reform wing of the movement. Indeed, the most notable feature of the growing militance of the last few years has been the approval of it even by those organizations and activists who do not engage in such tactics themselves. The movement seems willing to tolerate both insider and outsider strategies, recognizing the necessity of both in order to reach common goals. The deliberate manipulation of a spectrum of protest techniques bespeaks a political sophistication absent a decade earlier in the Dade County repeal campaign.

4. The stubborn resistance of the nation's top leadership, political and otherwise, to address some fundamental—and simple—issues posed by the epidemic has sparked the revival of a radical political analysis and a broad strategic vision within the movement.

The AIDS epidemic has once again given plausibility to understandings of gay and lesbian oppression as systemic; it has exposed the complex ways in which it is tied to a host of other injustices. The observation that most victims of the disease are either gay or of color, or both; the fact that the media and the federal health bureaucracy could be instantly mobilized by a disease that struck a few score members of the American Legion, but could look the other way as tens of thousands of gay men and IV drug users wasted away; the ability of the government to transport half a million personnel across the globe, and then provide for their food, shelter, clothing, *and* health care, while scarcely blinking an eye: all this and more has made AIDS an extraordinarily effective primer in politics.

One concrete result has been the initiative taken by the movement to break out of its ghettoized politics. Fighting AIDS effectively has made this a necessity, and the broad-based NORA coalition (National Organizations Responding to AIDS), conceived and shaped by gay activists, is the most obvious example. But movement leaders are not simply engaged in an unavoidable effort to draw others to their cause. They have effectively reached out to participate in coalition with other movements around issues of common concern. The passage in 1990 of the Hate Crimes Statistics Act and the Americans with Disabilities Act signify a coming of age of lesbian and gay activism.

## A FEW FINAL THOUGHTS

The good news is that the movement is stronger and more vital now than at any time in the past, a statement which could not have been made ten years ago. The sobering view is that it has taken a deadly epidemic to lead us to this point. And a cautious assessment requires me to acknowledge that the resolution of the crises of a decade ago is still incomplete and unstable.

Of the many changes that occurred in the 1980s, I am most confident of the continuing ability of men and women to work together. There are good reasons for optimism. Many of our organizations have built gender parity into their structure. Lesbians in large numbers have important leadership roles, nationally and locally, in the movement. Far more consciousness raising has occurred around sexism than around other issues of identity and oppression. The institutional legacy of lesbian-feminism remains strong enough that lesbians have a secure base from which to bargain. Without question, conflict and tension will continue to assert themselves, but I suspect that the progressive changes of the last ten years in this area are irreversible.

The issue of resources—particularly financial—is more troubling. Movement organizations, despite the growth in the budgets of many of them and despite greater sophistication in techniques of fund-raising, still groan under the burden of work loads swollen, paradoxically, by the movement's success: our agenda grows with each new victory. Any number of scenarios could restrict the growth, or even shrink the size, of the resource pie. What if a dramatic scientific breakthrough occurs in the treatment or prevention of AIDS? What if the budgetary crunch that state and local governments are facing deepens, and public money for AIDS dries up? Will contributions going to our political organizations be diverted to AIDS service work? If the movement wins a significant national victory in the next few years—rescinding the military's exclusion policy or passage of a federal civil rights bill, neither of which is beyond imagination—will donors grow complacent and think that the movement can close up shop?

On the question of racial and ethnic inclusion, there is cause for both optimism and caution. In some organizations and in some cities, commitments to inclusion have been made and are being acted upon. The impulse toward organization among lesbians and gays of color is so dynamic that their base for negotiation and dialogue is becoming stronger and stronger. Counterbalancing this is the simple fact that identity politics is always explosive: Will white organizations move fast enough to satisfy the expectations of people of color? Will some activists of color prove willing to absorb the inevitable frustrations, or will their autonomous organizing be transformed into a new separatism?

So far, most of the discussion about race and ethnicity has revolved around the issue of inclusion. Yet to be considered in any sustained way is the question of setting agendas. It's one thing to open the doors of organizations so that they encompass racial, ethnic, and class differences. It is quite another to reshape an organization's or a movement's agenda so that it incorporates the goals of these new constituencies. Profound change will occur when inclusion begins to affect the goals and direction of the movement. I suspect that the process, if we get far enough to engage in it seriously, will be tumultuous.

Already, it seems to me, the movement is taking small steps in this direction. Two issues that have risen to prominence in the last handful of years—the military's exclusion policy and family benefits—speak directly to the needs of working-class people, whatever their color. Can the movement go further? Is it willing, and able, to frame its agenda in ways that create broad coalitions for social change? Will the quest for domestic partnership rights be transformed into a drive for an inclusive national family policy? Will the organizing for access to drugs and medical care be redefined as a campaign for a system of national health care?

A final issue that bears watching is whether the movement can continue the elaborately choreographed dance in which "outsiders" and "insiders," local grass-roots activists and national lobbyists, paid professional staffers and volunteer laborers, all stay in step with one another. The history of social movements suggests that it will not be easy: the various places that people occupy in the spectrum of activities and functions are not simply different roles that they have taken. Often they represent sharply divergent visions of both the process of social change and the society one hopes to create. How do we negotiate the conflicts that always threaten to disrupt the movement?

One hopeful sign is that many key leadership roles in the movement, at both the national and local level, are held by activists who represent themselves as "progressive." As an identifying label, the word came into vogue in the late 1970s and early 1980s after a long dormancy. It seems to describe heirs of sixties radicalism who are willing to work for change "within the system" yet without abandoning a long-term vision of social transformation. Or, to adapt the language of gay emancipationists of a century ago, they are radical souls residing in the bodies of reformers. Many are able to speak with credibility and authority to both reformers and radicals, to local grass-roots militants as well as wealthy donors, to those comfortable in legislative corridors and to those at home in a picket line. Their flexible leadership has helped to move us closer to our goals over the last few years.

This sketch of the gay and lesbian movement has been a partial one: partial in that it is not based on exhaustive research and partial in that it is meant to give coherence to what has often seemed ornery and confusing. There are topics that I haven't attended to with the depth they deserve, such as the complex relationship between culture and politics, between communities and movements. I have also ignored the many crosscurrents of the 1970s and 1980s—for instance, the persistent thread of gay male radicalism, even at the height of the gay rights movement, or the continuing allegiance of some lesbians to a separatist vision, even in the era of AIDS. I am aware, too, that the experience of some cities (San Francisco, Boston, and Houston come to mind), at least on the surface, defies the construction I have given to events. Nonetheless, as I have rehearsed this overall analysis with groups of activists, it elicits nods of recognition.

I would love—of course—to believe that these signs of approval are evidence of the insightful accuracy of my inquiry. Though I suspect that at least some of what I have written will withstand closer scrutiny, I know that the affirmations

I've received are testimony to something else. The vast majority of us who are active in the gay and lesbian movement are saddled with a heavy burden of ignorance about our history of political struggle. The frenzy of activity that envelops us leaves little room for thoughtful reflection; the past vanishes before the image of the next task or crisis.

Community historians need to undertake the task of researching the history of lesbian and gay politics. We need studies of organizations, former and current. We need careful examination of issues—how have gays and lesbians worked with the churches, or the federal bureaucracy, or the Democratic Party? We need studies of geographic communities—from Boston to Seattle to San Diego to Atlanta—as well as studies of identity communities. The list is long. But only then will we have the richly textured history of emancipatory struggle that will preserve a collective memory of the past and serve as resource to meet today's—and tomorrow's—challenges.

## NOTES

1.  For useful surveys of the sociological literature on social movements see Doug McAdam, John D. McCarthy, and Mayer N. Zald, "Social Movements," in Neil J. Smelser, ed., *Handbook of Sociology* (New York: Sage Publications, 1988), 695–737; and Bert Klandermans and Sidney Tarrow, "Mobilization into Social Movements: Synthesizing European and American Approaches," *International Social Movement Research* 1 (1988): 1–38.

2.  One important exception is the study by Barry D. Adam, *The Rise of a Gay and Lesbian Movement* (Boston: Twayne, 1987).

3.  The analysis in this essay is informed by the following: my own experience in the gay movement since 1973; a reading of gay and lesbian publications, particularly *The Advocate*, *Gay Community News*, the *Body Politic*, *Lesbian Tide*, *Lavender Woman*, and *The Front Page*; a reading of the *New York Times* and the *Washington Post* for coverage of gay issues; research in the organizational records of the National Gay and Lesbian Task Force; and a reading of memoirs, journalistic accounts, and other analyses of lesbian and gay life and politics since Stonewall.

4.  Useful works on the homophile years include John D'Emilio, *Sexual Politics, Sexual Communities: The Making of a Homosexual Minority in the United States, 1940–1970* (Chicago: University of Chicago Press, 1983); Today Marotta, *The Politics of Homosexuality* (Boston: Houghton Mifflin, 1981); and Stuart Timmons, *The Trouble with Harry Hay: Founder of the Modern Gay Movement* (Boston: Alyson, 1990).

5. Allan Bérubé, *Coming Out Under Fire: The History of Gay Men and Women in World War Two* (New York: Free Press, 1990).

6. Useful works on radical gay liberation include Dennis Altman, *Homosexual: Oppression and Liberation* (New York: Avon, 1971); Karla Jay and Allen Young, *Out of the Closets: Voices of Gay Liberation* (New York: Douglas/Links, 1972); Donn Teal, *The Gay Militants* (New York: Stein and Day, 1971); Len Richmond and Gary Noguera, eds., *The Gay Liberation Book* (San Francisco: Ramparts Press, 1973); and Marotta, *The Politics of Homosexuality*.

7. The information on Shelley is drawn from an interview conducted by Jonathan Katz. I am grateful to Katz for allowing me access to the tape.

8. Quoted in Marotta, *The Politics of Homosexuality*, 88.

9. Ibid.

10. See Sara Evans, *Personal Politics: The Roots of Women's Liberation in the Civil Rights Movement and the New Left* (New York: Alfred A. Knopf, 1979).

11. For a partial list of GLF groups see the list of organizations at the end of Jay and Young, *Out of the Closets*, 375–403.

12. Useful works on gay rights activism include Teal, *The Gay Militants*, Marotta, *The Politics of Homosexuality*, and Arthur Bell, *Dancing the Gay Lib Blues* (New York: Simon & Schuster, 1971). All of these works focus on gay activism in New York City and thus highlight the need for historians and sociologists to study the evolution of activism in other cities in the 1970s.

13. On the Gay Academic Union see *The Universities and the Gay Experience: Proceedings of the Conference Sponsored by the Women and Men of the Gay Academic Union*, November 23 and 24, 1973 (New York, 1974).

14. The events and victories mentioned in this and the preceding paragraphs all deserve more detailed study and analysis by researchers.

15. A good description of this new public subculture can be found in Edmund White, *States of Desire: Travels in Gay America* (New York: Dutton, 1980).

16. Useful works on the evolution of lesbian feminism include Jay and Young, *Out of the Closets*; Marotta, *The Politics of Homosexuality*; Sidney Abbott and Barbara Love, *Sappho Was a Right-On Woman: A Liberated View of Lesbianism* (New York: Stein and Day, 1972); Nancy Myron and Charlotte Bunch, eds., *Lesbianism and the Women's Movement* (Baltimore: Diana Press, 1975); Michal Brody, ed., *Are We There Yet?: A Continuing History of Lavender Woman* (Iowa City: Aunt Lute, 1985); Alice Echols, *Daring to Be Bad: Radical Feminism in America, 1967–75* (Minneapolis: University of Minnesota Press, 1989); Sarah Lucia Hoagland and Julia Penelope, eds., *For Lesbians Only: A Separatist Anthology* (London: Onlywomen Press, 1988); and Ginny Vida, ed., *Our Right to Love: A Lesbian Resource Book* (Englewood Cliffs, N.J.: Prentice-Hall, 1978).

17. See Blanche Wiesen Cook, "The Historical Denial of Lesbianism," *Radical History Review* 20 (Spring/Summer 1979): 60–65.

18. Alice Echols has written extensively on the evolution of lesbian-feminist ideology and politics. See, especially, *Daring to Be Bad*, 210–241; "The Taming of the Id: Feminist Sexual Politics, 1968–1983," in Carole S. Vance, ed., *Pleasure and Danger: Exploring Female Sexuality* (Boston: Routledge and Kegan Paul, 1984), pp. 50–72; and "The New Feminism of Yin and Yang," in Snitow, Stansell, and Thompson, eds., *Powers of Desire: The Politics of Sexuality* (New York: Monthly Review Press, 1983), 439–459. "The Woman-Identified Woman" has been reprinted in many places. See Jay and Young, *Out of the Closets*, 172–177.

19. See Charlotte Bunch, "Learning from Lesbian Separatism," in Karla Jay and Allen Young, eds., *Lavender Culture* (New York: Jove/HBJ Publications, 1979), 433–444.

20. Women's Press Collective, *Lesbians Speak Out*, 2nd ed. (Berkeley, 1974), 139–140.

21. Charlotte Bunch, "Learning from Lesbian Separatism," in Jay and Young, *Lavender Culture*, 441.

22. See, for example, Thomas S. Szasz, *The Manufacture of Madness* (New York: Harper & Row, 1970); and R. D. Laing, *The Politics of Experience* (New York: Pantheon, 1967). The story of the American Psychiatric Association's reversal can be found in Ronald Bayer, *Homosexuality and American Psychiatry: The Politics of Diagnosis* (New York: Basic Books, 1981).

23. On the New Right and the gay movement, see Randy Shilts, *The Mayor of Castro Street: The Life and Times of Harvey Milk* (New York: St. Martin's Press, 1982); Gay Rights Writer's Group, *It Could Happen To You: An Account of the Gay Civil Rights Campaign in Eugene, Oregon* (Boston: Alyson, 1983); and Perry Deane Young, *God's Bullies: Native Reflections on Preachers and Politics* (New York: Holt, Rinehart and Winston, 1982).

24. For feminist statements against pornography see Laura Lederer, ed., *Take Back the Night* (New York: William Morrow, 1980), and Andrea Dworkin, *Pornography: Men Possessing Women* (New York: Perigee, 1981).

25. See "Butch-Femme Relationships: Sexual Courage in the 1950s," in Joan Nestle, *A Restricted Country* (Ithaca, N.Y.: Firebrand Books, 1987), 100–109.

26. On the Barnard Conference, see Carole S. Vance, ed., *Pleasure and Danger*.

27. On the experience and organizing efforts of gays and lesbians of color, see Cherrie Moraga and Gloria Anzaldua, eds., *This Bridge Called My Back: Writings by Radical Women of Color* (New York: Kitchen Table Press, 1983); Joseph Beam, ed., *In the Life: A Black Gay Anthology* (Boston: Alyson, 1986); and Barbara Smith, ed., *Home Girls: A Black Feminist Anthology* (New York: Kitchen Table Press, 1983).

28. The literature on the AIDS epidemic is vast. Useful works include Dennis Altman, *AIDS in the Mind of America* (Garden City, N.Y.: Anchor/Doubleday, 1986); Cindy

Patton, *Sex and Germs: The Politics of AIDS* (Boston: South End Press, 1985); Simon Watney, *Policing Desire: Pornography, AIDS, and the Media* (Minneapolis: University of Minnesota Press, 1987); Randy Shilts, *And the Band Played On: Politics, People, and the AIDS Epidemic* (New York: St. Martin's Press, 1987); Larry Kramer, *Reports from the Holocaust: The Making of an AIDS Activist* (New York: St. Martin's Press, 1989); Douglas Crimp, ed., *AIDS: Cultural Analysis, Cultural Activism* (Cambridge: MIT Press, 1988); and Douglas Crimp with Adam Ralston, *AIDS demo graphics* (Seattle: Bay Press, 1990).